The future of international environmental law

The future of international environmental law

Edited by David Leary and Balakrishna Pisupati

**United Nations
University Press**

TOKYO · NEW YORK · PARIS

The views expressed in this publication are those of the authors and do not necessarily reflect the views of the United Nations University.

United Nations University Press
United Nations University, 53-70, Jingumae 5-chome,
Shibuya-ku, Tokyo 150-8925, Japan
Tel: +81-3-5467-1212   Fax: +81-3-3406-7345
E-mail: sales@unu.edu   general enquiries: press@unu.edu
http://www.unu.edu

United Nations University Office at the United Nations, New York
2 United Nations Plaza, Room DC2-2062, New York, NY 10017, USA
Tel: +1-212-963-6387   Fax: +1-212-371-9454
E-mail: unuony@unu.edu

United Nations University Press is the publishing division of the United Nations
University.

Cover design by Mea Rhee

Printed in Hong Kong

ISBN 978-92-808-1192-6

Library of Congress Cataloging-in-Publication Data

The future of international environmental law / edited by David Leary and
Balakrishna Pisupati.
    p.   cm.
  Includes bibliographical references and index.
  ISBN 978-9280811926 (pbk.)
  1. Environmental law, International. I. Leary, David Kenneth. II. Pisupati,
Balakrishna.
  K3585.F88   2010
  344.04'6—dc22   2010025234

Contents

Contributors

Gudmundur Alfredsson is Professor in the Polar Law Master's Programs of the University of Akureyri, Iceland, and Invited Professor at the Law Faculty of the University of Strasbourg, France. He was Professor at Lund University, Sweden (1995–2008), and staff member with the United Nations Secretariat in New York and Geneva (1983–1995).

Dionysia-Theodora Avgerinopoulou is a Member of the Hellenic Parliament and a State Deputy. She is in charge of designing the environmental programme of her political party, New Democracy, in Greece. She is also the director of the European Institute of Law, Science and Technology (EILST) in Brussels, Belgium, and a specialist attorney in international law, environmental law and European Community law.

Donna Craig is a Professor of Law at the University of Western Sydney. She has over 30 years' experience in environmental law. Her research and publications emphasize social and human rights issues. She served as Regional Vice-Chair for the IUCN Commission on Environmental Law and is currently a Regional Governor of the International Council on Environmental Law.

Sébastien Duyck is a researcher at the Northern Institute for Environmental and Minority Law, University of Lapland, and has specialized in international environmental law, human rights law and the law of the sea. He holds a master's degree in Public International Law from the University of Helsinki and is currently writing a doctoral dissertation on public participation at the United Nations Framework Convention on Climate Change.

Robert M. Friedman is the Director for California at the J. Craig Venter Institute. Previously he was Vice President for Research at The Heinz Center. Earlier, he was a Senior Associate at the Office of Technology Assessment of the US Congress. He received his PhD from the University of Wisconsin, Madison, in Ecological Systems Analysis. He is a Fellow of the American Association for the Advancement of Science.

Michele S. Garfinkel is a policy analyst at the J. Craig Venter Institute. She held positions earlier at Columbia University's Center for Science, Policy and Outcomes, and at the American Association for the Advancement of Science. She holds an AB in Genetics from the University of California, Berkeley, and a PhD in Microbiology from the University of Washington.

Michael B. Gerrard is Andrew Sabin Professor of Professional Practice at Columbia Law School, where he teaches courses on environmental and energy law and directs the Center for Climate Change Law. He was previously managing partner of the New York office of the law firm Arnold & Porter LLP, and he chaired the American Bar Association's section of environment, energy and resources.

Michael Jeffery, QC, holds a Chair in Law at the University of Western Sydney (UWS), Australia. He currently serves as Head of the UWS Social and Environmental Research Group and Deputy Chair of the NSW Environmental Defenders Office Board of Management. He has previously served as Director of Macquarie University's Centre for Environmental Law, Deputy Chair of the IUCN's Commission on Environmental Law and Chair of the Environmental Assessment Board of the Province of Ontario (Canada).

Timo Koivurova is a Research Professor at the Northern Institute for Minority and Environmental Law, University of Lapland, and has specialized in various aspects of international law applicable in the polar regions. His current research focuses on the legal status of indigenous peoples, the law of the sea in Arctic waters, the role of law in mitigating/adapting to climate change, and the function and role of the Arctic Council.

David Leary is a Senior Research Fellow and environmental lawyer in the Faculty of Law at the University of New South Wales, Sydney, Australia. He is also a Visiting Research Fellow at the United Nations University Institute of Advanced Studies, Japan, and a member of the International Scientific Advisory Board of the Arctic Centre, University of Lapland, Finland. His research interests include, *inter alia*, international environmental law and the law of the sea.

Richard L. Ottinger is Dean Emeritus and Professor of Law, Pace Law School; Chair, IUCN Commission on Environmental Law's Climate and Energy Working Group; former Member, US Congress, chairing the House Subcommittee on Energy, Conservation and Power; a founding staff member, US Peace Corps;

graduate, Harvard Law School and Cornell University.

Balakrishna Pisupati currently coordinates activities on biodiversity-related multilateral environmental agreements in UNEP's Division for Environmental Law and Conventions (DELC). He holds a PhD in Genetics. He has worked extensively on science and policy linkages for the past 20 years in various capacities including as the Head of IUCN Regional Biodiversity Programme Asia, and Coordinator of the United Nations University Institute of Advanced Studies' Biodiplomacy Programme. His interests include conservation and development policy, sustainable development and environmental governance.

Ann Powers is Associate Professor of Law at Pace Law School's Center for Environmental Legal Studies, where she teaches a range of environmental courses focusing on the law of oceans and coasts, international environmental law, United Nations diplomacy and water quality. Her scholarship includes emerging ocean issues and water pollution trading programmes, among other subjects. Professor Powers' recent work has focused particularly on ocean and international issues, and she has worked with United Nations Environment Programme projects, and the World Conservation Union's (IUCN) Commission on Environmental Law and its Law Academy.

Rosemary Rayfuse is a Professor of International Law at the Faculty of Law, University of New South Wales in Sydney, Australia. She specializes in the law of the sea and is known internationally for her work in international fisheries law and high seas governance, including polar oceans governance.

Tullio Scovazzi is Professor of International Law at the University of Milano–Bicocca, Milan, Italy. He occasionally participates, as legal advisor for Italy, in international negotiations and meetings relating to the law of the sea, cultural matters and human rights.

Susan Shearing teaches environmental law at the University of Sydney Law School. Her teaching and research interests include biodiversity law, heritage law and protected areas management, water law and sustainable business and environmental regulation. She is a member of the Australian Centre for Climate and Environmental Law and the IUCN's World Commission for Protected Area.

Victor M. Tafur holds qualifications of J.D. from Pontificia Universidad Javeriana (Bogotá, Colombia) as well as an LL.M. and S.J.D. in Environmental Law from Pace University, New York, USA. He is an energy and environmental lawyer based in New York and a member of the Adjunct Faculty at Pace Law School as well as Visiting Professor of Environmental Law, Bard College, Center for Environmental Policy.

Preface

It has become increasingly obvious in our recent research, capacity-building and outreach activities that, while there is considerable information and understanding amongst states and other actors concerning the nature of their obligations under international environmental law, and key principles of environmental management more generally and their nexus to development, there has been little debate on how international environmental law should respond to a range of new and emerging issues. Simply put, there has been little debate on the future of international environmental law, what emerging issues it may need to tackle, and the relationship of those issues to development, human rights and other areas of international law.

Assessing the implementation experiences, utilitarian value and effectiveness of existing regimes developed to date offers us some valuable lessons on what we need to do to improve the effectiveness of international law into the future. This will be important for assessing what needs to be done in terms of improving the effectiveness of existing law, but also, importantly, how international environmental law should respond to new, emerging challenges. In order to contribute in a small way to moving forward in the development of the "third generation" of international environmental law, this publication aims to focus on international environmental law and the future challenges it faces.

A number of people and organizations have made this publication possible. At United Nations University Press we would especially like to thank Robert Davis for his patience and support, from inception of our idea for this book right through until its publication. Thanks also to Naomi Cowan for her help with the final steps in bringing the book to publication. Likewise we are grateful for the comments on our original manuscript provided by the three anonymous peer reviewers. Thanks also to Professor A.H. Zakri, Professor Govindan Parayil and Dr Jose Antonio Puppim de Oliveira at the United Nations University Institute of Advanced Studies for their support of this publication.

We are grateful to several colleagues at UNEP Division of Environmental Law and Conventions who participated in useful discussions with us during the editing process, and to Mr Bakary Kante for his support of this publication.

We are also grateful for the support provided by our research assistants, Nishad Kulkarni and Qi Jiang, who provided great support in proofing and formatting the manuscript for publication.

We would also like to thank all the authors for their contributions to this book and their timely cooperation in meeting editorial deadlines.

Finally, we are especially grateful for the financial support for this publication provided by Dr Kin-chung Lam and his company, eBizAnywhere Technologies Ltd. This support has been invaluable in ensuring that the book can be widely distributed to scholars and policymakers in developing countries and around the world.

David Leary, Sydney, Australia
Balakrishna Pisupati, Nairobi, Kenya
February 2010

1

Introduction

David Leary and Balakrishna Pisupati

International environmental law: Responding to a world of problems

In its *Global Environment Outlook (GEO 4)* published in 2007 the United Nations Environment Programme (UNEP) paints a bleak picture of the state of the global environment and the connection of environmental degradation with development and human well-being. In the introductory words to this report, UNEP observes:

> Imagine a world in which environmental change threatens people's health, physical security, material needs and social cohesion. This is a world beset by increasingly intense and frequent storms, and by rising sea levels. Some people experience extensive flooding, while others endure intense droughts. Species extinction occurs at rates never before witnessed. Safe water is increasingly limited, hindering economic activity. Land degradation endangers the lives of millions of people. This is the world today.[1]

Climate change is one of the most significant of the many global environmental challenges. While our understanding of the causes and impacts of climate change were slow to emerge, it is no understatement to say that climate change is the greatest threat facing humanity and all life on Earth today. While all regions of the world will be impacted by climate change, it is the poor and especially the developing countries that are the most vulnerable. A detailed examination of the projected impacts of climate change are beyond the scope of this chapter, but a few examples

The future of international environmental law, Leary and Pisupati (eds),
United Nations University Press, 2010, ISBN 978-92-808-1192-6

drawn from the *Fourth Assessment Report* of the Intergovernmental Panel on Climate Change (IPCC) are worth noting to highlight the nature and scale of the challenges posed by climate change. For example, the IPCC has noted that by 2020, in some parts of Africa, "yields from rain-fed agriculture could be reduced by up to 50%".[2] This in turn is projected to compromise agricultural production and further adversely affect food security and exacerbate malnutrition in Africa.[3] In Asia, coastal areas, especially the heavily populated megadelta regions in South, East and Southeast Asia, are projected to be at increased risk of flooding.[4] For small island communities, sea level rise is expected to exacerbate inundation, storm surge, erosion and other coastal hazards and threaten vital infrastructure, settlements and facilities upon which island communities rely.[5]

Climate change will not only affect humans and human communities. By 2020, significant loss of biodiversity is projected to occur in many of the world's ecologically rich sites such as the Great Barrier Reef in Australia.[6] There is also "a risk of significant biodiversity loss through species extinction in many areas of tropical Latin America".[7] While the loss of biodiversity is already occurring, and in part is caused by climate change, it is also the result of many other human impacts. Threats to biodiversity come from varied sources including habitat destruction such as deforestation and modification and destruction of ecosystems for industrial, agricultural and other activities, overexploitation of resources (through activities such as overfishing and hunting), pollution, introduced species, to mention but a few.

The loss of biodiversity is occurring at an alarming rate. An update of the *IUCN Red List* published in 2008, the world's leading source of information on the status of biodiversity, makes for sober reading. This update presented an assessment of only 44 838 of the several millions of species thought to exist on Earth. Key figures from this assessment worth highlighting include:

- There were 869 recorded extinctions, with 804 species listed as extinct and 65 listed as extinct in the wild;
- The number of extinctions increases to 1159 if the 290 critically endangered species tagged as "possibly extinct" are included;
- 16 928 species are threatened with extinction (3246 are critically endangered, 4770 are endangered and 8912 are vulnerable);
- 3796 species are listed as near threatened; and
- 5570 species have insufficient information to determine their threat status and are listed as data deficient.[8]

Climate change and the alarming rates of biodiversity loss are but two examples of the many environmental problems humanity has faced over the past few decades. These challenges are in turn closely linked to development and human well-being. The global community has taken steps to seek to tackle many of these environmental challenges. These attempts have seen a veritable bloom in the development of international environmental law. There are now more than 900 multilateral and over 1500 bilateral treaties and other international agreements dealing with environmental issues.[9] These are in addition to the thousands of "soft law" instruments such as declarations and plans of action which have been the product of environmental diplomacy in recent decades. But despite the proliferation of international environmental agreements, environmental degradation has proceeded and new environmental challenges have continued to emerge.

But given the experience, some might say the failure, of international environmental law to deal with existing environmental challenges before turning to consider new and emerging challenges (the subject matter of much of this book), it is useful to consider the history of international environmental law and what lessons we may learn from that history. With that in mind this chapter seeks to set the scene for subsequent chapters by briefly sketching the history of international environmental law and to suggest some lessons that might help shape approaches to new and emerging issues in international environmental law, such as those discussed in this book. The chapter will then conclude with an outline of the structure and content of the rest of this book.

The development of international environmental law: The convergence of environment and development

International environmental law has arguably now gone through four key phases in its development. While treaties dealing with access to fishery resources, for example, can be identified at least as far back as 1351 with the conclusion of a fishery treaty between England and Castile, it was not until the mid-nineteenth century that the first series of treaties dealing with what we would regard today as environmental issues began to emerge. These included a range of fishery treaties that sought to guard against overexploitation of certain fish stocks; the first treaty dealing specifically with the protection of migratory birds, the first regional wildlife protection convention and conventions dealing with polluted waterways.[10]

But the most significant development of this first phase of international environmental law was the emergence of key principles from two international arbitrations, both involving the United States. The first of these was the 1893 Pacific Fur Seal Arbitration[11] which involved a dispute between the United States and the United Kingdom in relation to the protection of fur seals in the Bering Sea from overexploitation. This case rejected any suggestion that states had the right to assert jurisdiction by enacting measures relating to the conservation of living resources outside their jurisdiction, even if that meant the extinction of the species.[12] Any such measure requires the consent of all states concerned.[13] The other major development during this first phase of the development of international environmental law was the emergence in the Trail Smelter Arbitration of the principle that "no state has the right to use or permit the use of its territory in such a manner as to cause injury by fumes in or to the territory of another or the properties or persons therein".[14] The Trail Smelter Arbitration is considered the pivotal case in the emergence of the duty to prevent transboundary environmental harm, which is now largely accepted as a principle of customary international law.

However, the emergence of international environmental law through decisions of arbitral tribunals and other international judicial bodies has been the exception rather than the rule. For the large part, international environmental law has emerged through bilateral and multilateral negotiation of treaties and "soft law" instruments such as declarations and plans of action.

During the first phase of the development of international environmental law most of the treaties that were developed were purely utilitarian in character; efforts at protecting or conserving specific species were motivated largely by their usefulness rather than environmental protection per se.[15] But by the late 1960s, a period that arguably represents the emergence of a second phase of the development of international environmental law, serious concerns were being expressed about growing evidence of environmental degradation and it was realized that this degradation was closely linked to unsustainable levels of economic development and population growth. A number of studies during this period predicted a very bleak future for humanity if these trends continued unabated. For example, the Club of Rome in its seminal study *The Limits to Growth*, concluded:

> If the present growth trends in world population, industrialization, pollution, food production, and resource depletion continue unchanged, the limits to growth on this planet will be reached sometime within the next one hundred years. The most probable result will be a rather sudden and uncontrollable decline in both population and industrial capacity.[16]

By the time of the lead-up to the United Nations Conference on the Human Environment (UNCHE) in Stockholm in 1972, an understanding was emerging that development and environmental issues were clearly interdependent. As early as 1962 the United Nations General Assembly,

in Resolution 1831 (XVII), noted that "to be effective measures to preserve natural resources, flora and fauna should be taken at the earliest
possible moment simultaneously with economic development, including
industrialization, and urbanization".[17]

Likewise in the run-up to the Stockholm conference the *Founex Report*
commented:

> ... concern for environment must not and need not detract from the com-
> mitment of the world community – developing and more industrialised alike –
> to the overriding task of development of the developing regions of the world
> ... the environment problem has to be placed in its proper perspective both in
> the developed and the developing countries. It should be treated as a problem
> of the most *efficient synthesis* of developmental and environmental concerns
> at different stages of social transitions ... it must be emphasized in all inter-
> national forums, including the Stockholm Conference, that it is for the devel-
> oped countries to reassure the developing world that their growing
> environmental concern will not hurt the continued development of the devel-
> oping world.[18]

How to bring about the "efficient synthesis" of developmental and environmental concerns, as suggested by the *Founex Report*, has been a key
theme in debate on global environmental issues in the subsequent forty
years, especially at pivotal diplomatic conferences such as the 1972
UNCHE in Stockholm, the 1992 United Nations Conference on Environment and Development (UNCED) in Rio de Janeiro and the World Summit on Sustainable Development (WSSD) in Johannesburg in 2002.
Woven through key documents emerging from these meetings, including
such "soft law" declarations as the Stockholm Declaration,[19] Agenda 21,[20]
the Rio Declaration[21] and the Johannesburg Declaration,[22] and numerous treaties negotiated since Stockholm, the right to development and
protection of the environment were increasingly linked.

The Stockholm Conference marked the beginning of the third and
modern era of international environmental law. The Stockholm meeting
produced a number of significant outcomes including the establishment
of UNEP and the adoption of the Stockholm Declaration[23] setting out
twenty-six Principles and an Action Plan containing 109 recommendations.[24] As Philippe Sands has observed:

> The Stockholm Conference set the scene for international activities at the re-
> gional and global level, and influenced legal and institutional developments up
> to and beyond UNCED. Developments in this period are of two types: those
> directly related to Stockholm and follow-up actions; and those indirectly re-
> lated thereto. The period was marked by: a proliferation of international envir-
> onmental organisations (including those established by treaty) and greater

efforts by existing institutions to address environmental issues; the development of new sources of international environmental obligations from acts of
such organisations; new environmental norms established by treaty; the development of new techniques for implementing environmental standards; including environmental impact assessment and access to information; and the formal
integration of environment and development, particularly in relation to international trade and development assistance.[25]

By the 1980s it was firmly recognized that measures aimed at environmental protection had to also take account of the need for development.
In particular the "efficient synthesis" of developmental and environmental concerns was given major impetus by the 1987 report of the World
Commission on Environment and Development, chaired by Norwegian
Prime Minister Gro Harlem Brundtland (the so-called Brundtland Report).[26] The Bruntland Report characterized this as the need to ensure
"sustainable development", that is, "development that meets the needs of
the present without compromising the ability of future generations to
meet their own needs".[27] The Brundtland Report led in turn to the convening of the UNCED (the Earth Summit) in Rio de Janeiro in Brazil in
1992. The Earth Summit adopted three non-binding instruments: the Rio
Declaration,[28] the UNCED Forest Principles[29] and Agenda 21. In addition the Convention on Biological Diversity[30] and the UN Framework
Convention on Climate Change[31] were opened for signature at the Earth
Summit.
   Following the Earth Summit it was clear that international environmental law had come of age. Today it is possible to discern the existence
of several key principles of international environmental law including
significant new principles such as the precautionary principle, the "polluter pays" principle and the principle of common but differentiated responsibility.[32] A number of these principles, such as the principle of
common but differentiated responsibility, as well as the idea of sustainable development reflected the synthesis of environmental and development concerns.

Has international environmental law failed?

Despite the proliferation of international environmental agreements,
environmental degradation has continued and new environmental challenges have continued to emerge. Why is it that, despite the huge volume
of international environmental law, the state of the global environment
has continued to worsen? There are many complex reasons for this and it
is possible to identify a number of key points that have been put forward.

Some argue that it is the sheer volume of international legal instruments or treaty congestion that is partly to blame. As Edith Brown Weiss has observed:

The number and variety of environmental agreements has reached the point that some critics ask whether they may not severely strain the physical and organizational capacity of countries to handle them. There are signs of treaty congestion, in the form of separate negotiating fora, separate secretariats and funding mechanisms, overlapping provisions and inconsistencies between agreements, and severe demands on local capacity to participate in negotiations, meetings of parties, and associated activities. This affects the international community as a whole, since there will always be limited resources to address difficult issues and some countries may suffer particular inequities in their ability to participate effectively in new regimes ... [w]ith such a large number of international agreements, there is great potential for overlapping provisions in agreements, inconsistencies in obligations, significant gaps in coverage, and duplication of goals and responsibilities ... [I]nternational environmental law has developed in a piecemeal, almost random, manner ... [T]reaty congestion also contributes to significant inefficiencies in implementing international agreements. There are usually separate secretariats, monitoring processes, scientific councils, financing mechanisms, technical assistance programs and dispute resolution procedures ... [F]inally, treaty congestion leads to overload at the national level in negotiating and implementing the agreements ... Even industrialised states with well-developed regulatory mechanisms and bureaucracies show signs of being overwhelmed. As attention shifts to the need to comply with existing agreements, the burden on the administrative capacity of states will become more acute.[33]

Clearly therefore, as new environmental challenges arise, careful thought needs to be given as to whether new law or institutions are needed, or whether it might be more appropriate for existing laws, mechanisms and institutions to be utilized or adapted to meet new environmental challenges.

Part of the explanation for failure of international environmental law to address global environmental challenges also lies in the fact that, throughout the development of international environmental law, little attention was paid to the "effectiveness" of this new body of law. The debate on the effectiveness of international environmental law more broadly, or regimes for specific issues, has received considerable attention in both the academic and policy literature in recent years. By far the most comprehensive and detailed examination of this concept so far is that provided by Chambers.[34] After reviewing numerous studies by legal scholars and social scientists (and international relations literature in particular) he characterizes effectiveness of international environmental law in the following terms:

... there are three critical elements to the measurement of effectiveness that we can be certain of establishing with the knowledge that we have now. The first is a measurement of a treaty's effectiveness based on its performance data and compared with its objectives. A second determinant of effectiveness, which has not been widely argued in the literature thus far and reflects a great deal of the legal analysis of why states comply with international rules without the enforceability of strong sanctions, is the robustness of the treaty itself. Modern treaties have various built-in systems that allow their parties to review a treaty's status through scientific mechanisms or effectiveness review systems, or that enable parties to learn and become familiarized with the problem the treaty is addressing. Combined with these review and learning mechanisms are additional built-in systems that allow treaty renegotiation and take on deeper commitments to tackling the problems they have been created to address.

A theory of effectiveness must also pay attention to the supporting components of the treaty which may not be binding on the parties directly but implementing these provisions enhances and enables parties to achieve the goals of the treaty. These include financing, national programmes, technology transfer, capacity-building, and even institutional parts of the treaty such as the treaty secretariat. Though measuring the implementation of these supporting components of the treaty from the viewpoint of behavioural change is again methodologically difficult, it is logical that these provisions do have an impact, and measuring the degree of implementation in terms of the number of programmes or the level of financing is also an important component of determining the effectiveness of a treaty. Though not a key legal requirement of treaty effectiveness, financing is nevertheless a crucial lesson that has been learned from treaty-making in the past.[35]

International responses to new and emerging environmental challenges should therefore be crafted with an eye to their "effectiveness". As suggested by Chambers, a wider, rather than narrow, conception of effectiveness appears appropriate.

Similarly, while the first generation of international environmental law paid lip service to the clear link between human well-being and the environment (most notably in the repeated articulation of concepts such as the right to development and, more recently, sustainable development), increasingly international environmental law has become fragmented and disconnected, especially from other areas of international law. International environmental law is increasingly viewed as something separate from human rights law and international trade law, for example. But the reality is that the issues touched upon by all these bodies of law are very much interlinked. Failure to see these linkages has also undermined the effectiveness of international environmental law. As one scholar has noted:

Traditionally, international environmental protection and international economic law have been treated separately. The focus has been on controlling specific pollutants or conserving particular species as ends in themselves. In the new model, the focus is on ecosystems conservation, pollution prevention, and a precautionary approach, not only as environmental goods but as integral to sustainable development.

In the quest for environmentally sustainable development, the focus will likely be on considering environmental concerns at the front end of the industrializing process, so as to prevent pollution, minimize environmental degradation, and use resources more efficiently. This should mean increasing concern with making the entire production system environmentally sound. International environmental law will need to reflect this emphasis by focussing on performance standards to prevent pollution and minimize degradation, rather than on liability for damage, and on providing incentives to companies to use environmentally sound processes. Environment and trade issues will be increasingly joined.[36]

The development of international law in the future will need to be developed mindful of these obvious but often forgotten interlinkages.

On a somewhat related note, the effectiveness of international environmental law in responding to new and emerging environmental challenges will also be partly dependent on us breaking out of the pernicious influence of the pervasive concept of state sovereignty in international law. Clearly to view international relations, international policy and international law as only shaped by the nation state is to deny the reality that a range of non-state actors now shape world affairs and responses to the major global environmental challenges of our times. There is some truth to the observation that we are witnessing the emergence of a "kaleidoscopic" international legal and political system.[37] That is to say:

At the same time as globalization and integration are increasing, there is increased fragmentation within States and pressures for decentralized decision making ... While there is growing integration and fragmentation, the international system is also becoming kaleidoscopic. Shifting, *ad hoc* coalitions and associations, as well as individuals are becoming important actors ... This stage in the evolution of the international system, with its emerging bottom-up empowerment, may be characterised as kaleidoscopic. It is informal, and the actors and coalitions constantly change.

These developments pose challenges for the international legal system and at the same time opportunities to strengthen and expand the foundations of international law. International law must operate in a new multi-layered system consisting of States, international institutions, private sector and nongovernmental organization networks, the wide range of formal transnational bodies, ... and the new kaleidoscopic pattern of informal coalitions and individual initiatives.[38]

However, international law (or international lawyers?) have been slow to realize the implications of these changes. While a "kaleidoscopic" world may be emerging, international lawyers still see the world through myopic "rose-coloured glasses", regarding only the nation-state as the legitimate bearer of rights and duties under international law. The effectiveness of international responses to new and emerging global environmental challenges will thus also, in part, depend on how they are crafted to reflect this new "kaleidoscopic" world. Non-governmental organizations, transnational corporations and intergovernmental organizations must have a role to play in shaping and implementing responses to these issues. Likewise legal, regulatory and policy responses will need to take many forms beyond the usual command-and-control instruments typically recognized by nation-state-centric models, and incorporate the other institutions which comprise regulatory systems – regulated entities themselves, their industry associations, and third parties, both public interest institutions and commercial actors.[39]

In broad terms all of these issues are related to the wider issue of "international environmental governance". But what does the term "governance" mean in the context of existing and emerging environmental challenges, which for the most part are not confined to one location, one country or even one region of the word? To understand that, we need to understand what we mean by "international" or, perhaps more appropriately, "global governance". As Rosenau has posited:

> Does it refer to a central authority that can exercise control over far-flung situations on a global scale? Or is it limited to the exercise of authority in particular situations, such as environmental threats ... which may be global in scope and especially dire? Or does it connote the sum of all diverse efforts of communities at every level to move towards goals while preserving their coherence from one moment to the next?[40]

In the context of global environmental challenges the notion of a central authority has dominated much of the debate on global environmental governance. Proposals have included an international environmental agency, an international environmental authority, a world environmental organization and an international environmental organization.[41] While theoretically possible, a central authority with respect to global environmental issues looks unlikely to become reality.

Realistically governance, and in particular environmental governance, now and into the foreseeable future will be about the "diverse efforts of communities at every level", as Rosenau has suggested. Thus, in considering the likely contours of the future of international law, we need to focus less on new laws or treaties, although these will still be significant, and more on governance. We need to take a much more holistic approach, looking beyond law as a solution to international environmental problems. Importantly our focus on environmental governance should emphasize achieving "good" environmental governance. By that term we mean governance that can produce measurable and verifiable improvements in the state of the global environment.

The structure of this book

This book aims to explore some of these themes in more detail; to explore the future of international environmental law, not from the narrow perspective of what new treaties or new institutions may emerge, but from the broader perspective of international environmental law as but one part of the overall future of environmental governance. The book aims to contribute to debate on the future of international environmental law, the emerging issues it may need to tackle, and the relationship of those issues to development, human rights and other areas of international law.

The book is structured in three parts. Assessing the implementation experiences and the effectiveness of contemporary international environmental law offers us some valuable lessons on what we need to do to improve the effectiveness of international environmental law into the future. This will be important for assessing what needs to be done in terms of improving the effectiveness of existing law, and also the way in which international environmental law will be part of overall global environmental governance into the future.

Part I, the experience to date, continues with Chapter 2, in which Ann Powers highlights that,while climate change and pollution affect all states and peoples around the world, small island developing states are especially vulnerable. Developing countries, and small island developing states in particular, already face major challenges in dealing with pollution. But responses to existing environmental challenges such as pollution are complicated by the new and emerging challenges presented by climate change. No response to an environmental issue can be considered in isolation from other issues, and as this discussion highlights, the difficulties which small island developing states and other vulnerable coastal states face in managing and effectively implementing existing regional and global environmental agreements are only exacerbated by climate change concerns. Treaty congestion is clearly a real and pressing issue for such countries, even before one factors in the challenges now presented by climate change.

Moving beyond climate change, in Chapter 3, Susan Shearing examines the key challenges that affect the capacity of countries to develop and implement effective biodiversity conservation regimes. Her analysis of those challenges reveals the critical importance of addressing the key drivers for biodiversity loss through economic measures and institutional reform. There is a brief overview of the international legal framework for biodiversity conservation, focusing on the Convention for Biological Diversity (CBD) and associated policies and initiatives. The chapter goes on to argue that, notwithstanding the ongoing challenges for effective national implementation of the CBD obligations relating to conservation and sustainable use of biodiversity, a range of examples drawn from northern and southern nations illustrate the extent to which some key mechanisms identified in the CBD itself, including protected areas networks, economic tools and the sectoral mainstreaming of biodiversity issues, are playing an important role in facilitating national approaches to biodiversity conservation. The chapter thus illustrates that the effectiveness of the CBD goes beyond formal compliance with the letter of the convention; effectiveness depends very much on how those obligations are translated into concrete action on the ground.

Chapter 4 by Tullio Scovazzi paints a picture of one of the success stories in international environmental law – the legal instruments applying to the protection of the Mediterranean environment, the so-called Barcelona system of marine pollution treaties. The Barcelona system has acted as a model for the UNEP regional seas treaties and this chapter highlights why it is important for international legal regimes to be able to adapt over time as new challenges emerge.

This is followed by Chapter 5 where Donna Craig and Michael Jeffery explore the role of public participation and access to information in achieving sustainable development and good environmental governance. They describe the close link between sustainable development and transparency and access to information in fostering good environmental outcomes. Clearly good environmental governance at the national and international level involves many actors and many stakeholders, and in this chapter the authors explore existing legal principles and "best practice" approaches to environmental governance highlighting public participation, and its relationship with the ever-evolving goals and complexities of ecologically sustainable development. In that regard they highlight the particularly significant model presented by the Aarhus Convention.

In the last chapter in Part I, Gudmundur Alfredsson, continuing some of the themes examined in Chapter 5, goes on to explore the connections between human rights law and the protection of the environment, with a particular focus on the rights of indigenous peoples. This chapter focuses in particular on the rights to land and resources of indigenous peoples and how these relate to environmental qualities; it covers the efforts at mainstreaming or incorporating human rights into other UN programme activities as well as human rights elements in international environmental instruments and how they are applied. A central question asked is whether environmental law can draw lessons from human rights law including, in particular, public access to and contributions to monitoring institutions. As this suggests, questions surrounding environmental governance are closely linked to developments in law and governance in other areas.

Part II of the book then goes on to explore the dynamics and challenges of a number of international legal regimes that are currently in transition. In Chapter 7, Michael Gerrard and Dionysia-Theodora Avgerinopoulou consider the challenges to environmental law posed by climate change, with a particular focus on the adaptation needs of both developed and developing countries. After considering the current status of international treaties relating to climate change, the chapter examines some of the key issues that need to be addressed beyond 2012. It also explores the interaction between international human rights provisions and climate change law. The authors argue in particular that climate change is becoming the public face of unsustainable development, and contend that new legal instruments will be required, but beyond that, developments in policy will also be important.

In Chapter 8, Timo Koivurova and Sébastien Duyck examine some key principles that could be used to sustainably address challenges in governing the Arctic Ocean. Significantly, as the first part of this chapter highlights, the environmental governance regime for the Arctic already clearly recognizes the legitimate expectations of and a role in decision-making for non-state actors, and in particular the indigenous peoples of the Arctic. As the authors make clear, future discussions in relation to the Arctic will focus on governance rather than on new treaties.

In Chapter 9, Rosemary Rayfuse examines the relevance of the Grotian legacy of freedom of the high seas for the future of international environmental law relating to the marine environment. She argues that the history of the law of the sea has been one of oscillation between freedom and restriction. Today, she argues, freedom of the high seas is not unlimited and an ever-increasing range of restrictions on this freedom now exists. Rayfuse goes on to consider what might replace the Grotian legacy in the future.

Part III examines a number of new and emerging issues for international environmental law to address. In Chapter 10 the editors of this book, David Leary and Balakrishna Pisupati, consider the implications of the emergence of nanotechnology. This chapter focuses on the emerging global debate on the need for new regulation to address perceived environmental and human health risks associated with nanotechnology. This analysis highlights that the response of policymakers, regulators and the legal system is very much a work in process. The chapter argues that it appears increasingly obvious that international responses to nanotechnology relate not so much to law, per se, but perhaps falls under the broader idea of international governance for nanotechnology. The evolution of this governance, perhaps eventually leading to new laws and treaties, will need to be driven by increased scientific understanding and a precautionary and adaptive framework of risk management.

This is followed, in Chapter 11, by Richard Ottinger and Victor Tafur's examination of the risks and opportunities posed by the emergence of biofuels as an alternative fuel source. The chapter focuses on emerging responses such as the development of appropriate standards to assure the sustainability of biofuel production, again highlighting the potential of governance mechanisms beyond new laws and treaties. New standards for sustainable biofuels appear initially to be most significant, pending development of any future treaty or other "hard law" responses.

In Chapter 12, Michele Garfinkel and Robert Friedman explore the emergence of yet another novel issue for international policymakers to consider, namely, synthetic biology. In this chapter the authors first describe the science and engineering of synthetic biology and synthetic genomics and then go on to discuss emerging societal concerns about the technologies. There has so far been little consideration of the implications of this issue for international environmental law, so this chapter will no doubt serve as the starting point for a debate on a new and as yet unconsidered challenge for international environmental law and policy. As the starting point for a new and significant debate, the chapter highlights that synthetic biology and synthetic genomics introduce novel problems for those concerned about the governance of biotechnologies generally. Responding to those challenges is both a legal and a broader policy and governance challenge.

In the concluding chapter the editors draw together the main conclusions from all the contributions and consider their implications for the future of international environmental law.

Notes

1. United Nations Environment Programme, *Global Environment Outlook (GEO-4): Environment for Development* (2007), p. 6; available at <http://www.unep.org/geo/geo4/report/GEO-4_Report_Full_en.pdf>.
2. Intergovernmental Panel on Climate Change, *Climate Change 2007-Synthesis Report: Contribution of Working Groups I, II and III to the Fourth Assessment Report of the Intergovernmental Panel on Climate Change*, (Geneva, Switzerland: IPCC, 2007), p. 11.

3. Ibid.
4. Ibid.
5. Ibid., p. 12.
6. Ibid., p. 11.
7. Ibid.
8. Jean-Christophe Vié, Craig Hilton-Taylor and Simon Stuart, *Wildlife in a Changing World: An Analysis of the 2008 IUCN Red List of Endangered Species* (Gland, Switzerland: IUCN, 2008), p. 16.
9. These figures are drawn from the University of Oregon's *International Environmental Agreements Database Project* website as at 21 August 2009; available at <http://iea.uoregon.edu/>.
10. For an overview of all these treaties see Philippe Sands, *Principles of International Environmental Law* (Cambridge: Cambridge University Press, 2003), pp. 26–30.
11. Behring Sea Fur Seals Fisheries Arbitration (Great Britain v United States), *Moore's International Arbitrations* (1893), p. 755.
12. Philippe Sands, "Unilateralism, Values and International Law", *European Journal of International Law*, vol. 11, no. 2 (2000), pp. 291–302, p. 293.
13. Ibid.
14. Trail Smelter Arbitral Tribunal Decision 11 March 1941, *American Journal of International Law*, vol. 35 (1941), pp. 684–736.
15. Bhrat H. Desahi, *Institutionalizing International Environmental Law* (New York: Transnational Publishers Inc., 2004), p. 71.
16. Donella H. Meadows, Dennis L. Meadows, Jørgen Randers and William W. Behrens III, *The Limits to Growth: A Report for the Club of Rome's Project on the Predicament of Mankind* (London: Pan Books Ltd, 1972), p. 23.
17. *Economic Development and the Conservation of Nature*, G.A. Resolution 1831 (XVII), UN GAOR, 17th Session, Supp. no. 17, UN Doc. A/RES/1831 (XVII) (1962).
18. *Fournex Report on Development and Environment*, submitted by a Panel of Experts Convened by the Secretary-General of the United Nations Conference on the Human Environment, 4–12 June 1971, Founex, Switzerland. Quoted in Desahi, *Institutionalizing International Environmental Law*, pp. 75–76 (emphasis added).
19. Declaration of the UN Conference on the Human Environment, Stockholm, 5–16 June 1972, contained in Report of the UN Conference on the Human Environment, UN Doc. A/CONF.48/14.
20. *Report of the UN Conference on Environment and Development*, A/CONF.151/26/ev.1 (vol. I) (1993).
21. Rio Declaration on Environment and Development, 31 ILM 874 (1992).
22. Johannesburg Declaration on Sustainable Development, A/CONF.199/L.6/Rev.2 (2002).
23. Declaration of the UN Conference on the Human Environment, Stockholm, 5–16 June 1972, contained in *Report of the UN Conference on the Human Environment*, UN Doc. A/CONF.48/14.
24. *Report of the UN Conference on the Human Environment*, UN Doc. A/CONF.48/14 and Corr.1 (1972).
25. Sands, *Principles of International Environmental Law*, p. 40.
26. *Report of the World Commission on Environment and Development: Our Common Future*; available at <http://www.un-documents.net/wced-ocf.htm>.
27. Ibid.
28. Rio Declaration on Environment and Development.
29. *Non-legally Binding Authoritative Statement of Principles for a Global Consensus on the Management, Conservation and Sustainable Development of All Types of Forests*, A/CONF.151/6/Rev.1, 13 June 1992.

30. Convention on Biological Diversity, Rio de Janeiro, 5 June 1992, entered into force 29 December 1993, 1760 UNTS 79; 31 ILM 818 (1992).
31. United Nations Framework Convention on Climate Change, Rio de Janeiro, 9 May 1992, entered into force 21 March 1994, 31 ILM 849 (1992).
32. A detailed examination of these principles is beyond the scope of this chapter but the reader is refered to texts on international environmental law such as Sands, *Principles of International Environmental Law*; and Patricia Birnie and Alan Boyle, *International Law and the Environment* (Oxford: Oxford University Press, 2002) for detailed examination of these principles.
33. Edith Brown Weiss, "New Directions in International Environmental Law", United Nations Congress on Public International Law, New York, 1995, reproduced in Donna Craig, Nicolas Robinson and Koh Kheng-Lian, *Capacity Building for Environmental Law in the Asian and Pacific Region* (Manila: Asian Development Bank, 2002), pp. 10–11.
34. William Bradnee Chambers, *Interlinkages and the Effectiveness of Multilateral Environmental Agreements* (Tokyo: United Nations University Press, 2008).
35. Ibid., pp. 128–129.
36. Weiss, "New Directions in International Environmental Law", p. 13.
37. Edith Brown Weiss, "International Law in a Kaleidoscopic World", paper presented at the Second Biennial General Conference of the Asian Society of International Law, Tokyo, 1–2 August 2009.
38. Ibid.
39. This conception of regulatory regimes draws on Peter N. Grabosky, "Discussion Paper: Inside the Pyramid: Towards a Conceptual Framework for the Analysis of Regulatory Systems", *International Journal of the Sociology of Law*, vol. 25, no. 3 (1997), pp. 195–201; and Weiss, "New Directions in International Environmental Law", p. 12.
40. James Rosenau, "Governance in a New Global Order", in David Held and Anthony McGrew (eds), *The Global Transformations Reader: An Introduction to the Globalization Debate* (Cambridge: Cambridge Polity Press, 2003), pp. 223–235, p. 224.
41. For an overview of these proposals see, for example, Steve Charnovitz, "A World Environmental Organization", *Columbia Journal of Environmental Law*, vol. 27, no. 2 (2002), pp. 323–362.

Part I

The experience to date

2

Climate change and pollution: Addressing intersecting threats to oceans, coasts and small island developing states

Ann Powers

Future developments in international law will take place in a number of forums, spurred by a range of environmental threats and related legal and policy issues. Two critical concerns will be the continuing impact of climate change on the global environment and the concomitant and often overlapping role of pollution in threatening human health and the environment. While both climate change and pollution may have impacts on states and peoples around the world, they cast an especially long shadow on ocean and coastal states, in particular on small island developing states (SIDS) and their vulnerable populations. These states are already feeling the effects of sea level rise attributable to climate change, or anticipate impacts in the near future. If predictions are correct, many may suffer inundation, increasing storm events, and the need to address displaced populations. For the most part the engine of the problem is greenhouse gas (GHG) emissions from land-based facilities, located primarily in developed or rapidly developing nations. In addition to warming the oceans and fuelling sea level rise, the emission of carbon dioxide, a particular greenhouse gas, has a direct impact on ocean waters, acidifying them, with dire effects for oceanic calcifying organisms such as coral reefs and shellfish. But the problems do not end there. Although climate change generally results from worldwide discharges to which small island and other vulnerable states contribute little, more localized sources of pollution can contribute to the degradation of their coastal environments. That may occasion the loss of fisheries and other coastal resources, and result in reduced employment opportunities, adverse economic impacts and

The future of international environmental law, Leary and Pisupati (eds),
United Nations University Press, 2010, ISBN 978-92-808-1192-6

perhaps eventual population displacement. This conjunction of climate change and pollution threats may be greater than the sum of the parts, and presents a peril of incalculable dimensions. Although efforts are being made at international, regional, national and local levels to respond to these threats, there are no ready solutions. Some of these efforts are described below, but first, a broader understanding of the problems is useful.

Fragile states

Although mainland coastal states are or may be severely impacted, witness Bangladesh, the nations most imperilled generally are small island developing states. Not only is the very existence of the islands often at risk, but wide swathes of ocean areas within SIDS Exclusive Economic Zones (EEZs) under the Law of the Sea Convention may be endangered.[1] While it might be more accurate to refer to these states as "large ocean states" rather than small island states,[2] under either sobriquet, they often lack the means to effectively protect and care for their far-flung environmental resources. Yet this semantic shift does emphasize the valuable resources for which SIDS are custodians and on which they depend.

The often impoverished nature of these island nation-states challenges their ability to control and properly address issues of climate change and pollution. At least 20% of SIDS still qualify as least developed countries (LDCs),[3] and the Secretary-General of the United Nations has taken particular note that, in the developing countries category, small island developing states are among the most vulnerable.[4] While SIDS make only a limited contribution to global climate change and can do little to mitigate that global problem, they may be able to influence many critical local pollution threats to their marine environments. The global and regional environmental conventions, treaties and protocols in place provide some protection and offer foundations for improvement and more comprehensive protection of marine resources. However, only through cooperation within the global community and with the development not only of international environmental law and programmes but efforts at every level of government, can we effectively address the dual threats of climate change and ocean degradation.

Environmental threats

Climate change impacts

Sea level rise from global warming, which could be as much as 0.8 to 2.0 metres by 2100,[5] threatens some low-lying, small islands with outright annihilation. The change in ocean levels will be due not only to melting of glaciers and polar ice, but also to thermal expansion of ocean waters from overall temperature increases.[6] The Intergovernmental Panel on Climate Change (IPCC) as far back at 1995 reported a 0.3 to 0.6 °C rise in mean surface temperature of the Earth compared to the late nineteenth century.[7] More recent studies indicate ocean warming and thermal expansion rates larger than previously thought,[8] and the *Climate Change Science Compendium 2009*, prepared by the United Nations Environment Programme (UNEP), shows that climate change is accelerating at a much faster pace than was previously comprehended by scientists. According to experts, new scientific evidence suggests the disturbing conclusion that important tipping points, leading to irreversible changes in major Earth systems and ecosystems, may already have been reached or even overtaken.

An increase in ocean levels holds disastrous effects for small islands, even if they are not completely inundated, since most of their population live in the coastal zones. Sea level rise, increased storm activity and climate change can affect food and water security, health and sanitation, as well as the lives and livelihoods of small island and coastal residents around the world. When these impacts are severe, they can lead to population displacement and migration.[9]

Many small islands are already experiencing extensive coastal erosion.[10] The South Pacific Regional Environment Programme reports that rising global sea levels have flooded small islets in Kiribati and Tuvalu, damaged coastal roads and bridges, and destroyed traditional burial places.[11] It is projected that in the Seychelles a 100 cm, or 39 inch, rise in sea level would claim 70% of the country's total land mass.[12] It is estimated that, if current trends continue, in a country such as the Maldives close to 80% of its atolls could be completely inundated. In a touching statement before the UN Human Rights Council in 2008 its Minister of Foreign Affairs noted that four children were born that morning in his capital city, who "will not have the opportunity to live out their lives in the country of their birth, on the islands that their ancestors have inhabited for the past three and a half millennia".[13]

In addition to raising sea levels, emissions of GHGs cause climate changes which seriously threaten the viability of ocean habitats and the viability of many SIDS themselves. Increased seawater temperature affects marine ecosystems and marine biodiversity, changing the distribution, abundance and biodiversity of marine organisms.[14] These same marine ecosystems are crucial to the global cycle of carbon and other greenhouse gases. Excess dissolution of carbon dioxide causes increased acidification of ocean water, thereby disrupting or destroying ocean ecosystems and threatening many marine life forms. The continuing decrease in pH, resulting from increased anthropogenic carbon dioxide emissions absorbed from the atmosphere into the oceans, will have negative environmental impacts, especially on oceanic calcifying organisms such as coral reefs.[15] Coral reefs are critical to small island communities, not only as breeding grounds for many fish and other marine species and subsistence for local fisheries, but also as tourist destinations. In addition, they provide natural barrier protection against storms, waves and floods.[16] Beyond climate change impacts, reefs are subjected to overfishing, unsustainable tourism practices, coastal development, pollution, disease and invasive species.[17]

Temperature changes may also cause or be connected with changing wind and rainfall patterns, which have already resulted in uncommon drought conditions on certain Indian Ocean and Pacific islands.[18] Extreme weather events such as storm surges, flash floods and tropical cyclones could increase in frequency and intensity as a result of changes in climate. All of these climatic phenomena can negatively affect populations and increase pressure on the already scarce land resources of SIDS.[19]

The impacts of climate change are not only physical, but economic. The IPCC estimates global warming may require developing countries to spend millions or even billions of dollars to adapt to changing climate conditions.[20] For example, Caribbean island states are projected to spend $1.1 billion in construction projects intended to combat sea level rise.[21]

Pollution effects from land-based sources and activities

Even without climate change impacts, many coastal and island nations are confronted with grave environmental threats from a variety of pollution sources, for the most part land-based (LBS, also termed land-based sources and activities or LBSA), or from undeveloped or underdeveloped waste management systems and especially poor land practices. It is estimated that 80 per cent of marine pollution comes from LBSA.[22] These sources of pollution exert adverse impacts on both marine and human systems. Especially vulnerable to land-based sources of pollution are a variety of valuable and fragile ecosystems, such as coral reefs. Particularly damaging to these coastal ecosystems is untreated wastewater that is being discharged into coastal waters. Nutrients released through sewage or fertilizer can cause eutrophication, or oxygen depletion, thereby reducing water quality and consequently damaging fish, coral and other marine populations.[23] These adverse effects alter food web dynamics and threaten a coastal state's entire marine ecosystem.[24] Nutrient pollution also increases the probability of disease outbreaks that kill fish and coral.[25] In addition to nutrient overloads, land-based sources of pollution frequently include chemical pollution from factories and activities such as mining or toxic dumping.[26] Toxic chemicals are especially dangerous because they bioaccumulate in fish and can disrupt hormone balances, hindering fish reproduction and altering food web dynamics and ecosystem functions.[27] Not only do these toxins bioaccumulate within a species, but they can biomagnify up the food chain. Plastics and floating debris have equally adverse consequences because they contain persistent organic pollutants such as polychlorinated biphenyls (PCBs). Once consumed by fish, marine mammals and seabirds, they too can negatively impact food web dynamics.[28]

Pollution additionally creates problems for human populations. Ocean pollution damages economically important marine species on which coastal and small island state economies often depend. Ocean pollution lowers the productivity of fisheries, which threatens the livelihood of local residents. Paralytic shellfish poisoning (PSP), ciguatera, or elevated mercury levels are severe health risks associated with nutrient pollution in coastal areas.[29] Economically, environmental degradation due to pollution of coastal waters spoils aesthetic values, recreation and tourism.[30] As industrial activities, agriculture and mining intensify throughout the world's regions, new synthetic compounds are developed. All too often, pollution from these compounds advances unregulated and unmonitored, with unfortunate results.[31] Many adverse environmental impacts to marine ecosystems and humans are observed on a daily basis, but sadly, many may remain undiscovered.[32]

As noted above, the parties most affected by land-based sources of pollution are the coastal communities that depend on the sea for subsistence, particularly SIDS, and developing states with substantial coastal exposure. The adverse impacts of ocean pollution on the most vulnerable populations, particularly from land-based sources, which often go unregulated, can be severe and may create poverty conditions or exacerbate existing hardship. Watershed management of coastal areas in many SIDS is undeveloped or ineffective, because these nations often lack adequate equipment, trained regulatory personnel, scientific data concerning water systems, or watershed planning and management organization.[33] The tenuous state of SIDS pollution control mechanisms are compounded by the fact that these states have authority over, and are responsible for, living resources in their 200-mile EEZs, which comprise much of the world's ocean space.[34] Despite this apparent wealth in ocean resources, many SIDS do not currently benefit from the resources within their EEZs due to the island states' inadequate capacity to manage their ocean resources. The states suffer from a lack of required technologies essential for development and a lack of capacity by the SIDS government to encourage proper and sustainable development.[35]

Environmental measures focused on reducing ocean pollution from land-based sources and activities are an important approach to achieving healthy and replenished marine ecosystems and to providing a platform for the sustainable use of coastal and ocean resources. As discussed below, international cooperation exists in varying forms and forums which help identify the scope, direction and extent of national and local actions to prevent, control, reduce and eliminate marine pollution from land-based sources and activities.[36] But identification of problems is not sufficient. Effective resolution of pollution problems requires technical and legal responses from every level of governance.

Addressing the problems

Cognisant of their imperilled condition, SIDS over the past decade have banded together in various international associations to focus attention on their plight and to pressure developed countries to curtail GHG emissions. The Alliance of Small Island States (AOSIS), a coalition of small island developing states and other low-lying coastal countries,[37] helps bring attention to developmental challenges and environmental issues facing SIDS, in particular the significant adverse effects of climate change.[38] The Alliance acts as "an ad hoc lobby and negotiating voice for Small Island Developing States (SIDS) within the United Nations system".[39] In order to assure that the islands' voices were heard in the process leading up to the UN Framework Convention on Climate Change (UNFCCC) negotiations in December 2009, AOSIS issued a Declaration on Climate Change calling for steep cuts in emissions and strict targets for temperature.[40]

In addition to AOSIS, the UN Office of the High Representative for the Least Developed Countries, Landlocked Developing Countries and the Small Island Developing States (UN-OHRLLS) supports the coordination of follow-up activities and assists in gathering support and resources for the implementation of the Programme of Action for the Sustainable Development of Small Island Developing States. It also performs group consultations with and advocacy work for SIDS with the applicable sections of the United Nations, in addition to working with civil society, media, academia and foundations.[41]

Additionally, the UN Department of Economic and Social Affairs (UN-ECOSOC) helps developing countries through analytic and policy support to transform the commitments made by the states at the international level into national policies. It further assists states by tracking their progress with internationally agreed development goals.[42] In spite of the benefits provided by these organizations to the SIDS, it is not clear which organization pre-eminently represents the issues concerning SIDS in international forums.[43]

The vulnerability of SIDS is due, not only to their fragile environmental ecosystems, but also by reason of their limited resources available for mitigating pollution and adapting to climate changes and sea level rise. In order to effectively handle the various environmental and social issues affecting SIDS, responses are needed from the global to local levels. Effective resolution, or at least mitigation, of the environmental challenges facing SIDS requires diligence on the part of both developed as well as developing countries to ensure that the legal mechanisms already available are properly employed, and that new legal mechanisms are developed. However, the legal mechanisms on each level are not comprehensive and, as demonstrated below, offer only fragmented approaches to addressing the environmental challenges facing SIDS. For the most part the mechanisms are in the form of international conventions and programmes, and these have in the past been focused primarily on addressing pollution and its impacts rather than climate change. Some efforts have been made to use courts and other tribunals as forums for addressing climate change, but those efforts have not yet been particularly effective.

Resorting to courts and tribunals

Litigation is especially problematic for addressing climate change because of the broad range of parties contributing to GHGs, and the procedural rules in most jurisdictions. Nonetheless, attempts have been made or threatened.[44] The utility of this type of approach may be more in focusing attention on the problem than in actually bringing emitters to court.[45] Cases brought before Human Rights Commissions have perhaps a greater chance of success,[46] since the link between climate change and human rights has already been recognized. In 2007, the Malé Declaration on the Human Dimension of Global Climate Change resulted from a Small Island States Conference on the Human Dimension of Global Climate Change. The agreement explicitly provided that "climate change has clear and immediate implications for the full enjoyment of human rights".[47] Subsequently, at the urging of the Maldives and other states, the United Nations Human Rights Council enacted Resolution 7/23, *Human Rights and Climate Change*, which asked the Office of the UN High Commissioner for Human Rights to undertake a study of the relationship between climate change and human rights.[48] However, substantive and procedural barriers remain.

Conventions and programmes

The UN Convention on the Law of the Sea

The 1982 UN Convention on the Law of the Sea (UNCLOS) provides a framework for the development and use of ocean resources. The

UNCLOS works as an overarching source of international ocean regulation by supplying basic principles and norms, and creating a foundation for more concrete rules, regulations and standards. These can be integrated into regional or locally specific agreements and national law. The principles agreed upon in UNCLOS guide the objectives of later international instruments relating to the effective and responsible use of ocean areas and resources.[49]

The UNCLOS is a valuable resource for addressing threats from LBSA because it provides that states shall adopt laws and regulations as well as take other measures that reduce, prevent and control pollution; including land-based sources of marine pollution.[50] The UNCLOS recognizes, when dealing with the LBSA of marine pollution, that action must be taken at global, regional and national levels. Article I of UNCLOS defines "pollution of the marine environment" as:

> ... the introduction by man, directly or indirectly, of substances or energy into the marine environment, including estuaries, which results or is likely to result in such deleterious effects as harm to living resources and marine life, hazards to human health, hindrance to marine activities, including fishing and other legitimate uses of the sea, impairment of quality for use of sea water and reduction of amenities.[51]

This definition provides a broad platform for addressing ocean pollution and for protecting valuable marine resources. Inclusion of estuaries ensures that LBSA deep within the responsible state are still subject to the conditions agreed upon in the UNCLOS. Likewise, terms such as "indirectly" and "likely to result" help avoid the narrowing of legal obligations by treaty members or within related regional protocols.

The UNCLOS builds on the definition of pollution through Part XII, which stipulates that states must "protect and preserve the marine environment".[52] They also must take all measures necessary to "prevent, reduce and control" pollution of the marine environment from any source.[53] This includes the "release of toxic, harmful or noxious substances, especially those which are persistent", from land-based sources, from or through the atmosphere.[54] Article 207 explains a state's obligations to prevent marine pollution from land-based sources.[55] Pollution under this article includes sources affecting and emanating from rivers, estuaries, pipelines and other such structures.[56] The UNCLOS additionally mentions prevention and reduction of marine pollution from and through the atmosphere.[57] In order to control and regulate marine pollution, states agree to take into account international rules, standards and recommended practices,[58] and they are advised to harmonize their policies on a regional basis.[59] Globally, member states should make an effort to create rules, practices and procedures through international organizations and diplomatic conferences to combat LBSA of marine pollution.[60] However, the UNCLOS recommends that these global initiatives take into account regional characteristics and the capacity of developing nations to comply, along with their need for economic development.[61]

The UNCLOS obligates states to meet the general requirements of the Convention but also to enhance national pollution prevention actions. When faced with pollution from LBSA that occurs within national land territory (land-based and airborne sources), the UNCLOS requires that national laws consider international rules and standards.[62] Recognizing that not all countries are able to modify their domestic legislation or development activities immediately, the UNCLOS provides that the measures each state employs must rely on the "best practicable means at [its] disposal and be in accordance with [its] capabilities".[63] Whether that provides sufficient guidance to protect the ocean environment may be open to question.

Convention on Biological Diversity

Other international treaties concerning environmental issues take a more generalized approach than the UNCLOS. The Convention on Biological Diversity (CBD) aims to protect biodiversity, provide for sustainable use of the components of biodiversity and encourage the sharing of benefits of genetic resources in an equitable manner.[64] The agreement applies to all ecosystems, species and genetic resources.[65] The CBD uses traditional conservation principles, but with an economic goal, to use biological resources sustainably. It calls for the development of national strategies and programmes for the conservation and sustainable development of biodiversity.[66] The CBD requires member states to identify processes and categories of activities that have or are likely to have significant adverse impacts on the conservation and sustainability of biological diversity.[67] Monitoring these impacts and their effects through sampling and other techniques offers a basis on which to strengthen national or regional environmental standards. Party nations are also required to develop or maintain necessary legislation and other regulatory provisions for the protection of threatened species and populations.[68] Through these treaty requirements, integrated marine and coastal area management approaches can emerge which protect and sustainably develop biodiversity in compliance with CBD provisions.[69]

The actual authoritative body comprised within the CBD is the Conference of Parties (COP), which includes the governments that have ratified the treaty, and other regional organizations. The COP is responsible for the measurement of progress on CBD requirements, the identification of new priorities and the establishment of work plans for member countries or organizations.[70] However, implementation of the CBD greatly depends on the initiative of individual countries. Compliance with the CDB also necessitates a cadre of dedicated nations willing to invest capital in the preservation of their natural resources, along with outside pressure from other countries or the public at large.

Integral to the successful operation of the CBD is the consistent sharing of knowledge and ideas, such as the best practices and policies for conservation of biodiversity, employing an ecosystem-based approach to sustainable use of natural resources. The CBD addresses threats to biodiversity by initiating projects founded in developmental planning, transboundary cooperation, involvement of local and indigenous populations in sustainable development management and the creation of thematic programmes covering the major biomes found on Earth.[71]

The most relevant CBD thematic programme for the SIDS is the Island Biodiversity Programme which seeks to address the issues peculiar to island habitats. Key challenges are the problems associated with the extreme vulnerability of endemic species.[72] The Island Biodiversity Programme seeks to address the specific island concerns and create a platform for the exchange of knowledge concerning the conservation of biodiversity.[73] In establishing the Programme the COP requested that parties apply targets and timeframes in a flexible manner, thereby providing a framework for the creation of national and regional targets, but taking into account particular nations' priorities and capacities.[74] Parties are also expected to consider differences in diversity between regions.[75] Progress may be tracked using existing national indicators, or national indicators may be established based on the list of global indicators used for assessing progress towards the 2010 Biodiversity Target.[76]

The goals of the Programme are to be achieved by implementation of fifty priority actions for parties.[77] The actions are intended to curb island biodiversity loss by 2010, thereby contributing to sustainable economic and environmental development for the SIDS.[78] The Programme priority actions integrate objectives of a number of key documents and programmes especially relevant to the SIDS. They include the Strategic Plan of the Convention on Biological Diversity,[79] the Barbados Programme of Action for the Sustainable Development of Small Island Developing States (BPoA),[80] the Plan of Implementation of the World Summit on Sustainable Development,[81] the Mauritius Strategy for the Further Implementation of the Barbados Programme of Action for the Sustainable Development of Small Island Developing States[82] and the Millennium Development Goals.[83]

A key mechanism used to implement these goals is the Global Island Partnership (GLISPA) which is used to mobilize leadership and aid in the conservation of island resources.[84] The partnership was first called for in Mauritius[85] and eventually implemented at the COP to the CBD in Brazil 2006.[86] The GLISPA advances island conservation and encourages sustainable development of SIDS through seven major strategies:

1. Inspire and recognize leadership and commitments to action for island conservation and sustainable livelihoods;
2. Strengthen partnerships to support implementation of commitments and to build local long-term conservation capacity;
3. Facilitate increased public and private funding for island priorities;
4. Promote targeted and cost-effective collaboration and exchanges among islands;
5. Engage in effective communication strategies on island issues;
6. Build linkages between all islands, regardless of political status;
7. Track progress on GLISPA commitments.[87]

So far the GLISPA has recorded some successful results including significant achievement on meeting conservation commitments by several countries, and progress by other countries establishing financial mechanisms for protecting biodiversity.[88]

Agenda 21

Agenda 21 was approved as a general policy document by the UN Conference on Environment and Development (UNCED) in Rio de Janeiro in 1992, and has made significant contributions to the development of LBSA protections in regional seas conventions and their protocols.[89] It established several new principles for the protection and preservation of ocean ecosystems, including a focus on sustainable development and integrated conservation methods, as well as economic incentives. Other principles of particular importance contained in Agenda 21 are the "polluter pays" principle and the precautionary principle, the latter aimed at preventing environmental harm as opposed to regulating sources of pollution after the fact.[90] The principles espoused in Agenda 21 have influenced subsequent global and regional conventions and have helped stimulate amendment or revision of existing treaties.[91]

Agenda 21 also established priority activities necessary for the sustainable development of SIDS, such as increasing scientific and technical knowledge, data and information, plans and response strategies, technology, human resources development and capacity-building.[92] It further stressed cooperation and involvement of the international community as an integral part to successful implementation of the prioritized activities.[93]

In carrying out the goals of Agenda 21, the World Conference on Sustainable Development issued, in 2002, the Johannesburg Plan of Implementation, in which it asked SIDS to thoroughly examine the implementation of the BPoA by 2004.[94] The ten-year review of the BPoA was held in Mauritius in January 2005. From this the Mauritius Strategy for the Further Implementation of the Programme of Action for the Sustainable Development of Small Island Developing States was created.[95] The Mauritius Strategy asserts that priority should be given to ocean and coastal issues, including action to complete delimitation of maritime boundaries of SIDS, assessment of seabed resources, effective monitoring and enforcement of their territories, implementation of sustainable fisheries strategies and development of sound ocean policies.[96] Like many other tasks, these efforts are costly and funds for their implementation limited.

Global Programme of Action

Integrating the ideals of the international treaties mentioned above, the Global Programme of Action for the Protection of the Marine Environment from Land-based Activities (GPA) and the Washington Declaration were adopted in 1995, by 108 governments and the European Commission, as an assertion of their commitment to protect and preserve the marine environment from adverse environmental impacts associated with LBSA.[97] The UN Environment Programme (UNEP) created the GPA Coordination Office and performs the secretariat function.[98] The broad, multi-sector, flexible approach of the GPA provides an appealing platform for government parties to strengthen collaboration and coordination on national, regional and global scales.

The GPA aims to prevent further degradation of the marine environment from LBSA by encouraging the states to recognize their duty to preserve and protect marine environmental resources.[99] The GPA assists states in taking actions, individually or jointly, that will lead to the prevention, reduction, control or elimination of adverse environmental impacts on the marine environment. In addition, it also aims to promote recovery from the adverse impacts of land-based activities.[100] Such actions will help achieve the aims of the Programme of Action to "contribute to maintaining and, where appropriate, restoring the productive capacity and biodiversity of the marine environment, ensuring the protection of human health, as well as promoting the conservation and sustainable use of marine living resources".[101]

The GPA recognizes that states face a plethora of environmental commitments flowing from Agenda 21 and other agreements and conventions. It therefore seeks to promote innovative financial mechanisms to generate needed resources in the protection and preservation of valuable marine resources.[102] To facilitate these goals the GPA recommends that states undertake specific activities. These include:

- The assessment and identification of problems based on factors such as food security, public health, coastal and marine resources, ecosystem health, and socioeconomic benefits.
- Establishment of priorities factoring in integrated coastal area management approaches, the correlation among the freshwater and marine ecosystems through the application of watershed management, applying environmental impact procedures, and integrating national actions with global and regional programmes.
- Setting management objectives of the identified and prioritized problems in terms of overall goals, targets and timetables, as well as specific targets for identified industries and areas.
- Identification, evaluation and selection of strategies and measures, including management approaches; such as specific measures, requirements and incentives of compliance, data collection, jurisdictional clarifications, development of environmental monitoring and quality reporting systems, and identification of finance sources available to cover costs associated with the management and administration of the state's strategies and programmes.
- Development of evaluation criteria for the effectiveness of state environmental protection programmes to ensure attainment of environmental and management goals. [103]

Through implementation of the above recommendations, governments can take positive steps that yield definite and traceable results, within boundaries of the states' respective policies, priorities and resources.[104] The implementation of these steps is the responsibility of governments, along with the inclusion of all stakeholders, namely local communities, public organizations, non-governmental organizations and the private sector.[105]

The GPA strengthens regional cooperation through encouragement of existing regional cooperative agreements and the creation of new arrangements to support effective action, strategies and programmes. These regional efforts are critical to effective abatement of adverse environmental impacts on marine resources from LBSA.

Regional seas conventions and LBSA protocols

Regional seas conventions and LBSA protocols are, in some cases, able to provide comprehensive and specific environmental agendas.[106] For instance, the Mediterranean LBSA Protocol addresses increased urbanization and coastal development as well as seasonal population increases due to tourism.[107] Other LBSA protocols emphasize addressing issues of economic inequalities and social development.[108] These regional protocols are more inclusive of land-based activities than previous versions and may create better environmental protections. For instance, protocols that include the regulation of watersheds beyond freshwater limits recognize that sources of LBSA may be farther inland than previously assumed.[109]

However, the same regional context which allows for very specific innovation and improvement of LBSA protocols also allows others to remain unchanged and less effective in the light of new evidence concerning pollution and climate change. For example, under the Caribbean Protocol, parties are required to adopt the minimum prescribed measures of control under its annexes but are not required to subscribe to all of the annexes.[110] This can make it more difficult to institute stronger standards consistently across a region in future annexes.[111] Similarly, some protocols list substances which are to be reduced and eventually phased out, while others list sources of pollution which are to be regulated, and still others only require pollutants to be taken into consideration when establishing pollution controls.[112]

Although many small island states have taken progressive steps, both technical and legal, to regulate and diminish marine pollution, pollution from LBSA continues to increase, especially from nutrients, sewage, marine litter and the physical alteration or destruction of habitats. These problems are partly due to the huge scale and diversity of human uses of ocean and coastal resources, the limited financial and human resources available (especially for SIDS), and the limited national participation in the GPA and regional LBSA protocols.

Adaptation

SIDS and other vulnerable states may be able to engage in some climate mitigation activities of local benefit, such as increasing use of non-fossil sources of power, but for the most part their contribution to reducing emissions is minute. They may, however, be able to play a much larger role grappling with pollution from land-based sources, given adequate economic and human resources. That is a large given, since mitigating pollution sources is not only time-consuming but extremely costly. One of the major needs is the construction or upgrading of sewage treatment plants – a good example of efforts that require technical expertise, a long timeframe and significant capital investment. Similarly, integrated coastal zone management and the provision of water and sewer infrastructure demand sophisticated planning systems and experienced staff. But the inescapable conclusion is that at least some adaptation, and perhaps a great deal, will be necessary in the various states.[113]

Adaptation may take many forms, from simple technical projects such as building seawalls and planting sea grasses, to evacuation of populations. While costs may vary, they are usually significant and often beyond the wherewithal of poor states. Further, they require careful planning efforts, for which many states do not have the skilled staff. These are difficult tasks and generally must be supported by sophisticated state infrastructure with stable and sustainable societies and governing structures.[114] Hampered by poverty, many SIDS and other vulnerable states are simply unable to rise to the task. Moreover, it is difficult to engender political support to address problems whose imminence and potential impact is not always obvious. The harder it is to predict when and where damage will occur, the more difficult it is to convince both public officials and the public that action much be taken now. And even if there is support for current action, the question of what to do and where to do it looms large. For that reason, improving information concerning local environmental systems is critical. That includes not only information-gathering and monitoring of local conditions, but modelling of those local ocean-climate systems. Again, these are expensive undertakings.

So where is the money to come from to provide states with the resources to plan and carry out adaptation? Three special funds have been created by the UNFCC which may provide assistance: the Special Climate Change Fund (SCCF), the Least Developed Countries Fund (LDCF) and an Adaptations Fund under the Kyoto Protocol. However, complicated application and monitoring requirements and insufficient technical resources have prevented full utilization of the funds by the SIDS and LDCs. Changes to the requirements, along with capacity-building and increased technology transfers, would help to change the situation. Funding may also be available for various projects through the Global Environmental Facility.[115] The most promising new source of money will result from the non-binding Copenhagen Accord, reached at the UNFCC meeting in December 2009. Developed countries agreed to provide funding for programs of mitigation and adaptation at $30 billion for the period 2010–2012, with the goal of increasing that funding to $100 billion a year by 2020. Funding for adaptation will be prioritized for the most vulnerable developing countries, including small island developing states.[116] How this fund will be established and operated, and the type of activities it will support, are not yet clear.

Other possibilities for underwriting climate change mitigation and adaptation activities might include drawing on money available in other funds, such as those targeted for global food security, along with energy-related taxes and levies on states. Whatever the sources, the millions of dollars now available, even the billions to become available, are a fraction of the amounts necessary to adequately implement adaptation programmes adequate to protect the lives and property of citizens of the world's most vulnerable areas.

Challenges

Despite the significant number of conventions, treaties, protocols and other initiatives available to aid in strengthening environmental understanding and management of coastal and island areas, progress has been slow. The Fourth Global Conference on Oceans, Coasts, and Islands: Advancing Ecosystem Management and Integrated Coastal and Ocean Management, in evaluating the Mauritius Strategy, emphasized that a substantial amount of additional work needs to take place,[117] and reports published in 2005 found merely 20 per cent of SIDS had developed specific institutions or interagency mechanisms utilizing integrated coastal and ocean management.[118] Just 7 per cent of SIDS had passed national coastal zone acts and 32 per cent possessed environmental impact assessment regulations and processes. While 63 per cent of SIDS had formulated national sea level rise adaptation plans, only 22 per cent had established national institutions to deal with climate change threats and adaptation issues.[119]

The obstacles blocking implementation of environmental conservation efforts include:
- the huge scale and breadth of human uses that have to be addressed;
- limited financing and human resources, especially for developing countries;
- limited national participation in GPA;
- lack of political priority and will;
- fragmented legal and institutional arrangements;
- lack of effective compliance and enforcement;
- limited adoption and implementation of global and regional agreements relating to LBSA;
- poverty, lack of public education and awareness;
- the limits inherent in a non-legally-binding approach.

In 2007, the International Union for the Conservation of Nature (IUCN) observed that, although many nations have made commitments under BpoA, implementation efforts still remain limited.[120] The effects of these efforts are in most situations unclear. Information available on organization websites is duplicative and out of date.[121] The IUCN also found a significant lack of coordination between the UN, donor agencies and multilateral organizations.[122] The lack of participation and concerted efforts to develop and implement the recommendations espoused in international agreements like the GPA have allowed the most serious LBSA of environmental degradation to continue with only minor abatement. In order to encourage more action in accordance with international environmental governance objectives it appears that more educational, financial and scientific support is needed.

The difficulties which SIDS and other vulnerable coastal states face in managing and effectively enforcing environmental agreements at the regional and global level are only exacerbated by climate change concerns. As described above, climate change affects SIDS much more drastically than larger nations, because of their limited ability to address sea level rise and the inherent vulnerability of island habitats (lack of habitable land, small amount of domestic resources and endemic species' poor adaptability). Some SIDS face complete inundation, and if current projections of sea level rise are correct, the resulting damages could include serious humanitarian crises.[123] Even if an island is not completely overflowed, a small rise in sea level can destroy a large percentage of its usable land. Sadly, these fragile states, that contribute little to the climate change problem, are those most affected and least able to deal with it.

Collaboration among SIDS and alignment of their environmental agendas to encourage both effective mitigation of local contributors to climate change and adaptation to changing climate conditions is a start, but will not solve the problem of global warming and associated sea level rise. Increased mitigation of GHG emissions by developed nations is critical, as are funding and other resources to assist SIDS in successfully adapting to the effects of sea level rise. Participation by industrialized nations includes not only capacity-building for adaptation techniques but also more emphasis on global environmental initiatives and programmes which curb climate changes sources within the industrialized countries themselves. It has been acknowledged in international agreements that the capacity and means to adapt to these climate phenomena are an absolute necessity for SIDS.[124] Furthermore, the committed support of the international community was recognized as a critical complement to the SIDS' own efforts in any response and long-term planning for the abatement of GHG emissions. It is especially important for identifying adaptation options and linking efforts to reduce vulnerability with the best available information.[125] For all of these tasks the global community, and particularly the developed states, must be prepared to commit exceptional sums of money. SIDS participation in pollution abatement and mitigation programmes will be in vain if the island and marine habitats they hope to preserve disappear under rising seas.

Acknowledgements

Ann Powers expresses deep appreciation for the excellent research assistance of David Wand, Pace '09, and Christopher Riti, Pace '10.

Notes

1. United Nations Convention on the Law of the Sea, art. 56, Montego Bay, 10 Dec. 1982, in force 16 November 1994, 1833 UNTS 397.
2. See, for example, Christen E. Loper, Miriam C. Balgos, Janice Brown, et al., *Small Islands, Large Ocean States: A Review of Ocean and Coastal Management in Small Island Developing States Since the 1994 Barbados Programme of Action for the Sustainable Development of Small Island Developing States (SIDS)*, Toward Mauritius 2005 Paper Series, 2005-1.
3. Global Forum on Oceans, Coasts, and Islands, *Recommendations for Action, Emanating from the 4th Global Conference on Oceans, Coasts, and Islands: Advancing Ecosystem Management and Integrated Coastal and Ocean Management in the Context of Climate Change*, Hanoi, Vietnam, 7–11 April 2008, p. 17; available at <http://www.globaloceans.org/sites/udel.edu.globaloceans/files/Chart-of-Recommendations_Oct-08.pdf>.
4. COP 8 Decision VIII/1, Island biodiversity, Para 10.
5. C.P. McMullen and J. Jabbour, *Climate Change Science Compendium 2009* (United Nations Environment Programme, Nairobi: EarthPrint, 2009), p. 27; available at <http://hqweb.unep.org/compendium2009/PDF/Compendium2009_fullreport.pdf>; see United Nations Department of Public Information, *Trouble in Paradise: Small Islands Struggle to Preserve Environments, Press Kit on Small Islands: Issues and Actions*, 22nd Special Session of the United Nations General Assembly (UNGASS) on Small Island Developing States New York, Sept. 1999, pp. 27–28, available at <http://www.un.org/esa/dsd/dsd_aofw_sids/sids_milemajomeetbpoa5_preskits_2.shtml>.
6. See DOE/Lawrence Livermore National Laboratory, "Ocean Temperatures and Sea Level Increases 50 Percent Higher than Previously Estimated", *Science Daily*, 19 June 2008; available at <http://www.sciencedaily.com/releases/2008/06/080618143301.htm>.
7. United Nations Department of Public Information, *Trouble in Paradise*, pp. 27–28.
8. DOE/Lawrence Livermore National Laboratory, "Ocean Temperatures and Sea Level Increases 50 Percent Higher than Previously Estimated".
9. Rosemary Rayfuse, "W(h)ither Tuvalu? International Law and Disappearing States", *University of New South Wales Faculty of Law Research Series* (2009), p. 9.
10. See C.P. McMullen and J. Jabbour, *Climate Change Science Compendium 2009*.
11. United Nations Department of Public Information, *Trouble in Paradise*, pp. 27–28.
12. Ibid.
13. Statement by His Excellency Mr. Abdulla Shahid, Minister of Foreign Affairs of the Republic of Maldives, at the Seventh Session of the Human Rights Council of the United Nations, Geneva, 4 Mar. 2008.
14. See B. Cicin-Sain (ed.), *Oceans and Climate Change: Issues and Recommendations for Policymakers and for the Climate Negotiations*, Policy Briefs prepared for the World Oceans Conference, 11–15 May 2009, Manado, Indonesia (Global Forum on Oceans, Coasts, and Islands, 2009), p. 3; available at <http://www.globaloceans.org/planning/pdf/Policy-Briefs-WOC2009.pdf>.

15. Ibid.
16. National Oceanic and Atmospheric Administration, *Why are Coral Reefs So Important?* (2009); available at <http://celebrating200years.noaa.gov/foundations/coral/side. html>.
17. International Coral Reef Action Network, *Threats to Reefs* (2009); available at <http:// www.icran.org/peoplereefs-threats.html>.
18. See United Nations Department of Public Information, *Trouble in Paradise*, pp. 27–28.
19. Ibid, pp. 27–28.
20. Ibid, pp. 27–28.
21. Ibid, pp. 27–28.
22. World Wildlife Federation International, *Problems: Ocean pollution* (2009); available at <http://www.panda.org/about_our_earth/blue_planet/problems/pollution/>.
23. Center for Ocean Solutions Pacific Ocean Library, *Pacific Ocean Threats & Impacts: Pollution* (2009); available at <http://www.centerforoceansolutions.org/library/pacific_ ocean/threats_and_impacts/pollution.html>.
24. Ibid.
25. Ibid.
26. Ibid.
27. Ibid.
28. Ibid.
29. Ibid.
30. Ibid.
31. Ibid.
32. Ibid.
33. UNEP, *From Barbados to Mauritius: The Programme of Action for Small Islands, Ten Years Later* (United Nations Department of Public Information, DPI/2348F, April 2004).
34. Third Global Conference on Oceans, Coasts and Islands, Panel 5, *Summary: Implementation of the Mauritius Strategy for Small Island Developing States (WSSD GOALS)* (2006); available at <http://www.globaloceans.org/sids/pdf/SIDSPanelReport.pdf>.
35. Ibid., p. 1.
36. UNEP, *Implementation of the GPA at Regional Level: The Role of Regional Seas Conventions and their Protocols* (2006); available at <http://www.unep.org/pdf/GPA/The_ Role_of_Regional_Seas_Conventions_and_their_Protocols.pdf>.
37. Alliance of Small Island States, *AOSIS Climate Change Summit* (2009); available at <http://www.sidsnet.org/aosis/>.
38. Ibid.
39. Ibid.
40. Alliance of Small Island States, *AOSIS Declaration on Climate Change 2009* (2009); available at <http://www.sidsnet.org/aosis/documents/AOSIS%20Summit%20Declaration%20Sept%2021%20final.pdf>.
41. UN-OHRLLS, *Small Island Developing States: UN-OHRLLS mandate on SIDS* (2009); available at <http://www.unohrlls.org/en/sids/181/>.
42. United Nations Mission Statement, *About DESA* (2009); available at <http://www. un.org/esa/desa/mission.html>.
43. Simon Rietbergen, Tom Hammond, Chucri Sayegh, et al., "Island Voices – Island Choices: Developing Strategies for Living with Rapid Ecosystem Change in Small Islands" (IUCN, 2007), p. 40; available at <http://data.iucn.org/dbtw-wpd/edocs/CEM-006.pdf>.
44. *Kivalina v ExxonMobil Corporation*, No. 08-1138 N.D. Cal., 26 Feb. 2008; available at <http://www.climatelaw.org/cases/country/us/kivalina/Kivalina%20Complaint.pdf> (common law nuisance suit against energy company emitters of carbon dioxide which

contributed to climate change damage to plaintiffs); Donna Green and Kirsty Rud-dock, "Could Litigation Help Torres Strait Islanders Deal with Climate Impacts?", *Sustainable Development Law & Policy*, vol. 9, no. 2 (2009); Peter Michael, "Water Rising in Dire Straits – Islanders Plan to Sue Major Climate Change Culprits", *Courier Mail*, 13 May 2009 (Torres Strait Islanders plan to file multimillion-dollar landmark legal case against large-scale Australian national greenhouse gas emitters).

45. See John Crump, "Snow, Sand, Ice, and Sun: Climate Change and Equity in the Arctic and Small Island Developing States", *Sustainable Development Law and Policy*, vol. 8, no. 3 (2008), p. 11 (Inuit lawsuit received international attention).

46. See, for example, *Petition to the Inter American Commission on Human Rights Seeking Relief from Violations Resulting from Global Warming Caused by Acts and Omissions of the United States* (2005); available at <http://www.earthjustice.org/library/legal_docs/petition-to-the-inter-american-commission-on-human-rights-on-behalf-of-the-inuit-circumpolar-conference.pdf> (on behalf of all Inuit of the Arctic regions of the United States and Canada).

47. Alliance of Small Island States, *Malé Declaration on the Human Dimensions of Global Climate Change* (2007); available at <http://www.manystrongvoices.org/_res/site/file/Background%20docs/Male_Declaration_Nov07.pdf>.

48. United Nations General Assembly, Human Rights Council, Promotion and Protection of all Human Rights, Civil, Political, Economic, Social and Cultural Rights, Including the Right to Development, *Human Rights and Climate Change*, A/HRC/7/L.21/Rev.1 (2008); <available at http://www.foreign.gov.mv/v2/Documents/L21%20item%203%20REV.1.pdf>.

49. See, generally, United Nations Convention on the Law of the Sea, Montego Bay, 10 December 1982, in force 16 November 1994, 1833 UNTS 397.

50. Ibid., art. 145

51. Ibid., arts. 1, 1(4).

52. Ibid., art. 192.

53. Ibid., art. 207(1).

54. Ibid., art. 207(5).

55. Ibid., art. 207.

56. Ibid.

57. Ibid., art. 212(1).

58. Ibid., art. 207(1).

59. Ibid., art. 207(3).

60. Ibid., art. 207(4).

61. Ibid.

62. See generally ibid., art. 207.

63. See ibid., art. 194(1).

64. Convention on Biological Diversity, Rio de Janiero, 5 June 1992, entered into force 29 December 1993, 1760 UNTS 79, art 1.

65. Ibid., art. 2 (defining "Biological Diversity" and "Genetic Resources").

66. Ibid., art. 6.

67. Ibid., art. 7(c).

68. Ibid., art. 8(k).

69. See, for example, AIDEnvironment, National Institute for Coastal and Marine Management/Rijksinstituut voor Kusten Zee (RIKZ), Coastal Zone Management Centre, the Netherlands, *Integrated Marine and Coastal Area Management (IMCAM) approaches for implementing the Convention on Biological Diversity* (Montreal, Canada: Secretariat of the Convention on Biological Diversity, 2004), CBD Technical Series no. 14.

70. CBD, COP-MOP; available at <http://www.cbd.int/biosafety/cop-mop/>.
71. See CBD, *History of the Convention*; available at <http://www.cbd.int/history/>.
72. See CBD, COP 8 Decision VIII/1, Island Biodiversity, Programme of Work on Island Biodiversity, A(2); available at <http://www.cbd.int/decision/cop/?id=11013>.
73. Ibid., at B para. 18.
74. Ibid., at A para. 8.
75. Ibid. at B para. 22.
76. Ibid., at A para. 8.
77. Ibid., at E.
78. Ibid., at E.
79. See CBD, COP 8 Decision VIII/1, Island Biodiversity, Programme of Work on Island Biodiversity, at B para. 19, 20. See also CBD.int., *Strategic Plan*; available at <http://www.cbd.int/sp/>.
80. CBD, COP 8 Decision VIII/1, Island Biodiversity, Programme of Work on Island Biodiversity, at B para. 19, 20; see also A para. 8; SIDSNET, *Report of the Global Conference on the Sustainable Development of Small Island Developing States, Bridgetown, Barbados: Global Conference on the Sustainable Development of Small Island Developing States*; A/CONF.167/9, 1994; available at <http://www.sidsnet.org/docshare/other/BPOA.pdf>.
81. United Nations, *Plan of Implementation of the World Summit on Sustainable Development* (2005); available at <http://www.un.org/esa/sustdev/documents/WSSD_POI_PD/English/WSSD_PlanImpl.pdf>.
82. United Nations, *Report of the International Meeting to Review the Implementation of the Programme of Action for the Sustainable Development of Small Island Developing States*, Port Louis, Mauritius (2005); available at <http://www.sidsnet.org/docshare/other/20050622163242_English.pdf>.
83. See CBD, COP 8 Decision VIII/1, Island Biodiversity, para. 8, 17, 19, 20; available at <https://www.cbd.int/decision/cop/?id=11013>. See also CBD.int., *What Needs to be Done*; available at <https://www.cbd.int/island/done.shtml>; United Nations, *The Millennium Development Goals Report 2009* (2009); available at <http://www.un.org/russian/millenniumgoals/pdf/mdgreport2009.pdf>.
84. See UNEP (Conference of the Parties to the Convention on Biological Diversity), *Decision Adopted by the Conference of the Parties to the Convention on Biological Diversity at its Ninth Meeting* (2008); available at <https://www.cbd.int/doc/decisions/cop-09/cop-09-dec-21-en.pdf>.
85. United Nations, *Report of the International Meeting to Review the Implementation of the Programme of Action for the Sustainable Development of Small Island Developing States*.
86. See CBD, *Global Island Partnership (GLISPA)* (2008); available at <http://www.cbd.int/doc/programmes/areas/island/glispa/glispa-brochure-en.pdf>.
87. CBD, *Strategy Objectives*; available at <http://www.cbd.int/island/strategy.shtml>.
88. CBD, *Milestones and Measurements of Success*; available at <http://www.cbd.int/island/Milestones.shtml>.
89. UNEP (Global Programme of Action for the Protection of the Marine Environment from Land-based Activities), *Implementation of the GPA at Regional Level: The role of regional seas conventions and their protocols 5* (2006); available at <http://www.unep.org/pdf/GPA/The_Role_of_Regional_Seas_Conventions_and_their_Protocols.pdf>.
90. UNDESA, *Agenda 21*, Section 2, Chapter 17, section 17.22; available at <http://www.un.org/esa/dsd/agenda21/index.shtml>.
91. See, for example, IMO, *1996* Protocol to the London Dumping Convention; available at <http://www.imo.org/Conventions/contents.asp?topic_id=258&doc_id=681#7>;   UNEP,

Regional Seas Conventions and Protocols, [Baltic, Mediterranean, Northeast Atlantic and Wider Caribbean]; available at <http://www.unep.ch/regionalseas/legal/conlist. htm>. See UNEP (Global Programme of Action for the Protection of the Marine Environment from Land-based Activities), *Implementation of the GPA at regional level: the role of regional seas conventions and their protocols*; available at <http://www. gpa.unep.org/documents/lbsa_protocols_for_the_english.pdf>.

92. See UNDESA, *Agenda 21*, Section 2, Chapter 17; available at <http://www.un.org/esa/ dsd/agenda21/index.shtml>.

93. Ibid.

94. United Nations, *Plan of Implementation of the World Summit on Sustainable Development*, Chapter VII, para. 61, p. 35 (2005); available at <http://www.un.org/esa/sustdev/ documents/WSSD_POI_PD/English/WSSD_PlanImpl.pdf>.

95. United Nations, *Report of the International Meeting to Review the Implementation of the Programme of Action for the Sustainable Development of Small Island Developing States*.

96. Ibid.

97. See generally UNEP, *Global Programme of Action for the Protection of the Marine Environment from Land-Based Activities*, UNEP (OCA)/LBA/IG.2/7: 1995 December; available at <http://www.gpa.unep.org/documents/full_text_of_the_english.pdf. See also http://www.gpa.unep.org/>.

98. Ibid.

99. Ibid., 7 (Pt. I, s. B, para. 3).

100. GPA, UNEP, *Aims of the Global Programme of Action*; available from <http://www. gpa.unep.org/content.html?id=181&ln=6>.

101. See UNEP, *Global Programme of Action for the Protection of the Marine Environment from Land-Based Activities*, Introduction, B: Aims of the Global Programme of Action, para. 3, UNEP (OCA)/LBA/IG.2/7: 1995 December; available at <http://www.gpa. unep.org/documents/full_text_of_the_english.pdf>.

102. UNEP (Global Programme of Action for the Protection of the Marine Environment from Land-based Activities), *Implementation of the GPA at Regional Level: The role of regional seas conventions and their protocols 5*.

103. See generally UNEP, *Global Programme of Action for the Protection of the Marine Environment from Land-Based Activities*. See also GPA, UNEP, *Aims of the Global Programme of Action*; available at <http://www.gpa.unep.org/content.html?id= 181&ln=6>.

104. UNEP (Global Programme of Action for the Protection of the Marine Environment from Land-based Activities), *Implementation of the GPA at Regional Level: the role of regional seas conventions and their protocols 6* (2006); available at <http://www.unep. org/pdf/GPA/The_Role_of_Regional_Seas_Conventions_and_their_Protocols.pdf>.

105. Ibid.

106. The Regional Seas Programme comprises thirteen different geographical programmes established under the auspices of the United Nations Environment Programme. Six are directly administered by UNEP. See at <http://www.unep.org/regionalseas/about/ default.asp>.

107. Protocol for the Protection of the Mediterranean Sea Against Pollution from Land-Based Sources (with annexes) 11, 17 May 1980; available at <http://www.gpa.unep.org/ content.html?id=280&ln=6>.

108. Ibid.

109. Ibid.

110. Ibid.

111. Ibid.

112. Ibid.
113. See M.L. Parry, O.F. Canziani, J.P. Palutikof, et al. (eds), *Climate Change 2007: Impacts, adaptation and vulnerability* (Cambridge: Cambridge University Press, 2007); available at <http://www.ipcc.ch/publications_and_data/publications_ipcc_fourth_assessment_report_wg2_report_impacts_adaptation_and_vulnerability.htm>; AOSIS and the UN Foundation, *Global Climate Change and Small Island Developing States: Financing Adaptation Green Paper Draft for Review* (2008); available at <http://www.un.int/wcm/webdav/site/suriname/shared/documents/papers/climatechangeaosis_GreenPaper_Feb52008_.pdf>.
114. See Jon Barnett, "Titanic States? Impacts and Responses to Climate Change in the Pacific Islands", *Journal of International Affairs*, vol. 59, no. 1 (2005), p. 210.
115. Ibid., pp. 212–216.
116. UN Framework Convention on Climate Change, *Copenhagen Accord*, FCCC/CP/2009/L.7, 2009; available at <http://unfccc.int/resource/docs/2009/cop15/eng/l07.pdf>.
117. Global Forum on Oceans, Coasts, and Islands, *Recommendations for Action, Emanating from the 4th Global Conference on Oceans, Coasts, and Islands*, p. 18.
118. Ibid.
119. Ibid.
120. Rietbergen et al., "Island Voices – Island Choices", p. 17.
121. Ibid., p. 17.
122. Ibid., pp. 12, 18.
123. See Rayfuse, "W(h)ither Tuvalu? International Law and Disappearing States", pp. 2, 9.
124. See, for example, United Nations, *Report of the International Meeting to Review the Implementation of the Programme of Action for the Sustainable Development of Small Island Developing States*.
125. Asia-Pacific Network for Global Change Research, Linking Science and Climate Change Policy. Overview address by Tuiloma Neroni Slade, Pacific Climate Change Conference, Raotonga, Cook Islands, April 2000.

3

Biodiversity

Susan Shearing

There is an alarming discrepancy between commitments and action. Goals and targets agreed by the international community in relation to sustainable development, such as the adoption of national sustainable development strategies and increased support to developing countries, must be implemented in a timely fashion. The mobilization of domestic and international resources, including development assistance, far beyond current levels is vital to the success of this endeavour.

Malmo Ministerial Declaration (2000)[1]

The United Nations has declared 2010 the International Year of Biodiversity,[2] urging member states to take advantage of an increased focus on biodiversity and to "increase awareness of the importance" of biodiversity through the promotion of actions at local, regional and international levels.[3] This initiative reflects the international consensus concerning the risks posed by the rate of decline in global biodiversity and the urgent need for action at all levels to address this trend. Increasingly, such measures are including the integration of climate change issues across a range of international agreements. However, the implementation of measures to conserve biodiversity at a national level remains problematic and can be exacerbated where there is a failure to recognize the critical relationship between the goals of poverty alleviation and improving the rate of biodiversity conservation.

This chapter provides an overview of issues affecting the capacity of nations to develop and implement policies for the conservation and sustainable use of biodiversity, in accordance with the objectives of the international legal framework established by the Convention on Biological

The future of international environmental law, Leary and Pisupati (eds),
United Nations University Press, 2010, ISBN 978-92-808-1192-6

Diversity.[4] An assessment of those challenges reveals the critical importance of addressing the key drivers for biodiversity loss through economic measures and institutional reform. It will be argued that, notwithstanding the ongoing challenges for effective national implementation of the CBD obligations relating to conservation and sustainable use of biodiversity, a range of examples drawn from northern and southern nations illustrate the extent to which some key mechanisms identified in the CBD itself, including protected areas networks, economic tools and the sectoral mainstreaming of biodiversity issues, are playing an important role in facilitating national approaches to biodiversity conservation.

The biodiversity challenge

The definition of biodiversity in the Convention on Biological Diversity (CBD) encompasses the diversity of life at all levels:

> ... the variability among living organisms from all sources including, *inter alia*, terrestrial, marine, and other aquatic ecosystems and the ecological complexes of which they are part; this includes diversity within species, between species and of ecosystems.[5]

The breadth of this definition, embracing genetic, species and ecosystem[6] diversity, is an emphatic recognition of the interconnectedness and interdependence of these "building blocks of life".[7]

Analysis of the "values" of biodiversity to humankind distinguishes between use (including food security, pharmaceutical products, fibres and ecosystem services such as water purification, pollination and pest control) and non-use values (such as intrinsic, cultural, spiritual and aesthetic values).[8] Through the sequestration and storage of carbon by terrestrial ecosystems (approximately 2400 Gt) and marine ecosystems (approximately 50 per cent of the global ecosystem uptake of carbon dioxide),[9] biodiversity and ecosystem services are also critical in addressing climate change and its impacts.

It is now well understood that failure to effectively address the causes of biodiversity loss has potentially catastrophic consequences. In particular, ecosystems can become destabilized and increasingly vulnerable to shocks and disturbances including hurricanes, floods and droughts. Given that biological diversity is fundamental to ecosystem conservation and sustainable use through the provision of ecosystem services, the linkages between biodiversity loss, ecosystem degradation and adverse impacts on human life are critical.[10] Loss of biodiversity and degraded ecosystem services can contribute (directly or indirectly) to increasing food insecurity, reduced material wealth and worsening of health and social relations.[11]

The 2005 United Nations Millennium Ecosystem Assessment (MEA) was initiated to establish a scientific basis for actions required to improve the conservation and sustainable use of ecosystems and their role in meeting human needs. It is the "largest-ever evaluation of the relationship between human well-being and ecosystems".[12] The MEA concluded that most of the human-created changes to the diversity of life on Earth, many of which are irreversible, represent a loss of biodiversity. Approximately 60 per cent (15 out of 24) of the ecosystem services examined during the MEA are being degraded or used unsustainably.[13]

The MEA[14] found that nearly all ecosystems have been significantly transformed through human action (for example, through conversion of land to cropland and increased reservoir storage). Further, there has been a 20–50 per cent conversion to human use in over half of the fourteen biomes assessed. The species extinction rate has been increased by as much as 1000 times over background rates typical over the planet's history over the past few hundred years.[15] The distribution of species on Earth is becoming more homogenous (that is, there is, on average, a diminution in the differences between the set of species at one location and the set of species at another location). Among cultivated species in particular there has been a significant global decline in genetic diversity.

Drivers of biodiversity loss

The key drivers of biodiversity loss are well understood. Encompassing both direct and indirect factors, in nearly every jurisdiction it is a combination of such drivers that leads to biodiversity loss, posing significant challenges to implementing the requisite changes at national level to improve conservation and sustainable use.

The direct causes of biodiversity loss, including habitat loss through land conversion, agricultural and forestry practices,[16] introduced species,[17] overexploitation of species[18] and pollution[19] have been recognized for many years. In its 2006 second assessment of the state of global biodiversity, the CBD Secretariat concluded that the direct drivers of biodiversity loss are projected to either remain at current levels or to increase in the near future.[20]

In recent years, the international community has focused on the impacts of anthropocentric climate change on biodiversity.[21] The link between the temperature of the Earth and the concentrations of greenhouse gases in the atmosphere (particularly carbon dioxide) is becoming increasingly well understood. In its 2007 *Fourth Assessment Report*,[22] the Intergovernmental Panel on Climate Change (IPCC) confirmed the significant impact of human activities since the pre-industrial period on the atmospheric concentrations of greenhouse gases, carbon dioxide, methane and nitrous oxides. The IPCC reported that, since the late 1800s, the average temperature of the surface of the Earth has increased by 0.74 °C, and is projected to increase by a further 1.1–6.4 °C by the year 2099. The IPCC reported that observed increases in sea level are consistent with warming. In particular, the global average sea level rose at an average rate of 1.8 mm per year between 1961 and 2003 and at an average rate of about 3.1 mm per year from 1993 to 2003.

Specific impacts of climate change in relation to species and ecosystems are expected to include the following:[23]

- Approximately 20–30 per cent of plant and animal species assessed so far are likely to be at increased risk of extinction if increases in global average temperature exceed 1.5–2.5 °C.
- Negative impacts on marine shell-forming organisms (e.g. corals) and their dependent species arising from the progressive acidification of oceans due to increasing atmospheric carbon dioxide.
- Significant impacts upon the resilience of many ecosystems due to an unprecedented combination of climate change, associated disturbances (e.g. flooding, drought, wildfire, insects, ocean acidification), and other direct drivers of biodiversity loss discussed above.
- Major changes in ecosystem structure and function, species' ecological interactions, and species' geographic ranges, with predominantly negative consequences for biodiversity. Wetlands, coral reefs, mangroves, cloud forests and Arctic ecosystems are projected to be particularly vulnerable.[24]
- Negative impacts upon ecosystem goods and services (e.g. water and food supply, where increases in global average temperature exceed 1.5–2.5 °C).

Ultimately, each of these direct drivers of biodiversity loss is caused by, and exacerbated through, the impact of more fundamental underlying or indirect drivers. According to leading economist, Jeffery D. Sachs:

> The great expansion in human population and economic activity over the past two centuries has come at the expense of other species with which we share the planet. Our own species' hunger for resources has led us to become the single most destructive force on Earth for the rest of life.[25]

There is little doubt that unsustainable rates of human population growth and natural resource consumption are placing unprecedented stress on biodiversity. The global population doubled over the last forty years to 6 billion in 2007 and is projected to grow to between 8.1 and 9.6 billion by 2050.[26]

An ongoing failure to attribute value within economic systems to bio-diversity and, in particular, the benefits provided by ecosystem services to human well-being has further contributed to biodiversity loss. As Salzman has argued, the basis for the failure of economies to attribute a market value to the ecosystems that underpin goods on which human well-being is reliant is not that such services are worthless, but that there is an absence of markets that can capture and directly express their value.[27] Such services comprise *provisioning services* (for example, food, water, timber and fibre); *regulating services* that affect climate, floods, disease, wastes and water quality; *cultural services* that provide recreational, aesthetic and spiritual benefits; and *supporting services* (e.g. soil formation, photosynthesis and nutrient cycling).[28]

Finally, in many jurisdictions there exist legal, political and institutional frameworks that facilitate overexploitation of natural resources, such as weak or non-existent law enforcement and lack of transparency and accountability of government and the corporate sector.[29] When these factors are combined with deficient scientific knowledge of biodiversity[30] and ecosystems, the challenges for development and implementation of effective measures to halt the rate of biodiversity loss can appear insurmountable.

International initiatives

International responses to the challenge of conserving biodiversity have encompassed an extensive range of soft law instruments[31] and legally binding treaties that are operative at regional, species and area levels. For example, numerous treaties address biodiversity conservation at a regional level, covering Africa, Europe, the Americas, the Pacific, Asia and the Antarctic.[32] In addition to regional treaties, a number of international instruments deal with the conservation of particular species (such as migratory species).[33] A key treaty operative at the species level is the Convention on International Trade in Endangered Species of Wild Fauna and Flora[34] that regulates trade in wild species. Other key instruments that touch upon biodiversity conservation are area-based agreements, in particular:

- Convention on Wetlands of International Importance Especially as Waterfowl Habitat (RAMSAR Convention);
- Convention Concerning the Protection of the World Cultural and Natural Heritage (World Heritage Convention); and
- United Nations Convention on the Law of the Sea (LOS Convention).[35]

Many of the regional, species- and area-based biodiversity-related treaties pre-date and are not supplanted by the CBD. However, while these treaties deal with the protection of particular species or biodiversity within specific areas, the CBD defines biodiversity comprehensively, including ecosystems, species and genetic resources. Further, the CBD was the first global agreement that recognized that, while nations hold sovereign rights over their biological resources, the conservation and sustainable use of biological diversity is "a common concern of humankind" and an integral part of sustainable development. The CBD also recognized the importance of all types of knowledge systems, including traditional knowledge, as relevant to the conservation and sustainable use of biodiversity. Accordingly, while the continued importance of other biodiversity-related treaties is acknowledged, this chapter focuses on issues affecting the implementation of the CBD at a national level, drawing on examples from a range of jurisdictions.

Convention on Biological Diversity

The CBD provides the key international legal framework for the protection of biodiversity.[36] Its objectives are framed in general terms: the conservation of biological diversity, the sustainable use of its components, and the fair and equitable sharing of the benefits arising out of the utilization of genetic resources.[37] The CBD does not prescribe targets, lists of species or habitats that are to be protected. It is a framework convention that leaves to the individual states parties themselves the responsibility to determine how most of its provisions are to be implemented. The CBD requires signatory countries "as far as possible and appropriate" to regulate or manage biological resources important for the conservation of biological diversity "whether within or outside protected areas[38] with a view to ensuring their conservation and sustainable use".[39]

From a national planning perspective, implementing the conservation and sustainable use objectives requires parties to identify important components of biodiversity,[40] develop national strategies, plans or programmes for the conservation and sustainable use of biodiversity, and integrate biodiversity conservation and sustainable use into relevant sectoral or cross-sectoral plans, programmes and policies.[41] Parties are to adopt economically and socially sound measures that act as incentives for biodiversity conservation,[42] and to establish a system of reserves and national parks for the in situ conservation and protection of biodiversity.[43]

In any jurisdiction, the preparation of national strategies, plans or programmes requires effective coordination between a variety of government departments and agencies in order to assess the sectoral impacts of activities on biodiversity management and to identify possible bases for integration of biodiversity issues across decision-making and national policy areas. As a minimum, this task involves an assessment of the status of biodiversity within the jurisdiction, the establishment of institutional structures vested with leadership responsibilities for developing a biodiversity strategy, and securing an adequate budget to enable these tasks.[44]

Significant obstacles to the implementation of CBD objectives at a national level include political and societal obstacles, institutional, technical and capacity-related obstacles, lack of accessible knowledge and information, lack of economic policy and financial resources, lack of collaboration and cooperation between key stakeholders, legal and juridical impediments, socioeconomic factors, natural phenomena and climate change.[45]

Particulars of such obstacles are included in the national reports to be prepared by states parties under the CBD (art. 26). For example, in its *Fourth National Report to the Convention on Biological Diversity*, Afghanistan included the following obstacles:[46]

- A deteriorating security situation affecting the ability of scientists, non-government organizations and government staff to safely visit areas of the country and undertake research, consultation and implementation activities;
- The extreme poverty of most rural Afghans makes implementation of biodiversity conservation impossible in the absence of economic benefits;
- Ineffective enforcement of prohibitions, decrees and laws;
- Lack of technical and administrative capacity on the part of government staff and institutions that impedes execution of planned activities.

Recognizing the ongoing challenge of addressing biodiversity loss, in 2002 the governing body of the CBD, the Conference of Parties established under art. 23 ("COP") adopted a Strategic Plan that called for urgent action and set a goal to "achieve by 2010 a significant reduction of the current rate of biodiversity loss at the global, regional and national level as a contribution to poverty alleviation and to the benefit of all life on earth"[47] (the "2010 Target"). A range of goals and targets was identified to assess progress in achieving the 2010 Target.[48]

One of the four broad goals included in the Strategic Plan relating to the national implementation of the CBD is "Goal 3: national biodiversity strategies and action plans [NBSAPs] and the integration of biodiversity concerns into relevant sectors [to] serve as an effective framework for achieving the objectives of the CBD."[49]

The Strategic Plan also adopted the Ecosystem Approach (EA) as the "overarching strategy for the integrated management of land, water and living resources" to be implemented in order to promote conservation and sustainable use in an equitable way. This approach recognizes the interconnectedness of all elements of an ecosystem and is based on the "application of scientific methodologies focused on levels of biological organisation which encompass the essential processes, functions and interactions among organisms and their environment".[50] Parties to the CBD are encouraged to apply the EA at a national level to balance the objectives of the CBD.[51]

The EA recognizes that the objectives of ecosystem management are societal choices and that management should be decentralized to the lowest appropriate level, with the effects of activities undertaken by ecosystem managers on adjacent and other ecosystems considered. Further, ecosystem management must be understood in an economic context and be based upon long-term objectives. Fundamental to the EA and the CBD is the recognition that all forms of relevant information (such as scientific, indigenous and local knowledge) should be considered and all relevant sectors of society and scientific disciplines should be involved in biodiversity management.[52]

Despite the aspirations of the Strategic Plan, the 2010 Target has been described by Sachs as "shockingly neglected".[53] It is difficult to argue against this assessment in the light of reviews undertaken to date. In its second periodic review (2006) of the status of implementation of the Strategic Plan goals, the CBD Secretariat concluded that, although it was "too soon to assess progress towards" the goals and targets set for 2010, on the basis of then current trends, it appeared "highly unlikely that all the targets aimed at addressing threats to biodiversity could be achieved globally by 2010" and that it would be a "major challenge" to meet targets to maintain the ecosystem services required to support human well-being over the next century.[54]

The actions required at a national level to meet the 2010 Target were identified in the 2006 periodic assessment as including:
- The development of national biodiversity strategies and action plans that include quantifiable targets;
- The implementation of NBSAPs through policy development and the enactment of enabling legislation; and
- The mainstreaming of biodiversity issues into national policies, and strategies for sustainable development and addressing poverty reduction through:
  - Systematic implementation of the EA as fundamental to achieving progress in the goal of mainstreaming biodiversity concerns into cross-sectoral programmes;
  - Incorporation of biodiversity into strategic and environmental impact assessment frameworks;

- Development of appropriate incentives for biodiversity conservation and the removal of disincentives; and
- Creation of markets for ecosystem services thereby placing an economic value on biodiversity and eco-services generally.

The link to human well-being and poverty reduction: The Millennium Development Goals

The relationship between biodiversity and human well-being is relatively well understood.[55] However, the livelihood impacts of degraded biodiversity on the poor are critical – biodiversity loss poses a disproportionate threat to the livelihoods of a significant proportion of the global population that lives in poverty.[56]

Climate change will further exacerbate the impacts of biodiversity loss on livelihoods. A recent report by Oxfam highlighted the critical link between climate change, depletion in crops and other biodiversity products, and poverty.[57] According to Oxfam:

> Without action, most of the gains that the world's poorest countries have made in development and ameliorating the harmful effects of poverty in the past 50 years will be lost, irrecoverable in the foreseeable future.[58]

Key among the threats identified is hunger, with rice and maize, some of the world's most vital staple crops, being susceptible to temperature variations and changing seasonal wealth patterns. The UN Food and Agriculture Organization (FAO) estimates that 75 per cent of the world's 1 billion poorest people are highly vulnerable to the impacts of climate change on crops and livestock. The FAO notes that those highly vulnerable also include more than 1.5 billion forest-dependent people, among the poorest in the world, and 200 million people dependent on fisheries.[59]

International recognition of the need to act decisively in relation to world poverty culminated in the United Nations Millennium Summit held in September 2000, at which the Millennium Declaration was adopted by member nations committing to a global initiative to reduce extreme poverty and improve lives. The Millennium Declaration included 48 key targets (the "Millennium Development Goals" or MDGs) to be achieved by 2015, encompassing the eradication of extreme poverty and hunger, achieving universal primary education, the promotion of gender equality and empowerment of women, a reduction in child mortality, improvement in maternal health, addressing HIV/AIDS, malaria and other diseases, and the creation of a global partnership for development.[60] The Millennium Declaration framework includes specific indicators and target dates to enable the international community to measure progress in achieving the MDGs.

The Declaration expressly recognized the linkage between poverty reduction and biodiversity loss through the inclusion of MDG 7– Ensure Environmental Sustainability. The MDG 7 targets include the integration of the principles of sustainable development in country practices and programmes and the reversal of the loss of environmental resources (Target A).[61]

In relation to biodiversity specifically, Target B (included in 2007) adopts the CBD Strategic Plan 2010 Target to effect a "significant" reduction in the rate of biodiversity loss.[62] To monitor the implementation of Target 7B, four indicators are identified: the proportion of land area covered by forest, the proportion of fish stocks within safe biological limits, the proportion of terrestrial and marine areas protected, and the proportion of species threatened with extinction.

According to the UN's *Millennium Development Goals Report*, 2008, significant progress is yet to be made with respect to the biodiversity indicators, with greater attention required for marine areas and terrestrial conservation, and the number of species threatened with extinction continuing to rise rapidly.[63]

The ongoing degradation of ecosystem services is clearly a significant barrier to achieving the MDGs. To some extent, it may be argued that there has been a failure to recognize explicitly the relationship between biodiversity and the MDGs. According to Pisupati and Warner,[64] the MDGs focus on developmental issues, and the inclusion of MDG7 does not incorporate reference to the role of biodiversity and natural resources and gives little or no guidance as to how national governments are to implement this MDG.[65] However, the need to recognize the economic benefits of biodiversity is an essential step in building links between biodiversity and development.

Indeed, the MDGs have been criticized as a less than effective framework for dealing with poverty reduction and sustainable development on a number of bases, including the separation of environmental sustainability into one of the eight "stand alone" MDGs rather than its integration across all MDGs.[66] As Pisupati and Warner argue, biodiversity plays an important role in achieving each of the MDGs. In their analysis of the MDGs and the 2002 Strategic Plan targets, Pisupati and Warner identify potential synergies between the MDGs and biodiversity conservation, stating that:

> The underlying causes of biodiversity loss are very similar to the underlying causes of poverty and include centralized planning, constraints on access and ownership, unregulated markets, weak political voice . . .[67]

They argue that achieving these synergies (in conjunction with initiatives under the United Nations Framework Convention on Climate Change) is critical to the goal of achieving sustainable development.[68]

This separation between sustainable development and the other MDGs in the MDG framework reflects the polarization between development and conservation communities that can occur in practice. Indeed, a failure to recognize the relationship between poverty reduction and biodiversity conservation is a matter of increasing concern in the context of achieving the MDGs.[69]

The post-2010 framework

According to Sachs, the 2010 Target is:

> ... the best-kept secret on the planet. The goal was set to modest fanfare but has now disappeared from the world's radar entirely. There are many good reasons, all relating to a lack of political leadership in all parts of the world.[70]

As noted above, it is difficult to disagree with this assessment, particularly given the poor progress to date in meeting the target. A revised and updated Strategic Plan, together with a revised Biodiversity Target to replace the 2010 Target, is to be considered at COP10.[71] The G8 Environment Ministers together with ministers from a number of other nations[72] recently agreed on a "common path toward biodiversity post 2010", acknowledging that:

> Notwithstanding the efforts and commitments to achieve the 2010 Target, direct and indirect drivers of biodiversity loss, aggravated by climate change, still continue. Furthermore, the world has been changing rapidly since the adoption of the 2010 Target. All of these drivers of biodiversity loss, causing mid- and long-term threats to biodiversity and identified on the basis of scientific research, should be considered in the development of the post-2010 framework.[73]

Further, Ministers agreed that:

> ... reform of environmental governance at all levels is essential to integrate biodiversity and ecosystem services into all policies, to turn the current weaknesses in economic systems into opportunities and to boost sustainable development and employment, taking particular account of the circumstances of developing countries.[74]

It is likely that the revised Strategic Plan will include a long-term vision (or 2050 Target) and a shorter-term mission (2020 Biodiversity Target), perhaps with an interim 2015 Target linked to the 2015 targets of the

MDGs. At the ninth meeting of the Conference of the Parties it was decided that the 2020 Target should be measurable. However, views differ as to whether or not the overall target should be, or can be, quantitative.[75]

In addition to the development of a new global Biodiversity Target, it has been suggested that the revised CBD Strategic Plan should provide a framework to enable the establishment of national (and where possible, quantitative) targets that may be implemented by nations in accordance with their particular priorities.[76] While the development of national targets has been embraced by some countries (including Ireland, South Africa and the United Kingdom) a more widespread adoption of this initiative would assist in assessing global progress towards implementation of CBD objectives.

The need to develop a workable revised Strategic Plan reflects the difficulties associated with the CBD as a framework for the global governance of biological diversity – effective implementation requires the regulation of resources and activities within national jurisdictions that have global, long-term impacts.

National implementation

According to the CBD Secretariat, implementation of the CBD at a national level is "far from sufficient".[77] To date, only sixty states parties have completed their Fourth National Report that is to be used by the COP to measure progress towards the 2010 Target.[78] For many nations, the capacity to develop a NBSAP remains the most significant impediment to achieving the CBD objectives.[79] In this regard, it is noted that financial assistance has been provided to over 140 eligible nations in preparing their NBASPs through the financial mechanisms established under the CBD.[80]

A further issue is the extent to which the NBSAPs have been implemented nationally to effectively integrate biodiversity concerns into relevant sectors.[81] From the CBD Secretariats review of analyses conducted by the United Nations Development Programme of country reports detailing progress on implementation of the MDGs and the World Bank of Poverty Reduction Strategy Papers, it was found that biodiversity concerns were rarely addressed in such documents.[82] This omission can be explained by the understandable focus of national governments in developing countries on the need to prioritize measures to deal with economic development and poverty reduction. However, as the MEA notes, a focus on short-term economic development may undermine the viability of a long-term resource base[83] and fails to recognize the critical role that biodiversity can play in working towards the achievement of the MDGs.

Indeed, actions that may be taken at a national level to help eradicate poverty can often result in further biodiversity loss, for example, through the expansion of cultivated land for agriculture. One of the key difficulties in implementing biodiversity conservation mechanisms in many developing countries lies in reconciling conflict between economic development and enhanced food supply achieved through such expansion and biodiversity outcomes.

The need for governments to weigh competing priorities is illustrated by the differing views regarding legislation[84] recently enacted by the Brazilian Government, that grants land rights to squatters occupying an area of land which covers 67.4 million hectares of land in the Amazon. The Brazilian Government argues that such legislation will benefit more than 1 million people, reduce conflict by conferring private ownership on the squatters and enable illegal tree-felling to be pursued more effectively. Small landowners who can prove they occupied lands before December 2004 will be given small areas of land free, while large areas will be sold off. However, environmental groups have argued that the law will not benefit impoverished farmers but will instead advantage wealthy farmers. They further argue that the law contradicts Brazil's policy on global warming through the reduction of greenhouse gas emissions, by making new areas available for deforestation.[85]

In the context of developing countries, the introduction of institutional changes in property rights can enable individuals and communities to exercise stewardship and enhance biodiversity conservation.[86] However, the creation of such rights needs to be undertaken following an analysis of key factors, including the population density. As Mellor has noted, employment and land reserve opportunities available in areas that are densely populated and where fertile agricultural land is found will clearly differ from such opportunities in land that supports only a small population through the rate of increase in land price incidental to development.

The following discussion considers a range of examples drawn from northern and southern nations that illustrate the role of protected areas, economic mechanisms and the sectoral mainstreaming of biodiversity issues as important tools for facilitating national approaches to biodiversity conservation.

Protected areas

While the CBD addresses both in situ and ex situ conservation measures, the emphasis of the CBD is on in situ conservation, that is, conservation within ecosystems and natural habitats or, in the case of domestic or cultivated species, in the surroundings where they have developed their distinctive properties.[87] Article 8(a) provides a framework for in-situ conservation, indicating a range of measures to be taken by each party "as far as possible and as appropriate" including establishing "a system of protected areas or areas where special measures need to be taken to conserve biodiversity".

The identification, establishment and management of protected areas together with conservation, sustainable use and restoration initiatives in adjacent land and seascape (art. 8(e)) have been a focus of biodiversity conservation planning in most jurisdictions. With increasing global understanding and concern regarding the impacts of climate change on biodiversity, protected areas are playing a critical role in the development of climate adaptation strategies, for example, by providing unbroken blocks of intact habitat for species and ecosystems to shift their ranges as conditions are altered through climate change impacts.

However, there are clear imbalances in global protection coverage across different biomes, ecosystems and habitats. In 2004, the COP agreed to adopt a *Programme of Work on Protected Areas* (PoWPA)[88] that aims to establish "comprehensive, effectively managed and ecologically representative national and regional systems of protected areas" by 2010 (in relation to terrestrial areas) and by 2012 (in relation to marine areas). The target is the "effective conservation" of at least 10 per cent of each of the world's ecological regions.[89]

Protected area coverage is one of the provisional indicators for assessing progress towards the 2010 Target.[90] As noted above, it is also an indicator for achieving the MDGs at a national level.[91] In assessing progress toward the 2010 protected area targets, Coad et al. analysed 113 962 protected areas.[92] They found that 11.3 per cent of national territories are covered by nationally designated protected areas (marine and terrestrial). Globally, 12.2 per cent of land is protected (exceeding the 10 per cent target) but only 5.9 per cent of the world's territorial seas are protected, falling well short of the 2012 target.

Undoubtedly there has been significant progress in the establishment of protected areas since the inception of the PoWPA – according to the CBD's *Year in Review 2008*, 2300 new terrestrial protected areas and 50 new marine areas, covering approximately 60 million hectares, have been established.[93] A key constraint for many jurisdictions is a lack of financial resources and expertise to enable the development and implementation of a protected areas system.[94]

Within any one jurisdiction, the proportion of land mass falling within the protected areas system may be small – of 236 nations assessed by Coad et al., the mean protection of terrestrial environments was 12.2 per cent, and 5.1 per cent for marine environments.[95] As Kiss has argued, protected areas are "on the whole too few, too small and too threatened to be relied upon as the sole instrument for conserving biodiversity".[96]

Factors affecting the extent of national terrestrial and marine protected area coverage include politics, security/stability, governance structures and socioeconomic imperatives. Even where protected areas are established, the effective protection afforded to biodiversity cannot be assured. Poaching, civil unrest and wars can impede the effective management of protected areas.[97] Further, approaches to management of areas are variable, depending upon national/regional priorities that affect political will and the availability of necessary resources (both financial and technical).[98]

The designation of protected areas can have significant consequences for local communities, particularly where the model of protected area adopted is exclusionary in nature, separating people from nature:

> Post-colonial governments maintained this protectionist approach, with centralized government institutions taking ownership of wildlife and forests, both within and outside protected areas.[99]

The devolution of biodiversity governance and management to local levels is a key principle of the Ecosystem Approach. The contrasting approaches to wildlife and forestry management in Tanzania[100] illustrate the critical role of effective local governance structures in achieving national biodiversity conservation goals and ensuring that a model of protected areas facilitates sustainable use and positive livelihood outcomes for local communities.[101]

Tanzania has one of Africa's highest levels of mammal, bird, amphibian, reptile and plant species diversity. This extensive diversity is supported by a broad range of habitats, including coastal mangrove forests, various types of wetlands, flood plains, tropical forests, grass plains, savannah woodlands, lakes and rivers.

Approximately 75 per cent of the population lives in rural areas and the majority of Tanzanians depend predominantly on biodiversity for their livelihoods. For example, wild plants, animals and fisheries provide a critical source of food, forests provide fuel and perform water catchment services, and land is critical for farming and livestock purposes. Tourism, based around wildlife, coral reefs and natural landscapes, has become an increasingly key component of Tanzania's macroeconomic prosperity.

Tanzania has one of the world's highest proportions of land under a reserve system.[102] An exclusionary protected area approach in national parks and game reserves has been in place since independence. There is no community participation in conservation management in game reserves, and extremely limited community use.

In 1974 unlicensed hunting was banned. However, the ban has been largely ineffectual due to a lack of local support for enforcement. An absence of incentives such as benefits or management rights has resulted in overexploitation of resources such as bushmeat by the local rural population. Further, community rights to hunt wildlife are extremely restrictive, with hunting permits unaffordable for most villagers. Such policies not only deprive local communities of vital resources, but also facilitate the depletion of biodiversity.

The Wildlife Policy (1998) and Wildlife Conservation Regulations (2002) altered the approach to wildlife management outside protected areas. The Wildlife Policy encourages all initiatives "to involve all stakeholders in wildlife conservation and sustainable utilisation, as well as in fair and equitable sharing of benefits". Communities can register Wildlife Management Areas (WMAs) on village land outside protected areas, and acquire rights to use and benefit from wildlife. Under a benefit-sharing formula the revenue from game fees is to be divided between WMAs (25 per cent), Tanzania Wildlife Protection Fund (25 per cent), district councils (15 per cent) and the Ministry of Natural Resource and Tourism (35 per cent).

However, the WMA system has had limited success,[103] with uncertainty concerning the allocation of rights and responsibilities and the distribution of benefits from tourism and hunting activities. Complexities associated with the regulatory requirements, EIA and numerous approval stages within the WMA framework have contributed to frustration among local communities and impeded implementation. A further issue is the requirement under the WMA system to create a new community-based organization to report to village councils. While village councils have been evolving in Tanzania for over thirty years, it takes time to create new institutions and develop necessary trust and accountability frameworks.

By contrast, Tanzania's 1998 National Forest Policy encourages participatory forest management within and outside the formal reserve system and seeks to integrate biodiversity values into forest management. Under the relevant legislation,[104] communities are permitted to register unreserved forest lands as village forests, to gain full ownership and management responsibility for such areas from the central government under a community-based forest management system (CBFM). A community can also enter into Joint Forest Management (JFM) agreements with the central or local government for devolved management on reserved forest land. Under such arrangements, forest management responsibility and returns are divided between government and forest communities. Such agreements have generally been negotiated in high-biodiversity catchment forests, where progress to devolve management responsibilities has traditionally been slow due to concerns that it will lead to ecosystem degradation.

Participatory forestry management is operating or being established in over 1800 villages and extends to 11 per cent of Tanzania's total forest cover (although JFM still covers only 1 per cent of government forest reserves). Where successfully adopted, it can result in recovery or maintenance of reserve or village forests through regeneration in degraded areas, reducing encroachment onto agricultural land and increasing biodiversity. However, CBFM has been less successful in areas with higher populations, ecological constraints (such as limited water availability) and where there has been resulting encroachment on village forests, leading to serious land conflicts.[105]

Zambia provides a further example of local initiatives linking biodiversity and positive livelihood outcomes, particularly through community-based natural resource management and tourism ventures. The South Luangwa Area Management Unit (SLAMU), a donor-funded programme that has been operational for twenty-three years, is one of southern Africa's first community-based wildlife management projects.[106] The role of local communities as co-managers in wildlife areas is formally recognized in the Zambian legislative framework.[107] This programme has resulted in a significant reduction in poaching in the national park, increased tourism investment and improved employment and business opportunities for local communities that share in income derived from tourism and associated activities.[108]

These examples[109] illustrate the challenges that arise in developing and resourcing local biodiversity management frameworks, and the biodiversity and livelihood benefits that can result where they are successfully implemented.

Economic tools: Valuing ecosystem services

Article 11 of the CBD calls upon parties to "adopt economically and socially sound measures that act as incentives for the conservation and sustainable use of the components of biodiversity". The use of incentives and the need to engage the private sector in order to do so have been considered repeatedly by the COP.[110]

Such incentives have a critical role to play in the conservation of biodiversity on land held outside protected areas, as part of national strategies to implement the objectives of the CBD. The conservation of biodiversity on private property is imperative for a number of reasons, including:

• The inadequate representation of some species of flora or fauna on lands falling within a nation's protected areas system.

- Threatened ecological communities may be found on private property which has fertile soil and flatter topography due to clearing and development.[111]
- An increasing recognition of the sustainable agriculture benefits to landholders of a conservation-oriented approach to property management through actions that conserve or enhance native vegetation and provide wildlife habitat.[112]
- The expense involved for governments to acquire private land for conservation purposes.
- The relative costs of maintaining habitat intact, contrasted to remediating degraded habitat.[113]
- In considering the role of biodiversity and carbon storage, the protected areas system accounts for 15 per cent of stored global carbon,[114] making the effective integration of conservation and sustainable use of biodiversity within and outside protected areas an essential component of climate change adaptation measures.

The challenge of protecting biodiversity outside protected areas can be significant. In many property law regimes, there is little incentive to encourage private owners to maintain habitat. Legal frameworks frequently reflect a conservation policy that has traditionally centred upon the public lands reserve system and to a significant extent ignored land in private ownership.[115]

In this context, economic mechanisms (including eco-service markets and payment schemes) are playing an increasingly important role in national regulatory frameworks seeking to promote biodiversity conservation. This is consistent with the Ecosystem Approach that calls for ecosystem management to be understood in an economic context and for priority to be accorded to the maintenance of ecosystem services through the conservation of ecosystem structures. Globally, total annual payments in 2007 under all payment schemes and markets for ecosystems services has been estimated at US$77 billion. These payments are projected to increase to approximately $300 billion by 2020.[116]

Clearly, the regulatory, fiscal and environmental services market mix adopted in a particular country will vary significantly, depending upon the national context, including economic, political, cultural, legal and social priorities. A number of examples are discussed below.

Market creation

The provision of environmental services has traditionally been viewed as the responsibility of the public sector, which has relied upon a combination of command-and-control regulation and tax-based incentives. However, a broad range of innovative market-based approaches has become more prominent in recent years as jurisdictions struggle with the failings associated with public regulation of environmental services.

Market-based instruments are seen as being capable of achieving environmental goals at significantly less cost than the conventional command-and-control approaches, and also create positive incentives for innovation and improvement.[117]

A more difficult issue is whether market-based approaches to environmental services result in greater equity in terms of the distribution of environmental burdens throughout society. While the "polluter pays" principle is a well-understood and accepted principle within international and domestic environmental law, it may be argued that, in the case of environmental services, the "provider–gets" principle should apply. According to this principle, those who provide an environmental benefit should be rewarded for doing so (or at least be compensated for their costs).[118] In many cases those who provide environmental services, such as rural land users, are poorer than the beneficiaries or consumers of those services. This heightens the importance of developing financial mechanisms which transfer resources from relatively rich consumers of environmental services to relatively poor suppliers.

Markets have been established in many jurisdictions for a variety of environmental services, including water quality, biodiversity, carbon and salinity credits. While markets for environmental services are particularly prevalent in northern nations such as the United States, increasingly such markets are developing in many other jurisdictions. The total size of all known regulated biodiversity offset transactions (drawn predominantly from the US mitigation markets) is approximately $3.4 billion annually, with some estimates that the global market could grow to 4.5 billion by 2010 and possibly 10 billion by 2020.[119]

Conservation/biodiversity banking/offset schemes

In a number of jurisdictions including the United States,[120] Australia and, most recently, France[121] conservation or biodiversity banking is used as a tool to promote positive biodiversity outcomes from land development proposals. Conservation banking involves "the establishment of land banks dedicated for conservation, which sell credits to developers who are required to purchase them to offset the environmental impacts of approved developments" on biodiversity.[122] The establishment of a legislative framework for offsets requires a transparent and effective integration of threatened species protection and planning laws.[123]

In the United States, the use of offsetting agreements within conservation banking approaches has been successful for some twenty years, stemming from the wetlands mitigation scheme established under the Federal Clean Water Act 1972. Under both state and federal US endangered species legislation, the power to require developers to mitigate for the adverse impacts of their activities on endangered species is provided.[124]

In Australia, recent amendments to threatened species legislation in some state jurisdictions enable the creation of biodiversity site banks and for biodiversity credits to be traded to offset the impacts of development. For example, in New South Wales, the biodiversity offsets scheme established under the Threatened Species Conservation Amendment (Biodiversity Banking) Act 2006 seeks to protect "biodiversity values".[125]

Sheahan has identified a range of issues common to the implementation of biodiversity mitigation schemes in the United States and Australia, including:

- The need for the mitigation of environmental impacts to be scientifically valid, consistently applied and rigorously enforced;
- The need to take into account the "time lag" of mitigation;
- The scheme needs to be capable of protecting the greatest area of habitat and to share economic benefits to the greatest number of landholders; and
- The scheme should ensure the legal security of the biodiversity bank site through the creation of a conservation easement, covenant or other registered agreement.[126]

Such issues are of general application to the design and implementation of biodiversity banking/offsets schemes.

Increasingly, developing countries are considering the role of regulated biodiversity offsets, particularly in the context of resources exploration within protected areas. For example, in Uganda the possibility of introducing a biodiversity offset scheme is being considered by the Uganda Wildlife Authority to enable mitigation of the impacts of oil drilling on species within national parks.[127]

Tradable reserve rights

Under the Brazilian Forest Code (1965), legal reserves of native or regenerated forest were required to be established on private property. While the size of the legal reserves varies depending upon the location of the property, in the south of the country it is normally approximately 20 per cent of private land while, in the north, it is somewhere between 50 and 80 per cent which must be reserved.

Provisional Regulation (Medida Provisoria) 2166-67 of 2001 allows landholders to satisfy the requirement from one property through the establishment of a legal forest reserve located on another. In some cases, the offsite legal reserve may be owned by another party, enabling a market in legal reserve rights to develop. As many properties do not comply with the legal reserve requirement under the 1965 Forest Code, increased enforcement of the law has led to significant interest in a number of policies which may permit trade of legal reserve obligations, allowing landholders with insufficient legal reserve to purchase offsetting reserve at different sites.[128]

Fiscal measures

Globally, a wide range of taxation and spending or "fiscal policy" mechanisms are used by governments to achieve biodiversity conservation. However, measures aimed at removing disincentives to adopting sustainable land use or agricultural practices and/or encouraging philanthropic conservation of ecologically sensitive land (such as conservation covenants, easements and donations of land) are being used in a number of jurisdictions, including the United States, the United Kingdom, Canada and Australia.[129]

According to the MEA, land use change is likely to maintain its position as the leading direct cause of biodiversity loss until at least 2050. In many jurisdictions, the role of agri-environmental payment or subsidy programmes implemented at national or state and provincial levels is critical in providing payments to agricultural producers in return for the provision of environmental services.

Eco-service payment schemes are well established in most developed countries including the United States, Canada, Australia and the United Kingdom.[130] Such payment schemes are also emerging in developing countries. For example, in 1996 Costa Rica established the Payments for Environmental Services programme which introduced a national compensation system for the provision of environmental services under the Forestry Law 7575 (1996). The programme recognizes environmental services provided by forest ecosystems, including biodiversity conservation and mitigation of greenhouse gas emissions.[131] The government contracts with landowners for the services provided by their lands. Landowners are committed to managing or protecting their contracted forest for twenty years (or fifteen in the case of reforestation).[132]

In Mexico, a number of biodiversity-related national payment-based mechanisms have been implemented. For example, under the Law of Sustainable Rural Development,[133] payments are made to producers who change their agricultural activities towards more sustainable use of their land, according to its productive capacity and ecological viability. Mexico has also introduced legislation aimed at promoting access to local and international markets for environmental services, particularly in relation to carbon sequestration and biodiversity of forest ecosystems. The legislation seeks to encourage landowners and holders of agricultural land to convert to agriforest systems. Under this legislation,[134] payments are made to landowners to protect biodiversity and for conversion to or improvement of agriforestry systems.

A range of initiatives for the implementation of fiscal measures is developing in Brazil, a biologically mega-diverse country. While command-and-control instruments still prevail as the key mechanisms for enabling the conservation and sustainable use of biodiversity,[135] localized initiatives include a green value added tax in a number of states,[136] linked to the creation of protected areas, financial compensation to farmers who maintain on their properties permanent preservation areas of native vegetation,[137] and a state incentive programme for the production of hardwoods and associated carbon sequestration programme in Sao Paulo.[138]

In China, environmental policymakers are increasingly focusing on the development and use of "eco-compensation mechanisms" that provide payments for ecosystem services including watershed ecosystem services, carbon, biodiversity conservation and anti-desertification services. The importance of such initiatives is reflected in State Council Release no. 39 [2005], State Council Decision Regarding Using the Scientific Development View to Strengthening Environmental Protection, that states that the government ". . . should improve eco-compensation policy, and develop eco-compensation mechanisms as quickly as possible".[139]

The Chinese Government has initiated key eco-service payment schemes, including expenditure of in excess of RMB 130 billion on the Conversion of Cropland to Forests and Grassland (CCFG) programme. Over 9 million hectares of cropland have been reforested under this programme that involves direct payments to individual farmers to retire and afforest or plant grasses on sloping or marginal cropland.[140]

Sectoral mainstreaming of biodiversity issues

Article 6 of the CBD calls upon parties to integrate biodiversity conservation and sustainable use into relevant sectoral or cross-sectoral plans, programmes and policies. Mainstreaming the conservation and sustainable use of biodiversity across all sectors of the national economy, the society and the policy-making framework has been described as "a complex challenge at the heart of the Convention".[141]

The CBD Secretariat has emphasized the need to focus on sectors such as land use planning, agriculture, forestry and fisheries. These sectors give rise to a number of the key direct drivers for biodiversity loss outlined in Part A.[142] The 2002 Strategic Plan emphasizes the role of tools such as the Ecosystem Approach and the use of strategic environmental assessment in achieving effective integration.

To date, three key approaches to mainstreaming biodiversity issues have involved integration of biodiversity into:
- economic sectors (such as agriculture, forestry, fisheries, tourism, education and health);

- cross-sectoral policies and strategies (finance, national development and poverty eradication); and
- spatial planning approaches to land use, especially at state and municipal levels.

As national governments strive to develop frameworks for dealing with climate change threats and to implement adaptation plans, the need to ensure that biodiversity conservation forms a part of national climate strategies is likely to result in further efforts to integrate biodiversity issues across sectors. This is particularly likely where the economic security of a nation and the livelihoods of its people are threatened by climate change impacts.[143]

Land use planning

In all jurisdictions, one of the key challenges for policymakers lies in developing a legal framework that effectively integrates biodiversity conservation into strategic land use planning, to enable a landscape approach to biodiversity. Even where legislation seeks to integrate biodiversity concerns into planning and development decision-making, failure to identify biodiversity values on a landscape basis and to build conservation measures into applicable planning instruments may result in little reduction to rates of biodiversity loss.

In one Australian jurisdiction,[144] recent changes to threatened species legislation enable biodiversity certification of environmental planning instruments (the planning scheme for an area) by the relevant Minister where the Minister is satisfied that the environmental planning instrument seeks to promote the conservation of threatened species, populations and ecological communities. In deciding whether to confer certification, the Minister must consider, among other things:

- the likely social and economic consequences of implementing the environmental planning instrument;
- the most effective and efficient use of resources for conserving threatened species, population and communities; and
- the principles of ecologically sustainable development.

The biodiversity certification legislation is integrated into the land use regulatory framework to avoid a site-by-site approach to development decisions. Rather, consideration of biodiversity values is undertaken at the land use planning stage. The effect of certification of an environmental planning instrument is that a development that requires consent under the land use legislation no longer requires site-specific threatened species assessment.

While biodiversity certification of an area is potentially an important initiative in addressing biodiversity loss, that objective may be compromised where there is a lack of political will and/or government agency cooperation, inadequate resourcing, ineffective integration into the land use planning framework and poor monitoring mechanisms.[145]

Another example is the ecological and economic zoning policy implemented in the Brazilian state of Acre. This policy underpins land use planning and decision-making related to agrarian reform and rural resettlement, the development of economic sectors, the protected areas system, demarcation of indigenous lands and water resources management. The critical role of biodiversity conservation and sustainable use is reflected in the zoning approach: 50 per cent of the state is protected either as formal protected areas (10 per cent), indigenous lands (14 per cent), or conservation and sustainable use areas (26 per cent). It has been estimated that the use of such policies has resulted in an 80 per cent reduction in deforestation in Acre since 2002.[146]

Economic and cross-sectoral policies and strategies

The relationship between the mainstreaming of biodiversity issues through embedding biodiversity within relevant decision-making frameworks and across economic sectors (particularly tourism)[147] and the achievement of the MDGs is critical.

As noted above,[148] a major issue is the extent to which NBSAPs have been implemented nationally to effectively integrate biodiversity concerns into relevant sectors and, in particular, the integration of biodiversity into poverty reduction schemes. There is some evidence that nations are beginning to more closely align their national biodiversity strategies with poverty reduction programmes through long-term strategic cross-sectoral plans. For example, in Cambodia the development of the NBSAP has been linked to the goal of poverty reduction and the achievement of the Cambodia MDGs that are "the cornerstones of the country's development policies and strategies".[149]

A recent case study by Aongola et al.[150] examined the challenges and opportunities inherent in mainstreaming environmental issues in development in Zambia. The Zambian economy is highly dependent on sectors that are underpinned by the environment: the mining, agriculture, tourism and forestry sectors contribute the largest proportion of Zambia's gross domestic product and export value. Zambia is typical of developing countries for which the value of environmental assets is disproportionately significant compared to other assets in assessing the national wealth.[151] Its environmental assets include World Heritage sites, minerals, fertile agricultural land, abundant water resources and biodiversity. However, in common with other nations, Zambia faces the challenges identified earlier in this chapter in managing its environmental assets, including biodiversity. Deforestation[152] and subsistence poaching are particular drivers of biodiversity loss. While the proportion of land included in protected areas is high (41.5 per cent),[153] a significant number of national parks are considered to be degraded in their environmental status.[154] In its 2008 MDG Progress Report, Zambia indicated that MDG7, Environmental Sustainability, is the only MDG target that is "unlikely" to be met.[155]

Recent policy and legislative initiatives have identified opportunities for environmental concerns (including biodiversity issues) to be integrated across national planning strategies. For example, the *Fifth National Development Plan 2006–2010* calls for "mainstreaming environmental issues into national development programmes and enforcement of existing laws and policies to protect the environment". The Plan includes a commitment to expand the protected areas system and a range of planning initiatives to promote sustainable development, including the incorporation of provisions for strategic and environmental assessment; biological diversity impact assessment and management in all economic and development activities; and maintenance of a representation of ecosystems.

Sectoral integration of environmental management has been initiated through the development of specialist environmental units within line ministries and institutions responsible for key sectors of the Zambian economy, including the mining, roads and electricity sectors.[156]

The proposed Urban and Regional Planning Act provides for integrated development plans (IDPs) for both urban and regional areas that incorporate sectoral plans, dealing with wildlife and environmental management in addition to issues such as agricultural land use, energy networks and heritage. The sectoral plans are to integrate international environmental law obligations.[157] Critically for resourcing and implementation, the plans will be used by the Ministry of Finance and National Planning as components in budget and economic planning procedures.[158]

The Environmental Council of Zambia has developed a range of environmental impact assessment (EIA) guidelines for project level assessment in different sectors (including fisheries and forestry) to assist in understanding and compliance with EIA requirements under the relevant legislation.[159] The Zambia Wildlife Authority has likewise prepared sectoral EIA guidelines for protected areas. However, in common with many jurisdictions, the Zambian EIA process faces issues regarding the level of political will to recognize and address environmental issues, transparency and timely decision-making.[160] While EIA has been used as a mainstreaming tool in Zambia for many years, it is not yet regarded as an essential part of the decision-making process.[161] Further, strategic environmental assessment (SEA) is not required under planning legislation and this remains an area for reform at the policy level.[162]

While these measures contribute to progressing the mainstreaming of environmental issues across sectors and within decision-making frameworks, Aongola et al. conclude that:

> ... despite progress, environmental issues are not integrated adequately or systematically into Zambia's development policy, budget and institutions. We conclude that there is no systematic approach to environment-development links.[163]

Effective mainstreaming of biodiversity conservation and sustainable use is a long-term process requiring significant institutional change to ensure the development of a coherent mainstreaming policy that addresses the loss of biodiversity arising as a secondary consequence of activities in economic sectors (such as agriculture, forestry, fisheries and urban development).

Conclusion

In 2008, the IUCN Red List of Threatened Species included 44 838 species, 38 per cent of which are threatened with extinction.[164] Projections for the global community's ability to meet the 2010 Target indicate that success is unlikely. In addition to the well-known causes of biodiversity loss, the devastating impacts of climate change on biodiversity call for urgent action from the international community. Effective national implementation of measures to conserve biodiversity and its sustainable use is a challenge for all nations, but particularly for those struggling with the demands of devising and implementing measures to alleviate poverty. By drawing on examples from a range of nations, it can be seen that, notwithstanding the many and varied challenges to biodiversity conservation and sustainable use, a number of the key mechanisms identified in the CBD are facilitating the objectives of the Convention. The revised Strategic Plan and Biodiversity Target to be agreed in 2010 will be critical in setting the future course for global biodiversity protection – the issue for many nations will be whether political will to act decisively can match international rhetoric.

Notes

1. Ministers of Environment and heads of delegation meeting in Malmö, Sweden, 29–31 May 2000, on the occasion of the First Global Ministerial Environment Forum, held in pursuance of UN General Assembly Resolution 53/242 of 28 July 1999; available at

<http://www.pnuma.org/deramb/MalmoMinisterialDeclaration.php> (accessed 16 June 2009).

2. A/RES/61/203; available at <http://www.un.org/Docs/journal/asp/ws.asp?m=A/RES/61/203>.

3. Ibid., p. 4.

4. United Nations, *Treaty Series*, vol. 1760, no. 30619 (CBD). Other biodiversity-related conventions are the Convention on International Trade in Endangered Species of Wild Fauna and Flora, Washington DC, 3 March 1973, entered into force 1 July 1975, 12 ILM 1085 (1975); the Convention on Wetlands, Ramsar, 2 February 1971, entered into force 21 December 1975, 11 ILM 963 (1972); the Convention on the Conservation of Migratory Species of Wild Animals, Bonn, June 1979, entered into force 1 November 1983, 19 ILM 15 (1980); and the Convention Concerning the Protection of World Cultural and Natural Heritage, Paris, 16 November 1972, entered into force 17 December 1975, 11 ILM 1358 (1972) (World Heritage Convention).

5. CBD, art. 2.

6. CBD, art. 2 defines "ecosystem" as follows: "a dynamic complex of plant, animal and micro-organism communities and their non-living environment interacting as a functional unit".

7. James Salzman, Zaelke Durwood and David Hunter, *International Environmental Law and Policy* (New York: West Publishing Company, 2002), p. 912.

8. Ibid., p. 918.

9. Secretariat of the Convention on Biological Diversity, *Draft Findings of the Ad Hoc Technical Expert Group on Biodiversity and Climate Change, London, 17–21 November 2008*, para. 15; available at <http://www.cbd.int/doc/meetings/cc/ahteg-bdcc-01/other/ahteg-bdcc-01-findings-en.pdf>.

10. World Resources Institute, *Millennium Ecosystem Assessment: Ecosystems and Human Well-being: Biodiversity Synthesis* (2005), p. 22; available at <http://www.millenniumassessment.org/documents/document.354.aspx.pdf>.

11. Ibid., pp. 30–32.

12. Secretariat of the Convention on Biological Diversity, *Global Biodiversity Outlook 2* (2006), p. 58; available at <http://www.cbd.int/doc/gbo/gbo2/cbd-gbo2-en.pdf>.

13. Only four ecosystems examined were found to have been enhanced, namely, crops, livestock, aquaculture and carbon sequestration. Where modifications were found to have enhanced an ecosystem service, such change generally arose due to a trade-off to other services. World Resources Institute, *Millennium Ecosystem Assessment: Ecosystems and Human Well-being: Biodiversity Synthesis*, p. 5.

14. Secretariat of the Convention on Biological Diversity, *Global Biodiversity Outlook 2* (2006), p. 58.

15. World Resources Institute, *Millennium Ecosystem Assessment: Ecosystems and Human Well-being: Biodiversity Synthesis*, p. 3.

16. According to the MEA, this is particularly significant with respect to terrestrial ecosystems due to deforestation and cultivation: for example, the MEA reports that cultivated systems (defined as "areas in which at least 30 per cent of the landscape is in croplands, shifting cultivation, confined livestock production, or freshwater aquaculture in any particular year") cover 24 per cent of the Earth's surface. Ibid., p. 51.

17. Particularly with respect to freshwater and island habitats: ibid., p. 53.

18. This is particularly evident among marine species, trees and animals hunted for food. The demand for resources at the global level exceeds the biological capacity of the Earth by approximately 20 per cent: Secretariat of the Convention on Biological Diversity, <http://www.cbd.int/cepa/messages.shtml>. The MEA notes that fishing pressures in some marine systems have resulted in a reduction in the biomass of fish

targeted in fisheries by 90 per cent relative to pre-industrial fishing levels. World Resources Institute, *Millennium Ecosystem Assessment: Ecosystems and Human Wellbeing: Biodiversity Synthesis* (2005), p. 51.

19. Increasing levels of nutrient loading (especially nitrogen and phosphorus) into ecosystems, particularly terrestrial, freshwater and coastal ecosystems, has resulted in the creation of "dead zones" in various parts of the world. For example, the loss of wetlands in the Mississippi watershed of the United States, combined with high nutrient loads from intensive agriculture in the region, has contributed to the creation of a low-oxygen "dead zone", incapable of supporting animal life, which extends, on average at mid-summer, 16,000 square kilometres into the Gulf of Mexico. Secretariat of the Convention on Biological Diversity, *Global Biodiversity Outlook 2* (2006), p. 15.

20. Ibid, p. 62.

21. In this regard, see Secretariat of the Convention on Biological Diversity, *Connecting Biodiversity and Climate Change Mitigation and Adaptation: Report of the Second Ad Hoc Technical Expert Group on Biodiversity and Climate Change* (2009); available at <http://www.cbd.int/doc/publications/cbd-ts-41-en.pdf>.

22. IPCC, *Fourth Assessment Report Climate Change 2007: Synthesis Report Summary for Policy Makers*, released 17 November 2007; available at <http://www.ipcc.ch/pdf/assessment-report/ar4/syr/ar4_syr_spm.pdf>.

23. *IPCC: Summary for Policymakers*, in Martin L. Parry, Osvaldo F. Canziani, Jean P. Palutikof, Paul J. van der Linden and Clair E. Hanson (eds), *Climate Change 2007: Impacts, Adaptation and Vulnerability: Contribution of Working Group II to the Fourth Assessment Report of the Intergovernmental Panel on Climate Change* (Cambridge: Cambridge University Press, 2007), p. 11; available at <http://www.ipcc-wg2.org/>.

24. CBD Secretariat, *Draft Findings of the Ad Hoc Technical Expert Group on Biodiversity and Climate Change, London, 17–21 November 2008.*

25. Jeffrey D. Sachs, *Common Wealth: Economics for a Crowded Planet* (New York: Penguin Press, 2008), p. 139.

26. CBD Secretariat, *Global Biodiversity Outlook 2* (2006), p. 49.

27. Salzman et al., *International Environmental Law and Policy*, p. 916.

28. World Resources Institute, *Global Biodiversity Outlook 2* (2006), p. 22.

29. Krystyna Swiderska, Dilys Roe, Linda Siegele and Maryanne Grieg-Gran, *The Governance of Nature and the Nature of Governance: Policy that Works for Biodiversity and Livelihoods* (2009), p. 11; available at <http://www.iied.org/pubs/display.php?o=14564IIED>.

30. According to UNEP, current best estimates of the number of species globally vary between 5 and 30 million, of which approximately 2 million have been described by science. UNEP, *Global Environment Outlook 4: Environment for Development* (2007); available at <http://www.unep.org/geo/geo4/media/>.

31. Most notably, Stockholm Declaration on the Human Environment, 16 June 1972, 11 ILM 1416 (1972); *World Conservation Strategy: Living Resource Conservation for Sustainable Development* (IUCN-UNEP-WWF, 1980); The World Charter for Nature, 28 October 1982, 22 ILM 455 (1983); *Report of the World Commission on Environment and Development: Our Common Future* (Brundtland Commission) (Oxford: Oxford University Press, 1987); Rio Declaration on Environment and Development, 14 June 1992, 31 ILM 874 (1992); United Nations Conference on Environment and Development, Agenda Item 21 (Agenda 21), A/CONF.151/26, 31 ILM 814 (1992).

32. For example, Africa: African Convention on the Conservation of Nature and Natural Resources, *Algiers*, 15 September 1968, entered into force 16 June 1969, 1001 UNTS 3; Europe: Convention on the Conservation of European Wildlife and Natural Habitats, Bern, 19 September 1979, entered into force 1 June 1982, 1284 UNTS 209; Benelux

Convention Concerning Hunting and the Protection of Birds, Brussels, 10 June 1970, 1 July 1972, 847 UNTS 255 (Benelux Convention); Benelux Convention on Nature Conservation and Landscape Protection, Brussels, 8 June 1982, entered into force 1 October 1983, UNEP Reg. p. 207; Convention on the Protection of the Alps, Salzburg, 7 November 1991, entered into force 6 March 1995, 1917 UNTS 315 (Alpine Convention). Americas: Convention on Nature Protection and Wild Life Preservation in the Western Hemisphere, 12 October 1940, entered into force 30 April 1942, 161 UNTS 193 (Western Hemisphere Convention); Convention for the Conservation of Biological Diversity and the Protection of Priority Wild Areas in Central America, 5 June 1992, entered into force 20 December 1994. Asia: *ASEAN* Agreement on the Conservation of Nature and Natural Resources, July 1985, not yet in force, 15 EPL 64. Antarctic: The Antarctic Treaty, 1 December 1959, entered into force 23 June 1961, 402 UNTS 71; Protocol on Environmental Protection to the Antarctic Treaty, 4 October 1991, entered into force 14 January 1998, [1999] ATS no. 6. Pacific: Convention on the Conservation of Nature in the South Pacific, 12 June 1976, entered into force 26 June 1990, [1990] ATS no. 41.

33. For example, Convention on the Conservation of Migratory Species of Wild Animals, Bonn, 23 June 1979, entered into force 1 November 1983, 1651 UNTS 356; Agreement for the Protection of Migratory Birds and Birds in Danger of Extinction and their Environment, Australia-Japan, Tokyo, 6 February 1974, entered into force 30 April 1981, 1241 UNTS 385; Agreement for the Protection of Migratory Birds and their Environment, Australia-China, Canberra, 20 October 1986, entered into force 1 September 1988, 1535 UNTS 243; International Convention for the Regulation of Whaling, Washington DC, 2 December 1946, entered into force 10 November 1948, 161 UNTS 72.

34. Convention on International Trade in Endangered Species of Wild Fauna and Flora, Washington DC, 3 March 1973, entered into force 1 July 1975, 993 UNTS 243 (CITES).

35. Convention on Wetlands of International Importance Especially as Waterfowl Habitat, Ramsar, 2 February 1971, entered into force 21 December 1975, 996 UNTS 245 (RAMSAR Convention); Convention Concerning the Protection of World Cultural and Natural Heritage, Paris, 16 November 1972, entered into force 17 December 1975, 11 ILM 1358 (1972) (World Heritage Convention); United Nations Convention on the Law of the Sea, Montego Bay, 10 December 1982, in force 16 November 1994, 1833 UNTS 397, 21 ILM 1261 (1982) (LOS Convention).

36. At the date of writing, there are 191 state parties to the Convention. See <http://www.cbd.int/convention/parties/list/>.

37. CBD, art. 1.

38. The CBD, in art. 2, defines "protected area" as a "geographically defined area which is designated or regulated and managed to achieve specific conservation objectives".

39. CBD, art. 8(c).

40. CBD, art. 7.

41. CBD, art. 6.

42. CBD, art. 11.

43. CBD, art. 8(a).

44. See Kenton R. Miller and Steven M. Lanou (eds), *National Biodiversity Planning: Guidelines Based on Early Experiences around the World* (Washington DC: World Resources Institute/UNEP/IUCN, 1995); available at <http://www.cbd.int/nbsap/guidance-tools/guidelines.shtml>.

45. These obstacles were noted by the Conference of the Parties (COP) of the Convention at COP 6 (Decision VI/26) and included in the Appendix to the Strategic Plan. See

Strategic Plan for the Convention on Biological Diversity, para. 11; available at <http://www.cbd.int/sp/>.

46. Islamic Republic of Afghanistan, *Afghanistan's Fourth National Report to the Convention on Biological Diversity* (2009); available at <https://www.cbd.int/doc/world/af/af-nr-04-en.pdf>.

47. *Strategic Plan for the Convention on Biological Diversity*. The 2010 Target was supported in the Johannesburg Plan of Implementation of the 2002 World Summit on Sustainable Development; available at <http://www.un.org/esa/sustdev/documents/wssd_poi_pd/english/wssd_PlanImpl.pdf>.

48. COP Decision VII/30, UNEP/CBD/COP/DEC/VII/30, 13 April 2004.

49. *Strategic Plan for the Convention on Biological Diversity*.

50. COP5 Decision V/6, UNEP/CBD/COP/5/23, Nairobi, 15–26 May 2000.

51. Ibid.

52. See CBD, art. 8(j).

53. Sachs, *Common Wealth: Econonics for a Crowded Planet*, p. 153.

54. CBD Secretariat, *Global Biodiversity Outlook 2* (2006), p. 59.

55. Dilys Roe (ed.), *The Millennium Development Goals and Conservation – Managing Nature's Wealth for Society's Health* (London: IIED/UNEP, 2004), p. 3.

56. For example, in rural Zimbabwe, biodiversity provides 37 per cent of the total household income with the poorest 20 per cent of the community deriving 40 per cent of their total income from environmental products, while the richest 10 per cent derive only 29 per cent from such products. IUCN, *Biodiversity Brief 1: The Links Between Biodiversity and Poverty*; available at <http://www.undp.org/biodiversity/biodiversitycd/BioBrief1-poverty.pdf>.

57. Oxfam International, Briefing Paper, *Suffering the Science – Climate Change, People and Poverty* (2009); available at <http://www.oxfam.org.uk/resources/policy/climate_change/downloads/bp130_suffering_science.pdf>.

58. Ibid., p. 5.

59. World Food Programme, *UN food agencies urge climate change action to avert hunger* (2007); available at <http://www.wfp.org/news/news-release/un-food-agencies-urge-climate-change-action-avert-hunger>.

60. See *Millennium Development Goals*; available at <http://www.un.org/millenniumgoals/>.

61. Goal 7 Targets: Integrate the principles of sustainable development into country policies and programmes and reverse the loss of environmental resources; halve, by 2015, the proportion of people without sustainable access to safe drinking water; and achieve, by 2020, a significant improvement in the lives of at least 100 million slum dwellers. See <http://www.un.org/millenniumgoals/environ.shtml>.

62. Target B was incorporated into the framework for the MDGs in 2007 as Target 7.B Resolution A/RES/61/1 adopted by the General Assembly of the United Nations. See <http://mdgs.un.org/unsd/mdg/Resources/Attach/Indicators/ares60_1_2005summit_eng.pdf>.

63. United Nations, *The Millennium Development Goals Report* (2008); available at <http://www.un.org/millenniumgoals/pdf/The%20Millennium%20Development%20Goals%20Report%202008.pdf>.

64. Balakrishna Pisupati and Emilie Warner, "Biodiversity and the Millennium Development Goals", *Asian Biotechnology and Development Review* (2003), p. 15; available at <http://www.undp.org/biodiversity/mdgandbiodiversity.html>.

65. Ibid., p. 17.

66. Roe, *The Millennium Development Goals and Conservation*, p. xix.

67. Pisupati and Warner, "Biodiversity and the Millennium Development Goals", p. 28.

68. Ibid., p. 34.
69. Roe, *The Millennium Development Goals and Conservation*, p. viii.
70. Sachs, *Common Wealth: Economics for a Crowded Planet*, p. 145.
71. Executive Secretary, CBD Secretariat, *Revision and Updating of the Strategic Plan: Synthesis/Analysis of Views*, UNEP/CBD/SP/PREP/1, 2009; available at <http://www.cbd.int/doc/meetings/ind/emind-02/official/emind-02-07-cbd-sp-en.pdf>.
72. These countries included Australia, Brazil, the Czech Republic, Sweden, Egypt, India, Indonesia, South Africa, Mexico and the Republic of South Korea.
73. *Carta di Syracusa* on Biodiversity; available at <http://www.cbd.int/doc/g8/g8-declaration-siracusa-carta-en.pdf>.
74. Ibid.
75. CBD Secretariat, *Revision and Updating of the Strategic Plan: Synthesis/Analysis of Views*, UNEP/CBD/SP/PREP/15 June 2009; available at <http://www.cbd.int/sp/>.
76. CBD Secretariat, *Revision and Updating of the Strategic Plan: Synthesis/Analysis of Views*.
77. Secretariat of the Convention on Biological Diversity, *Global Biodiversity Outlook 2* (2006), p. 53.
78. See National Reports and NBSAPs; available at <https://www.cbd.int/reports/search/>.
79. CBD Secretariat, *Global Biodiversity Outlook 2* (2006), p. 53. At the time of writing, 166 state parties had completed a NBSAP with 25 still to do so: <http://www.cbd.int/nbsap/>.
80. See <http://www.cbd.int/nbsap/financial.shtml>.
81. CBD Secretariat, *Global Biodiversity Outlook 2* (2006), p. 53.
82. Of 100 country reports analysed, UNDP found that seventeen included targets for forest coverage or protected areas under MDG7. See CBD Secretariat, *Global Biodiversity Outlook 2* (2006), p. 53.
83. CBD Secretariat, *Global Biodiversity Outlook 2* (2006), p. 69.
84. Provisional Measure 458/2009.
85. Under the new law, small landowners who can prove they occupied lands before December 2004 will be handed small pieces of land free, while large areas will be sold off at knockdown rates. See "Brazil Grants Land Rights to Squatters Living in Amazon Rainforest" (2009); available at <http://www.guardian.co.uk/environment/2009/jun/26/amazon-land-rights-brazil>.
86. John W. Mellor, *Poverty Reduction and Biodiversity Conservation: The Complex Role for Intensifying Agriculture* (WWF Macroeconomics Programme Office, 2002), p. 2.
87. CBD, art. 2.
88. COP7 Decision VII/28.
89. COP7 Decision VII/30.
90. COP8 Decision VIII/15.
91. MDG, Indicator 7.6: Proportion of terrestrial and marine area protected.
92. Lauren Coad, Neil Burgess, Lucy Fish, et al., "Progress towards the Convention on Biological Diversity Terrestrial 2010 and Marine 2012 Targets for Protected Area Coverage", *Parks*, vol. 17, no. 2 (2008), pp. 35–42, p. 36.
93. CBD Secretariat, *The Convention on Biological Diversity Year in Review 2008* (2009); available at <http://www.cbd.int/doc/reports/cbd-report-2008-en.pdf>.
94. UNEP/CBD/COP/8/29. *Review of Implementation of the Programme of Work on Protected Areas for the Period 2004-2006*; available at <http://www.cbd.int/doc/meetings/cop/cop-08/official/cop-08-29-en.pdf>. The Report notes, at para. 48, that "Forty of the 50 reporting countries indicated identifying gaps and barriers that impede effective establishment and management of protected areas. From the information provided, some of the common constraints are: limited financial resources; lack of trained personnel;

competing needs on land for agriculture and recreation; lack of intersectoral coordination; compensation issues and land tenure rights. Many countries, including developed countries noted an inadequacy in investments for protected areas."

95. Coad et al., "Progress towards the Convention on Biological Diversity Terrestrial 2010 and Marine 2012 Targets for Protected Area Coverage", p. 38.

96. Agnes Kiss, *Making Biodiversity Conservation a Land Use Priority* (2002); available at <http://www2.gsu.edu/~wwwcec/special/AgiBookChapter2002.pdf>.

97. See, for example, the threats posed by armed conflict to the Okapi Wildlife Reserve, one of the protected areas in the Democratic Republic of Congo listed under the World Heritage Convention: <http://www.unep-wcmc.org/sites/wh/pdf/Okapi%202.pdf>.

98. Coad et al., "Progress towards the Convention on Biological Diversity Terrestrial 2010 and Marine 2012 Targets for Protected Area Coverage", p. 41.

99. Swiderska et al., *The Governance of Nature and the Nature of Governance*, p. 21.

100. Considered both within and outside protected areas.

101. The discussion of this case study is drawn from Swiderska et al., *The Governance of Nature and the Nature of Governance*, pp. 90–93.

102. 26 per cent of the country is under strict protection.

103. According to Swiderska et al., *The Governance of Nature and the Nature of Governance*, p. 92: "The WMA pilot phase was launched in January 2003, and by the end of 2006, only four out of the 16 pilot WMAs had been gazetted. By October 2007, a total of nine WMAs had been gazette and issued with user rights. Another five WMAs were still in the process of being gazetted, while one WMA was stopped due to conflicts between villages."

104. Land and Village Land Acts (1999) and the Forest Act (2002).

105. Swiderska et al., *The Governance of Nature and the Nature of Governance*, p. 95.

106. See discussion of the South Luangwa Area Management Unit in Aongola et al., "Creating and Protecting Zambia's Wealth. Experience and Next Steps in Environmental Mainstreaming", *Natural Resource Issues* no. 14 (International Institute for Environment and Development, 2009), pp. 40–43; available at <http://www.iied.org/pubs/pdfs/17502IIED.pdf>.

107. The Wildlife Act (1998) and the National Parks and Wildlife Policy.

108. Aongola et al., "Creating and Protecting Zambia's Wealth", p. 42. However, concerns have arisen as to the extent to which the expectations of local communities involved in community-based natural resource management under this programme have been met. See Musole M. Musumali, Thor S. Larsen and Bjorn P. Kaltenborn, "An Impasse in Community-based Natural Resource Management Implementation: The Case of Zambia and Botswana", *Oryx*, vol. 41, no. 3 (2007), pp. 306–313.

109. See also Abebe H. Gebremariam, Million Bekele and Andrew Ridgewell, *Small and Medium Forest Enterprises in Ethiopia* (2009), IIED Small and Medium Forest Enterprise Series no. 26, FARM-Africa and IIED; available at <http://www.iied.org/pubs/search.php?s=FSME>.

110. See Decision III/18, Decision IV/10, Decision IV/15 and Decision VIII/17, VIII/25 and VIII/26; available at <http://www.cbd.int/decisions/>.

111. Carl Binning and Mike Young, *Native Vegetation Institutions, Policies and Incentives* (Synthesis Report to Land and Water Resources R & D Corporation and Environment Australia National Program on Rehabilitation, Management and Conservation of Remnant Vegetation, Canberra, 2000), p. 11.

112. Paul Bateson, *Incentives for Sustainable Land Management: Community Cost Sharing to Conserve Biodiversity on Private Lands, A Guide for Local Government* (Melbourne: Environment Australia, 2001), p. 3.

113. For example, the Australian experience to date has shown that it is seven times more cost effective to conserve intact native ecosystems than attempting to re-establish such ecosystems once they have been cleared or significantly degraded. Commonwealth of Australia, *Directions for the National Reserve System – A Partnership Approach* (Report prepared by National Reserve System Taskforce of the NRM Ministerial Council's Land, Water and Biodiversity Committee, 2004), p. vi.

114. UNEP-WCMC, *State of the World's Protected Areas: An annual review of global conservation progress* (2008), p. 32.

115. Binning and Young, *Native Vegetation Institutions, Policies and Incentives*, p. 11.

116. Michael T. Bennett, *Markets for Ecosystem Services in China: An Exploration of China's "Eco-Compensation" and other Market-Based Environmental Policies* (2009), p. 13; available at <http://www.forest-trends.org/documents/files/doc_2317.pdf>.

117. Robert N. Stavins, *Experiences with Market-Based Environmental Policy Instruments* (Discussion Paper 01-58, 2001), pp. 2–3; available at <http://www.rff.org/documents/RFF-DP-01-58.pdf>.

118. Stefano Pagiola, Natasha Landell-Mills and Joshua Bishop (eds), "Market-based Mechanisms for Forest Conservation and Development", in *Selling Forest Environmental Services: Market-based Mechanisms for Conservation and Development* (London: Earthscan, 2002), p. 6.

119. Forest Trends and the Ecosystem Marketplace, *Payments for Ecosystem Services: Market Profiles* (2008), p. 19; available at <http://ecosystemmarketplace.com/documents/acrobat/PES_Matrix_Profiles_profor.pdf>.

120. See <http://speciesbanking.com/pages/dynamic/about_us.landing_page.php>.

121. See <http://www.liberation.fr/terre/0101566503-un-premier-site-pour-compenser-les-degats>.

122. Mark Sheahan, *Credit for Conservation: A report on conservation and mitigation banking in the USA, and its applicability to New South Wales* (Canberra: Winston Churchill Memorial Trust of Australia, 2001), p. 8; available at <http://www.churchilltrust.com.au/site_media/fellows/Sheahan_Mark_-_2001.pdf>

123. For an overview of the use of biodiversity offsets globally in the context of the possible use of offsets in England, see Jo Treweek et al., *Scoping Study for the Design and Use of Biodiversity Offsets in an English Context* (Final Report to Defra [Contract NE 0801], 2009); available at <https://statistics.defra.gov.uk/esg/reports/env.asp>.

124. See discussion of the California Endangered Species Act and the US Federal Endangered Species Act in Sheahan, *Credit for Conservation*, pp. 15–16.

125. Defined in s 4A, Threatened Species Conservation Act as including "the composition, structure and function of ecosystems, and includes (but is not limited to) threatened species, populations and ecological communities, and their habitats". The NSW biobanking and offsets scheme commenced on 1 July 2008. See Threatened Species Conservation Amendment (Biodiversity Banking) Act 2006, which inserts a new Pt 7A into TSCA, and the Threatened Species Conservation (Biodiversity Banking) Regulation 2008.

126. Sheahan, *Credit for Conservation*, p. 6.

127. See Gerald Tenywa, *Uganda: Environmentalists want biodiversity offsets* (2009); available at <http://allafrica.com/stories/200908121006.html>.

128. Kenneth N. Chomitz, Timothy S. Thomas and Antonio Salazar P. Brandao, "The Economic and Environmental Impact of Trade in Forest Reserve Obligations: A Simulation Analysis of Options for Dealing with Habitat Heterogeneity", *Revista de Economia e Sociologia Rural*, vol. 43, no. 4 (2005), pp. 657–682.

129. Allens Consulting Group, *Building a Stronger Social Coalition: A discussion paper proposing measures to encourage increased philanthropy to benefit the environment and*

create a stronger civic culture in Australia (prepared for the Steering Group on Incentives for Encouraging Private Conservation, 2002); available at <http://www.
allenconsult.com.au/resources/ACG_Philanthropy_Main_2002.pdf>.

130. For example: United States: the Conservation Reserve Program administered by the
US Department of Agriculture is the largest ecosystem service payment system in the
world, providing annual rental payments and sharing the cost of conservation practices
on farmland: see <http://www.nrcs.usda.gov/programs/crp/>.

Canada: The 5-year Greencover Canada Program enabled landowners to access funding and technical assistance to improve grassland management practices, protect water
quality, reduce greenhouse gas emissions and enhance biodiversity and wildlife habitat.
The programme finished in March 2009 and has been replaced by initiatives under
the Growing Forward programme. See <http://www4.agr.gc.ca/AAFC-AAC/display-
afficher.do?id=1200339470715&lang=eng>.

European Union: Council Regulation (EC 1698/2005) created an instrument to finance
rural development through the European Agricultural Fund for Rural Development
(EAFRD) which entered into force on 1 January 2007. See Council Regulation (EC)
1698/2005 of 20 September 2005 on Support for Rural Development by the European
Agricultural Fund for Rural Development (EAFRD); available at <http://europa.eu/
legislation_summaries/agriculture/general_framework/l60032_en.htm>.

United Kingdom: the Natural England programme provides financial incentives
to farmers and land managers who deliver effective environmental management of
their land. See <http://www.naturalengland.org.uk/information_for/farmers_and_land_
managers/default.aspx>.

131. The other eco-services recognized under the legislation are hydrological services (including water for human consumption, irrigation and energy production) and the provision of scenic beauty for recreation and ecotourism: see Pagiola et al., *Selling Forest
Environmental Services*, p. 40.

132. The financing mechanism is a National Forestry Fund which offers government payments to private forestry owners in protected areas. Payments vary according to the
activity undertaken and are made over a five-year period. In return for payments,
landholders agree to cede their environmental service rights to the National Forestry
Fund. At the end of the contract period, a landholder is free to renegotiate the price or
sell the rights to other parties. The landowner's obligation under the contract runs with
the land – it is recorded in the public land register and applies to future purchasers of
that land. The National Forestry Fund can sell the rights to clearly identified environmental services which it has purchased from the landowner to buyers at local national
and international levels. Pagiola et al., *Selling Forest Environmental Services*, p. 41.

133. The programme was introduced in 2001 and, by 2004, 2 437 957 hectares of land was
covered. The payment amount under this legislation depends upon the type of the crop
– the focus is upon payments to producers in regions of oversupply and assistance is
targeted to areas where crop conversion is required in terms of making better use of
natural resources. See <http://www2.oecd.org/agr-envdbo/SearchResult.asp?Type=
Par488>.

134. The General Law of Sustainable Forestry Development 2004. See <http://www2.
oecd.org/agr-envdbo/SearchResult.asp?Type=Par489> and <http://www2.oecd.org/agr-
envdbo/SearchResult.asp?Type=Par491>.

135. Brazil, *Third National Report to the Convention on Biological Diversity* (2005); available at <http://www.cbd.int/doc/world/br/br-nr-03-en.pdf>.

136. For example, in the states of Parana, Sao Paulo and Minas Gerais: ibid.

137. Bill no. 4160, 2004, discussed in Brazil, *Third National Report to the Convention on
Biological Diversity*.

138. State Program for Incentives to the Production of Hardwoods: Decree 46818 of 10 June 2002, discussed in Brazil, *Third National Report to the Convention on Biological Diversity*.

139. State Council (of the People's Republic of China) (2005), referred to in Bennett, *Markets for Ecosystem Services in China*, p. 14.

140. Bennett, *Markets for Ecosystem Services in China*, p. 13.

141. CBD Strategic Plan, available at <http://www.cbd.int/sp/>.

142. CBD Secretariat, *Global Biodiversity Outlook 2* (2006), p. 53.

143. See for example, Samoa Ministry of Natural Resources, Environment and Meteorology, *National Adaptation Programme of Action*, 2005; available at <http://unfccc.int/resource/docs/napa/sam01.pdf>.

144. Threatened Species Conservation Amendment Act 2004 (NSW).

145. See assessment of the NSW scheme in Isabelle Connolly and Martin Fallding, "Biocertification of Local Environmental Plans: Promise and Reality", *Environmental and Planning Law Journal*, vol. 26, no. 2 (2009), pp. 128–152.

146. UNEP/CBD Secretariat, *Mainstreaming Biodiversity: Workshops on national biodiversity strategies and action plans* (2009), p. 20; available at <http://www.cbd.int/doc/publications/cbd-brochure-nbsap-ws-en.pdf>.

147. See examples drawn from a variety of jurisdictions in UNEP/CBD Secretariat, *Mainstreaming Biodiversity: Workshops on national biodiversity strategies and action plans*.

148. See CBD Secretariat, *Global Biodiversity Outlook 2* (2006), p. 53.

149. According to Cambodia's *Draft Fourth National Report to the Convention on Biological Diversity*, p. 19, available at <http://www.cbd.int/reports/search/?type=nr-04>. "The NBSAP was developed with a clear vision on 'Equitable Economic Prosperity and Improved Quality of Life through a Sustainable Use, Protection and Management of Biological Diversity.' It highlights more protection beyond the minimum standard as set by the Convention. The Strategy provided a framework for action at all levels that would enhance our ability to ensure the productivity, diversity and integrity of our natural systems and, as a result, our ability as a nation to reduce poverty and improve the quality of life of all Cambodians."

150. Aongola et al., "Creating and Protecting Zambia's Wealth".

151. 27 per cent, excluding biodiversity, compared to 26 per cent in all low income countries and 2 per cent in OECD countries: ibid., p. 2.

152. Zambia has the fifth highest deforestation rate in the world and the second highest rate in Africa. Ibid., p. 4.

153. Republic of Zambia, *Millennium Development Goals Progress Report* (2008), p. 25; available at <http://www.undp.org.zm/joomla/attachments/005_Zambia%20MDGs%20Progress%20Report%20Zambia%202008.pdf>.

154. Ibid., p. 6.

155. Impediments to achieving MDG7 in Zambia include: lack of framework environmental policy approach at the national level that supports mainstreaming of principles of sustainable development throughout all sectors of the economy; pressure for unsustainable exploitation of land arising from high poverty levels and the lack of alternative sources of livelihoods in rural areas; weak coordinating mechanisms in the public environmental sector bodies; poor environmental policy implementation and enforcement of laws, particularly at local levels; inadequate data and weak/non-existent monitoring systems concerning forest inventories and animal populations. Ibid., p. v.

156. Aongola et al., "Creating and Protecting Zambia's Wealth", p. 27.

157. Ibid., p. 25.

158. In Zambia, as in many jurisdictions, the issue of securing land tenure is critically important in relation to biodiversity issues. Much of the land is held under traditional

tenure systems that do not, in many cases, have clearly defined property rights and environmental degradation has been due, to some degree, to inadequately defined property rights.

159. Environmental Protection and Pollution Control Act, Act no. 12 of 1990.
160. Aongola et al., "Creating and Protecting Zambia's Wealth", p. 36.
161. Ibid, p. 56.
162. However, some private sector entities have undertaken SEA as part of their planning approach to ensure that strategic investment decisions can be supported and to meet the requirements of prospective financing partners: see discussion of a strategic environmental assessment commissioned by Biomax Zambia Ltd for oil palm development. Ibid., p. 38.
163. Ibid., p. 59.
164. See <http://www.iucn.org/about/work/programmes/species/red_list/>.

4

Implementation of environmental legal regimes at regional level: The case of the Mediterranean Sea

Tullio Scovazzi

The implementation of a general obligation at the regional level

The Mediterranean is a regional sea surrounded by the territories of 22 states.[1] The bordering countries, all of which have ancient historical and cultural traditions, differ as far as their internal political systems and levels of economic development are concerned. Highly populated cities, ports of worldwide significance, extended industrial areas and renowned holiday resorts are located along the shores of the Mediterranean. Important international navigation routes cross the Mediterranean, connecting the Atlantic and the Indian Oceans through the strait of Gibraltar and the Suez Canal. The Mediterranean region is an area of major strategic importance and, in certain cases, of high political tension. The protection of the Mediterranean environmental balance, which is especially fragile because of the very slow exchange of waters, is a particularly serious concern.

With regard to the legal framework which applies to the Mediterranean environment, under the United Nations Convention on the Law of the Sea (UNCLOS),[2] "States have the obligation to protect and preserve the marine environment" (art. 192).[3] In this aim they are bound to cooperate on a global and, as appropriate, regional basis in formulating and elaborating international rules, standards and recommended practices and procedures, taking into account characteristic regional features (art.

The future of international environmental law, Leary and Pisupati (eds),
United Nations University Press, 2010, ISBN 978-92-808-1192-6

197).[4] These general obligations must be fulfilled through the adoption, individually or jointly, of measures addressing pollution from all sources, such as the operation of ships, land-based activities, exploitation of the seabed and dumping of wastes.

In general terms, an obligation to cooperate implies a duty to act in good faith in pursuing a common objective and in taking into account the requirements of the other interested states. In practice, such an obligation can have several facets (information, consultation, negotiation, joint participation in preparing environmental impact assessments or emergency plans), depending on the circumstances.

As stated by the International Court of Justice, "... the parties are under an obligation to enter into negotiations with a view to arriving at an agreement, and not merely to go through a formal process of negotiation ...; they are under an obligation so to conduct themselves that the negotiations are meaningful, which will not be the case when either of them insists upon its own position without contemplating any modification of it".[5]

The obligation to cooperate applies at both the global and the regional level. While general concerns need to be faced on a world scale, regional or sub-regional treaties are the best tool to take into account the particularities of a specific marine area. The number of treaties which have so far been concluded to protect the marine environment is ever increasing. In many regional seas, both treaties having a worldwide scope and treaties having a regional (or even sub-regional) scope are applicable at the same time. It often happens that the same subject matter (for example, pollution from dumping) is regulated by two or more treaties and that complex legal questions of coordination arise.[6]

Fortunately, the UNCLOS, the only global treaty on the law of the sea, specifies that its provisions on the protection of the environment are without prejudice to the specific obligations assumed by states under special conventions and agreements concluded previously which relate to the protection and preservation of the marine environment, and to agreements which may be concluded in furtherance of the general principles set out in the UNCLOS itself.[7] It adds that specific obligations assumed by states under special conventions, with respect to the protection and preservation of the marine environment, should be carried out in a manner consistent with the general principles and objectives of the UNCLOS.[8]

While presenting several innovative aspects, the legal instruments applying to the protection of the Mediterranean environment, comprising the so-called Barcelona system, are consistent with the general principles and objectives of the UNCLOS, to which they bring an added value.

The Barcelona system

The Barcelona system[9] is a notable example of fulfilment of the obligation to cooperate for the protection of a semi-enclosed sea.[10]

On 4 February 1975 a policy instrument, the Mediterranean Action Plan (MAP), was adopted by an intergovernmental meeting convened in Barcelona by the United Nations Environment Programme (UNEP). One of the main objectives of the MAP was to promote the conclusion of a framework convention, together with related protocols and technical annexes, for the protection of the Mediterranean environment. This occurred on 16 February 1976 when the Convention on the Protection of the Mediterranean Sea against Pollution and two protocols were opened for signature in Barcelona. The Convention, which entered into force on 12 February 1978, is chronologically the first of the so-called regional seas agreements concluded under the auspices of UNEP.

In the years following the 1992 Rio Conference on Environment and Development, several components of the Barcelona system underwent important changes. In 1995, the MAP was replaced by the Action Plan for the Protection of the Marine Environment and the Sustainable Development of the Coastal Areas of the Mediterranean (MAP Phase II). Some of the legal instruments were amended. New protocols were adopted, either to replace the protocols which had not been amended or to cover new subjects of cooperation.

The present Barcelona legal system includes a framework convention and seven protocols, namely:

(a) The Convention on the Protection of the Mediterranean Sea against Pollution[11] which, as amended in Barcelona on 10 June 1995, changed its name to Convention for the Protection of the Marine Environment and the Coastal Region of the Mediterranean (the Convention) when the amendments entered into force on 9 July 2004;

(b) The Protocol for the Prevention of the Pollution of the Mediterranean Sea by Dumping from Ships and Aircraft 1976, in force from 12 February 1978, which will change its name, as amended in Barcelona on 10 June 1995, to the Protocol for the Prevention and Elimination of Pollution of the Mediterranean Sea by Dumping from Ships and Aircraft or Incineration at Sea (the Dumping Protocol) when the amendments come in force;[12]

(c) The Protocol Concerning Co-operation in Combating Pollution of the Mediterranean Sea by Oil and Other Harmful Substances in Cases of Emergency 1976, in force from 12 February 1978, which has been replaced by the Protocol Concerning Cooperation in Preventing Pollution from Ships and, in Cases of Emergency, Combating Pollution of the Mediterranean Sea 2002 (the Emergency Protocol) which has been in force from 17 March 2004;

(d) The Protocol for the Protection of the Mediterranean Sea against Pollution from Land-Based Sources 1980, in force from 17 June 1983, which, as amended in Syracuse on 7 March 1996, changed its name to Protocol for the Protection of the Mediterranean Sea against Pollution from Land-Based Sources and Activities (the Land-Based Protocol) when the amendments came into force on 11 May 2008;

(e) The Protocol Concerning Mediterranean Specially Protected Areas 1982, in force from 23 March 1986, which has been replaced by the Protocol Concerning Specially Protected Areas and Biological Diversity in the Mediterranean 1995 (the Areas Protocol) which has been in force since 12 December 1999;

(f) The Protocol Concerning Pollution Resulting from Exploration and Exploitation of the Continental Shelf, the Seabed and its Subsoil 1994 (the Seabed Protocol) which is not yet in force;

(g) The Protocol on the Prevention of Pollution of the Mediterranean Sea by Transboundary Movements of Hazardous Wastes and their Disposal 1996 (the Wastes Protocol), which has been in force since 18 December 2007;

(h) The Protocol on Integrated Coastal Zone Management in the Mediterranean 2008 (the Coastal Zone Protocol) which is not yet in force.

The updating and the additions to the Barcelona legal system show that the parties consider it as a dynamic body capable of being subject to re-examination and improvement, whenever appropriate.[13] Each of the new instruments contains important innovations, which will be reviewed below. The protocols display a certain degree of legal imagination in finding constructive ways to address complex environmental problems.

The Convention

The Convention, as amended in 1995, retains its character of a framework treaty that has to be implemented through specific protocols. It also retains what, in 1976, was seen as a major innovation, that is, the possibility of participation by the European Economic Community (now the European Union or EU) and by similar regional economic groupings of which at least one member is a coastal state of the Mediterranean Sea and which exercise competence in fields covered by the Convention.[14] In fact, the EU is a party to the Convention and some of its protocols, together with seven Mediterranean states which are EU members (Cyprus, France, Greece, Italy, Malta, Slovenia and Spain).

In 1995 the geographical coverage of the Convention was extended to include all maritime waters of the Mediterranean Sea, irrespective of their legal status.[15] However, the sphere of territorial application of the Barcelona legal system is flexible, in the sense that the area of application of any protocol may be extended. For example, and for obvious reasons, the Seabed Protocol applies also to the continental shelf, the seabed and its subsoil. The Land-Based Protocol applies also to the "hydrologic basin" of the Mediterranean Sea Area, this being "the entire watershed area within the territories of the Contracting Parties, draining into the Mediterranean Sea Area".[16] The application of the Convention may also be extended to "coastal areas as defined by each Contracting Party within its own territory",[17] as was recently done with the Coastal Zone Protocol.

The amended text of the Convention recalls and applies to a regional scale the main concepts embodied in the instruments adopted by the 1992 Rio Conference – the Declaration on Environment and Development and the Programme of Action[18] (Agenda 21), such as sustainable development, the precautionary principle, the integrated management of the coastal zones, the use of best available techniques and best environmental practices, as well as the promotion of environmentally sound technology, including clean production technologies. For the purpose of implementing the objectives of sustainable development, the parties are called to take fully into account the recommendations of the Mediterranean Commission on Sustainable Development, a new body established within the framework of the MAP Phase II.

A new provision, art. 15, relates to the right of the public to have access to information on the state of the environment and to participate in the decision-making processes relevant to the field of application of the Convention and the protocols. Nothing, however, is said as regards the equally important question of access of the public to justice.

Compliance with the Convention and the protocols, as well as with the decisions and recommendations adopted during the meetings of the parties, is assessed on the basis of the periodic reports that the parties are bound to transmit to the secretariat at regular intervals.[19] Such reports, which are examined by the biannual meetings of the parties, relate to the legal, administrative or other measures taken by the parties, their effectiveness and the problems encountered in their implementation. The meeting of the parties can recommend, when appropriate, the necessary steps to bring about full compliance with the Convention and the protocols and to promote the implementation of decisions and recommendations.[20] Specific reporting obligations are found in the protocols.[21]

In 2008 the meeting of the parties adopted the procedures and mechanisms on compliance and established a compliance committee. The committee's objective is "to facilitate and promote compliance with the obligations under the Barcelona Convention and its Protocols, taking into account the specific situation of each Contracting Party, in particular those which are developing countries".[22]

The Dumping Protocol

The Dumping Protocol applies to any deliberate disposal of wastes or other matter from ships or aircraft, with the exception of wastes or other matters deriving from the normal operations of vessels or aircraft and their equipment, which are considered as pollution from ships. The protocol, as amended in 1995, presents two major changes with respect to the previous text.

First, the protocol applies also to incineration at sea, which is prohibited.[23] Incineration is defined as "the deliberate combustion of wastes or other matter in the maritime waters of the Mediterranean Sea, with the aim of thermal destruction and does not include activities incidental to the normal operations of ships and aircraft".[24]

Second, the protocol is based on the idea that the dumping of wastes or other matter is in principle prohibited, with the exception of five categories of matters specifically listed, including dredged materials, fish waste and inert uncontaminated geological materials. The original protocol was based on the idea that dumping was in principle permitted, with the exception of the prohibited matters listed in Annex I (the so-called black list) and the matters listed in Annex II (the so-called grey list) which required a prior special permit. The logic of the original text is thus fully reversed in order to ensure better protection of the environment.[25]

The Land-Based Protocol

The Land-Based Protocol applies to discharges originating from land-based points and diffuse sources and activities. Such discharges reach the sea through coastal disposals, rivers, outfalls, canals or other watercourses, including groundwater flow, through run-off and disposal under the seabed with access from land.

The protocol, as amended in 1996, takes into account the objectives laid down in the Global Programme of Action for the Protection of the Marine Environment from Land-based Activities, adopted in Washington in 1995 by a UNEP intergovernmental conference. The Programme is designed to assist states in taking individual or joint actions leading to the prevention, reduction and elimination of what is commonly regarded as the main source (about 80 per cent) of pollution of the marine environment.[26]

As already stated,[27] the amended protocol enlarges its application to the "hydrologic basin of the Mediterranean Sea Area". To face land-based pollution of the sea, action must primarily be taken where the polluting sources are located, that is, on the land territory of the parties. The Land-Based Protocol provides that parties shall invite states that are not parties to it and have in their territories parts of the hydrological basin of the Mediterranean Area to cooperate in the implementation of the protocol. However, a party cannot be held responsible for any pollution originating on the territory of a non-party state.

With the aim of eliminating pollution deriving from land-based sources, the parties "shall elaborate and implement, individually or jointly, as appropriate, national and regional action plans and programmes, containing measures and timetables for their implementation".[28] The parties shall give priority to the phasing out of inputs of substances that are toxic, persistent and liable to bioaccumulate.[29] These kinds of substances were not specifically mentioned in the original protocol.

The amended protocol was the subject of extensive negotiations, not only among the parties but also between the non-governmental environmental organizations and the organizations representing the chemical industry, as regards the crucial question of how to implement the obligation "to prevent, abate, combat and eliminate to the fullest possible extent pollution".[30] Finally the following solution was found satisfactory by all. On the one hand, the environmentalists accepted that their initial request, that is, an absolute ban by the year 2005 of any kind of discharge and emission of substances which are toxic, persistent and liable to bioaccumulate, would be impossible to achieve because of its serious economic and social repercussions. On the other hand, the chemical industry agreed to be bound by measures and timetables of a legally obligatory nature, provided that they related to specific groups of substances and were adapted to the specific requirements of the circumstances.

The procedural machinery to achieve what was agreed upon is embodied in art. 15. It provides that the meeting of the parties adopts, by a two-thirds majority, the short-term and medium-term regional plans and programmes, containing measures and timetables for their implementation, in order to eliminate pollution deriving from land-based sources and activities, in particular to phase out inputs of substances that are toxic, persistent and liable to bioaccumulate. These measures and timetables become binding on the 180th day following the date of their notification, for all the parties which have not notified an objection. The result is a mechanism that is intended to be both realistic and effective.

Major changes were also made with respect to the annexes. Annex I relates to the "elements to be taken into account in the preparation of action plans, programmes and measures for the elimination of pollution from land-based sources and activities". It provides that in preparing action plans, programmes and measures, the parties "will give priority to substances that are toxic, persistent and liable to bioaccumulate, in particular to persistent organic pollutants (POPs), as well as to wastewater treatment and management". It lists nineteen categories of substances and sources of pollution which will serve as guidance in the preparation of action plans, programmes and measures, including, as first entry, the organohalogen compounds and substances which may form such compounds in the marine environment.[31] Annex II relates to the "elements to be taken into account in the issue of the authorizations for discharges of wastes" and Annex III to the "conditions of application to pollution transported through the atmosphere". Finally, Annex IV gives the "criteria for the definition of best available techniques and best environmental practice".[32]

The Areas Protocol

The 1995 Areas Protocol is very different from the 1982 protocol, and formally distinct from it.[33] The new protocol is applicable to all the marine waters of the Mediterranean, irrespective of their legal status, as well as to the seabed, its subsoil and to the terrestrial coastal areas designated by each party, including wetlands. Previously, the application of the 1982 protocol was limited to the territorial sea of the parties and did not cover the high seas. The extension of the geographical coverage of the instrument was seen as necessary to protect highly migratory marine species (such as marine mammals) which, through their natural behaviour, cross the human-drawn, artificial boundaries on the sea.

The aim to establish marine protected areas on the high seas gave rise to some difficult legal problems due to the lack of territorial jurisdiction in these waters. As some coastal states have not yet established an exclusive economic zone (EEZ), there are in the Mediterranean extents of waters located beyond the 12-mile territorial limit which still have the status of high seas. However, if every coastal state was to proclaim an exclusive economic zone, the high seas would disappear in the Mediterranean, as no point in this semi-enclosed sea is located more than 200 nautical miles from the nearest land or island. Another delicate question was the possibility of establishing marine protected areas in waters where the maritime boundaries have yet to be agreed upon by the interested countries. There are in the Mediterranean several cases where a delimitation of the territorial seas or other maritime zones is particularly complex because of local geographic characteristics.

In order to overcome these difficulties, the new protocol includes two very elaborate disclaimer provisions (art. 2(2) and 2(3)) which have two important aims. First, the establishment of intergovernmental cooperation in the field of the marine environment cannot prejudice other legal questions which have a different nature and are still pending, such as those relating to the nature and extent of marine jurisdictional zones or to the drawing of marine boundaries between adjacent or opposite states. Second, the very existence of such legal questions cannot jeopardize or delay the adoption of measures necessary for the preservation of the ecological balance of the Mediterranean.

The Areas Protocol provides for the establishment of a list of specially protected areas of Mediterranean importance (SPAMI List).[34] The SPAMI List may include sites which "are of importance for conserving the components of biological diversity in the Mediterranean; contain ecosystems specific to the Mediterranean area or the habitats of endangered species; are of special interest at the scientific, aesthetic, cultural or educational levels".[35] The procedures for the establishment and listing of SPAMIs are specified in detail in the protocol. For instance, as regards an area located partly or wholly on the high seas, the proposal must be made "by two or more neighbouring parties concerned" and the decision to include the area in the SPAMI List is taken by consensus by the contracting parties during their periodic meetings.

Once the areas are included in the SPAMI List, all the parties agree "to recognize the particular importance of these areas for the Mediterranean" and – this is also important – "to comply with the measures applicable to the SPAMIs and not to authorize nor undertake any activities that might be contrary to the objectives for which the SPAMIs were established".[36] This gives to the SPAMIs and to the measures adopted for their protection an *erga omnes partes* effect. As regards the relationship with third countries, the parties are called to "invite States that are not Parties to the Protocol and international organizations to cooperate in the implementation"[37]of the protocol. They also "undertake to adopt appropriate measures, consistent with international law, to ensure that no one engages in any activity contrary to the principles and purposes"[38] of the protocol. This provision is aimed at facing the potential problems arising from the fact that treaties, including the Areas Protocol, can create rights and obligations only among parties.

The Areas Protocol is completed by three annexes, which were adopted in 1996 in Monaco. They are the "Common criteria for the choice of protected marine and coastal areas that could be included in the SPAMI

List" (Annex I), the "List of endangered or threatened species" (Annex II) and the "List of species whose exploitation is regulated" (Annex III).

At the Meeting of the Contracting Parties held in 2001 the first twelve SPAMIs were recorded in the SPAMI List, namely the island of Alborán (Spain), the sea bottom of the Levante de Almería (Spain), Cape Gata-Nijar (Spain), Mar Menor and the East coast of Murcia (Spain), Cape Creus (Spain), Medas Islands (Spain), Columbretes Islands (Spain), Port-Cros (France), the Kneiss Islands (Tunisia), La Galite, Zembra and Zembretta (Tunisia) and the French-Italian-Monegasque sanctuary for marine mammals (so-called Pelagos sanctuary, jointly proposed by the three States concerned and covering also high seas waters).[39] Thirteen other SPAMIs have subsequently been added, namely the Cabrera Archipelago (Spain) and Maro-Cerro Gordo (Spain) in 2003, Kabyles Bank (Algeria), Habibas Islands (Algeria) and Portofino (Italy) in 2005, Miramare (Italy), Plemmirio (Italy), Tavolara–Punta Coda Cavallo (Italy) and Torre Guaceto (Italy) in 2008, Bonifacio Mouths (France), Capo Caccia – Isola Piana (Italy), Punta Campanella (Italy) and Al-Hoceima (Morroco) in 2009.

The Seabed Protocol

The Seabed Protocol relates to pollution resulting from exploration and exploitation of the seabed and its subsoil. Several of its provisions set out obligations incumbent on the parties with respect to activities carried out by operators, who can be private persons, either natural or juridical. This kind of obligation is to be understood in the sense that each party is bound to exercise the appropriate legislative, executive or judicial activities in order to ensure that the operators comply with the provisions of the protocol. The definition of "operator" is broad. It includes not only persons authorized to carry out activities, for example the holder of a licence, or who carry out activities (for example, a subcontractor), but also any person who does not hold an authorization but is *de facto* in control of activities. The parties are under an obligation to exercise due diligence in order to make sure, within the seabed under their jurisdiction, that no one engages in activities which have not previously been authorized or which are exercised illegally.

All activities in the Seabed Protocol area, including erection of installations on site, are subject to prior written authorization by the competent authority of a party. Before granting the authorization, the authority must be satisfied that the installation has been constructed according to international standards and practice and that the operator has the technical competence and the financial capacity to carry out the activities.

Authorization must be refused if there are indications that the proposed activities are likely to cause significant adverse effects on the environment that could not be avoided by compliance with specific technical conditions. This obligation can be seen as an application of the precautionary principle. Special restrictions or conditions may be established for the granting of authorizations for activities in specially protected areas.

The parties are bound to take measures to ensure that liability for damage caused by activities to which the protocol applies is imposed on operators, who are required to pay prompt and adequate compensation. They shall also take all measures necessary to ensure that operators have and maintain insurance cover or other financial security in order to ensure compensation for damages caused by the activities covered by the protocol.[40]

The Wastes Protocol

The Wastes Protocol is applicable to a subject matter already covered, on the world scale, by the Basel Convention on the Control of Transboundary Movements of Hazardous Wastes and Their Disposal 1989.[41] The Basel Convention allows its parties to enter into regional agreements, provided that they stipulate provisions which are not less environmentally sound than those of the Basel Convention itself. This means that, to have some purpose, a regional instrument on movements of wastes should bring some "added value" to the rights and obligations already established under the Basel Convention. In the specific case, this occurs in at least three instances.

First, while the Basel Convention does not apply to radioactive wastes, the Wastes Protocol covers also "all wastes containing or contaminated by radionuclides, the radionuclide concentration or properties of which result from human activity".[42]

Second, unlike the Basel Convention, the Wastes Protocol applies also to a particular kind of substances which are properly to be considered products instead of wastes, as they are not intended for disposal. These are the "hazardous substances that have been banned or are expired, or whose registration has been cancelled or refused through government regulatory action in the country of manufacture or export for human health or environmental reasons, or have been voluntarily withdrawn or omitted from the government registration required for use in the country of manufacture or export".[43]

Third, the Wastes Protocol clarifies an important question that was not settled in precise terms by the Basel Convention: what are the rights of the coastal state if a foreign ship carrying hazardous wastes is in transit through its territorial sea? The Basel Convention, which is applicable to both land and marine transboundary movements of hazardous wastes, provides in general that movements may only take place with the prior written notification by the state of export to both the state of import and the state of transit and with their prior written consent. However, as far as the sea is concerned, the Basel Convention contains a disclaimer which protects both the sovereign rights and jurisdiction of coastal states, on the one hand, and the exercise of navigational rights and freedoms, on the other. Because of its wording, this provision is open to different interpretations and, indeed, has been interpreted in opposite ways by states inclined to give priority to one or the other solution. In fact, under the Basel Convention, doubt remains as to whether the export state has any obligation to notify the coastal transit state or to obtain its prior consent. The conflicting alternatives pose a dilemma between notification and authorization, on the one hand, and neither notification, nor authorization, on the other.

The Wastes Protocol gives a definite answer to the question by providing for an intermediate solution, consisting of a "notification without authorization" scheme. The transboundary movement of hazardous wastes through the territorial sea of a state of transit may take place only with the prior notification by the state of export to the state of transit. The approach adopted by the Wastes Protocol strikes a fair balance between the interests of maritime traffic and the protection of the marine environment. On the one hand, ships carrying hazardous wastes keep the right to pass, as their passage is not subject to authorization by the coastal state. On the other, the coastal state has a right to be previously notified, in order to know what occurs in its territorial sea and to be prepared to intervene in cases of casualties or accidents during passage which could endanger human health or the environment.[44] Yet transparency can only lead to cooperation, while maintaining secrecy does not seem a promising way to ensure protection of the marine environment.

The Emergency Protocol

The 2002 Emergency Protocol has replaced the previous 1976 protocol. As in the case of the Areas Protocol, the changes with respect to the previous instrument were so extensive that the parties decided to draft a new instrument, instead of merely amending the old text. The adoption of a strengthened legal framework for combating pollution from ships is particularly important in view of the increasing maritime traffic and transport of hazardous cargo within and through the Mediterranean. The Emergency Protocol takes into account lessons learned from the *Erika* tanker accident in 1999.

It is true that pollution from ships is an issue where, typically, regulation at the world level is most appropriate. All the technical rules, such as those relating to requirements in respect of design, construction, equipment and manning of ships, need to be adopted at a global and uniform level. Navigation, which is the traditional cornerstone of the regime of oceans and seas, would be impossible if different and conflicting provisions on technical characteristics of ships were adopted at the domestic or regional level. Article 211 of the UNCLOS, relating to pollution from vessels, explicitly refers to "generally accepted international rules and standards established through the competent international organization or general diplomatic conference". It would also be unrealistic to try to modify the allocation of enforcement powers among the flag state, the port state and the coastal state, set out in arts. 217, 218 and 220 of the UNCLOS, which were the outcome of difficult negotiations.

The Emergency Protocol acknowledges in the preamble the role of the International Maritime Organization (IMO), which is the competent international organization in the field of safety of navigation, and the importance of cooperating in promoting the adoption and the development of international rules and standards on pollution from ships within the framework of IMO. This is a clear reference to the various conventions which have been concluded under the sponsorship of IMO[45] and to the competences that IMO has long been exercising as regards safety of shipping (such as decisions on traffic separation schemes, ships' reporting systems, areas to be avoided, and so on). All such instruments and competences are in no way prejudiced by the Emergency Protocol.[46]

However, it is also true that regional cooperation has a role to play in the field of pollution from ships. For instance, international cooperation for prompt and effective action in taking emergency measures against pollution needs to be organized at the regional level. The first Emergency Protocol already provided for the setting up of an institutional framework for actions of regional cooperation in combating accidental marine pollution: the Regional Marine Pollution Emergency Response Centre for the Mediterranean Sea (REMPEC), which is administered by IMO and UNEP and is located in Malta.

The Emergency Protocol is not limited (as was the former instrument) to emergency situations. It also covers some aspects of pollution from ships and aims at striking a fair balance between action at the world level and action on a regional scale. For instance, art. 15, relating to environmental risk of maritime traffic, provides that "in conformity with generally accepted international rules and standards and the global mandate of the International Maritime Organization, the Parties shall individually, bilaterally or multilaterally take the necessary steps to assess the environmental risks of the recognized routes used in maritime traffic and shall take the appropriate measures aimed at reducing the risks of accidents or the environmental consequences thereof".

The "added value" brought by the new protocol may be found in several of its provisions. It covers not only ships, but also places where shipping accidents can occur, such as ports and offshore installations. The definition of the "related interests" of a coastal state that can be affected by pollution has been enlarged to include "the cultural, aesthetic, scientific and educational value of the area" and "the conservation of biological diversity and the sustainable use of marine and coastal biological resources".[47] A detailed provision on reimbursement of costs of assistance has been elaborated.

The Emergency Protocol sets out a number of obligations directed to the masters of ships sailing in the territorial sea of the parties, including ships flying a foreign flag, namely: to report incidents and the presence, characteristics and extent of spillages of oil or hazardous and noxious substances; to provide the proper authorities, in case of a pollution accident and at their request, with detailed information about the ship and its cargo and to cooperate with these authorities. The obligations in question, which have a reasonable purpose and do not overburden ships, do not conflict with the rights of innocent passage and freedom of navigation provided for in the UNCLOS. The lessons arising from the *Erika* accident are particularly evident in the provision according to which the parties shall define strategies concerning reception in places of refuge, including ports, of ships in distress presenting a threat to the marine environment.

The 2008 Coastal Zone Protocol

To confirm the dynamic character of the Barcelona legal system, a new protocol, relating to the integrated coastal zone management, was opened for signature in 2008. It addresses the increase in anthropic pressure on the Mediterranean coastal zones which is threatening their fragile equilibrium and provides Mediterranean states with the legal and technical tools to ensure sustainable development throughout the shores of this regional sea.[48] It is the first treaty ever adopted which is specifically devoted to the coastal zone.

The Coastal Zone Protocol defines "integrated coastal management" as "a dynamic process for the sustainable management and use of coastal zones, taking into the account at the same time the fragility of coastal ecosystems and landscapes, the diversity of activities and uses, their interactions, the maritime orientation of certain activities and uses and their impact on both the marine and land parts".[49]

The precise delimitation of the geographical coverage of the protocol gave rise to lengthy discussion during the negotiations. The final solution was both precise and flexible in the form of art. 3. The seaward limit of the coastal zone is the external limit of the territorial sea;[50] the landward limit of the coastal zone is the limit of the competent coastal units as defined by parties. However, parties may establish different limits, in so far as certain conditions occur.

Article 6 of the protocol lists a number of general principles of integrated coastal zone management. For instance, the parties are bound to formulate "land use strategies, plans and programmes covering urban development and socio-economic activities, as well as other relevant sectoral polices".[51] They shall take into account in an integrated manner "all elements relating to hydrological, geomorphological, climatic, ecological, socio-economic and cultural systems", so as "not to exceed the carrying capacity of the coastal zone and to prevent the negative effects of natural disasters and of development". The parties are also required to take into account the diversity of activities in the coastal zone and to give priority "where necessary, to public services and activities requiring, in terms of use and location, the immediate proximity of the sea".

Article 8 of the protocol provides for the establishment of a 100-metre zone where construction is not allowed. However, "adaptations" are allowed "for projects of public interest" and "in areas having particular geographical or other local constraints, especially related to population density or social needs, where individual housing, urbanisation or development are provided for by national legal instruments". Other important obligations of the parties relate to "limiting the linear extension of urban development and the creation of new transport infrastructure along the coast", to "providing for freedom of access by the public to the sea and along the shore" and to "restricting or, where necessary, prohibiting the movement and parking of land vehicles, as well as the movement and anchoring of marine vessels in fragile natural areas on land or at sea, including beaches and dunes".

Some provisions of the protocol deal with specific activities, such as: "agriculture and industry", "fishing", "aquaculture", "tourism, sporting and recreational activities", "utilization of specific natural resources" and "infrastructure, energy facilities, ports and maritime works and structure",[52] as well as with certain specific coastal ecosystems, such as "wetlands and estuaries", "marine habitats", "coastal forests and woods" and "dunes".[53] Due emphasis is granted to risks affecting the coastal zone, in particular climate change[54] and coastal erosion.[55]

The Guidelines on Liability and Compensation

On 18 January 2008, the meeting of the parties to the Convention, held in Almeria, adopted a set of Guidelines for the Determination of Liability and Compensation for Damage resulting from Pollution of the Marine Environment in the Mediterranean Sea Area (the Guidelines).[56] The Guidelines, which are the outcome of lengthy works of elaboration,[57] present several elements of interest. As it would be impossible to discuss all the aspects of this instrument, the remarks below will focus on a few selected issues.

The Guidelines, as the name clearly implies, are not mandatory in nature for the parties.[58] Rather than drafting a protocol (and waiting for the number of ratifications needed for its entry into force), the parties chose instead a step-by-step approach, starting with a soft-law instrument. During the discussion on this question, some states called for prudence, remarking that several treaties relating to environmental liability and compensation had not yet come into force and there were doubts as to when they would actually come into force. As a first step, the parties decided to strengthen their cooperation in the field of liability and compensation through the adoption, in their national legislation, of a set of provisions which are as uniform as possible, being based on the model of the Guidelines.

As regards their scope, the Guidelines in principle apply to all the subject matters covered by the so-called Barcelona system, that is, "to the activities to which the Barcelona Convention and any of its Protocols apply".[59] In the determination of the scope of the Guidelines, it should also be taken into account that they have a complementary character and do not intend to prejudice any environmental liability and compensation regimes which exist or may exist in the future,[60] as listed in the Appendix to the Guidelines.

From the theoretical point of view, the most interesting aspect of the Guidelines is the distinction they make between two kinds of damage resulting from the pollution of the marine environment, namely, "traditional damage" and "environmental damage", and the classification they provide of the entries falling under either of them. The first kind of damage, that is traditional damage, comprises four categories:

For the purpose of these Guidelines, "traditional damage" means:
(a) loss of life or personal injury;
(b) loss of or damage to property other than property held by the person liable;
(c) loss of income directly deriving from an impairment of a legally protected interest in any use of the marine environment for economic purposes,

incurred as a result of impairment of the environment, taking into account savings and costs;
(d) any loss or damage caused by preventive measures taken to avoid damage referred to under sub-paragraphs (a), (b) and (c).[61]

In the light of the Guidelines, traditional damage is intended as the damage suffered by persons, either natural or juridical, such as individuals and private or public entities, including the state. The damage can consist in bodily injuries or loss of life, in loss or deterioration of property and in loss or reduction of earnings. The adjective "traditional" simply means that it is accepted that this kind of damage can be compensated under well-established general principles of law, as they have been for hundreds of years in the national legislation of most countries.

The second kind of damage is typical of cases of pollution of natural components, including marine waters. It is suffered by the environment as such (*per se*), determining a negative change in the quality of a natural component:

For the purpose of these Guidelines, "environmental damage" means a measurable adverse change in a natural or biological resource or measurable impairment of a natural or biological resource service which may occur directly or indirectly.[62]

The categories comprising the "environmental damage" are the following:

Compensation for environmental damage should include, as the case may be:
(a) costs of activities and studies to assess the damage;
(b) costs of preventive measures including measures to prevent a threat of damage or an aggravation of damage;
(c) costs of measures undertaken or to be undertaken to clean up, restore and reinstate the impaired environment, including the cost of monitoring or control of the effectiveness of such measures;
(d) diminution in value of natural or biological resources pending restoration;
(e) compensation by equivalent if the impaired environment cannot return to its previous condition.[63]

The first three categories of environmental damage relate to costs that are borne by a person, in many cases the state or another public entity, especially where there is a need to take urgent measures or where the liable operator cannot be identified.[64] These costs can be calculated in precise monetary terms, corresponding to the sum of the invoices for the measures taken.

Regarding the last two categories of "environmental damage", the Guidelines follow an advanced approach, based on the model of some legislative texts, such as European Union Directive 2004/35/CE of 21 April 2004 on environmental liability, with regard to the prevention and remedying of environmental damage.[65] This instrument makes a distinction between "primary remediation", that is, "any remedial measure which returns the damaged natural resources and/or impaired services to, or towards, baseline condition", "complementary remediation", that is, "any remedial measure taken in relation to natural resources and/or services to compensate for the fact that primary remediation does not result in fully restoring the damaged natural resources and/or services" and "compensatory remediation", that is, "any action taken to compensate for interim losses of natural resources and/or services that occur from the date of damage occurring until primary remediation has achieved its full effect".[66] According to this logic, accepted also by the Guidelines, compensation for environmental damage includes the cost of the re-establishment of the condition that existed before the pollution (primary remediation, covered by Guideline D, para. 10(a)–(c)), the cost of compensation by equivalent action to be taken elsewhere if the polluted environment cannot fully return to its previous condition (complementary remediation, covered by para. 10(e) of the Guideline), as well as the value of the diminution of the quality of natural components during the time when restoration is pending (compensatory remediation or interim compensation, covered by para. 10(d) of the Guideline). Neither complementary nor compensatory remediation can be assessed in precise monetary terms. Both correspond to a damage suffered by the environment itself and are paid by the liable operator to the state or another public entity, as a trustee of the public interest in the preservation of the quality of the environment.

On the complex issue of the assessment of damage that cannot be determined in precise monetary terms, the Guidelines avoid any reference to specific criteria, such as the habitat equivalency analysis or others that are also sometimes proposed. They provide in general that:

> ... in assessing the extent of environmental damage, use should be made of all available sources of information on the previous condition of the environment ....[67]

An important condition is put on what is received as complementary and compensatory compensation. It must be earmarked for environmental purposes:

> When compensation is granted for damage referred to in paragraph 10(d) and (e), it should be earmarked for intervention in the environmental field in the Mediterranean Sea Area.[68]

The Guidelines channel liability[69] onto the operator,[70] who can avail himself of limitations of liability on the basis of international treaties or relevant domestic legislation.[71] However, the question of compulsory insurance for the operators, which could be seen as linked to the benefit of limitation of liability, was the subject of lengthy discussions, due partly to the lack of a sufficiently developed market for insuring environmental damage. In consideration of the doubts expressed, Guideline K postpones to the future the question of a financial security scheme:

> The Contracting Parties, after a period of five years from the adoption of these Guidelines, may, on the basis of an assessment of the products available on the insurance market, envisage the establishment of a compulsory insurance regime.[72]

While the basic rule is that the operator should pay for the damage, there may be cases where the operator is unknown, or unable to pay, or the amount of compensation goes beyond the limit of his liability. The question of the establishment of a Mediterranean Compensation Fund (MCF) was the subject of discussions that, for the time being, could not reach a generally agreed solution.[73] Here again the parties were careful to reserve the possibility of further action in the future:

> The Contracting Parties should explore the possibility of establishing a Mediterranean Compensation Fund to ensure compensation where the damage exceeds the operator's liability, where the operator is unknown, where the operator is incapable of meeting the cost of damage and is not covered by financial security or where the State takes preventive measures in emergency situations and is not reimbursed for the cost thereof.[74]

Concluding remarks

When it was originally drafted, the Barcelona system served as an example for the elaboration of other UNEP regional seas instruments. It may play a similar role again today, after the updating and additions that it has undergone. The Barcelona system has been adapted to the evolution of international law in protection of the marine environment, and has addressed concrete problems in a clear and sensible way. It is to be regretted that some of the newer or updated protocols are taking too long to come into force. Governments are sometimes led by different reasons to balance environmental needs with other interests, and may be hesitant to promptly endorse the most advanced instruments. But the fact remains that all the present new or updated instruments of the Barcelona system constitute effective tools in preserving a common natural heritage and in facing the common concerns of the states bordering the Mediterranean. The framework convention and protocols bring an added value to the general obligation to cooperate in the protection of the marine environment already embodied in the UNCLOS and in customary international law.

Instances of such added value can be found in the establishment of the category of Specially Protected Areas of Mediterranean Importance, in the flexible but binding procedure for the phasing out of pollution by substances discharged through land-based sources, in the provision of the innovative regime of "notification without authorization" for hazardous wastes transiting through the territorial sea, and in the very decision to devise an international instrument applicable to the typically domestic field of the management of the coastal zone.

Notes

1. Spain, the United Kingdom (as far as Gibraltar and the sovereign base areas of Akrotiri and Dhekelia are concerned), France, Monaco, Italy, Malta, Slovenia, Croatia, Bosnia and Herzegovina, Montenegro, Albania, Greece, Cyprus, Turkey, Syria, Lebanon, Israel, Egypt, Libya, Tunisia, Algeria, Morocco. This paper does not consider the Black Sea, a semi-enclosed sea connected to the Mediterranean by the straits of Dardanelles and Bosporus.
2. Montego Bay, 10 December 1982, in force 16 November 1994, 1833 UNTS 397, 21 ILM 1261 (1982) (UNCLOS).
3. The UNCLOS also provides that states are bound to take measures "necessary to protect and preserve rare or fragile ecosystems as well as the habitat of depleted, threatened or endangered species and other forms of marine life" (art. 194(5)).
4. Part IX of the UNCLOS, relating to enclosed or semi-enclosed seas, confirms that international cooperation in several fields, including the protection of the environment, is particularly suited in the case of countries surrounding the same regional sea. The Mediterranean fully fits the definition of enclosed or semi-enclosed sea, namely "a gulf, basin or sea surrounded by two or more States and connected to another sea or the ocean by a narrow outlet or consisting entirely or primarily of the territorial seas and exclusive economic zones of two or more coastal States" (art. 122).
5. Paragraph 85 of the judgment of 20 February 1969 in the *North Sea Continental Shelf Cases (Federal Republic of Germany v Denmark/Federal Republic of Germany v The Netherlands)* (1969) ICJ 1. In the *MOX Plant Case* (Ireland v United Kingdom) (Provisional Measures) (2002) 41 ILM 405, the International Tribunal for the Law of the Sea found that the parties were bound, as a provisional measure, to enter into consultations with regard to possible consequences arising out of the commissioning of a nuclear plant (para. 89 of the order of 3 December 2001). The Tribunal confirmed that the duty to cooperate is a fundamental principle in the prevention of pollution of the marine environment under the UNCLOS and general international law (*Mox Plant Case*, para. 82).
6. As provided for in the Vienna Convention on the Law of Treaties, Vienna, 22 May 1969, 27 January 1980, 1155 UNTS 331 (1969), the legal tools for tackling the problem of potentially overlapping treaties derive from the combination of different criteria (*ratione*

temporis, ratione personae and *ratione materiae*). A conflict between treaties arises only if two successive treaties have been concluded by the same parties and regulate in a different way the same subject matter. From a logical point of view and assuming, for the sake of simplicity, that all the parties to the earlier treaty are also parties to the later one, the following questions need to be addressed: (a) whether the provisions of two different treaties relate to the same subject matter; (b) if so, whether one of the two treaties specifies that it is subject to the other; (c) if not, whether the two provisions in question are really incompatible, considering that the special rules (with respect to their subject matter or their territorial application) prevail over the general ones; (d) finally, if the provisions in question remain incompatible, those of the later treaty prevail.

7. UNCLOS, art. 237(2).
8. Ibid.
9. On the Barcelona system see Evangelos Raftopoulos, *Studies on the Implementation of the Barcelona Convention: The Development of an International Trust Regime* (Athens: Ant. N. Sakkoulas Publishers, 1997); José Juste Ruiz, "Regional Approaches to the Protection of the Marine Environment", in Kalliopi K. Koufa, *Thesaurus Acroasium*, Vol. 31 (Athens-Thessaloniki: Sakkoulas Publications, 2002), p. 402; Evangelos Raftopoulos and Moira L. McConnell (eds), *Contributions to International Environmental Negotiation in the Mediterranean Context* (Athens, Ant. N. Sakkoulas-Bruylant Publishers, 2004); Tullio Scovazzi, "The Developments within the 'Barcelona System' for the Protection of the Mediterranean Sea against Pollution", *Annuaire de Droit Maritime et Océanique*, Vol. 26 (2009), pp. 201–218.
10. Other treaties, that do not belong to the Barcelona system, are relevant for the Mediterranean marine environment, such as the Agreement on the Conservation of Cetaceans of the Black Sea, Mediterranean Sea and Contiguous Atlantic Area, Monaco, 24 November 1996, entered into force 1 June 1997, 36 ILM 777 (1996) (ACCOBAMS) and, at the sub-regional level, the Agreement between France, Italy and Monaco on the Protection of the Waters of the Mediterranean Shore, Monaco, 10 May 1976, 1 March 1981, 1976 (RAMOGE).
11. Barcelona, 16 February 1976, entered into force 12 February 1978, 1102 UNTS 27; 15 ILM 290 (1976).
12. The amendments will come into force on the thirtieth day following receipt by the depositary of notification of their acceptance by three-quarters of the parties to the amended protocol.
13. As regards transparency within the Barcelona system, under an amendment adopted in 1988 to the Rules of procedure for meetings and conferences of the parties to the Convention, "the Executive Director [of UNEP] shall, with the tacit consent of the Contracting Parties, invite to send representatives, to observe any public sitting of any meeting or conference, including the meetings of technical committees, any international non-governmental organization which has a direct concern in the protection of the Mediterranean Sea against pollution". Non-governmental organizations, representing both the environmentalist interests and other interests, such as those of the industrial sector, participate as observers at the meetings of the Barcelona legal system and are granted the right to take the floor. They provide a notable and competent contribution to the discussions.
14. UNCLOS, art. 30.
15. Taking into consideration the present multiform legislation of Mediterranean states, such waters can have the legal status of maritime internal waters, territorial seas, fishing zones, ecological protection zones, exclusive economic zones or high seas.
16. Land-Based Protocol, art. 3(b).
17. Ibid., art. 1, para. 2.

18. Doc A/CONF.151/26, vol. I (12 August 1992).
19. The secretariat functions are carried out by the UNEP (art. 17), through the UNEP/ MAP, located in Athens.
20. Barcelona Convention, art. 18, para. 2.
21. See, for example, art. 23 of the Areas Protocol.
22. See Irini Papanicolopulu, "Procedures and Mechanism on Compliance under the 1976/1995 Barcelona Convention on the Protection of the Mediterranean Sea and its Protocols", in Tullio Treves, Laura Pineschi, Attilla Tanzi, et al. (eds), *Non-Compliance Procedures and Mechanisms and the Effectiveness of International Environmental Agreements* (The Hague: Asser Press, 2009), pp. 155–169.
23. Dumping Protocol, art. 7.
24. Ibid., art. 3, para. 5.
25. At a global level, the 1996 Protocol to the Convention on the Prevention of Marine Pollution by Wastes and Other Matter introduces a similar reversal of the logic followed in the parent convention. It is also based on the assumption that the parties shall prohibit the dumping of any wastes or other matter with the exception of those listed in an annex. In the 2000 report on Oceans and the Law of the Sea by the United Nations Secretary-General, the 1996 Protocol was seen as a "milestone in the international regulations on the prevention of marine pollution by dumping of wastes" and "a major change of approach to the question of how to regulate the use of the sea as a depository for waste materials" (UN Doc A/55/61 of 20 March 2000, para. 159). The same could equally be said about the Dumping Protocol.
26. The Global Programme of Action strongly encourages action on a regional level as crucial for successful actions to protect the marine environment from pollution from land-based activities: "This is particularly so where a number of countries have coasts in the same marine and coastal area, most notably in enclosed or semi-enclosed seas. Such cooperation allows for more accurate identification and assessment of the problems in particular geographic areas and more appropriate establishment of priorities for action in these areas. Such cooperation also strengthens regional and national capacity-building and offers an important avenue for harmonizing and adjusting measures to fit the particular environmental and socio-economic circumstances. It, moreover, supports a more efficient and cost-effective implementation of the programmes of action" (para. 29).
27. *Supra*, under the heading "The Convention".
28. Land-Based Protocol, art. 5(2).
29. Land-Based Protocol, art. 1.
30. Ibid.
31. Priority is given to aldrin, chlordane, DDT, dieldrin, dioxins and furans, endrin, hexachlorobenzene, mirex, PCBs and toxaphene.
32. The criteria listed in Annex IV of the Land-Based Protocol are literally taken from the Convention for the Protection of the Marine Environment of the North-East Atlantic, Paris, 22 September 1992, entered into force on 25 March 1998, 32 ILM 1069, (1992) (OSPAR). In fact, the state which proposed the criteria in question simply presented a photocopy of the relevant OSPAR annex. However, unlike the case of literary works, copying is by no means illegal in the process of drafting a legal text. In the case in question, copying was tantamount to paying tribute to the wisdom of the drafters of another regional sea treaty.
33. The 1995 Areas Protocol implements the objectives set forth in Agenda 21. According to this instrument, states, acting individually, bilaterally, regionally or multilaterally and within the framework of the IMO and other relevant international organizations, should assess the need for additional measures to address degradation of the marine environment. This should be done, inter alia, by taking action to ensure respect for areas which

are specially designated, consistent with international law, in order to protect and preserve rare or fragile ecosystems: para. 17.30. Agenda 21 stresses the importance of protecting and restoring endangered marine species, as well as preserving habitats and other ecologically sensitive areas, both on the high seas (para. 17.46(e) and (f)) and in the zones under national jurisdiction (para. 17.75(e) and (f)). In particular, "States should identify marine ecosystems exhibiting high levels of biodiversity and productivity and other critical habitat areas and provide necessary limitations on use in these areas, through, inter alia, designation of protected areas" (para. 17.86). On the protocol see Tullio Scovazzi (ed.), *Marine Specially Protected Areas: The General Aspects and the Mediterranean Regional System* (The Hague: Kluwer Law International, 1999); Valentin E. Bou Franch and Margarita Badenes Casino, "La Protección Internacional de Zonas y Especies en la Región Mediterránea", *Anuario de Derecho Internacional* (1997), p. 33.

34. The existence of the SPAMI List does not prejudice the right of each party to create and manage marine protected areas which are not intended to be listed as SPAMIs.

35. Areas Protocol, art. 8, para. 2.

36. Ibid., art. 8, para. 3.

37. Ibid., art. 28, para. 1.

38. Ibid., art. 28, para. 2.

39. On 25 November 1999 France, Italy and Monaco signed an agreement in Rome on the creation in the Mediterranean Sea of a sanctuary for marine mammals. This is the first international agreement ever adopted with the specific objective of establishing a sanctuary for marine mammals. The area covered by the sanctuary, which extends over 96,000 km^2, includes waters which have the legal status of maritime internal waters, territorial sea, ecological protection zone and high seas. It is inhabited by the eight cetacean species regularly found in the Mediterranean, namely, the fin whale (*Balaenoptera physalus*), the sperm whale (*Physeter catodon*), Cuvier's beaked whale (*Ziphius cavirostris*), the long-finned pilot whale (*Globicephala melas*), the striped dolphin (*Stenella coeruleoalba*), the common dolphin (*Delphinus delphis*), the bottlenose dolphin (*Tursiops truncatus*) and Risso's dolphin (*Grampus griseus*). In this area, the water currents create conditions favouring phytoplankton growth and abundance of krill (*Meganyctiphanes norvegica*), a small shrimp that is preyed upon by pelagic vertebrates. Under the agreement, the parties undertake to adopt measures to ensure a favourable state of conservation for every species of marine mammal and to protect them and their habitat from negative impacts, both direct and indirect. They prohibit in the sanctuary any deliberate "taking" (defined as "hunting, catching, killing or harassing of marine mammals, as well as the attempting of such actions") or disturbance of mammals. Non-lethal catches may be authorized in urgent situations or for in-situ scientific research purposes. There is a direct connection between the Sanctuary Agreement and the Areas Protocol. As provided for in the former, as soon as the Areas Protocol "enters into force for them, the Parties will present a joint proposal for inclusion of the sanctuary in the list of specially protected areas of Mediterranean importance". This was actually done in November 2001 by France, Italy and Monaco.

40. On the subject of liability and compensation, see Wastes Protocol, para. 11.

41. Basel, 22 March 1989, 1673 UNTS 126, 28 ILM 657 (1989) (Basel Convention).

42. Wastes Protocol, Annex 1, para. A.

43. Wastes Protocol, art. 3, para. 1(d).

44. The "notification without authorization" scheme of the Wastes Protocol is fully compatible with the international law of the sea, as embodied in the UNCLOS. Under the UNCLOS section on innocent passage in the territorial sea, passage must be innocent, i.e. "not prejudicial to the peace, good order or security of the coastal State" (art. 19(1)). Any act of wilful and serious pollution contrary to the UNCLOS is incompatible with

the right of innocent passage (art. 19(2)(h)). Foreign ships have the right to pass (art. 17), but nowhere in the UNCLOS is it said that they have the right to pass secretly or covertly. Moreover, under art. 22(1) and (2) of the UNCLOS, some particularly dangerous ships, namely, "tankers, nuclear-powered ships and ships carrying nuclear or other inherently dangerous or noxious substances may be required to confine their passage" to sea lanes designated or prescribed by the coastal state. An obvious question can be asked in this respect: how could a coastal state exercise its right to prescribe sea lanes for ships carrying noxious substances if it were not even entitled to know that a foreign ship is carrying these substances?

45. Such as the Convention for the Prevention of Pollution from Ships, Oslo, 15 February 1973, 1340 UNTS 184 as amended by the Protocol 1978 which entered into force 2 October 1983 (MARPOL), the Convention on Oil Pollution Preparedness, Response and Co-operation, London, 30 November 1990, entered into force 13 May 1995, 1891 UNTS 51; 30 ILM 773 (1990), the Convention on the Control of Harmful Anti-Fouling Systems on Ships 2001, London, 5 October 2001, entered into force 17 September 2008, IMO Doc AFS/CONF/26 (2001) or the Convention for the Control and Management of Ships' Ballast Waters and Sediments, London, 13 February 2004, not yet in force.

46. The Emergency Protocol also acknowledges "the contribution of the European Community to the implementation of international standards as regards maritime safety and the prevention of pollution from ships". The European Union has enacted a number of legal instruments relating to the control and prevention of marine pollution from ships which apply to its member states, in addition to rules adopted under the aegis of the IMO.

47. Emergency Protocol, art. 1(d).

48. See *Report by the Coordinator for the 15th Meeting of the Contracting Parties*, 21 November 2007, Doc UNEP(DEP)/MED IG 17/3, p. 7.

49. Coastal Zone Protocol, art. 2(g).

50. Presently 12 nautical miles for most Mediterranean states, with the exceptions of the United Kingdom (3 nautical miles), Greece (6 nautical miles) and Turkey (6 nautical miles in the Aegean Sea).

51. Article 17 provides for the definition by parties of a common regional framework for integrated coastal zone management in the Mediterranean. Under art. 18, parties are bound to formulate a national strategy for integrated coastal zone management and coastal implementation plans and programmes consistent with the common regional framework.

52. Coastal Zone Protocol, art. 9(2).

53. Coastal Zone Protocol, art. 10.

54. Coastal Zone Protocol, art. 22.

55. Coastal Zone Protocol, art. 23.

56. For text, see Report of the meeting, 18 January 2008, Doc UNEP(DEPI)/MED IG 17/10, p. 133.

57. On the preparatory works, see Lorenzo Schiano Di Pepe, "Introducing an International Civil Liability Regime for Damage to the Marine Environment in the Mediterranean Sea Area", *Environmental Liability* (1999), pp. 8–12; Tullio Scovazzi, "The Mediterranean Guidelines for the Determination of Environmental Liability and Compensation: The Negotiations for the Instrument and the Question of Damage that Can Be Compensated", in *Max Planck Yearbook of United Nations Law* vol. 9 (2009), pp. 183–211.

58. From here on the term "parties" refers to the parties to the Barcelona Convention.

59. *Guidelines on Liability and Compensation*, Guideline A, para. 4.

60. See Guideline B, para. 5.

61. Guideline D, para. 14.

62. Guideline D, para. 9.
63. Guideline D, para. 10.
64. "The legislation of the Contracting Parties should require that the measures referred to in paragraph 10(b) and (c) are taken by the operator. If the operator fails to take such measures or cannot be identified or is not liable under the legislation implementing these Guidelines, the Contracting Parties should take these measures themselves and recover the costs from the operator where appropriate" (Guideline E, para. 16).
65. *Official Journal of the European Union*, no. L 143 (30 April 2004).
66. Annex II, para. 1(a), (b) and (c). Interim losses are defined in the Directive as "losses which result from the fact that the damaged natural resources and/or services are not able to perform their ecological functions or provide services to other natural resources or to the public until the primary or complementary measures have taken effect. It does not consist of financial compensation to members of the public" (Annex II, para. 1(d)).
67. *Guidelines on Liability and Compensation*, Guideline D, para. 11.
68. Guideline D, para. 13.
69. The basic standard of liability is strict liability (see Guideline G, para. 19).
70. Guideline F, para. 17. The operator is defined as "any natural or juridical person, whether private or public, who exercises the *de jure* or *de facto* control over an activity covered by these Guidelines, as provided for in paragraph 4" (Guideline F, para. 18).
71. Guideline I, para. 25.
72. Guideline K, para. 28.
73. If a fund were to be established, the complex question should be addressed of whether it would be financed by the states, by the operators concerned, or by both of them, and a system would have to be developed to assess the respective contributions.
74. *Guidelines on Liability and Compensation,* Guideline L, para. 29.

5

Non-lawyers and legal regimes: Public participation for ecologically sustainable development

Donna Craig and Michael Jeffery, QC

Introduction

Sustainable development, though a complex concept, has become the underlying goal of environmental governance both globally and locally. The concept was articulated in its most popularized form by the 1983 report of the World Commission on Environment and Development.[1] In the past few years, despite the debate surrounding the meaning and scope of the concept of sustainability, the policy objective for all international, national and sectoral environmental agencies has become sustainable development (or ecologically sustainable development – ESD – in the preferred Australian terminology).

International laws subsequent to the Report of the World Commission on Environment and Development (the Brundtland Report) have ESD as their fundamental objective. The Rio Declaration, Agenda 21 and several environmental conventions, such as the Convention on Biological Diversity[2] (CBD) and the United Nations Framework Convention on Climate Change[3] are examples of this. Agenda 21[4] recognizes the reality that the integration of environment and development is essential to address the worsening of poverty, ill-health, the widening gap between rich and poor nations, disparities within nations and the continuing deterioration of ecosystems. In addition, the key definitions and framework of the Millennium Development Goals[5] (with a strong emphasis on the principles of sustainability and poverty alleviation) are now reflected in most international legal instruments and policies relating to sustainable development,

The future of international environmental law, Leary and Pisupati (eds), United Nations University Press, 2010, ISBN 978-92-808-1192-6

such as the United Nations World Summit on Sustainable Development (WSSD)[6] and the associated Plan of Implementation, (2002).[7]

Apart from the debate surrounding the significance of the concept of sustainable development, there is the challenge of how to achieve ESD and how to determine success in achieving it. Scholars have developed different theories in an attempt to determine how sustainable development can be assessed.[8] Sustainability indicators have been proposed as parameters for measuring the effectiveness of policies in achieving ESD. However, unlike with economic indicators such as the gross domestic product, consensus on ESD indicators has proved difficult, as the very concept is an ideal as opposed to a quantifiable goal. While the jury is still out on how success in achieving ESD can be measured, there is agreement on the possibility of identifying overarching principles that would facilitate the achievement of ESD. There is recognition, however, that the process of environmental policy-making, and implementation in general, is closely linked to politics and political values. This introduces a complex array of factors, which explains why the incorporation of these overarching principles into the development and implementation of policy will not, of itself, guarantee ESD.

The achievement of ESD presupposes, among other things, the identification of clear environmental goals and norms. As environmental norms are rarely self-implementing, management systems are required at all levels to determine how these environmental goals can best be attained and how environmental rules may be most effectively observed. This process of identifying goals and the management systems necessary to achieve ESD is the task of environmental governance.[9]

The concept of environmental governance encompasses the relationships and interactions among government and non-government structures, procedures and conventions, where power and responsibility are exercised in making environmental decisions.[10] It concerns *how* the decisions are made, with a particular emphasis on the need for citizens, interest groups, and communities generally, to participate and have their voices heard.[11] Therefore, the concept does not apply to the province of government alone,[12] and the term "governance" must be distinguished from "government".[13] It is imperative that we study the actions of the government in terms of environmental policy- and decision-making, but we must also observe how citizens take on their own responsibility and develop environmental initiatives. As an extension of the concept of environmental governance, *good environmental governance* is measured by the effectiveness of strategies and initiatives implemented to achieve environmental goals, the ultimate goal being ESD.

The challenge of developing sustainable environmental policy has been described as a wicked problem, on the grounds that the issues contained are particularly difficult.[14] This is true in so far as some of the features of environmental policy and sustainability are complex, because of a variety of factors: inter alia, their novelty, interconnectedness, uncertainty and their variable spatial and temporal scales.[15] These features, together with the interconnectedness required if sustainability is to be achieved, mean that, unlike traditional policy formulation, where, historically, a fragmented approach to policy development and implementation has been used for the different sectors, in the case of environmental policy the process must be integrative.[16]

Further, ESD requires a restructuring of economic, social and environmental relations and this restructuring is often not in the interest of political expediency,[17] particularly with respect to traditional political ideologies. This introduces an additional complexity in environmental governance. Environmental governance cannot be divorced from the wider issues of political culture, values and social tensions.[18] The current stalemate in the arena of environmental governance and global climate change is a manifestation of the intricacies.

This chapter examines some of the existing legal principles and "best practice" approaches to environmental governance, highlighting public participation and always having regard to the evolving goals and complexities of ESD.

Elaboration of the principles for sustainable development

Despite the challenges in developing management systems that foster sustainability, some strides have been taken in the elaboration of environmental governance and the identification of principles that promote good environmental governance.

The Aarhus Convention,[19] although it presently applies primarily to the region of Europe, has global significance for the promotion of environmental governance. The Convention, which has the current status of forty signatory states plus the European Community, and 44 parties who have ratified or acceded to it,[20] contains three main pillars: the right of the public to access information about the environment, the requirement for public participation in certain environmental matters and the public's access to courts and tribunals of law for environmental matters.

The Convention develops one of the most fundamental and crucial principles of environmental governance, the need for civil participation in environmental issues, which shall constitute the subject of discussion in this chapter. This right has its origin in the Rio Declaration on Environment and Development.[21] Principle 10 of the Declaration states:

Environmental issues are best handled with participation of all concerned citizens, at the relevant level. At the national level, each individual shall have appropriate access to information concerning the environment that is held by public authorities, including information on hazardous materials and activities in their communities, and the opportunity to participate in decision-making processes. States shall facilitate and encourage public awareness and participation by making information widely available. Effective access to judicial and administrative proceedings, including redress and remedy, shall be provided.[22]

Agenda 21 also recognizes this principle by advocating for the inclusion of major social groups in environmental governance. A large section of this document is devoted to strengthening the role of major groups, with particular reference to women, children and youth, indigenous people and their communities, NGOs, local authorities, workers and trade unions, business and industry, scientific and technological communities, as well as farmers. ESD requires that environmental governance incorporate ecological, social, economic and cultural research, strategies and processes. This integrative approach of ESD makes participation by a cross-section of actors in environmental governance essential. Public participation in environmental governance has thus become a hallmark feature of international environmental law.

The Rio Declaration and Agenda 21, as well as other international environmental laws providing for public participation, identify principles necessary for environmental governance to achieve sustainability. However, these principles must be elaborated and translated into legal frameworks and rights. The Aarhus Convention, though a regional instrument, is important as it seeks to develop the legal rights arising from the principle of public participation. The Convention has rightly been described as *"by far the most impressive elaboration of principle 10 of the Rio Declaration"*.[23] It provides explicit linkages between environmental rights and human rights. Commencing with the preamble, it states in the 7th and 8th paragraphs:

Recognising also that every person has the right to live in an environment adequate to his or her health and well-being, and the duty, both individually, and in association with others, to protect and improve the environment for the benefit of present and future generations, . . .
    Considering that, to be able to assert this right and observe this duty, citizens must have access to information, be entitled to participate in decision-making and have access to justice in environmental matters, and acknowledging in this regard that citizens may need assistance in order to exercise their rights.[24]

The linkage of environmental rights to human rights is important as it constitutes a move from the mere encouragement of policymakers and implementers to include the public in some processes of governance, to the definition of the right of the public to take part in the process of environmental governance. The understanding of public participation in the context of a right facilitates its implementation, as it provides the public with enforcement mechanisms used in human rights.

Apart from recognizing the right to public participation, the Aarhus Convention grants the public rights of access to information and imposes obligations on public authorities to provide this information. Access to environmental information leads to a well-informed public, who are more able to question the actions of government. These factors are a prerequisite if public participation in environmental governance is to be meaningful. Article 4 outlines when it is appropriate for access to information to be denied, these circumstances being when the public authority does not have the information requested;[25] when it is unreasonable to provide the information;[26] and when confidentiality is in the public interest,[27] for example, with intelligence or national security information. Moreover, information can be refused if disclosure will adversely affect factors such as the course of justice[28] and intellectual property rights.[29] Subsequent meetings of the parties to this convention have gone further and given direction on the development of the procedural aspects of this right. For instance, at the first Meeting of the Parties to the Convention,[30] the parties noted the revolution in electronic information technology as being very important to the promotion of environmental governance. The Meeting's declaration called on parties to the Convention to make government environmental information progressively available electronically, but for these services to be kept under frequent review.[31] The Meeting of the Parties stressed that the Convention was largely about building partnerships between an empowered civil society and the government, and that the public had responsibility for sustainable development too. It was stated:

> The engagement of the public is vital for creating an environmentally sustainable future. Governments alone cannot solve the major ecological problems of our time. Only through building partnerships within a well-informed and empowered civil society, within the framework of good governance and respect for human rights, can this challenge be met.[32]

The Aarhus Convention is a good example of the elaboration of the procedural aspects of public participation required in environmental governance in order to ensure that ESD is achieved. To this extent, the Convention is a clear advance in the area of environmental governance. It is an instrument that is being considered for its merits not only by European countries, but also by many countries around the world. The Convention has led to the development of directives, by the European Union Parliament, which have the effect of moving the principle of public participation from an ideal to a reality.

Directive 2003/35/EC of the European Parliament and of the Council of 26 May 2003 provided for public participation in respect of the drawing up of certain plans and programmes relating to the environment and amending, with regard to public participation and access to justice, Council Directives 85/337/EEC and 96/61/EC.

In December 2004, the Environment Council gave the green light for the EU to ratify the Aarhus Convention and also reached political agreement on a Regulation that will apply the Convention's provisions to Community institutions and bodies. This new directive on public access to environmental information (Directive 2003/4/EC) entered into force on 14 February 2005, thus becoming binding for all European Union member states.

The proposed Directive on Access to Justice (COM 2003 624) grants citizens the right to initiate administrative or judicial procedures against public authorities for omissions or acts that do not comply with environmental law. It is also intended to provide a framework for the implementation, at the level of the Community and the member states, of the third pillar of the Convention; access to justice in environmental matters. The directive recognizes the need to move from theory to practice for environmental law to be effective.

Few countries or regions have elaborated the right to public participation in the context of their environmental governance systems. Much more remains to be done for the principle of public participation to form an integral part of environmental governance on the global and local scenes. The following section seeks to re-examine the right to public participation and to make proposals on how public participation can be better integrated into environmental governance in the future.

Public participation: Non-lawyers and legal regimes

Public participation has been defined in a variety of ways, the import of most of these definitions being the participation of the "lay public" in environmental decision-making.[33] The assumption is that room must be made, presumably by the "experts", for the public in environmental governance, which is understood as fundamentally a policy and legal regime. Understood in this way, it becomes necessary to justify the presence of the public in what could appear to be a fairly complex regime that has often been left to experts and elected representatives. ESD calls for a re-conceptualization of this traditional presumption of the distinction between the "expert" and the public. With the need to integrate environmental issues with the economic and social issues, experience has shown that the public may well be the experts on the issues involved in environmental governance.[34] Besides, as Philip Wendells observed: "*Law is nothing unless close behind it stands a warm, living public opinion.*"[35] The law depends on the sanction of the public for its effective implementation. This re-conceptualization of the concept of public participation contributes to its integration in the process of environmental policy development and implementation.

However, the potential contribution of the public must not be overrated, a risk ever present in the discourse on public participation in governance. The public cannot be expected to resolve all the issues that present themselves in the course of environmental governance. Misconceptions in the understanding of the role and limits of public participation can adversely affect the integration of the principle into environmental governance and its capacity to contribute to the achievement of ESD.

Public participation in governance is not a novel concept. The right of individual citizens and groups to participate in shaping decisions and policies that affect them is a well-recognized human right.[36] Discourse on the rationale for public participation in environmental governance has analysed its exact nature, to determine whether public participation is an end or a means to an end. In international environmental law instruments, for example, the principle tends to be expressed as a means to an end. Principle 10 of the Rio Declaration, for instance, presents public participation as a useful tool for resolving environmental issues. However, public participation in the context of democracy and emancipation in environmental governance can be regarded as an end.[37] It could be argued that the objective of governance, environmental governance included, is democracy, and thus public participation is a central goal of good environmental governance.

In this chapter, it is recognized that public participation can be both a means and an end but, regardless of its nature, it must be analysed and evaluated in the context of ESD. If a means, then the quality of public participation should be determined by the extent to which it contributes to the achievement of the end. If regarded as an end, it is imperative that this participation be empowering in so far as it is one of the elements of ESD.

Just as democracy in government is not an absolute good, public participation in environmental governance has benefits but is not devoid of risks. One of the fundamental risks of the incorporation of public participation into environmental decision-making is that it increases the cost in terms of money and time of the process. The values expressed may not always be aligned with ESD. Public participation may also trigger, or highlight, differences in interests of the various stakeholders.[38] However, these risks can be mitigated through sound environmental governance principles. Besides, often the cost of failing to include public participation is, in the long run, much more than the costs associated with public participation. In the context of ESD the case for public participation is thus stronger.

As mentioned earlier, public participation has functional benefits. In broad terms these benefits fall into three main categories.[39] First, public participation contributes to the quality of decision-making. This is because the very nature of environmental governance and ESD incorporates factors which are primarily in the purview of the public. Such factors include, but are not limited to, social cultural needs of the people, which are a necessary ingredient if environmental governance is to achieve ESD. Second, public participation increases legitimacy in the environmental governance process and this, in the long run, facilitates in the implementation and enforcement of environmental policies and laws. Finally, the process of public participation builds local capacities which ultimately improve the quality of life of the public, thus contributing to ESD.

In recognition of the benefits of public participation, in most jurisdictions it is no longer acceptable to argue against public participation in environmental decision-making processes. Nevertheless, the challenge lies in ensuring that this participation is genuine and not mere co-option or consultation.[40] In some instances, such as the elements of environmental impact assessment (EIA), the very legal process itself works well only when systems of consulting the stakeholders, and general public, are well developed. The Aarhus Convention, as noted earlier, has codified the processes at the international level requiring public participation in environmental decisions, access to environmental information, and access to justice to ensure that environmental procedures will be followed.

Following the identification of the principle of public participation as essential to ESD, governments have sought to incorporate the principle into their respective environmental governance mechanisms. However, the common strategy has been to identify specific instances in environmental decision-making where public participation is necessary and to provide for this.[41] Checklists are used as a means of ensuring that the public have been informed and/or consulted. The result is that participation becomes simply "procedural" and ad hoc, a far cry from the situation envisaged in the concept of ESD. This approach to environmental governance has led to dissatisfaction. Increasingly, participants are weary of participation where they have no say in determining the terms of reference, scope of research and the procedures for decision-making but are only included just before roll-out of the action plan or project. They see the policy and management context as flawed in terms of ESD and feel that their participation does not make a difference in the decision or process because entrenched vested interests and practices have captured the agenda. These fundamental concerns, raised in many participation processes, often need to be addressed through long-term institutional and policy change based on ESD. This can only be achieved through a re-thinking of environmental governance systems.

Developing integrated participatory processes based on ecologically sustainable development

In order to achieve an integrated public participatory process, an integrated approach to environmental governance must be adopted. This is an onerous task for many governments as most of them are structured along sectoral lines. The management of resources making up the environment is frequently based on a fragmented system dealing with particular aspects of the environment. In such a scenario, the process of integrating public participation in the various sectors and at the various levels of the governance process becomes a challenge.

Few jurisdictions have achieved this level of integration. The New Zealand Resource Management Act constitutes an attempt to develop a legal framework for an integrated approach to environmental governance, and by extension to establish an integrated public participatory process.[42] This Act, passed in 1991, has the objective of promoting sustainable management of all physical and natural resources. The Act identifies public participation as a policy feature and thus provides for its inclusion at the various levels of environmental governance.

Drawing from the experience so far on public participation processes, it is possible to develop some best practice rules and principles for the development of an integrative participatory process which would facilitate the achievement of ESD. This would involve the re-examination of the process of formulating and implementing environmental policy so as to integrate the contribution of the public at all levels. The following section discusses the main features of such a process.

Determination of strategic policy direction, legal framework and management objectives

If environmental governance is to successfully achieve ESD, the primary step of problem formulation and thus determination of strategic policy direction must be reconsidered. As ESD requires the integration of environmental concerns with social and economic issues, the identification of the problem and charting of policy direction to resolve the problem will require the input of various parties. Apart from experts in the different fields, the input of the public would be indispensable at this stage.[43] The exact mode and level of public participation would depend on the specific issues at hand and is thus outside the scope of this chapter. However, it is important for legal frameworks on environmental governance to safeguard the right of the public to be involved at this stage and to provide guidelines for the procedural aspects of this participation, so as to ensure that participation is not merely procedural.

Sustainability also requires that decision-makers not only identify and seek to meet current legal and policy requirements but should also be proactive in developing ESD policies for the long-term future (e.g. twenty to thirty years). The policy directives need not be static. Knowledge of ESD will grow and public attitudes will change. Therefore, the strategic policy, legal framework and management objectives should be periodically reviewed, taking into account the input of the public along with the other steps in the integrated ESD process described below.

Research: biophysical, social, cultural and economic

In order to achieve ESD, the policy process must be driven by research that cuts across the different spheres of development. Even at this stage the involvement of the public, though perhaps to a limited extent, is necessary.[44] Research might include projects involving:
(i)   developing baseline data on regions;
(ii)   undertaking ecosystem studies and related social, cultural and economic studies;
(iii)   preliminary identification of research priorities and research undertaken;
(iv)   preliminary identification of critical issues and threatening processes for ESD planning and management;
(v)   preliminary stakeholder identification having regard to (i), (ii), (iii) and (iv) above;
(vi)   preliminary identification of ESD policy and implementation options;
(vii)   preliminary identification of options for reviewing, monitoring and evaluating ESD policy and implementation.

Scoping and ecologically sustainable development policy

There are rarely enough resources to undertake all of the tasks, outlined above, to a satisfactory extent and standard. Research needs to serve applied policy-making and implementation in order to make ESD a reality. This involves choices about priorities to be given to strategies, objectives, research, critical issues and endangering processes in the operations of the agency. Scoping is a participatory "round table" of stakeholders (including government) and experts which convenes to make these hard choices in a transparent and informed way. Parties involved need to take responsibility for their choices. Scoping of EIA and strategic impact assessment (SIA) in the United States and Canada has led to greatly improved efficiency and coordination between and within governments and with other stakeholders. These choices in the scoping process will be critical to ESD, and "informed choice" often requires further research as well as timely and adequate access to information and expertise. Effective scoping needs to be interactive and carefully planned and resourced. Conflict resolution approaches are important. Participants in the scoping process need to be accorded the power and resources of "partners" in ESD. Initial choices may be informed by interest-based values, but this process can be educative in the normative sense (evolving wider public interest values in participants) as well as in the technical sense (evolving increased knowledge and resources). The ESD scoping process should:

(i)   review identification of critical issues and threatening processes for ESD planning and management and identify research priorities and gaps in existing research in relation to them;
(ii) determine research priorities and feedback to the scoping process and wider stakeholders;
(iii) review stakeholder identification and resource, and facilitate additional participants in the scoping process where necessary;
(iv) develop and implement public participation strategy relating to the critical issues and identification of threatening processes and the formulation of ESD policy;
(v)   communicate to wider stakeholders the scoping recommendations and agency and other government actions based on them.

Ecologically sustainable development policy implementation

This phase involves several elements including the selection of the policy instrument, the planning of the actual implementation process and the determination of the means to ensure enforcement and compliance.[45]

The involvement of the public in the selection of the policy instrument contributes to the effective implementation of the policy in the long run. The nature and level of participation in this process of selecting the policy instrument depends on the nature of the problem sought to be addressed by the policy. Some policy instruments, by their very nature, require public participation: for example, the use of education and training to achieve a particular sustainability goal will necessarily require the inclusion of the public as they would be the object of the education and training.

The implementation plan is a dynamic process rather than a static task.[46] The objective of this plan is to set out the means of using the policy instruments chosen to achieve the ESD policy strategy identified earlier. The public could assist in providing feedback on early experiences with implementation instruments chosen.

It is important to identify the most effective means to ensure that the policy instruments chosen achieve their goal. The involvement of the public to varying degrees in the determination of the enforcement and compliance mechanism contributes to the success of a policy instrument in so far as, more often than not, the object of the policy is the public and consequently they are also the object of the enforcement and compliance mechanism. Even where the subject of the policy instrument is not the public, their participation in determining the plan of enforcement and compliance is still important. Their having been involved in designing the compliance and enforcement mechanism will ensure that they understand it and thus will facilitate their subsequent participation in the actual compliance and enforcement mechanism during implementation.

Periodic review of overall environmentally sustainable development policy and implementation process

Every public participation strategy needs to be applied flexibly and needs modification. The effectiveness of the ESD strategy is dependent on its ensuring that public participation is not viewed as merely a separate strategy at some stage of ESD, but rather that it is inherent in each one, although the form and intensity may vary. Participation drives the forging of new partnerships, conflict resolution, cross-sectoral decision-making, focused and applied research, developmental education and the co-ordination of decision-making within and between levels of government and other stakeholders. Public participation, in itself, cannot "guarantee" that ESD will be realized, but the proposed approaches to public participation will be an essential and important part of ESD policy and implementation.

Evaluation of public participation in environmental decisions

Best practice in public participation is dependent on the ability and skills of practitioners and the very specific context in which participation occurs. There is a common experience that public participation that works well on one occasion may not be as successful when applied elsewhere or in a different situation. There is very little useful literature available on the criteria for evaluating public participation.

IUCN has prepared a resource kit for sustainability assessment[47] to help incorporate social concerns in appraising, planning, implementing and evaluating conservation initiatives. It argues that what constitutes "effective participation" in a conservation initiative could include the following (and various combinations of the following):

* Local actors assessing their needs and resources, and recognizing the opportunities offered by the conservation initiative;
* Local actors taking part in collecting information, and project managers sharing information with them;
* Local actors contributing to planning and decision-making at district, regional and national level;
* Local actors being consulted on key issues in the project cycle, including project objectives, design and management;
* Local actors contributing to planning and decision-making at local level;
* Local actors taking part in decision-making during project implementation;
* Local actors providing labour and resources to implement the conservation initiative;
* Local actors initiating action (i.e. local groups identifying and responding to new needs in a project, and taking initiative for their own sake; this is different to deciding on tasks identified by project management);
* Local actors assuming specific responsibilities for the conservation initiative;
* Local actors acquiring benefits from the conservation initiative;
* Local actors developing effective partnerships with other social actors, while agreeing on an equitable sharing of the rights and responsibilities in conservation;
* Local actors taking part in the evaluation of the initiative.

Evaluation also needs to have reference to the short- and long-term objectives of the decision or process. However, public participation evaluation should also be considered in the context of other objectives and performance criteria. The problem of evaluating public participation processes requires further research and cannot be resolved at this stage, but the above criteria provide useful reference points in reviewing public participation programmes. The principles of good environmental governance identified by the Aarhus Convention can also provide useful criteria for ensuring effective public participation. The following section identifies two areas in which public participation is crucial (enforcement and compliance) and seeks to determine the efficacy of current management systems for public participation.

Effective public participation in compliance and enforcement

Both in "North" and "South" nations, there are several fundamental regulatory and institutional elements that are prerequisites for effective citizen participation: access to information, clear environmental standards, recognition of environmental rights and a citizen cause of action, standing, affordability, and an independent and informed judiciary. It is recognized that political, legal and institutional capacity, experience and resources vary greatly and affect the actual implementation of these prerequisites. However, it is not a clear "North" and "South" divide. For example, the Aarhus Convention was developed in Eastern Europe; most of the constitutions providing a right to environmental quality (and related procedural rights) are in "South" nations that emerged from colonialism after World War II. Constitutional guarantees are poorly developed in "North" nations such as the United Kingdom and the United States. Generally, there are very significant implementation, compliance and enforcement issues in "South" nations. Some nations, such as India, are exceptional world leaders in public interest environmental law through their Supreme Court decisions. In such nations, the constitution and judiciary can play a very important role when political and civil society institutions often fail to protect the environment and develop ESD strategies. However, it will become necessary for this political and institutional capacity to develop in order to entrench ESD in the long term.

Susan Casey-Lefkowitz has argued that more than a willing citizenry is required for effective public participation.[48] If even one of these regulatory and institutional elements is missing, citizens find it very difficult to participate in the environmental enforcement process. Many countries have developed creative solutions to meeting one or more of these requirements, but only a few countries meet enough of them to allow for effective citizen participation in enforcement.[49] Enforcement and compliance is a crucial and continuing focus for environmental law and ESD. It is timely to undertake a more detailed examination of the role of public participation in these processes, particularly in the context of national laws.

National and comparative approaches to enforcement and compliance

Access to information

Access to information is the foundation of all effective public participation. For environmental enforcement, the public needs access to specific information about relevant standards, as well as specific facility permits, discharges, monitoring data as well as access to information on databases, such as toxic release information contained in the United States pollutant register system. In many nations, access to this type of information is limited, not allowed, or are not systematically and reliably collected in up-to-date databases. Finally, the public needs to have a remedy, such as an appeal, for violations of access to information requirements. Mere policy rarely serves this purpose.

In many nations, constitutional and national laws grant the public the right to have access to information, but fail to provide more detailed regulations or guidelines stating how this shall happen.[50] Access to information concerning permit conditions and regulatory standards is also necessary to verify whether a violation has taken place. It is fairly well accepted that the public has the right to access information concerning regulatory standards, but very few legal systems have a clear right to access information concerning decisions affecting a regulated entity (e.g. permits, licences and approvals) and monitoring data. The requirement for a citizen or NGO to independently undertake these tests or gather data is usually fatal to their complaint or litigation.

Publicly accessible pollution databases originated in the United States and the initiative is slowly spreading to other jurisdictions. The US Emergency Planning and Community Right-to-know Act (EPCRA) imposes extensive self-monitoring and reporting requirements on certain industries that use and release extremely hazardous chemicals. This data often proves very useful to citizens who access it, but there are continuing concerns related to self-monitoring, reporting and voluntary codes of conduct.

Defining environmental standards

The legal processes of enforcement and compliance tend to work most efficiently when environmental standards are clearly defined and the issues in dispute relate to applying the standard to factual situations and establishing breaches. The more ill-defined the standard, such as references to "harmful", "negligent" or "knowingly", the less likely that enforcement and compliance will be effective. Citizens need to be able to bring actions for environmental damage.

Recognition of environmental rights, standing and a cause of action

Gradually some jurisdictions have developed environmental rights that extend beyond the infringement of property and other financial interests. The expansion of constitutional and human rights (to life and environmental quality) approaches has assisted in this process. Citizens usually need to rely on a public interest or constitutional right. However, the existence of the right is not enough, in itself. Citizens will need standing and funding to bring a suit and an appropriate cause of action before a tribunal or court. Australia (New South Wales) has pioneered "open" standing provisions that allow any person to have standing to enforce compliance with many environmental laws.[51] However, issues related to funding, class actions and the risk of cost awards (for unsuccessful action) remain unresolved.

Role and independence of judiciary

Some civil law jurisdictions have a judiciary that may be closely aligned with the executive branch of government. This may create entrenched problems with compliance and implementation, particularly where there is no history and tradition of democratic governance. The separation of powers and independence of the judiciary is central to compliance and enforcement. It is also necessary to adequately resource (an often over-burdened) judiciary and provide appropriate training and access to environmental expertise. Judicial training programmes have been undertaken by the United Nations Environmental Programme (UNEP), AusAid (in Indonesia) and the World Conservation Union (IUCN) Commission on Environmental Law.

An insight into the role of an independent judiciary is provided by the Supreme Court of India. The world-renowned activist lawyer, M.C. Mehta, has been able to effectively use the judiciary to fill the gap in areas where the executive and legislative branches of government have failed to provide the leadership necessary to curtail widespread environmental degradation. He provides a unique example of what an exceptionally passionate, talented and determined individual can accomplish. Mehta is best known for the remarkable results he obtained in his very first environmental case and his ongoing crusade to save the Taj Mahal, a national treasure, from gradual decay in the face of industrial air pollution and neglect.[52]

This litigation, initiated by Mehta in 1984, sought to have the court interpret the Indian constitution's right-to-life provision to include a right to a healthy environment. The result of this case was that the court closed more than 600 offending industries in the vicinity of the Taj Mahal and forced new industries to meet stringent environmental pollution standards.

Mehta then turned his attention to convincing the court to curtail pollution emanating from the disposal of waste from government-owned factories into the Ganges (Holy Ganga) River (covering eight states) posing a threat to the life and health of people;[53] improving the unfortunate exploitation of children under laws dating back to British colonial rule and has become involved in a multitude of other important environmental causes. Mehta, since 1984, has won more than forty landmark decisions on environmental issues, a distinction that earned him a UNEP Global 500 award (1993), the Goldman Environmental Prize for Asia (1998) and the Ramon Magsaysay Foundation Public Service award for Asia (1997).[54]

Citizen involvement in monitoring

There are some precedents in international law for the involvement of non-state parties in monitoring (human rights regimes and the International Labour Organization). In some nations, governments use citizen monitoring which may already be taking place.[55] For example, in the United States, some citizen organizations have begun harbour watch programmes to identify oil spills or other emissions in local harbours.[56]

The successful citizen initiative to save New York's Hudson River that began more than thirty years ago, known as the "Riverkeepers", is a good example of how the citizenry of almost any local community can be effectively mobilized to defend the place in which they live and the environmental heritage to which they are entitled.[57] This community-led initiative has now spread throughout the globe to monitor and protect river and coastal ecosystems.

Most EIA regulations in various countries do not explicitly require any monitoring. EIA laws in Indonesia provide a positive example that links EIA to development or planning consent conditions and monitoring. However, there is poor institutional capacity, expertise and implementation. Where national EIA legislation does require some type of monitoring, it rarely specifies whether that includes citizen participation.

Citizen complaints and role of ombudsmen

This is the most common mechanism for public input in environmental enforcement. It usually involves a government administrative process for citizens to file an environmental grievance or allegation of harm. The state or municipal government reviews the matter and is required to formally respond (usually within a specified period).

Some jurisdictions have an independent complaint body or designated ombudsman at the national or local levels that is usually funded by, but independent of, the government. The type of complaints that can be dealt with and the powers of the ombudsman are usually governed by statutory rules. Their powers are usually to undertake an inquiry, publish a public report and make recommendations. Some ombudsmen or Commissioners for Environment (for example, in New Zealand) may report directly to Parliament. Their effectiveness depends very much on publicity and the legitimacy, independence and authority of the ombudsman or complaint body.

Mediation and negotiation

This is an increasingly common approach to dispute resolution. Significant concerns remain about the adequacy of stakeholder identification and participation (for example, adequacy of public interest, disadvantaged and minority group representation). Confidentiality clauses impede transparency and monitoring. Finally, some issues relating to ESD may not be amenable to mediation or negotiation when ecological thresholds and public goods (such as clean air and water) are involved.

Transboundary and international enforcement

The International Court of Justice (ICJ) had a growing number of environmental cases and it established a special environmental chamber in 1993. NGOs can submit information to the ICJ based on art. 50 of the ICJ Statute, which allows such organizations to provide opinions as experts. The ICJ has used this power in a way that is similar to recognizing intervenors or "friends of the court". A coalition of national and international environmental and human rights organizations from Slovakia, Hungary, the United States and Switzerland filed a brief with the ICJ and were accepted as "friends of the court" in the case concerning the Gabcikovo-Nagymaros Hydropower Project between Hungary and Slovakia. This formal intervention was accepted by the court.[58]

The environmental side-agreement to the North American Free Trade Agreement (NAFTA) created several mechanisms for public participation in promoting the enforcement of national environmental laws in the United States, Mexico and Canada.

Similarly, the European Court of Justice (ECJ) plays a key role in the enforcement of European Community Directives. This includes environmental directives. Citizens have the ability to petition the European Parliament for enforcement action or implementation. The ECJ may require domestic legal remedies to be exhausted before dealing with the matter, or may appoint an ombudsman. The possibility of a citizen remedy exists under this system but significant legal and procedural barriers deter many complainants.

Complex legal issues remain about the extent to which environmental laws have a transboundary effect and are amenable to enforcement through national courts (for example, can an Australian law be enforced by Australian courts for breaches that occur outside the Australian Antarctic jurisdiction?). Conflict of law issues often arise for governments as well as "jurisdictional" issues. It is often the case that the larger an environmental problem or damage (affecting a river basin or many nations), the less likely there is to be an effective remedy. The legal position of intervening NGOs and citizens is much more tenuous than the position of governments in these situations. For this reason, there is a continuing focus on compliance and enforcement mechanisms under environmental treaties, and the role of NGOs.

The trend towards harmonization is increasing with international standard-setting through global and regional environmental and trade treaties and agreements. Compliance and enforcement is more likely to be available to governments and citizens in regional political and trade regimes such as NAFTA and the European Community.

The World Bank and the Asian Development Bank are examples of multilateral development institutions that have created a method for citizen participation in enforcement of internal bank policies and procedures in bank-financed projects. The World Bank created an Inspection Panel in 1994 to investigate claims filed by affected parties and to review the bank's compliance with its own policies and procedures.

There are some very important non-government resources and networks that can assist citizens seeking to participate in decisions and enforce international and national environmental law. The Environmental Law Alliance Worldwide (ELAW) is a global network of public interest environmental lawyers that shares information in defence of the environment. ELAW uses email and electronic databases to give these attorneys access to vital scientific and legal information for use in their cases. Freedom of information laws may mean that crucial information and data may be more available and accessible in some jurisdictions.

The International Network for Environmental Compliance and Enforcement (INECE) is an international network focusing on environmental law compliance and enforcement. INECE is collaborating with nations, organizations and professionals to assist them to effectively comply with and enforce environmental laws through networking, capacity-building and cooperation.

Many initiatives have been undertaken with the purpose of building capacity in local NGOs and government officials and developing their expertise in environmental enforcement, but the challenge is ongoing.

Innovative approaches to public participation

We have already discussed the importance of early, timely and adequately resourced public participation in determining issues, priorities, values and the scoping of studies, decision processes and inquiries. Similarly such participation may be necessary in enforcement priority-setting such as prosecution guidelines. This involves some risks, as public participation may have positive and negative consequences. However, the "capture" of government regulators by corporations and their timidity in prosecuting often provides a poor track record that can easily be improved. The challenge is how to involve the public in long-term strategies such as corporate environmental improvement, monitoring and audit programmes as well as ESD strategies.

Citizen participation in the context of environmental proceedings has evolved in most jurisdictions with a focus on how to ensure the citizens' right to participate as a party, regardless of the citizens' financial ability to do so in an effective manner. In some respects, the public and certain judiciaries have almost entirely overlooked the dynamics of the environmental litigation process. Without adequate resources to properly prepare a case for hearing, to retain experienced counsel and expert witnesses, and to participate fully throughout the entire proceeding, standing translates into little more than "participatory tokenism". One of the tools that has been used to reduce participatory tokenism is intervenor funding.

In 1989 the Province of Ontario, Canada, embarked on a groundbreaking experiment designed to facilitate public participation in the decision-making process, in the form of the Intervenor Funding Project Act.[59] Although, regrettably, this legislation has since been repealed, it represented at the time a quantum leap forward in providing, on the one hand, the financial means by which an intervenor's right to participate was transformed into the ability to effectively participate, while at the same time providing the decision-maker with a more informed and substantive factual basis upon which to base its decision.

Some jurisdictions in Canada followed suit, providing *intervenor funding* based on a variety of different statutory models.[60] New South Wales relied upon such mechanisms as the Environmental Defenders Office. In addition, the open standing provisions referred to above were reinforced by the court soon[61] evidencing a reluctance to award costs against intervenors that were acknowledged to be motivated by and acting in the public interest, and this was followed by a further reluctance to order security for costs to be posted by public interest litigants.

Access to justice is now accepted in the international arena as one of the essential pillars contributing to good environmental governance. The inability of parties in opposition to effectively present their case seriously undermines the concept of public participation as well as the integrity of the entire environmental decision-making process. There is little doubt that the introduction of appropriate intervenor funding programmes would increase the cost of project approval to some degree, although there is little evidence to suggest that the costs would be excessive or the programmes open to widespread abuse. Such has not been the case, by and large, with respect to the many and varied legal aid systems including the operation of Environmental Defender Offices now entrenched in almost all jurisdictions in the western world. Democracy has a price, and it is now generally recognized that balance and broad representation of competing interests are essential in maintaining the social stability and economic well-being of countries which rely upon democratic institutions to develop policies and programmes designed to further the public interest.

Conclusion

It is now a well-accepted principle that public participation and social and cultural values are necessary for the achievement of ESD. Contemporary environmental law at the global, regional and national levels mostly acknowledge these principles. However, serious concerns remain about the adequacy of public participation in the making of crucial environmental decisions (including policies, plans and projects). Participation is a methodology as well as an "end" or value in achieving ESD. This chapter argues that good policies and laws must pay closer attention to the type of issues to be resolved, as well as the purpose and context of decision-making processes. Public and private resources are scarce and citizens have limited time and priorities.

The most important level of decision-making for ESD strategies remains the determination of public policy options, choices and values. Increasingly many of these decisions are being made by the private sector or by an unelected public body or officials. The need for the application of the precautionary principle, good applied research and inquiry and the engagement with civil society is more important than ever. Participation strategies have largely evolved in isolated areas such as EIA or other planning laws. The role of the public in good governance and integrated approaches to ESD has not received a great deal of recent legal attention, because of the political sensitivity and legal complexity of the issues, that are not amenable to resolution by law alone. However, there is considerable evidence that law could play a far more significant role, particularly in implementing the principles developed under the Aarhus Convention that are central to environmental governance and good governance generally.

However, as noted in various sections in this chapter, there is a real danger of overrating what public participation, per se, is capable of achieving in environmental governance. Current trends indicate that public participation has become an exit gate for "experts" and representatives of the public in governance positions, where attempts at solving environmental problems have failed. It would be unfair and unrealistic to expect the public to resolve all the problems faced in the attempt to achieve ESD. Strategies to improve the process must therefore not overlook the fact that public participation is a useful tool for achieving ESD, but it is not the only tool in the toolbox.

Acknowledgement

The authors wish to gratefully acknowledge the assistance of their PhD student, Elizabeth Gachenga, in the preparation of this chapter.

Notes

1. *Report of the World Commission on Environment and Development*, UN Doc A/Res/42/187, (1987).
2. Convention on Biological Diversity, Rio de Janeiro, 5 June 1992, entered into force 29 December 1993, 1760 UNTS 79 (1992).
3. United Nations Framework Convention on Climate Change, 1771 UNTS 107; S. Treaty Doc no. 102-38; UN Doc. A/AC.237/18 (Part II)/Add.1; 31 ILM 849 (1992).
4. *Agenda 21, Programme of Action for Sustainable Development*, UN GAOR, 46th Sess., Agenda Item 21, UN Doc A/Conf.151/26 (1992).
5. United Nations Millennium Declaration, UN Doc. A/Res/55/2 (2000).
6. *Report of the World Summit on Sustainable Development*, UN Doc. A/CONF.199/20 (2002).
7. Plan of Implementation of the World Summit on Sustainable Development; available at <http://www.un.org/esa/sustdev/documents/WSSD_POI_PD/English/WSSD_PlanImpl.pdf>.
8. Peter P. Rogers, Kazi F. Jalal and John A. Boyd, *An Introduction to Sustainable Development* (2008).
9. Jacob Pak, Ken Conca and Matthias Finger, *The Crisis of Global Environmental Governance: Towards a New Political Economy of Sustainability* (New York: Routledge, 2008).
10. Richard E. Saunier and Richard A. Meganck, *Dictionary and Introduction to Global Environmental Governance* (London: Earthscan, 2009), p. 3.
11. John Graham, Bruce Amos and Tim Plumptree, *Governance Principles for Protected Areas in the 21st Century*, Durban, World Parks Congress 2003 (2003), p. iii.
12. John Scanlon and Francoise Burhenne-Guilmin (eds), *International Environmental Governance – An International Regime for Protected Areas* (Gland, Switzerland and Cambridge, UK; IUCN, 2004), p. 2.
13. Ibid., pp. 1–2.
14. Robert F. Durant, Daniel J. Fiorino and Rosemary O'Leary, *Environmental Governance Reconsidered: Challenges, Choices and Opportunities* (Cambridge, MA: MIT Press, 2004).

15. Stephen Dovers, *Environment and Sustainability Policy: Creation, Implementation, Evaluation* (Sydney: Federation Press, 2005), pp. 43–49.
16. Ibid. p. 50.
17. James Connelly and Graham Smith, *Politics and the Environment: From Theory to Practice* (New York: Routledge, 2008).
18. Michael Carley and Ian Christie, *Managing Sustainable Development*, 2nd edn (London: Earthscan, 2002), p. 44.
19. Convention on Access to Information, Public Participation in Decision-Making and Access to Justice in Environmental Matters, Aarhus, 25 June 1998, entered into force on 30 October 2001, 2161 UNTS 447; 38 ILM 517 (1999).
20. List of parties to the Treaty available at the United Nations Treaty Collection, <http://treaties.un.org/Pages/ViewDetails.aspx?src=TREATY&mtdsg_no=XXVII-13&chapter=27&lang=en#1>.
21. Rio Declaration on Environment and Development, UN Doc. A/CONF.151/26 (vol. I); 31 ILM 874 (1992).
22. Ibid, Principle 10.
23. Kofi A. Annan, Former Secretary-General of the United Nations; available at <http://www.unece.org/env/pp/>.
24. *Report of the World Commission on Environment and Development*. See Preamble, paras. 7 and 8. The linkage between environmental rights and human rights is further articulated in the stated objective of the Convention (art. 1) as follows: "In order to contribute to the protection of the right of every person of present and future generations to live in an environment adequate to his or her health and well being, each party shall guarantee the rights of access to information, public participation in decision-making, and access to justice in environmental matters in accordance with the provisions of this Convention."
25. Ibid., art. 4(3)(a).
26. Ibid., art. 4(3)(b).
27. Ibid., art. 4(3)(c).
28. Ibid., art. 4(4)(c).
29. Ibid., art. 4(4)(e).
30. Held in Lucca, Italy, 21–23 October 2002.
31. Meeting of the Parties to the Convention on Access to Information, Public Participation in Decision-making and Access to Justice in Environmental Matters, *Draft Lucca Declaration* (2002), paras. 14 and 27; available at <http://www.participate.org/conferences/mp.pp.2002.crp.1.e.pdf>.
32. Ibid., para. 1.
33. Thomas C. Beirerle and Jerry Cayford, *Democracy in Practice: Public Participation in Environmental Decisions* (Washington, DC: RFF Press, 2002).
34. Aarón E. Zazueta, *Policy Hits the Ground: Participation and Equity in Environmental Policy Making* (Washington, DC: World Resources Institute, 1995), p. 9.
35. Wendell Phillips, *Speeches, Lectures and Letters* (Boston: Walker, Wise & Co, 1864).
36. Sharon Beder, *Environmental Principles and Policies: An Interdisciplinary Approach* (Sydney: University of New South Wales Press, 2006).
37. Frans H.J.M. Coenen, *Public Participation and Better Environmental Decisions: The Promise and Limits of Participatory Processes for the Quality of Environmentally Related Decision-making* (Dordrecht: Springer, 2008), p. 2.
38. Zazueta, *Policy Hits the Ground*.
39. Coenen, *Public Participation and Better Environmental Decisions*.
40. Daniel Robinson, "Public Participation in Environmental Decision-making", *Environmental and Planning Law Journal*, vol. 10, no. 5 (1993), pp. 320–335.

41. An example of this is the provision for public participation in the United Nations Framework Convention on Climate Change, art. 6.
42. Resource Management Act 1991 (New Zealand).
43. Dovers, *Environment and Sustainability Policy*, p. 75.
44. Sally Eden, "Public Participation in Environmental Policy: Considering Scientific, Counter-scientific and Non-scientific Contributions", *Public Understanding of Science*, vol. 5, no. 3 (1996), pp. 183–204.
45. Dovers, *Environment and Sustainability Policy*, pp. 105–127.
46. Ibid., p. 114.
47. IUCN, *Resource Kit for Sustainability Assessment* (2009); available at <http://74.125.93.132/custom?q=cache:pxLk3P0XfOEJ:cmsdata.iucn.org/downloads/resource_kit_c_eng.pdf+IUCN+Resource+Book&cd=7&hl=en&ct=clnk&client=pub-2748287108348956>.
48. Susan Casey-Lefkowitz, "A Comparative Look at the Role of Citizens in Environmental Enforcement", *National Environmental Enforcement Journal*, vol. 12, no. 5 (1997), pp. 29–42.
49. Ibid.
50. Ibid.
51. Environment Planning and Assessment Act 1979 (New South Wales), ss 123 and 124.
52. *M.C. Mehta v Union of India* (1996) 4 SCALE SP 29.
53. *M.C. Mehta v Union of India and Others*, Writ Petition Civil no. 3727 of 1985.
54. M.C. Mehta has recently published a four-volume hardcover book entitled *In The Public Interest* (New Delhi: Praktiti Publications, 2009), detailing his career in public interest environmental litigation. Volumes 2, 3 and 4 contain compilations of judgments and orders of the Supreme Court of India relating to his cases as well as some of the various notifications issued by authorities. See also a pre-publication book review of Volume 1 by Professor Michael Jeffery, QC, in the *Macquarie Journal of International and Comparative Environmental Law*, vol. 5, no. 2 (2008), pp. 211–214.
55. Meeting of the Parties to the Convention on Access to Information, Public Participation in Decision-making and Access to Justice in Environmental Matters, *Draft Lucca Declaration*, 2002, available at <http://www.participate.org/conferences/mp.pp.2002.crp.1.e.pdf>.
56. Ibid.
57. For a full account of this type of environmental initiative see John Cronin and Robert F. Kennedy Jr., *The Riverkeepers* (New York: Simon & Schuster, 1999).
58. *Gabcikovo-Nagymaros Project (Hungary v. Slovakia)*, Judgment, [1997] ICJ Reports 7.
59. RSO 1990 c. I-13 (repealed 1996). One should note that a government formed by a political party other than the one responsible for its enactment in 1988 subsequently repealed this legislation.
60. In 1991 Manitoba followed Ontario, and Alberta introduced intervenor funding legislation in 1994.
61. *Oshlack v Richmond River Council* (1998) 193 CLR 72.

6

Human rights and the environment

Gudmundur Alfredsson

Environmental and human rights concerns overlap in significant ways.[1] Our lives, cultures, food, drinking water and sanitation, health, and homes are clearly affected by the environment. The same is true for the use and value of property. Empowerment, that is, opportunities to participate in political and economic policy and decision-making, as well as access to national and international justice, has an obvious impact on these situations and our responses to them. Respect for the freedoms of information, association and expression is necessary. So is non-discrimination. Poor and marginalized persons and groups need special attention, as they are most likely to face the consequences of environmental problems, often with dramatic results such as displacement, refugee flows, migration and relocation. Ways of life, from agriculture and fisheries to endless other cultural characteristics, will not be the same with pollution and ongoing and expected changes in the climate, ocean currents and rivers.

On a grander scale, global warming and rising sea levels will not only bring about population movements, but whole countries may go under water. It has been repeatedly in the news that the Maldives is looking at choices for protecting its islands against the encroaching sea, but questions about alternative territory for refuge or even resurrection of the state elsewhere are also being examined.[2] In line with these and similar concerns, the UN Human Rights Council, in the preamble to Resolution 7/23 of 28 March 2008,[3] recognized the particular vulnerability to the adverse effects of climate change of low-lying and small island countries, countries with low-lying coastal, arid and semi-arid areas, and areas liable

The future of international environmental law, Leary and Pisupati (eds),
United Nations University Press, 2010, ISBN 978-92-808-1192-6

to floods, drought and desertification.[4] In other places, new opportunities may arise as receding glaciers and sea ice make land and seabed areas more accessible. Even in these instances, territorial questions and the race for access to, control over and benefits from land and natural resources will inevitably put pressure on local and often marginal populations, including indigenous peoples, and their ways of life and cultures.

In this chapter, very much by way of examples rather than exhaustive listings, the connections in human rights instruments and monitoring work between certain well-established rights and the environment will be surveyed; emphasis will be placed on the rights to land and resources of indigenous peoples and how these relate to environmental qualities; efforts at mainstreaming or incorporating human rights into other UN programme activities will be described; and human rights elements in international environmental instruments and their application will be identified. By way of conclusion, one of the questions asked will be whether environmental law can draw lessons from human rights law including, in particular, public access and contributions to monitoring institutions.

The environment in human rights texts

To a large extent, in the human rights field, the application of human rights to environmental issues has meant reliance on a series of well-established human rights. A series of such connections between the environment and certain human rights has been established. These would include the rights to life, food, water, health, home, property and political participation, the freedoms of information, association and expression, and cultural rights. Environmental considerations also play a significant role as concerns the rights of indigenous peoples. The rules of equal enjoyment and the prohibition of discrimination in the enjoyment of these rights apply across the board.

Global instruments and monitoring efforts

In a general comment on the right to life set forth in art. 6 of the International Covenant on Civil and Political Rights (ICCPR), the Human Rights Committee, in charge of monitoring state compliance with the Covenant, noted that the "expression 'inherent right to life' cannot properly be understood in a restrictive manner, and the protection of this right requires that States adopt positive measures". It would therefore be desirable for states parties "to take all possible measures to reduce infant mortality and to increase life expectancy, especially in adopting measures to eliminate malnutrition and epidemics".[5]

Under the first Optional Protocol to the ICCPR, the Human Rights Committee has the competence to examine complaints received from individuals and sometimes individuals speaking on behalf of groups, after they have exhausted domestic remedies. The Committee has considered petitions about waste and radiation as threats to the right of life, without finding violations.[6]

In general, comments on the right to adequate housing,[7] the right to adequate food[8] and the right to water[9] under the International Covenant on Economic, Social and Cultural Rights, the Committee on Economic, Social and Cultural Rights has linked respect for these rights to environmental issues. In a general comment on the right to health, the Comment states at para. 4 that the express wording of art. 12(2) "embraces a wide range of socio-economic factors that promote conditions in which people can lead a healthy life, and extends to the underlying determinants of health, such as food and nutrition, housing, access to safe and potable water and adequate sanitation, safe and healthy working conditions, and a healthy environment". The comment goes on to specify in significant detail the legal obligations of states parties.[10] In the context of the state reporting procedure, Committee members have from time to time requested specific information about environmental harm that threatens human rights.[11] Now that the Committee on Economic, Social and Cultural Rights will acquire the ability to receive complaints when a newly adopted Optional Protocol to the Covenant enters into force, it will be interesting to see how soon they will have an opportunity to entertain complaints with environmental content.[12]

Likewise on health rights, the Committee on the Elimination of Discrimination against Women (CEDAW) has linked environment to the right to health in concluding observations on state reports, expressing concern about the situation of the environment and its impact on women's health.[13]

In art. 24(2)(c) of the 1989 UN Convention on the Rights of the Child, it says that states parties shall take appropriate measures to combat disease and malnutrition "through the provision of adequate nutritious foods and clean drinking water, taking into consideration the dangers and risks of environmental pollution". Furthermore, under art. 24(2)(e), information on hygiene and environmental sanitation and education is to be provided to all segments of society.

When examining state reports, the Committee on the Rights of the Child (CRC) has issued observations calling for better compliance with art. 24(2)(e). In concluding observations, the CRC has recommended to a state that it "take all appropriate measures ... to prevent and combat the damaging effects of environmental pollution and contamination of water supplies on children and to strengthen procedures for inspection". On another occasion, the Committee recommended that a state party "increase its efforts to facilitate the implementation of sustainable development programmes to prevent environmental degradation, especially as regards air pollution".[14]

Among the dozens of special investigative procedures under the UN Human Rights Council, there is a Special Rapporteur on Toxic Waste, operating under an original mandate set forth in Commission on Human Rights Resolution 1995/81. According to this and many subsequent resolutions, the mandate holder is authorized to investigate the effects of illicit dumping of toxic and dangerous products and wastes on the enjoyment of human rights, in particular on the rights of everyone to life and health, examine and receive communications on the illicit traffic and dumping of toxic and dangerous products and wastes, make recommendations on adequate measures to control, reduce and eradicate the illicit traffic in, transfer and dumping of toxic and dangerous products and wastes, and produce annually a list of the countries and transnational corporations engaged in such practices.[15] In para. 1 of Resolution 9/1 of 24 September 2008, the UN Human Rights Council strongly condemned "the dumping of toxic and dangerous products and wastes that have a negative impact on human rights".

In Resolution 9/1, para. 5(b), the Human Rights Council specifically drew the attention of the Special Rapporteur on Toxic Waste to the human rights responsibilities of transnational corporations and other business enterprises that dump toxic and dangerous products and wastes, to the question of rehabilitation of and assistance to victims, and to the question of ambiguities in international instruments that allow the movement and dumping of toxic and dangerous products and wastes, and any gaps in the effectiveness of the international regulatory mechanisms.

By Resolution 7/22 of 28 March 2008, also under the so-called special procedures, the Human Rights Council authorized the appointment of an independent expert on the issue of human rights obligations related to access to safe drinking water and sanitation. The tasks of the mandate holder include developing a dialogue with governments, relevant UN bodies, the private sector, local authorities, national human rights institutions, civil society organizations and academic institutions in order to identify and exchange views on best practices related to access to safe drinking water and sanitation, and making recommendations that could help in the realization of the Millennium Development Goals.[16]

At UNESCO, the 1972 Convention on the Protection of the World Cultural and Natural Heritage describes methods of cooperation for safeguarding the natural heritage which is increasingly threatened by the deterioration of the environment. States parties undertake to protect property forming part of the cultural and natural heritage situated on their territory and suitable for protection against disappearance, deterioration, destruction, abandonment, natural catastrophes or the outbreak or threat of an armed conflict. According to the Convention, "deterioration or disappearance of any item of the cultural or natural heritage constitutes a harmful impoverishment of the heritage of all the nations of the world" (art. 11).

In addition, this survey of global and regional instruments could be extended to humanitarian law,[17] refugee law,[18] human security,[19] international labour standards, and good governance in relation to such issues as health and safety conditions in the workplace, damage resulting from conflicts, and climate refugees. In the UN Global Compact, human rights and the environment are highlighted in one and the same instrument, intended for business to follow. One can also refer to the human rights–environment linkage in the Voluntary Guidelines to Support the Progressive Realization of the Right to Adequate Food in the Context of National Food Security, adopted in 2004 by the General Council of the Food and Agriculture Organization of the United Nations.[20]

It goes without saying that all of the above-mentioned rights must be exercised without discrimination of any kind as to race, colour, sex, gender, language, religion, political or other opinion, national, ethnic or social origins, property, birth, disability or other status.

Regional instruments and monitoring work

According to art. 24 of the 1981 African Charter on Human and Peoples' Rights, "All peoples shall have the right to a general satisfactory environment favorable to their development." The African Commission on Human and Peoples' Rights, entrusted with monitoring compliance with the Charter, has not dwelled much on environmental rights. The topic has come up in two working groups of the Commission, on Indigenous Populations/Communities in Africa and on Economic, Social and Cultural Rights. In its complaints capacity, in the case *The Social and Economic Rights Action Center and the Center for Economic and Social Rights v Nigeria*, the African Commission found that several articles of the Charter, including art. 24, had been violated, and appealed to the Nigerian Government to ensure respect for the rights relating to life, health and the environment of Ogoniland.[21]

The approach of the African Charter is based on peoples' rights, as a solidarity right under the so-called third generation of human rights, which raises a handful of problems. It is, of course, to be welcomed when a group such as the Ogonis is able to benefit. At the United Nations, in something of a parallel scenario, establishing peoples as holders of the right to development has contributed to a stalemate for more than twenty years. There is no serious ongoing monitoring work in relation to the UN Declaration on the Right to Development, adopted by the General Assembly in Resolution 41/128 of 4 December 1986,[22] since its meaning remains unclear, in part because of the peoples' provision. After all, if peoples have the right and the peoples are represented by governments, and these same governments represent the states that are supposed to guarantee the right, maybe there is a good reason for hesitation. Instead, the United Nations is increasingly engaged in a human rights-based approach to development.[23]

Article 11 of the 1988 Additional Protocol to the American Convention on Human Rights in the area of Economic, Social and Cultural Rights,[24] entitled "Right to a healthy environment", reads: "1. Everyone shall have the right to live in a healthy environment and to have access to basic public services. 2. The states parties shall promote the protection, preservation and improvement of the environment." The Inter-American Commission on Human Rights and the Inter-American Court on Human Rights have decided a number of cases relating to indigenous peoples where the environment has been a factor in alleged rights violations.[25]

With no direct reference to the environment in the European Convention on Human Rights, the European Court on Human Rights, in addressing issues with environmental aspects, has made use of other provisions in the Convention. Article 8 of the Convention can apply to environmental issues if, for example, pollution is directly caused by the state or the state has not sufficiently regulated private activities.[26] The Court has most often considered these problems with respect to the right to respect for the home, as provided for in art. 8, since it has been difficult to prove a causal link between the reported deterioration of an applicant's health and pollution. Within the framework of art. 8, the question can be posed in terms of positive or negative obligations of the state.

As concerns positive obligations, the Court has emphasized that a state must put in place adequate legislative and administrative measures which are aimed at effective prevention of damage that might be caused to the environment and to health.[27] The Court's case law has identified detailed obligations as concerns the decision-making process leading to the authorization and functioning of projects that may have an effect on the environment.[28] On several occasions, the Court has underlined the importance of public access to studies and other information evaluating danger to the environment.[29] Finally, there must be an effective appeal procedure in place.[30] In a recent case which concerned the exploitation of gold mines near populated areas, the Court, for the first time, referred to the precautionary principle and positive obligations in terms of art. 8 that are derived from this principle. The Court found that a state had failed to assess in advance the potential risks that the gold mine might have on the environment and the health of the population, and had neglected to take the necessary measures to protect the private lives and homes of the applicants.[31]

The methods employed by human rights monitoring institutions, now described, that is the ability to initiate an examination through complaints, access to the monitoring processes by individuals, groups and NGOs, and the appointment of independent experts to scrutinize country performances would certainly enhance the effectiveness of environmental protection.

The rights of indigenous peoples

It has long been said that the environment has never been and will never be endangered by indigenous peoples, as long as their cultures are traditional and untouched by outside influences. Customary indigenous ways of life are often based on fishing, gathering, herding and hunting, and these depend to a very large extent on the Earth being in a healthy state. In recognition of this close relationship, international human rights instruments, when dealing with the rights of indigenous peoples, directly address the environment, as well as self-governance and the rights to land and resources that would serve the same end. Primary among these instruments are the 2007 UN Declaration on the Rights of Indigenous Peoples and the 1989 ILO Convention on Indigenous and Tribal Peoples in Independent Countries (ILO Convention no. 169). The substance of case law from the Human Rights Committee in its supervision of the International Covenant on Civil and Political Rights, by and large, coincides with these instruments.

According to art. 27 of the ICCPR, members of minority groups shall not be denied the right, in community with other members of their group, to enjoy their own culture, to profess and practice their own religion, or to use their own language. In a general comment, on art. 27, the Human Rights Committee observed "that culture manifests itself in many forms, including a particular way of life associated with the use of land resources, especially in the case of indigenous peoples. That right may include such traditional activities as fishing or hunting and the right to live in reserves protected by law. The enjoyment of those rights may require positive legal measures of protection and measures to ensure the effective participation of members of minority communities in decisions which affect them."[32]

Under the first Optional Protocol to the same Covenant, in response to complaints received from individuals, and sometimes individuals speaking on behalf of groups, after they have exhausted domestic remedies, the Human Rights Committee has in a series of findings confirmed the protection of land rights and traditional economic activities of indigenous peoples as part of their culture.[33]

In General Recommendation no. 23 on indigenous peoples, the Committee on Elimination of Racial Discrimination has endorsed the same or similar rights to land, resources and political participation.[34]

The UN 2007 Declaration on the Rights of Indigenous Peoples, in a preambular paragraph, recognizes that respect for indigenous knowledge, cultures and traditional practices contributes to sustainable and equitable development and proper management of the environment. In art. 26, which stipulates the right of indigenous peoples to own, use, develop and control the lands, territories and resources that they possess by reason of traditional ownership and other traditional occupation or use, it says in para. 3 that "States shall give legal recognition and protection to these lands, territories and resources. Such recognition shall be conducted with due respect to the customs, traditions and land tenure systems of the indigenous peoples concerned." Article 28 provides that indigenous peoples have the right to redress, including just, fair and equitable compensation, for damage to their lands, territories and resources.

The key environment provision of the Declaration is in art. 29:

1. Indigenous peoples have the right to the conservation and protection of the environment and the productive capacity of their lands or territories and resources. States shall establish and implement assistance programmes for indigenous peoples for such conservation and protection, without discrimination.
2. States shall take effective measures to ensure that no storage or disposal of hazardous materials shall take place in the lands or territories of indigenous peoples without their free, prior and informed consent.
3. States shall also take effective measures to ensure, as needed, that programmes for monitoring, maintaining and restoring the health of indigenous peoples, as developed and implemented by the peoples affected by such materials, are duly implemented.

According to its preamble, the rights recognized in the Declaration constitute minimum standards for the survival, dignity and well-being of the indigenous peoples of the world. Within the special procedures programme of the UN Human Rights Council, a Special Rapporteur is entrusted with monitoring of state compliance with the human rights and fundamental freedoms of indigenous peoples.[35] Also under the Council, indigenous representatives can participate in and make statements on their concerns at an Expert Mechanism on the Rights of Indigenous Peoples.[36] The UN Permanent Forum on Indigenous Issues, a subsidiary body of the Economic and Social Council (ECOSOC), has a mandate to discuss indigenous issues related to economic and social development, culture, the environment, education, health and human rights. The Permanent Forum is also open to participation by indigenous groups.[37]

The ILO Convention concerning Indigenous and Tribal Peoples in Independent Countries 1989 (Convention no. 169) contains numerous references to the lands, resources and the environment of indigenous peoples. Article 2 provides that actions respecting indigenous peoples shall be developed with the participation of the peoples concerned; art. 4 provides that special measures for safeguarding the environment of such peoples are to be adopted consistent with their freely expressed wishes; arts. 6 and 7 provide that states parties must consult indigenous peoples and provide for their participation in formulating national and regional development plans that may affect them; art. 7(3) provides that environmental impact assessments of planned development activities must be done with the cooperation of the peoples concerned; "Governments shall take measures, in cooperation with the peoples concerned, to protect and preserve the environment of the territories they inhabit" according to art. 7(4); and there is a stipulation for the right to remedies in art. 12. Part II of the Convention, in particular arts. 14 and 15, addresses land issues, including the rights to own land and to participate in the use, management and conservation of these natural resources pertaining to their lands. Governments are required by art. 30 to make known to the peoples concerned their rights and duties. Some 20 states have ratified the Convention, most of them in Latin America.[38]

The mainstreaming of human rights

For a long time, international human rights law has been interpreted narrowly and employed in something of a splendid isolation, as this approach to a sensitive topic generally suited governments. Human rights were thus thought of and treated in corners of international organizations, mostly separate from other programme activities. With the 1993 World Conference on Human Rights seeking the integration of human rights into other work programmes of the United Nations,[39] more importantly with the repeated calls for the mainstreaming of human rights in the United Nations by former Secretary-General Kofi Annan, and through political backing to human rights mainstreaming by the 2005 World Summit,[40] the walls around human rights have started coming down, and we increasingly see references to and the use of human rights in the context of and relation to other international issues. It is now generally acknowledged that a human rights dimension is relevant and applicable to international and internal peace and security, from the prevention of violent conflicts to the restoration of peace after conflict, development, humanitarian relief, elections, good governance, anti-corruption, economic cooperation, trade, the activities of transnational corporations, and so on. The same is true for human rights and the environment, and this linkage is now more and more frequently on the table, as indicated by the survey above. A look at the output of the UN Human Rights Council reveals a continuing trend of this kind, but one can ask whether some of these links are still merely rhetorical and not practical in terms of actual change leading to human rights and environmental improvements.

In a preambular paragraph to Resolution 10/4 on human rights and climate change, adopted on 25 March 2009, the Council pointed out that, while these implications affect individuals and communities around the world, the effects of climate change will be felt most acutely by those segments of the population who are already in vulnerable situations owing to factors such as geography, poverty, gender, age, indigenous or minority status, and disability. In para. 3 of the same resolution, the Council encouraged relevant special procedure mandate holders and the Office of the High Commissioner for Human Rights (OHCHR) to give consideration to the issue of climate change within their respective mandates.

In the preamble to Resolution 10/12 of 26 March 2009, on the right to food, the Council noted that environmental degradation, desertification and global climate change are factors contributing to destitution and desperation, causing a negative impact on the realization of the right to food, in particular in developing countries.

The UN Human Rights Council adopted Resolution 9/6 of 24 September 2008 concerning a follow-up to the seventh special session on the negative impact of the worsening of the world food crisis on the realization of the right to food for all. In para. 3 the Council encouraged "States to mainstream the human rights perspective in building and reviewing their national strategies for the realisation of the right to adequate food for all." In a preambular paragraph to the same resolution, the Council recognized the complex character of the current global food crisis as a combination of several major factors, with negative impact by, *inter alia*, environmental degradation, drought and desertification, global climate change, natural disasters and the lack of the necessary technology, and that a strong commitment from national governments and the international community as a whole is required to confront the major threats to food security.

In a joint statement of 7 December 2009 to the Climate Change Conference in Copenhagen, some twenty special procedure mandate holders warned that a "weak outcome of the forthcoming climate change negotiations threatens to impinge upon human rights". They went on to observe: "Adaptation or mitigation measures, such as the promotion of alternative energy sources, forest conservation or tree-planting projects and resettlement schemes must be developed in accordance with human rights norms."[41]

In the above-mentioned resolutions, the Human Rights Council and its Special Rapporteurs have highlighted that the adverse effects of climate change will be felt most acutely by people who are already in vulnerable situations owing to such factors as geography, poverty, gender, age, indigenous or minority status, and disability. In June 2009, a Council panel stressed that a human rights perspective was indispensable to the ongoing negotiations leading to the Copenhagen Climate Change Conference in December 2009. In an opening statement, Deputy High Commissioner for Human Rights Kyung-wha Kang observed that "Climate change is related not only to environmental factors but also to poverty, discrimination and inequalities – this is why climate change is a human rights issue."[42] An analytical study by the OHCHR found that climate change-related impacts have a range of implications for the effective enjoyment of human rights, and human rights obligations and commitments can inform and strengthen policy-making in the area of climate change, promoting policy coherence, legitimacy and sustainable outcomes.[43]

In these and other resolutions, the Human Rights Council has expressly relied on a long series of instruments and reports. In addition to the Charter of the United Nations, human rights texts such as the *Universal Declaration of Human Rights*, *the International Covenant on Economic, Social and Cultural Rights*, *the International Covenant on Civil and Political Rights* and the *Vienna Declaration and Programme of Action* have been brought up. Reports and recommendations by human rights treaty bodies and special procedures have also been quoted. On the environment side, references have been made to the UN Framework Convention on Climate Change, as well as the relevant provisions of a series of declarations, resolutions and programmes of action adopted by major UN conferences, summits and special sessions and their follow-up meetings, such as the Bali Action Plan of the 2007 United Nations Climate Change Conference, 2005 World Summit Outcome, the Rio Declaration on Environment and Development, Agenda 21, the Programme for the Further Implementation of Agenda 21, the Johannesburg Declaration on Sustainable Development, and the Plan of Implementation of the World Summit on Sustainable Development.

Human rights in environmental instruments

In a 1996 advisory opinion on the use of nuclear weapons, the International Court of Justice placed the human being, if not human rights, at the centre of environmental law. The Court recognized "that the environment is not an abstraction but represents the living space, the quality of life and the very health of human beings, including generations unborn. The existence of the general obligation of states to ensure that activities within their jurisdiction and control respect the environment of other States or of areas beyond national control is now part of the corpus of international law relating to the environment."[44]

Significant references to human rights in environmental texts may have appeared before environmental concerns seriously entered human rights instruments and monitoring work. The growth in that process, however, seems to have slowed down, presumably for the same or similar reasons that often make the mainstreaming of human rights a contentious issue, namely the desire of many governments to limit their exposure to human rights, as well as the tendency of governments to politicize human rights in intergovernmental forums. That tendency has been seen to slow down human rights work, and it is understandable when policy- and law-makers in other fields try to avoid that type of situation.

The 1972 Declaration of the UN Conference on the Human Environment (known as the Stockholm Declaration)[45] established, in Principle 1, a foundation for linking human rights and environmental protection, declaring that man has a fundamental right to freedom, equality and adequate conditions of life, in an environment of a quality that permits a life of dignity and well-being. It also announced the responsibility of each person to protect and improve the environment for present and future generations. In Resolution 45/94 of 14 December 1995, entitled "Need to ensure a healthy environment for the well-being of individuals", the UN General Assembly recognized in operative para. 1 "that all individuals are entitled to live in an environment adequate for their health and well-being".

The 1992 Rio Declaration on Environment and Development[46] refers, in Principle 10, to appropriate access to environment information held by public authorities, the opportunity to participate in decision-making processes, and effective access to judicial and administrative proceedings, including redress and remedy. Other Principles of the Declaration dwell on the participation of women, youth, indigenous peoples and local communities, and specific links are made between environment and development in relation to the need of individuals, groups and organizations to participate in environmental impact assessment procedures and to know about and participate in decisions, particularly those that potentially affect their communities.

A series of subsequent global and regional instruments with a focus on environmental protection[47] relate to the themes that were brought up in the Stockholm and Rio texts, that is, access to information, public awareness, participation, as well as non-discrimination and special measures relating to the roles of women, indigenous peoples and local communities. Some of the texts call for access to justice via judicial or other institutions, as well as the right to remedies such as claiming compensation or other relief for damage caused by environmental harm. This trend is likely to continue; it was pointed out above that the human rights community would be present and promoting the human rights issues at the 2009 Copenhagen Climate Change Conference.

From a human rights perspective, the most frequently quoted text is the 1998 Convention on Access to Information, Public Participation in Decision-Making and Access to Justice in Environmental Matters (known as the Aarhus Convention).[48] It is a treaty open to states members of the UN Economic Commission for Europe (ECE), with arts. 17 and 19 providing for possible openings. The preamble states that "every person has the right to live in an environment adequate to his or her health and well-being, and the duty, both individually and in association with others, to protect and improve the environment for the benefit of present and future generations".

On the official website, it is proudly proclaimed that the Aarhus Convention "adopts a rights-based approach".[49] It seeks to guarantee rights of access to information, public participation in decision-making and access to justice in environmental matters. The Convention prohibits discrimination on the basis of citizenship, nationality or domicile against persons seeking to exercise their rights under the Convention. In particular, art. 1 refers to the goal of protecting the right of every person of present and future generations to live in an environment adequate to health and well-being. The Convention establishes minimum standards, that is, a "floor" and not a "ceiling", but it does not prevent a state party from adopting measures which go further in the direction of providing access to information, public participation or access to justice.

Under the Aarhus Convention, public authorities should proactively collect, update and disseminate legislative and policy documents, and international instruments relating to the environment and other information, and respond to specific requests without a requesting person having to state his or her interest. Information has to be made available within one month or, in exceptional cases, up to three months. The obligations are mainly those of public authorities, that is, governmental bodies from all sectors and at all levels, and bodies performing public administrative functions. Although the Convention does not focus on the private sector, privatized bodies with public responsibilities in relation to the environment, which are under the control of the aforementioned types of public authorities, are also covered by the definition. Bodies acting in a judicial or legislative capacity are excluded. States parties must obtain information on proposed and existing activities which could significantly affect the environment, including private sector activities. States parties must also ensure that consumer information on products is available.

The Aarhus Convention lists a number of exceptions to the obligation to inform, taking into account other political, economic and legal interests. A state may refuse to provide information if it is not in its possession; the request is manifestly unreasonable or too general; it concerns material not completed or the internal communications of a public authority; or if disclosure would adversely affect, *inter alia*, the confidentiality of public proceedings, international relations, national defence or public security, criminal investigations or trials, commercial and industrial secrets, certain personal data, and the interests of a third party. All exceptions are to be read restrictively, and a state can provide broader information than provided for by the Convention. Where non-exempt information can be separated from that not subject to disclosure, the non-restricted information must be provided. Refusal to provide information must be in writing and with reasons given for the refusal. Special disclosure obligations arise in case of imminent threat to human health or the environment.

To enhance the effectiveness of the Convention, states parties must provide information about the type and scope of information held by public authorities, the basic terms and conditions under which it is made available, and the procedure by which it can be obtained. The Convention foresees the establishment of electronic sites that would be publicly accessible and contain reports on the state of the environment, texts of environmental legislation, environmental plans, programmes and policies, and other information that could facilitate the application of national law.

Public participation is required under the Aarhus Convention in regard to environmental plans, programmes, policies, laws and regulations as well as all decisions on whether to permit or renew permission for industrial, agricultural and construction activities listed in an Annex to the Convention, as well as other activities which may have a significant impact on the environment. On specific projects, the public must be informed in detail about the proposed activity early in the decision-making process, and must have access to all relevant information, including the

site, description of environmental impacts, measures to prevent and/or reduce the effects, a non-technical summary, an outline of the main alternatives, and any reports or advice given. Public participation can be through
writing, hearings or inquiry. All public comments, information, analyses
or opinions shall be taken into account by a ratifying state in making its
decision. All decisions must be made public, along with the reasons and
considerations on which the decision is based. In order to facilitate meaningful participation, states parties are to promote environmental education and to recognize and support environmental associations and groups.

According to art. 9 of the Aarhus Convention, each state party must
offer the option of judicial review as well as a possible remedy if a request for information is denied. The proceedings must take place before
an independent and impartial body established by law. Standing to challenge information denials is limited to members of the public having a
sufficient interest or maintaining impairment of a right, as well as environmental NGOs. Standing to challenge violations of environmental law is
open to the public, including NGOs "where they meet the criteria, if any,
laid down in national law".

As to compliance procedures and enhancement of public participation
at the international level, art. 10 states that primary review of implementation rests with the Meeting of the Parties, at which certain NGOs may
participate as observers. Significantly, art. 15 of the Convention allows for
a provision on compliance review which mandates the establishment by
the Meeting of the Parties of a "non-confrontational, non-judicial and
consultative" arrangement for compliance review, which "shall allow for
appropriate public involvement and may include the option of considering communications from members of the public on matters related to
this Convention". Such a petition procedure has indeed been established,
marking an important first step in enhancing the effectiveness of international environmental agreements, and the first several cases have been
decided by the Aarhus Convention's Compliance Committee of independent experts serving in a personal capacity.[50] The Convention acknowledges its broader implications, expressing a conviction that its
implementation will "contribute to strengthening democracy in the region of the UNECE".

It is, of course, noteworthy that the Aarhus Convention remains essentially a European and Central Asian endeavour, and one can only hope
that efforts to expand the coverage will eventually succeed. As Kofi
Annan observed, "Although regional in scope, the significance of the
Aarhus Convention is global. It is by far the most impressive elaboration
of principle 10 of the Rio Declaration, which stresses the need for citizen's participation in environmental issues and for access to information

on the environment held by public authorities. . . . As such it is the most ambitious venture in the area of environmental democracy so far under-taken under the auspices of the United Nations."[51]

Concluding remarks

The most frequently employed human rights approach to the environ-ment, by several global and regional human rights instruments and moni-toring bodies, as surveyed above, relies on the use of a variety of specific rights as they relate to the environment. Monitoring reports and cases have thus, for the most part, not been based on a separate right to a safe and sound environment, but rather on a series of specific human rights. While instances of noise, deforestation, water pollution, toxic waste and other types of environmental harm have brought about the complaints, the decisions have been made on the basis of the rights to a home, cul-ture, health and so on. The question nevertheless arises whether or not an explicit right to a safe and environmentally sound environment, as in-deed a few of the instruments quoted above pursue, would improve the protection and further the international values represented by environ-mental law and human rights.

As Special Rapporteur of the UN Sub-Commission on Prevention of Discrimination and Protection of Minorities, Fatma Zohra Ksentini was entrusted with the task of undertaking a study on human rights and the environment. In Annex I to her final report in 1994,[52] she set forth Draft Principles on Human Rights and the Environment with some twenty-two quite far-reaching and detailed principles of rights and duties. The second of these reads: "All persons have the right to a secure, healthy and ecologically sound environment." The Sub-Commission in Resolution 1994/27 of 26 August 1994 welcomed, but did not endorse, the conclu-sions and recommendations contained in the final report as well as the draft principles, and the Commission on Human Rights as the parent body did not pursue the matter in a direct manner. Subject to serious drafting, the right to a clean and sound environment can add value, not instead of but in addition to the reliance on a series of specific rights.

The question could be posed: does human rights law hold lessons for environmental law? Indeed, it can be argued that some human rights achievements could serve as models for other areas such as the environ-ment where people are directly affected. When a human rights treaty is ratified, a state party commits itself under international law to provide for the standards in national law and to make available national avenues of redress with effective remedies, through access to mainly independent and impartial courts and/or national human rights institutions.[53] In addition to this access to national justice, several of the most significant human rights treaties also allow access to international justice by way of appeals of administrative practices and national court decisions to regional courts, quasi-judicial international treaty bodies and international investigators. With some variations, this access is provided to individuals, minority groups and indigenous peoples and NGOs who can in this manner challenge the governments of the countries in which they live. There is little doubt that this type of opening has served human rights well, not only in terms of the case law produced, but also as an educational and motivating factor for the public. The same is true for special procedures based on instruments other than treaties. There would seem to be every reason to employ this approach beyond the Aarhus Convention to many environmental texts, and both treaties and declarations, thus allowing direct public participation, motivation and involvement. And the number of environment complaints submitted under the human rights procedures is surprisingly low.

And finally, in answer to the question raised above, whether some of the links made between human rights and the environment, such as those in resolutions of the UN Human Rights Council, are more rhetorical than practical in terms of leading to actual change: yes, undoubtedly they are, but one would like to see them as building blocks that will in due course result in more concrete action. After all, it is a real challenge, as with many other cross-cutting issues and disciplines, that many human rights lawyers (the present author included), diplomats and activists are not familiar with environmental law and that many environmental lawyers, diplomats and activists still have more to learn about human rights law. This expanded knowledge would seem to be a prerequisite for a human rights-based approach to the environment and the successful mainstreaming of human rights in environmental law.

Notes

1. Six background papers prepared for a joint OHCHR-UNEP seminar on 16 January 2002 on human rights and the environment (for the report of the seminar, see UN Doc E/CN.4/2002/109) constitute an excellent survey of linkages between human rights and the environment in international human rights and environment instruments. See in particular Dinah Shelton, "Human Rights and Environment Issues in Multilateral Treaties Adopted between 1991 and 2001", Background paper no. 1; Dinah Shelton, "Human Rights and the Environment: Jurisprudence of Human Rights Bodies", Background paper no. 2; and Jonas Ebbesson, "Information, Participation and Access to Justice: the Model of the Aarhus Convention", Background paper no. 5. The Background Papers are available at <http://www2.ohchr.org/english/issues/environment/environ/> (accessed 4 July 2009). For an earlier survey, see Gudmundur Alfredsson and Alexander Ovsiouk,

"Human Rights and the Environment", *Nordic Journal of International Law*, vol. 60, no. 1–2 (1991), pp. 19–27.

2. Selma Oliver, "A New Challenge to International Law: The Disappearance of the Entire Territory of a State", *International Journal on Minority and Group Rights*, vol. 16, no. 2 (2009), pp. 209–243.

3. For the text of this resolution and other resolutions of the Human Rights Council mentioned in this chapter, see the website of the UN Office of the High Commissioner for Human Rights at <http://www.ohchr.org> under Human rights bodies.

4. For information about cross-cutting environmental and human rights issues, see the UNESCO website pages on national and regional enabling environments on the Inter-Sectoral Platform on Small Island Developing States, at <http://portal.unesco.org/en/ev.php-url_id=29602&url_do=do_topic&url_section=201.html>. All websites noted in this chapter were in July 2009.

5. Office of the High Commissioner for Human Rights, *General Comment no. 6 on Article 6 of the Covenant*, 1982, para. 5. The text is available at <http://www.unhchr.ch/tbs/doc.nsf/(Symbol)/84ab9690ccd81fc7c12563ed0046fae3?Opendocument>.

6. Communication no. 67/1980 (EHP v Canada), and Communication no. 645/1995 (Bordes and Temeharo v France). See below on complaints involving indigenous peoples' rights under art. 27 of the ICCPR.

7. *General Comment no. 4*, 1991; available at <http://www.unhchr.ch/tbs/doc.nsf/(Symbol)/469f4d91a9378221c12563ed0053547e?Opendocument>.

8. *General Comment no. 12*, 1999; available at <http://www.unhchr.ch/tbs/doc.nsf/(Symbol)/3d02758c707031d58025677f003b73b9?Opendocument>.

9. Economic and Social Council, *General Comment no. 15* on the right to water (articles 11 and 12), 2002; available at <http://daccessdds.un.org/doc/UNDOC/GEN/G03/402/29/PDF/G0340229.pdf?OpenElement>.

10. Economic and Social Council, *General Comment no. 14* on the right to the highest attainable standard of health, 2000; available at <http://www.unhchr.ch/tbs/doc.nsf/(Symbol)/40d009901358b0e2c1256915005090be?Opendocument>.

11. See examples provided by Shelton, "Human Rights and the Environment: Jurisprudence of Human Rights Bodies".

12. General Assembly Resolution 63/117, *Optional Protocol to the International Covenant on Economic, Social and Cultural Rights*, adopted on 10 December 2008.

13. See examples provided by Shelton, "Human Rights and the Environment: Jurisprudence of Human Rights Bodies".

14. Quoted by Dinah Shelton, "Human Rights and the Environment: Jurisprudence of Human Rights Bodies", Background paper no. 2, n 1 above.

15. Special Rapporteur to the UN High Commissioner for Human Rights, *Special Rapporteur on the Adverse Effects of the Movement and Dumping of Toxic and Dangerous Products and Wastes on the Enjoyment of Human Rights*; available at <http://www.ohchr.org> under Issues and Environment.

16. For a description of the early activities of the independent expert, see <http://www2.ohchr.org/english/issues/water/iexpert/index/htm>.

17. On the website of the International Committee of the Red Cross <http://www.icrc.org> there is a long list of instruments, reports and publications about the protection of the environment in conflict situations.

18. UN High Commissioner for Refugees, *UNHCR Environmental Guidelines*, June 1996; available at <http://www.unhcr.org/refworld/docid/42a01c9d4.html>.

19. For one recent study, see Dan Kuwali, "From the West to the Rest: Climate Change as a Challenge to Human Security in Africa", *African Security Review*, vol. 17, no. 3 (2008), pp. 18–38.

20. The Guidelines are available at <http://www.fao.org/righttofood/publi_01_en.htm> (accessed 15 July 2009). The FAO maintains pages on the right to food and links to food security at <http://www.fao.org/righttofood/index_en.htm>.

21. The text of the communication, no. 155/96 (2001), is available at <http://www1.umn.edu/humanrts/africa/comcases/155-96.html>. See also the website of the African Commission at <http://www.achpr.org/english/_info/news_en.html>.

22. Available at <http://www.unhchr.ch/html/menu3/b/74.htm>.

23. Relevant UNDP publications include *Access to Justice* Practice Note and *Human Rights in UNDP* Practice Note, both accessible at <http://www.undp.org/governance/practice-notes.htm>; and *Indicators for Human Rights Based Approaches to Development in UNDP Programming: A Users' Guide*, March 2006, at <http://www.undp.org/governance/docs/HR_guides_HRBA_Indicators.pdf>.

24. Inter-American Commission on Human Rights. See <http://www.cidh.org/basicos/english/basic5.prot.sn salv.htm>.

25. For case summaries, see Shelton, "Human Rights and the Environment: Jurisprudence of Human Rights Bodies".

26. *Lopez Ostra v Spain*, Application no. 16798/90; *Guerra v Italy*, Application no. 14967/89; *Surugiu v Romania*, Application no. 48995/99; *Powell and Rayner v the United Kingdom*, Application no. 9310/81; and *Moreno Gómez v Spain*, Application no. 4143/02. These and subsequently quoted cases can be accessed on the website of the Court at <http://www.echr.coe.int/ECHR/EN/Header/Case-Law/HUDOC/HUDOC+database/>.

27. *Budayeva v Russia*, Application nos. 15339/02, 21166/02, 20058/02, 11673/02 and 15343/02, paras. 129–132.

28. *Oneryildiz v Turkey*, Application no. 48939/99, para. 90; and *Hatton and Others v the United Kingdom*, Application no. 36022/97, para. 128.

29. *Guerra v Italy*, para. 60; *McGinley and Egan v The United Kingdom*, Application nos. 21825/93 and 23414/94, para. 97.

30. *Hatton and Others v the United Kingdom*, para. 128.

31. *Tatar v Romania*, Application no. 67021/01, para. 112. For analysis of these and other cases, see also Alan Boyle, "Environment and Human Rights", in *Max Planck Encyclopedia of Public International Law* (Max Planck Institute for Comparative Public Law and International Law and Oxford University Press, 2010); available at <http://www.mpepil.com>.

32. Office of the High Commissioner for Human Rights, General Comment no. 23 on Article 27 of the Covenant, para. 7; available at <http://www.unhchr.ch/tbs/doc.nsf/(Symbol)/fb7fb12c2fb8bb21c12563ed004df111?Opendocument>.

33. Some of the well-known cases are: *Bernard Ominayak, Chief of the Lubicon Lake Band v Canada*, Communication no. 167/1984, views adopted on 26 March 1990; *Kitok v Sweden*, Communication no. 197/1985, views adopted on 27 July 1988; *Apirana Mahuika et al. v New Zealand*, Communication no. 547/1992, views issued 16 November 2000. The texts of the Committee's views are available at the website of the UN Office of the High Commissioner for Human Rights at <http://www.ohchr.org> under Human rights bodies. For a listing of additional cases, see Shelton, "Human Rights and the Environment: Jurisprudence of Human Rights Bodies".

34. See <http://www.unhchr.ch/tbs/doc.nsf/(Symbol)/73984290dfea022b802565160056fe1c?Opendocument>.

35. For an account of the Special Rapporteur's activities, see <http://www2.ohchr.org/english/issues/indigenous/rapporteur/>.

36. The activities of the Expert Mechanism are described at <http://www2.ohchr.org/english/issues/indigenous/ExpertMechanism/index.htm>. This Mechanism replaced the better-known UN Working Group on Indigenous Populations (1982–2006).

37. The Permanent Forum's website is at <http://www.un.org/esa/socdev/unpfii/>.
38. For the ILO website on indigenous and tribal peoples, go to <http://www.ilo.org/indigenous/lang--en/index.htm>.
39. Paragraph 4 in Part I and para. 1–3 of Part II of the Vienna Declaration and Programme of Action. For the text, see <http://www2.ohchr.org/english/law/vienna.htm>.
40. Para. 126 of General Assembly Resolution 60/1 of 16 September 2005, entitled 2005 World Summit Outcome.
41. As quoted at <http://www.ohchr.org/en/NewsEvents/Pages/DisplayNews.aspx?NewsID= 9667&LangID=e>.
42. See <http://www.ohchr.org/EN/NewsEvents/Pages/Humanrightskeytoclimatechangenegotiations.aspx> (accessed 25 June 2009).
43. <http://www.ohchr.org/EN/NewsEvents/Pages/OHCHRanalyticalstudyClimateChange.aspx> (accessed 25 June 2009).
44. *Legality of the Threat or Use of Nuclear Weapons* (Advisory Opinion) (1996) ICJ Reports 226, para. 29.
45. Available at <http://www.unep.org/Documents.Multilingual/Default.asp?DocumentID= 97&ArticleID=1503>.
46. Adopted by the 1992 UN Conference of Rio de Janeiro on Environment and Development, available at <http://www.unep.org/Documents.Multilingual/Default.asp?document ID=78&articleID=1163>.
47. For a survey of these instruments in one time period, see Shelton, "Human Rights and Environment Issues in Multilateral Treaties Adopted between 1991 and 2001".
48. The website of the Aarhus Convention, including its text, list of ratifying states and institutions serving it, is at <http://www.unece.org/env/pp/mop3.htm>. See also Ebbesson, "Information, Participation and Access to Justice: The Model of the Aarhus Convention". For analysis of these and other cases see also Boyle, "Environment and Human Rights".
49. At <http://www.unece.org/env/pp/contentofaarhus.htm>.
50. For a listing of cases and the Compliance Committee's conclusions, see <http://www.unece.org/env/pp/pubcom.htm>.
51. As quoted at <http://www.unece.org/env/pp/>.
52. In UN document E/CN.4/Sub.2/1994/9.
53. For a prime example, see article 2(2) of the ICCPR.

Part II

International legal regimes in transition

7

Development and the future of climate change law

Michael B. Gerrard and Dionysia-Theodora Avgerinopoulou

Introduction

The success or failure of multilateral environmental agreements (MEAs) on climate change will affect the everyday lives of billions of people worldwide for generations to come. The United Nations Framework Convention on Climate Change[1] (UNFCCC) and its principal implementing instrument, the Kyoto Protocol,[2] are the main global MEAs on climate change. This chapter briefly summarizes them and then delineates the core issues currently under international negotiations that are going to shape future global climate change law and policy. Recent scientific findings challenge world leaders to alter their nations' development paths and set aside short-term economic interests in order to achieve substantial cuts in the emissions of greenhouse gases (GHGs). Several of the world's leading GHG emitters have refused to undertake serious GHG emission reduction commitments, either saying they will not move until others have gone first, or denying any responsibility. The long-term necessity for action by every nation is easy to forget amid the pressing developmental needs of the developing countries and the need to maintain the quality of life for the population in the developed countries.

The first part of this chapter examines the current status of the climate change MEAs. It also discusses the core issues that those treaties leave open to be determined by the ongoing negotiation process for the adoption of the next implementing protocol to the UNFCCC that may succeed the Kyoto Protocol and shape the "post-2012" climate change

The future of international environmental law, Leary and Pisupati (eds),
United Nations University Press, 2010, ISBN 978-92-808-1192-6

regime. Core issues under negotiation include questions on where to set GHG emission reduction targets for industrialized countries, and whether developing countries should undertake any emission reduction obligations. Special consideration is given to the upcoming role of the newly devised categories among developing nations, especially the rapidly developing economies. New agreements will need to address GHG emission sources that cross national borders, especially international shipping and aviation, and the destruction of forests, the key non-energy contributor to GHG emissions. International agreement is also needed on implementing and financing mitigation policies and on decision-making concerning geoengineering methods that might help reduce the effects of climate change.

The second part of the chapter acknowledges the challenges posed to international environmental law by the unavoidable rise in temperature and, under this perspective, it chiefly discusses the adaptation needs for both developed and developing countries. States and international institutions need to reorganize existing institutions and policies in order to cope with the new realities. Adaptation also includes preparedness programmes for natural disasters and humanitarian crises at both the national and international levels, as well as strategies to effectively prepare for forced migration in the future due to climate change. Lastly, the chapter discusses the interaction between international human rights provisions and climate change law. Climate change impacts put an additional stress on the enjoyment of fundamental human rights, especially by vulnerable populations. International human rights dispute settlement forums have recently begun facing climate change-related disputes.

The chapter concludes that climate change is becoming the public face of unsustainable development. New instruments of law and policy should be devised in order to successfully address the new realities that climate change poses for global human and natural systems. To this end, it recapitulates some of the main themes to be negotiated in connection with the adoption of the post-2012 global legal regime.

Mitigation policies under the current and future international climate change regime

Current status of the international climate change regime

In 1992, the UNFCCC was adopted as the first global treaty on climate change. It established an overall, comprehensive structure for dealing with the main aspects of climate change. As of 26 August 2009 the UNFCCC has been ratified by 193 parties.[3] The UNFCCC is based on the principles of: (a) inter-generational and intra-generational responsibility of the parties, namely, that parties are obliged to participate in the achievement of the goals set by the UNFCCC "in accordance with their common but differentiated responsibilities and capabilities";[4] (b) the special consideration of developing countries "that are particularly vulnerable to the adverse effects of climate change";[5] (c) precautionary measures;[6] (d) the promotion of sustainable development by policies and measures that are integrated with national development programmes; and (e) cooperation among the parties "to promote a supportive and open international economic system that would lead to sustainable economic growth and development in all Parties, particularly developing country Parties".[7] These are the principles that should guide the efforts toward the achievement of the main objective of the UNFCCC, namely the "stabilization of greenhouse gas concentrations in the atmosphere at a level that would prevent dangerous anthropogenic interference with the climate system".[8]

As a framework convention, the UNFCCC includes very general provisions. The details of their meaning and the methods and institutions for implementing them need to be further specified. The Kyoto Protocol is the first implementing agreement for the UNFCCC. It was signed in Kyoto, Japan, in December 1997 and entered into force on February 2005. As of 26 August 2009, the Kyoto Protocol has been ratified by 188 parties to the UNFCCC and the European Community, including thirty-six industrialized nations, with the prominent exception of the United States.[9] The Kyoto Protocol specified the percentages by which industrialized countries should reduce their collective GHG emissions by 2012.[10] It introduced innovative finance mechanisms that would help in the achievement of the emissions reduction target, the so-called "flexibility mechanisms" that include: (a) emissions trading or cap-and-trade; (b) Joint Implementation (JI); and (c) the Clean Development Mechanism (CDM), a special mechanism designed to include projects in developing countries. For the functioning of these mechanisms, the Kyoto Protocol created the carbon credits or emissions reduction units (CERs), which gave rise to the carbon markets and may emerge as the largest commodity in the world.[11]

Climate change represents one of the primary drivers for investment in clean technology (cleantech) today. According to a report by the World Bank, the value of the global carbon market was approximately US$64 billion in 2007, up from approximately $31 billion in 2006.[12] The European Union Emissions Trading Scheme (EU ETS) alone accounted for approximately $50 billion of this market, with the Japanese carbon market also being a significant segment. Europe and Japan currently make up a dominant portion of the market.[13] Cleantech investment, including energy efficiency, renewable energy, carbon capture and storage, measuring and monitoring equipment, and other technologies will continue rising. However, it is notable that, when first introduced, the EU ETS presented some flaws, most prominently shown by the extreme price volatility, though this has moderated. The designers of the post-Kyoto mechanisms face the challenge of devising the most effective and least market-distorting ways to reduce unpredictability and maintain market confidence.

From scientific uncertainty to clear scientific consensus

Initially, certain officials in the United States and some of the other major GHG emitters invoked scientific uncertainty surrounding questions regarding anthropogenic sources of climate change, the degree of severity of the phenomenon and the appropriate measures to combat climate change, as grounds for their refusal to ratify the Kyoto Protocol. However, in response to popular demand and the overwhelming scientific evidence presented by the Intergovernmental Panel on Climate Change (IPCC) and other prestigious national scientific institutions, most of the signatory parties to the UNFCCC, apart from the United States, eventually ratified the Kyoto Protocol.

The vagueness of the phrases and terms in the provisions of both the UNFCCC and the Kyoto Protocol reflects the scientific uncertainty which prevailed in the past, regarding both their objectives and the specific policies to combat climate change. For instance, according to Article 2, the UNFCCC seeks "stabilization of greenhouse gas concentrations in the atmosphere at a level that would prevent dangerous anthropogenic interference with the climate system". The UNFCCC does not, however, stipulate what the level of the "dangerous anthropogenic interference" (DAI) with the climate environment should be. Neither did the agreement associate this objective with any specific emission reduction target or any upper threshold in the temperature rise. In a separate paragraph (not related to the DAI goal) it merely "urged" Annex I countries to reduce their GHG emissions to 1990 levels by 2000, mixing its binding legal nature with soft law. Nor is a subsequent interpretation of the meaning of this provision an easy matter, since assessing what actions lead to DAI involves complex scientific and evaluative judgements. There continues to be scientific dispute over where to set the threshold after which the anthropogenic interference with the climate system will become dangerous. It would ordinarily be desirable to set a goal that embodies a comfortable margin of safety, but even small increments in where the goal is set can have serious effects on economic and social development. Thus, setting the goals is a matter of enormous scientific, economic and political complexity and difficulty. Fortunately, the global scientific community has largely moved on from the question of whether human activities are contributing to climate change.

Where to set the target?

In the 2007 *IPCC Fourth Assessment Report*[14] ("AR4"), the most authoritative recent study of climate change and its global impacts, carbon dioxide levels in the atmosphere in 2005 were estimated at 379 parts per million (ppm). Since 2005, other research institutions estimated carbon dioxide levels to have increased up to 382 ppm by 2007[15] and to have reached 387 ppm by July 2009.[16] The report found that high levels of emissions are certain to continue in the short to mid-term. Discussion has, therefore, centred on identifying a point at which emissions concentration might be stabilized in future, to keep adverse impacts to a minimum. Until recently, the international scientific community mostly held that the threshold at which carbon dioxide should be stabilized is 450 ppm carbon dioxide equivalents (CO_2 eq). Such an atmospheric level was thought to result in a rise of temperature of no more than 2 °C, a rise that would lead to managable impacts on the state of the natural environment.[17] Recently however, the world-renowned climate change scientist, Dr James Hansen, argued that the proposed threshold and the subsequent emissions reduction percentages that scientists had been proposing were products of miscalculations, and were not adequate to keep the temperature at safe levels to "effectively avoid the dangerous anthropogenic interference with the environment".[18] Dr Hansen urged that the actual target should be to stabilize carbon dioxide concentration at a level of 350 ppm CO_2 eq.[19]

Even with the less ambitious targets for atmospheric concentrations, the international community has fallen far short of adopting the emissions reduction targets necessary to succeed in avoiding the most serious impacts of climate change. According to IPCC AR4, in order to achieve the much less stringent target of 490–535 ppm, global emissions could still peak by 2020 and then fall sharply by 2050 to 80 to 85 per cent below 2000 levels. Despite the fact that there is scientific agreement over the necessity to adopt the aforementioned targets, most of the developed countries (Annex I countries) have stated their intention to adopt less stringent targets than necessary, while developing countries have declared their firm intention not to undertake any emission reduction obligation under the future protocol. These positions will likely make the attainment of safe thresholds extremely difficult, if not impossible.

On 9 July 2009 there was a positive development in the international negotiations: the group of the eight most industrialized countries of the world (G8), an unofficial but politically influential forum, met in Rome, Italy. Under the leadership of the United States President, Barack Obama, the group decided that participating countries will reduce their emissions by 80 per cent by 2050. The G8 requested that the developing countries should reduce their emissions by 50 per cent within the same timeframe. In addition, there was a general agreement that the average temperature should not rise more than 2 °C. This was the first time that the United States had made a commitment on the international stage to reduce its emissions. President Obama reaffirmed his intention to become involved and to do his best to secure ratification of the upcoming protocol by the US Congress. However, the G8 meeting did not produce any announcement regarding short- and medium-term emissions reduction targets, which raises questions about the final achievement of the long-term goals.

Negotiations toward the post-2012 era

The first commitment period for the implementation of the Kyoto Protocol ends in 2012. Negotiations over terms for the second commitment period have been ongoing since December 2005, in order to shape the so-called "post-2012" law and policy architecture. At the 2007 UN Climate Change Conference in Bali, the Conference of the Parties (COP14) of the UNFCCC decided to launch a "roadmap" in order "to enable the full, effective and sustained implementation of the Convention through long-term cooperative action, now, up to and beyond 2012, in order to reach an agreed outcome and adopt a decision at its fifteenth session" in Copenhagen, Denmark, on December 2009 (the Bali Action Plan).[20] In subsequent meetings, the COP produced a "Revised Negotiating Text" (RNT) in which the parties stated their proposals and their main points of agreement regarding the post-2012 protocol and the overall global climate change governance regime.[21] The Bali Action Plan, the RNT and unilateral statements by the parties include the most recent information on the development of the international negotiations, which form the subject of this chapter.

Major issues that the framers of the post-2012 regime will have to decide upon include the adoption of an implementing protocol, pursuant to article 17 of the UNFCCC that will succeed the Kyoto Protocol, and shape the new mitigation and adaptation strategies. Fundamental questions regarding the new world mitigation strategy include the following:
1. By how much are the industrialized countries willing to reduce their emissions of GHGs?
2. What are major developing countries, such as China and India, willing to do in order to reduce the growth of their emissions?
3. How is the help needed by developing countries to engage in reducing their emissions going to be financed? And how is that money going to be managed?

4. How will deforestation be reduced? How will countries with large forests be compensated for avoiding deforestation and for replacing forests that have been cleared?
5. Will economic sectors generating seriously important amounts of GHG emissions, such as international shipping and aviation, be eventually regulated in relation to climate change?

Discussions also include questions on the appropriate baseline year, namely, whether it should be either 1990, which is the benchmark year that the United Nations uses for the emission reduction calculations, or a later year, such as 2000 or 2005, an alternative that some of the industrialized nations prefer. Many developing countries support 1990 as the base year, because this would force rich nations to cut back their emissions more sharply, leaving developing nations more room to expand their economies. Another question is which should be the main time line for the emission reduction. At present, there are two main time lines; the first refers to emission targets up to 2020 and the second up to 2050. Lastly, establishing additional interim targets would aid monitoring and enforcement of mitigation commitments.

Copenhagen Conference

The Fifteenth Conference of the Parties was held in Copenhagen, Denmark, in 2009. The results fell far short of those hoped for in the Bali Action Plan. On the final day of the conference, the leaders of twenty-eight major countries agreed on a three-page document, the Copenhagen Accord. The COP itself did not formally adopt the Copenhagen Accord, but merely "took note" of the document.

The most important elements of the Copenhagen Accord are:
1. The parties reaffirm the need to "urgently combat climate change" and agree that global temperature increases should be limited to 2 °C.
2. The parties agree that financial assistance should be provided to the least developed countries, small island developing states and Africa, to help them adapt to climate change.
3. The parties were given until 31 January 2010 to submit their domestic mitigation targets, actions and policies. (A total of fifty-five countries have done so.)
4. Implementation of these targets, actions and policies by the developed countries will be subject to monitoring, reporting and verification under rigorous and transparent procedures. Implementation by developing countries will be subject to domestic measuring, reporting and verification subject to "international consultation and analysis".
5. The developed countries collectively commit to an amount "approaching" $30 billion for the period 2010–2012 to help developing countries

with emissions mitigation, adaptation, and reduction in deforestation. The developed countries will also mobilize $100 billion annually by 2020 for these purposes.

This final item – providing substantial funds to the developing countries – is a major accomplishment of COP 15. The relative contributions of different developed countries to these sums has not been decided. It appears that a significant portion of these funds may come from private sector purchases of offsets from developed countries, under the Kyoto Protocol's Clean Development Mechanism or whatever succeeds it. There is concern, however, that some of the money will be at the expense of previously provided international development assistance. The contribution of the United States is likely to come in large part from international offsets as part of a cap-and-trade system; but that is contingent on US legislation.

Another important accomplishment is that the major emerging economies, most notably China, India and Brazil, for the first time committed to take actions to reduce their emissions. These commitments are not always quantified emissions reductions; China, for example, has committed to a decrease in its emissions intensity (that is, amount of GHG emitted per unit of economic activity). However, as a practical measure COP 15 eliminated the distinction made by the Kyoto Protocol that the world is sharply divided between developed and developing countries, and only the former have obligations to reduce their GHG emissions.

The selection of a 2 °C temperature rise objective was highly controversial. Many of the small island states and some African nations objected that this degree of warming would drown them; they called instead for a 1.5 °C objective. The Copenhagen Accord calls for a reassessment of this goal and other items in 2015, to reflect the latest science available at that time. However, it is far from clear that even this 2 °C objective will be met – national commitments do not seem to add up to nearly achieving that goal.

At the end of COP 15, the future of the UNFCCC process was unclear. The conference had fallen far short of expectations, the requirement for unanimous votes had blocked adoption of several positions that the great majority of the delegates appeared to support, and the overall negotiations were generally thought to have been cumbersome. COP 16 will be held in Mexico in November–December 2010; it is expected that several, much smaller, groupings of major economies will meet frequently throughout 2010 in an effort to resolve many of the most difficult issues.

Prospects for mitigation by the industrialized countries

As discussed above, according to the available scientific data regarding the safe threshold before DAI occurs, Annex I countries should reduce their GHG emissions by at least 25 per cent by 2020, relative to their 1990 emissions. In the long run, Annex I countries should further reduce their emissions by 80 per cent by 2050. It is noteworthy that not all countries are expected to be able to reduce their emissions to this extent. The international climate agreements distinguish between large and small states, even for developed countries, so that some type of flexibility can be maintained with respect to mitigation obligations. Due consideration should be given to comparability of effort among the nations.[22] Achieving an overall global level of GHG emissions reduction will require effort by all countries: most importantly, by the most industrialized countries, which are the major economies and most of the major GHG emitters, and by the rapidly developing countries, most notably China, India and Brazil. Among the industrialized countries, those with the largest GHG emissions are, in descending order, the United States, the twenty-seven countries of the European Union as a whole (EU-27), Russia, Japan, Canada and Australia. China has recently surpassed the United States as the largest emitter.

Position and participation of the United States

As the world's largest economy and the first or second – depending on the year of measurement – largest source of GHGs, there will never be an effective global plan to address GHG emissions without the active participation and leadership of the United States.[23] However, the United States is the only industrialized country that has not ratified the Kyoto Protocol. One of the major reasons the Senate did not ratify the Kyoto Protocol (in addition to the lack of binding commitments by China and the other rapidly developing countries) was the scientific uncertainty, in some quarters, surrounding the connection between the phenomenon of global warming and anthropogenic interference with climate, despite the overwhelming scientific indications to this end. Only in February 2007 did the White House of President George W. Bush for the first time recognize the scientific authority of the IPCC and declared that the work of the IPCC "captures and summarizes the current state of the climate science and will serve as a valuable source of information for policy makers ... including the finding that the Earth is warming and that human activities have very likely caused most of the warming of the last 50 years".[24] The subsequent change of governing party brought a change in United States foreign relations, including the participation of the United States in the global alliance to combat climate change. President Barack Obama, after his inauguration on 20 January 2009, made climate protection a top priority of his administration. Since their takeover of Congress in the 2006 election, Democrats have held the majority in both legislative bodies, the House of Representatives and the Senate. Consequently, there are now stronger prospects than in the previous eight years for vigorous domestic legislation and leadership at the international level in the fight for mitigation of and adaptation to climate change. President Barack Obama and congressional leaders have proposed a "cap-and-trade" bill that would return United States emissions back to 1990 levels by 2020, namely a more than 15 per cent reduction from current levels. The so-called Waxman-Markey bill, which seeks to reduce United States GHG emissions 17 per cent below 2005 levels by 2020, was approved by the House of Representatives in June 2009. As of February 2010, there was considerable uncertainty concerning the prospects for passage of a counterpart bill in the Senate. The rules of the Senate currently require at least sixty of the one hundred senators to support a bill before it may be adopted, and fewer than sixty senators have pledged support for cap-and-trade legislation for GHGs.

President Obama has demonstrated his willingness on behalf of the United States to participate in the climate change negotiations. Nonetheless, the emission reduction target promoted by the Waxman-Markey bill is not so bold so as to give the United States a leading role in the negotiations, and the continuing uncertainty over prospects in the Senate further diminish President Obama's negotiating position.

A new role for the developing nations regarding mitigation

According to the principle of "common but differentiated responsibility", developing countries have undertaken no emission reduction obligation under either the UNFCCC or the Kyoto Protocol. Developing countries are the non-OECD countries plus Mexico, South Korea and Turkey, excluding countries with economies in transition (pursuant to the terms used by the UNFCCC and Kyoto Protocol: non-Annex I countries). Developing countries are divided into further groups which may well enjoy differentiated treatment under the new protocol. One such group is the least developed countries (LDCs), which will have no emission reduction obligations, while they may receive additional financial and technical assistance in order to adapt to climate change impacts.

A second group is the newly devised "rapidly developing countries" or "rapidly developing economies" (RDEs). Countries in this group have a better capacity than other developing countries to undertake mitigation obligations; among them, Brazil, China, India, Indonesia and Mexico are participants in the Major Economies Forum. Brazil, South Africa, India and China have formed themselves into the "BASIC" group, and played a significant role in Copenhagen. In addition to their capacity to combat climate change, the RDEs are or will soon become major GHG emitters. Until now, the burden of reducing GHG emissions has mostly fallen on the states that produced in the past and are responsible for "historic emissions". During recent decades, however, the RDEs, with their growing economies and consequent growing need to consume energy and other natural resources, have started contributing meaningfully to global warming. To understand the importance for these countries to undertake GHG mitigation obligations, one must take into account the high and continuously increasing rates of GHG emissions. For instance, in 1990, the combined GHG emissions of China and India added up to 57 per cent of the US total,[25] by 2000 they equalled US emissions,[26] and by the year 2006, China alone surpassed the United States.[27] Although emitting less than one-quarter of anthropogenic sources of carbon dioxide now, developing nations in total are expected to emit about two-thirds of the new emissions to the atmosphere. Moreover, between 2005 and 2030, GHG emissions from non-OECD countries are expected to increase by an average of 2.5 per cent each year.[28]

A new international agreement needs to establish an intermediate category for this second group of developing countries (the RDEs), in order to provide for obligations that these countries should undertake, even though lesser than the obligations to be imposed upon industrialized nations. It further ought to provide for incentives that would promote the development of efficiency, so that the economic activity of RDEs becomes less energy-intensive, primarily through the adoption of new technologies and investment in less carbon-intensive sectors, such as the services sector. A major question, therefore, is whether the RDEs will agree to undertake emission reduction obligations under the new international agreements. Next, the chapter discusses the positions of China, India and Brazil, three countries included in both the RDEs and the Major Economies Forum.

Positions and participation of China, India and Brazil

It is estimated that China is currently the world's largest GHG producer, and its emissions are increasing rapidly, along with economic growth and rising energy demand.[29] China's emissions have grown by about 80 per cent since 1990, strongly driven by increased consumption of electricity generated from coal. It is, thus, crucial that China commits to control its emissions in the post-2012 era. On the eve of the Copenhagen conference, China stated that it would reduce carbon dioxide emissions per unit of GDP (i.e. its emissions intensity) in 2020 by 40–45 per cent compared to 2005 levels. India, Asia's third largest economy (after China and Japan), has stated that it will not accept cuts in its GHG emissions, since such cuts could potentially undermine the energy consumption, transportation needs and even food security of its people. India may be the second most populous nation, however, it is responsible for only 4.6 per cent of global carbon dioxide emissions, while the United States produces 20.9

per cent of global emissions. Brazil has denounced GHG emission reduction obligations for developing countries under an upcoming protocol.[30]

In general, the majority of developing countries adopt the position that only countries responsible for historic emissions – namely, the industrialized countries – should undertake emission reduction obligations, while they themselves should not compromise their pace of development. Their stance is that it might be appropriate for them to undertake mitigation action at the national level, provided that they receive adequate financing and relevant technology transfer from developed countries or international institutions to this end.

Nationally appropriate mitigation actions

In view of the positions of the participating countries in the negotiations, post-Kyoto agreements are expected to impose some soft obligations upon developing countries. According to the RNT, "each developing country Party shall, in accordance with Article 4.1 of the UNFCCC, elaborate a low-carbon emissions development strategy" and "[D]eveloping country Parties shall commit to integrate low-carbon/emissions development strategies covering all key emitting sectors into national and sectoral strategies, and have them in place as soon as possible and no later than 2012."[31]

New themes in future climate change international regulation

Financing investments in mitigation technology and technology transfer

The Copenhagen Accord provides that nationally appropriate mitigation actions by developing countries will be voluntary and contingent on financial and technical support by developed countries, thus establishing a link to the financial and technology mechanism designed under the UNFCCC. The Copenhagen Accord also declares an intent to establish the Copenhagen Green Climate Fund "as an operating entity of the financial mechanism of the Convention to support projects, programme, policies and other activities in developing countries related to mitigation including REDD-plus, adaptation, capacity-building, technology development and transfer".[32]

The Copenhagen Accord also declared that "[i]n order to enhance action on development and transfer of technology we decide to establish a Technology Mechanism to accelerate technology development and transfer in support of action on adaptation and mitigation that will be guided by a country-driven approach and be based on national circumstances and priorities".[33]

"REDD-plus"

There are estimations that a vital contribution to the reduction of carbon dioxide concentrations up to 50 per cent of the total carbon reduction could come from regulating activities related to the forestry sector and land use change.[34] Tropical deforestation is one of the largest causes of global GHG emissions. Current estimates are that 17–20 per cent of global carbon dioxide emissions emanate from tropical deforestation. In addition, tropical rainforests continue to sequester carbon at a rate of a few tonnes of carbon dioxide per hectare each year. It is, thus, vital to preserve them. Furthermore, the cloud cover over tropical rainforests provides an insulation belt, which can reduce the local ground temperature by as much as 5 °C. This insulating effect is lost after forests are cleared. Without conserving tropical forests, it may be impossible to stabilize carbon and avoid the disastrous impacts of global warming.[35]

Under the current legal regime, forest carbon trading is only possible through CDM projects that only allow afforestation and reforestation projects. Carbon credits from other forestry-related projects can only be traded and sold in the voluntary carbon market. At the UNFCCC's COP 13 in Bali, a new mechanism was discussed to deal with emissions from deforestation and degradation of tropical forests in developing countries, commonly referred to as REDD (reducing emissions from deforestation and degradation).[36] In Copenhagen substantial progress was made on establishing an enlarged REDD mechanism, REDD-plus, that would include, in addition to REDD, a financial incentive scheme for developing countries that conserve and sustainably manage their forests, based on verifiable changes in carbon stocks, that could have trading value. The REDD-plus mechanism will encompass activities which reduce anthropogenic GHG emissions from deforestation and forest degradation, and increase anthropogenic removals from afforestation, reforestation and enhancement of forest carbon in developing countries.

The Clean Development Mechanism and emerging technologies

A further question relates to use of the CDM to produce CERs, not only through application of tested and proven technologies for mitigation, as has been the case until now, but also from the development and application of research projects in emerging technologies. This question has been raised especially in relation to carbon sequestration projects. Carbon sequestration includes both biological sequestration and carbon capture and storage (CCS) mechanisms.[37] Biological sequestration refers to the capacity of plants to take up carbon dioxide through the process of photosynthesis, and then store it in plant biomass and in soil organic matter. Pilot projects using biological sequestration techniques include, for example, the use of algae to absorb carbon. CCS mechanisms refer to the use of engineered systems to capture carbon dioxide before it is emitted into the atmosphere, and then to inject it into reservoirs for long-term storage. The use of emerging technologies such as the integrated gasification combined cycle (primarily for coal-fired electric power plants, and also for waste management, cement and glass manufacture, and iron and steel manufacture) should be encouraged by the new protocol, not only by the provision for economic incentives via the CDM, but also through other flexible emission trading mechanisms.

Geoengineering

Some UN scientists hold that the upcoming legal regime should support research and development (R&D) and application of geoengineering.[38] The United States National Academy of Sciences defined the new term "geoengineering" as "options that would involve large-scale engineering of our environment in order to combat or counteract the effects of changes in atmospheric chemistry".[39] Geoengineering proposals fall into at least three broad categories:

1. Reducing the levels of atmospheric GHGs through large-scale manipulations. GHG remediation projects seek to remove GHGs from the atmosphere, e.g. iron fertilization of the oceans.[40]
2. Creating a cooling influence on Earth by reflecting sunlight, e.g. solar radiation management projects seek to reduce the amount of sunlight striking the Earth and thus counteract global warming.[41]
3. Various hydrological geoengineering projects aiming to change the climate without directly or indirectly removing GHGs, or directly influencing solar radiation. These principally act by limiting Arctic sea ice loss. Keeping the Arctic ice is seen by many commentators as vital, due to its role in the planet's albedo and in keeping methane, an important GHG, locked up in permafrost.[42]

Some reports present geoengineering as a very attractive solution, finding some techniques to be capable of reversing the warming effect of a doubling of the level of carbon dioxide in the atmosphere when compared to pre-industrial levels.[43] Some say the use of geoengineering techniques might be unavoidable in the global effort to keep the Earth's temperature within safe limits. Further, some geoengineering techniques can be achieved at little cost. On the other hand, it could be difficult to safely predict the effectiveness and ancillary impacts of several techniques, since climate modelling is a science with large margins of inaccuracy. Various criticisms have been made of geoengineering, pointing out potential disadvantages or downsides of some of the techniques which may need to be monitored or controlled, or may alternatively weigh against a particular technique. Techniques that block some sunlight, while allowing GHG emissions to continue, could have unpredictable impacts on ecosystems that depend on sunlight. This approach would also allow rising concentrations of carbon dioxide in the atmosphere, some of which is converted into carbonic acid when it comes into contact with ocean water, adding to the acidification of the oceans, a serious ecological problem in its own right. Some of the techniques themselves may have serious side effects and cause significant foreseen or unforeseen harm. For example, ozone depletion is a risk of some geoengineering techniques, notably those involving sulfur delivery into the stratosphere. For this reason, opposition to some early schemes has been intense, with respected environmental groups campaigning against them.

Thus far there is no international legal framework to directly regulate the development and application of geoengineering techniques. One relevant international agreement relates to the weaponization of geoengineering, which is generally prohibited by the 1977 Environmental Modification Convention (ENMOD).[44] Taking into account the potential contribution that geoengineering could have in climate change mitigation, as well as the potential dangers that geoengineering experiments and applications would bring with them, it is necessary that a legal framework be adopted to address geoengineering as a whole. The regulatory framework would need to include the basic policy and legal principles upon which geoengineering could be conducted, and special provisions regulating comprehensive impact assessment, R&D, safety issues, international consultations, financial facilitation for research and, possibly, application of geoengineering technologies.

Transition from the fuel-based economy to a low-carbon economy

It is primarily coal, oil and, to a lesser extent, natural gas that create GHG emissions contributing to climate change. The fulfilment of the main obligation in the UNFCCC for the parties to stabilize their GHG emissions requires the parties to create or find alternative or substitute sources of energy to replace potentially dangerous hydrocarbons and facilitate sustainable development.[45] This is a challenging enterprise for numerous reasons.

First, a post-Kyoto regime introducing deep cuts in fossil fuel emissions will, among others, bring considerable geopolitical changes in the distribution of wealth among countries. For instance, the added strategic significance of low-carbon fuels in a carbon-constrained world could bolster the position of a natural gas-rich country such as Russia, while severely undermining the strategic importance of the Middle East countries in global politics. The world political power reallocation is a factor that should be taken into account when predicting the possibilities for the transition to a low-carbon economy.

Second, the demand for energy is exploding internationally, and all forecasts, including those from the IEA and the United States Department of Energy, agree that GHG emissions will increase steeply during the foreseeable future.[46] One indicator is that the construction of power generation facilities is expanding as populations increase, especially in developing nations, leading to a risk of run-away global warming.[47] In order to respond to the increasing demand for energy and at the same time lower GHG emissions, there is an urgency that the world economy moves toward the use of renewable, low-carbon energy sources, such as wind, solar power and biomass, as well as new alternative energy-generating technology. It is similarly urgent to develop and apply energy-efficient technologies so that the need for power can be minimized.

International finance that is necessary for power capacity construction in developing countries should not flow independent from certain environmental metrics, but should aim to finance alternative technologies. The new protocol should offer strong incentives for the move to a green, low-carbon economy.

A question that remains open at the international level is the use of nuclear energy as a climate change strategy. There is much divergence in the approaches of different countries to the use of nuclear power as an alternative energy resource. On the one hand, nuclear energy is non-carbon-based, except during uranium mining and processing, and can be generated in abundance. Some countries, such as India recently, have found an additional pro-nuclear argument by invoking the need to combat climate change.[48] They choose not to join the Nuclear Non-Proliferation Treaty (NPT) and opt instead for a nuclear future. On the other hand, the issues of nuclear waste management, nuclear proliferation and safety remain unresolved, and there is widespread public opposition in many countries, even to the peaceful uses of nuclear power, as memories of the disasters at Chernobyl and Three Mile Island still survive. There are also serious economic and timing questions with respect to the large-scale expansion of nuclear power, and the issue of whether the large amount of capital required could be better deployed towards renewable energy and energy efficiency.

International aviation and shipping transportation

One of the most important fields that has not been subject to international climate change regulation is transportation. The IPCC calculates that transportation contributes 23 per cent of global energy-related GHG emissions.[49] International maritime shipping accounts for 11.8 per cent of the total contribution of the transportation sector to carbon dioxide emissions, with aviation representing 11.2 per cent, rail transport 2 per cent and road transportation the biggest share, 72.6 per cent.

Carbon dioxide and other GHG emissions related to transportation are inversely proportional to fuel economy.[50] More stringent fuel economy standards and fuel-related energy-saving technologies should be high on the list of ways to mitigate GHG emissions from transportation. Suitable substitutes might include low-carbon electricity, natural gas, propane, hydrogen or second-generation biofuels.[51] However, fuel economy is just one way to cope with the impact of transportation on global warming. Further incentives for investment in infrastructure should be provided in order to facilitate, for example, more widespread commercialization of electric vehicles, since the electrification of personal transportation seems to be crucial for mitigation. Land development patterns that encourage use of public transport are another essential element.

The international dimensions of transportation, and especially international aviation and maritime transportation, are among the sectors currently under consideration for inclusion in the future global emissions trading scheme under the upcoming protocol. According to the RNT, international maritime shipping and aviation sectors need to play their part in limiting emissions.[52] Global sectoral approaches could address emissions that cannot be attributed to any particular economy. Multilateral collaborative action would be the most appropriate means to address emissions from international aviation and the maritime transport sectors, and for this reason the International Civil Aviation Organization (ICAO) and the International Maritime Organization (IMO) should proceed to global regulation in connection with the processes for the adoption of the new protocol. In cooperation with these two intergovernmental organizations, the parties to the climate change regime are expected to commence negotiations in 2010 on two global sectoral agreements, addressing international aviation and maritime emissions, respectively, with a view to concluding the agreements in 2011.

The inescapable realities that adaptation to climate change poses to international environmental law

This part of the chapter looks at natural disaster and humanitarian crisis preparedness, national security and human rights dimensions of adaptation to climate change.

Development of adaptation policies

The Earth's ecosystems are already experiencing a rise in the average global temperature of about 0.8 °C in comparison to pre-industrial levels.[53] Projections by the IPCC and other bodies show the planet continuing to get warmer for many years, even in the unlikely event that the most optimistic projections of human action are realized. As discussed in the first part of the chapter, all current indications are that the developing world will not accept measures that seriously impede its development, while the developed world will not accept measures that seriously diminish current lifestyles. Thus, at least in the absence of breathtaking and unanticipated technological breakthroughs, the adverse effects projected by the IPCC and others will probably occur. Accordingly, new policies need to be developed to prepare human and natural ecosystems for adaptation to climate change. In view of the above, international law will have, *inter alia*, to: (a) adapt to the new circumstances that global warming will create and, especially, to protect the world's most vulnerable regions; (b) cope with future climate disasters, including droughts, floods and resulting mass migrations; (c) deal with national security concerns; and (d) protect human rights.

Adaptation is the second pillar in the fight against climate change, next to mitigation, and is vital for the increase of the world's resilience to climate change impacts. Adaptation is one of the main objectives of the UNFCCC,[54] one of the five key building blocks required for a "strengthened future response to climate change" by the Bali Action Plan, and the theme of the Nairobi Work Programme on impacts, vulnerability and adaptation to climate change (NWP).[55] The latter has as its main purpose to help countries improve their understanding and assessment of the impacts of climate change and make improved decisions on practical adaptation actions and measures.[56] Up to the present, however, there have been no comprehensive studies or global action plans addressing even the fundamental aspects of research, design and application of adaptation policies. Vital sectors of the economies of many countries – (especially, developing countries), such as agriculture, fisheries and tourism, will be adversely affected by climate change impacts. However, there has been only limited planning on how these sectors will cope with climate change.

In addition, the way that countries will adapt those sectors to face the impacts of climate change will also affect their mitigation efforts. For example, climate change will affect new sustainable land management policies that will shape the role of soils in carbon sequestration and GHG emissions. Numerous adaptation technologies must be employed in a variety of settings and may include, for example, infrastructure construction (dykes, sea walls, harbours and railways), building design and structure, and technology related to drought-resistant crops. The distribution of climate change impacts is expected to vary considerably among regions and countries. Developing countries, and particularly the poorest and most marginalized populations within these countries, will be the most adversely affected by the impacts of climate change and the most vulnerable to its effects, due to their limited ability to adapt to the upcoming circumstances. Lastly, adaptation policies should differ according to the vulnerability of each region.

Adaptation via natural disaster and humanitarian crisis preparedness

Climate change is already increasing the intensity and frequency of natural disasters.[57] For instance, precipitation events are becoming more severe due to climate change; heavier rainfall and shifts in rainfall patterns mean increased likelihood of both flash flooding and drought. Hurricane intensity has increased significantly in the last fifty years. Extreme temperature highs may cause deadly heatwaves, while lack of precipitation is associated with unusual drought and with secondary effects, such as forest wildfires in areas of drought. Natural disasters and increased risks due to climate change affect not only developing countries, but also developed countries with natural disaster preparedness mechanisms in place. However, mechanisms, as well as institutions and policies, designed in the era before climate change may prove to be inadequate to face the climate change challenge, and thus may need to be reshaped. The mega-fires in 2007 destroyed thousands of hectares of forests in the developed, North Mediterranean countries.[58] All the affected countries had fire prevention programmes and competent agencies in place, but these had been designed to cope with forest fires that were regular in extent and force and not with the fast-paced and high-temperature fires that were generated by drought over extensive forest regions. Thus, even existing natural disaster preparedness projects need to be adapted in both developed and developing countries in order to face the new challenges that climate change generates.

In many developing countries, primarily LDCs, humanitarian crises will occur due to natural disasters. A report on the human impacts of climate change, presented by the Global Humanitarian Forum headed by former UN Secretary-General Kofi Annan, estimates that global warming already counts for some 300,000 deaths per year and that it could rise to half a million casualties by the year 2030.[59] Similar numbers are also supported by other analyses such as that by Oxfam International.[60] The Global Humanitarian Forum qualified impact of climate change on humanitarian issues as a "silent crisis". Kofi Annan described global warming as the "greatest emerging humanitarian challenge of our time", while of all forms of humanitarian crisis, the IPCC posited as early as 1990 that "the gravest effects of climate change may be those of human migration".

Forced migration

Apart from the humanitarian aspects, forced migration will also be a major issue of national security at the transnational level and especially regarding bilateral relationships between neighbouring countries. Climate change threatens to dramatically increase human movement both within states and across state borders. Although there can be no accurate estimates of actual numbers of displaced persons, many suggest that between 200 and 250 million people will be displaced by environmental causes more or less related to climate change before 2050.[61]

Forced migration is already an acute issue of national security for the small island states. Back in 2001, the people of the island nation of Tuvalu reached agreement with New Zealand for the latter to accept an annual quota of refugees fleeing due to expected inundation of their island because of rising sea levels.[62] Since then, the people of Kivalina, Alaska, have said they will also need to evacuate their homes for similar reasons.[63] Papua New Guinea's Carteret Islands in the Pacific have been the first low-lying island to evacuate their population due to climate change. In 2005, a political decision was reached to evacuate the Carterets and resettle their population of 2600 on the larger Bougainville Island, since the Carterets may be completely submerged as soon as 2015. The issue of forced migration for the thirty-nine island nations is so widespread that their respective governments formed the Alliance of Small Island States in 1990 to serve as an advocate for them.[64]

In addition to small island states, in future scenarios it is projected that rising sea levels and the associated disappearance of low-lying coastal lands could conceivably lead to massive migration, involving hundreds of millions of people, in Central America, South Asia and Southeast Asia. For instance, in Bangladesh, one of the most densely populated countries in the world, the risk of coastal flooding is growing and could leave some 30 million people searching for higher ground, while 20 per cent of the country's total landmass could be submerged under the sea water.

Migration on this unprecedented scale requires a global institutional response, as well as several changes in the interpretation of international legal instruments relating to other traditional notions of forced migration. The Copenhagen Accord did not refer to climate change refugees at all. There is at present no internationally agreed definition on what it means to be an "environmental migrant", a "climate change refugee" or a "environmentally displaced person". People migrating for environmental reasons do not fall within any one particular category provided by the existing international legal framework, and the aforementioned terms have no legal meaning under international refugee law. Questions on definitions have clear governance implications, forming the appropriate location of environmental migration both procedurally – as an international, regional, or local responsibility – and thematically, for instance, a subject under the existing refugee protection framework or under the UNFCCC regime. In order for the international community to effectively adapt to forced migration, additional institutional arrangements are necessary, while existing international legal instruments should be revised.[65]

Safeguarding national security

Natural disasters and forced migration, as well as infectious diseases, food and water shortages, may lead to the collapse of weak and failing states and may create new and additional national security considerations. Climate change can act as a multiplier of national instability phenomena, while the severity of these threats to national security depends on the number of degrees of rise in temperature and its consequences. The higher the temperature rises, the more serious could be the national security issues created. Current predictions of global temperature rise lead in turn to scenarios involving armed conflict between nations, at least unless effective adaptation measures are put in place.[66]

Climate change can lead to the flooding of major coastal cities, the destruction of vital infrastructure such as main transportation links, and other socially and economically catastrophic impacts. Climate change impacts will worsen existing problems, such as poverty, social tensions, environmental degradation, ineffectual leadership and weak political institutions. State failure might be a result of extensive global warming as well although, according to an assessment conducted in the United States, climate change alone is unlikely to trigger failure in any state up to 2030.[67] In the short term, climate change can threaten domestic stability in some states and potentially contribute to intrastate or, less likely, interstate conflict, particularly over access to increasingly scarce water resources. An illustrative case study is that of Darfur, Sudan, where UNEP's environment and conflict analysis found that regional climate variability, water scarcity and the steady loss of fertile land are important underlying factors in the conflict:[68]

> The decrease in the availability of fertile land and water has been compounded by the arrival of people displaced from conflict-affected areas in southern Sudan during the civil war ... as climate change may further compound water and land stresses, Darfur and indeed the entire Sahel region – recently dubbed "ground zero" for climate change[69] – will need to place adaptation at the center of their development and conflict prevention plans. In addition to resolving the long-standing ethnic tensions in Darfur, durable peace will indeed depend on addressing the underlying competition for water and fertile land.[70]

On the international level, the opening of new northerly sea routes and the access to untapped natural resources in the Arctic enabled by global warming could generate conflict. There are predictions that Arctic waters could be ice-free in summers by 2013, much earlier than previously thought. The United States, Russia and Canada are among the countries attempting to claim jurisdiction over Arctic territory alongside Nordic nations. The North Atlantic Treaty Organization (NATO) has started preparing for an intensified "scramble for resources" as melting glaciers and sea ice open up previously inaccessible areas to exploitation, and is ready to deploy troops in the Arctic, in order to safeguard stability in the region in cooperation with other institutional allies, such as the Arctic Council and the European Union.[71] The potential for wars related to climate change impacts is so profound that on 17 April 2007 the United Nations Security Council (UNSC) debated whether the potential for global warming to cause wars brought it within the UNSC's authority over international peace and security. The majority of countries, many international institutions and the United Nations itself supported a "long-term global response" to deal with climate change. Such response should include unified efforts including measures adopted by the UNSC.[72] Ultimately, climate change will completely reshape our perceptions around national and global security.

How climate change discourse has shaped international human rights law

Climate change is already undermining the realization of a broad range of internationally protected human rights, primarily including the rights to water, food, health and property, and rights associated with livelihood, culture, migration, resettlement and personal security in the event of conflict.[73] The primary binding source texts for human rights are the 1966 International Covenant on Civil and Political Rights[74] (ICCPR) and the International Covenant on Economic, Social and Cultural Rights[75] (ICESCR), both of which derive from the 1948 Universal Declaration of Human Rights.[76] Regional binding agreements on human rights protection also exist within Europe, the Americas and Africa.[77] These international instruments discuss primarily the "old" harms on human rights and not the new and additional future harms posed by climate change. In order to address this gap, the Office of the High Commissioner for Human Rights produced a Report that was endorsed by the tenth special session of the Human Rights Council.[78] The Report advocated for a human rights-based approach to climate change mitigation, and adaptation strategies that would promote the empowerment of individuals and groups as active agents of change and not as passive victims. The Report also highlighted the impact of climate change on those already living in vulnerable situations due to poverty, gender, age, minority status and disability. In the same session, the Human Rights Council adopted a resolution on human rights and climate change, stressing particularly the protection of the right to housing and to an adequate standard of living for poor populations under threat.[79]

An illustrative example on how climate change could directly affect the fulfilment of human rights is its impacts on available water resources. Scientists predict that global warming will have significant impacts on water resources around the world, leading to shortage of potable and irrigable water and consequently food in some regions. Some areas will become wetter and others drier, resulting in more frequent and severe droughts and related famines in some regions and higher flood risks in others.[80] Shifts in temperature and precipitation are also expected to have serious adverse effects on water quality, such as ecological disruptions to fish, plant and wildlife populations, blooms of nuisance algae and losses or impairments to both coastal and inland wetlands.[81] According to the IPCC Report, *Climate Change and Water*, "observed warming over several decades has been linked to changes in the large-scale hydrological cycle such as increasing atmospheric water vapour content.... Changes in water quantity and quality due to climate change are expected to affect food availability, stability, access and utilisation."[82]

Within the climate change debate, there is a recent evolution in the literature and political discourse relating to the "right to development"[83] to what have been called "greenhouse development rights" (GDR).[84] According to this approach, the right to development leads to a framework for mitigation and adaptation strategies by suggesting these strategies should take priority to ensure the enjoyment of the fundamental human rights already threatened by current low levels of development.[85] Thus, human rights dimensions introduce additional checks and balances to the global, regional and domestic climate change policies.

Lastly, it is notable that litigants have also started to use human rights instruments and dispute settlement forums in order to address harms caused by climate change. Petitions have been filed with several international commissions concerning the adverse effects of climate change on indigenous peoples or protected sites. For instance, in December 2005, the Chairperson of the Inuit Circumpolar Conference, on behalf of herself and all affected Inuit regions in the United States and Canada, filed a petition against the United States with the Inter-American Commission on Human Rights, the investigative arm of the Organization of American States. The petition alleged that the United States infringed the human rights of the plaintiffs by degrading the Arctic, in large part due to the failure of the United States to curb its GHG emissions.[86] Because the

United States did not accept the jurisdiction of the tribunal, the Commission could not accept the petition as admissible. It did, however, invite the petitioners to a public hearing where the issue of joint liability of the states was at least raised, at this point theoretically. Human rights litigation involving climate change cases has only just started. This trend seems likely to grow.[87] However, there are several issues to be resolved before submissions become successful, such as the proof of causal link and attribution of liability.

Concluding remarks

Climate change poses certain inescapable realities. These will pose serious challenges for international environmental law. In our view, the inescapable realities are as follows. First, the planet will continue to get warmer for many years, even if the most optimistic projections of human action are realized, and these projections are much more optimistic than what is likely to actually happen. Thus, the adverse effects projected by the IPCC and others will probably occur. Second, the developing world will not accept measures that seriously impede its development. Third, the developed world will not accept measures that seriously diminish current lifestyles.

In view of the above, we believe international law will face the following tasks:

- Coping with future climate disasters (e.g. droughts, floods, agricultural failures, resulting mass migrations);
- Managing the large flows of money and other resources that will be necessary to deal with these future disasters, including determining who will pay, who will get the money and through what mechanisms;
- Managing the diffusion and adoption of new technologies, such as carbon capture and storage, and technologies for renewable energy and energy efficiency;
- Developing mechanisms to finance energy efficiency and renewables, and in particular to align incentives and rewards;
- Dealing with growing demands for geoengineering as a solution, and determining how the world community will make decisions on what measures to adopt and how to pay for them.

Notes

1. United Nations Convention on Climate Change, Rio de Janeiro, 4 June 1992, entered into force 21 March 1994, 31 ILM 849; available at <http://unfccc.int/2860.php>.

2. Kyoto Protocol to the United Nations Framework Convention on Climate Change, Kyoto, 11 December 1997, entered into force 16 February 2005, 37 ILM 22; available at <http://unfccc.int/essential_background/kyoto_protocol/items/1678>.

3. See "List of Signatories and Ratification of the Convention" at the official website for the UNFCCC; available at <http://unfccc.int/files/na/application/pdf/unfccc_ratification_20090826.pdf>.

4. See UNFCCC, Preamble and art. 3(1).

5. Ibid., art. 3(2) and art. 4(4).

6. Ibid., art. 3(3).

7. Ibid., art. 3(5).

8. Ibid., art. 2.

9. See *Kyoto Protocol Status of Ratification*; available at <http://unfccc.int/files/kyoto_protocol/status_of_ratification/application/pdf/kp_ratification_20090826corr.pdf>.

10. United Nations Environment Programme, *Industrialized Countries to Cut Greenhouse Gas Emissions by 5.2%*; available at <http://unfccc.int/cop3/fccc/info/indust.htm>.

11. See Irwin Speizer, "A Convenient Truth", *Institutional Investor (Americas Edition)*, vol. 42, no. 5 (2008), pp. 96–101.

12. The World Bank, *State and Trends of the Carbon Market 2008* (2008); available at <http://siteresources.worldbank.org/NEWS/Resources/States&Trendsformatted06May 10pm.pdf>.

13. New Carbon Finance Press Release, *Economic Researchers Predict $1 Trillion US Carbon Trading Market by 2020* (2008); available at <http://www.newcarbonfinance.com/download.php?n=new_carbon_finance_press_release_us_carbon_market2.pdf&f=filename&t=ncf_downloads>.

14. Rajendra K. Pachauri and Andy Reisinger (eds), Intergovernmental Panel of Climate Change, *IPCC Fourth Assessment Report (AR4), Climate Change 2007*: Synthesis Report, Contribution of Working Group I, II and III to the Fourth Assessment Report of the Intergovernmental Panel on Climate Change, (Geneva: IPCC, 2007), p. 104.

15. See, for example, Brian Dawson and Matt Spannagle, *The Complete Guide to Climate Change* (New York: Routledge, 2009), p. 68.

16. Visit <http://co2now.org> stating monthly data on CO_2, as measured by the United States National Oceanic and Atmospheric Administration (NOAA) and the Mauna Loa Observatory.

17. In the late 1980s, the Advisory Group on Greenhouse Gases (AGGG) determined that a 2°C increase was "an upper limit beyond which the risks of grave damage to ecosystems, and of non-linear responses, are expected to increase rapidly". Frank R. Rijsberman and Robert J. Swart, *Targets and Indicators of Climate Change* (Stockholm: Stockholm Environment Institute, 1990), pp. 28–39; Greenpeace, *Carbon Logic – The Argument against New Oil* (2000); available at <http://archive.greenpeace.org/climate/artic99/html/content/factsheets/carbonlogic2.html>; see also Kanchan Chopra et al. (eds), *Millennium Ecosystem Assessment, Ecosystem and Human Wellbeing: Policy Responses* (2005), p. 375, supporting the threshold of 2°C.

18. See, among others, James Hansen et al., "Climate Change and Trace Gases", *Philosophical Transactions of the Royal Society A*, vol. 365 (2007), pp. 1925–1954; James Hansen, "Can We Still Avoid Dangerous Human-made Climate Change?" (2006); available at <http://www.columbia.edu/~jeh1/2006/NewSchool_20060210.pdf>, pp. 965–66l; James Hansen et al., "Target Atmospheric CO_2: Where Should Humanity Aim?" *Open Atmospheric Science Journal*, vol. 2 (2008), pp. 217–231.

19. Visit also the official website of 350.org, an international campaign dedicated to building a movement to unite the world around solutions to the climate change crisis and promoting first and foremost the adoption of 350 ppm as a threshold, available at <http://www.350.org>.

20. See Decision 1/CP.13, *Bali Action Plan*, 2007; available at <http://unfccc.int/resource/docs/2007/cop13/eng/06a01.pdf#page=3.

21. "Revised Negotiating Text", Ad Hoc Working Group on Long-Term Cooperative Action under the Convention, Sixth Session, Bonn, 1–7 June 2009, UN Framework Convention on Climate Change, Distr. General, FCCC/AWGLCA/2009/INF.1, 22 June 2009, GE.09-61746 (RNT).

22. Ibid., p. 77.

23. Carl Pope, "Next Year in Copenhagen: Concrete US Actions Are Necessary before the Copenhagen Conference of the Parties", *Environmenal Law Reporter News & Analysis*, vol. 39 (2009), p. 10070.

24. Office of Science and Technology Policy, Executive Office of the President, "Intergovernmental Panel on Climate Change Finalizes Report" (2007); available at <http://france.usembassy.gov/root/pdfs/press070202.pdf>.

25. Calculated from Energy Information Administration, *Emissions of Greenhouse Gases in the United States 2004* (US Department of Energy, December 2005), p. 4; available at <ftp://ftp.eia.doe.gov/pub/oiaf/1605/cdrom/pdf/ggrpt/057304.pdf> (accessed 1 May 2010).

26. Calculated from UNFCCC Greenhouse Gas Inventory Data; available at <http://unfccc.int> (accessed 1 May 2010).

27. Netherlands Environmental Assessment Agency, "China Now No.1 in CO2 Emissions: US in Second Position" (2006); available at <http://www.pbl.nl/en/dossiers/Climatechange/moreinfo/Chinanowno1inCO2emissionsUSAinsecondposition.html> (accessed 1 May 2010); see also International Energy Agency, *World Energy Outlook 2007* (2007); available at <http://www.worldenergyoutlook.org> (accessed 1 May 2010).

28. See *Trade and Climate Change*, WTO/UNEP Report (2009); available at <http://www.unep.org/documents.multilingual/default.asp?documentid=589&articleid=6235&l=en>, p. viii.

29. See resources on China and Climate Change at the website of Pew Center for Global Climate Change; available at <http://www.pewclimate.org/policy_center/international_policy/china.cfm>.

30. However, the most important point of Brazil's position regarding the negotiations relates to its recent negative stance towards a scheme that would allow developed nations to gain carbon credits by supporting forest conservation. See discussion below.

31. See "Revised Negotiating Text", p. 85.

32. Copenhagen Accord, para 10, p. 3; available at <http://unfccc.int/resources/docs/2009/cop15/eng/107.pdf> (accessed 1 May 2010).

33. Ibid., para 11, p. 3.

34. Copenhagen Climate Council, "Summary for Policy Makers", p. 11.

35. See The Prince's Rainforests Project, *Rainforests and Climate Change* (2009); available at <http://www.rainforestsos.org/pages/rainforests-and-climate-change>.

36. At COP 13 in Bali, member states adopted Decision 2/CP.13 calling for "meaningful action to reduce emissions from deforestation and forest degradation in developing countries". See para. 1(b)(iii) of the Bali Action Plan.

37. See, for example, David J. Hayes and Joel C. Beauvais, "Carbon Sequestration", in Michael B. Gerrard (ed.) *Global Climate Change and US Law* (New York: American Bar Association, Section on Environment, Energy and Resources, 2007), p. 691–741.

38. *Innovation in Responding to Climate Change: Nanotechnology, Ocean Energy and Forestry*, UNU-IAS Report (2008); available at <http://www.ias.unu.edu>.

39. Committee on Science, Engineering and Public Policy (COSEPUP), *Policy Implications of Greenhouse Warming: Mitigation, Adaptation, and the Science Base* (1992); available at <http://books.nap.edu/openbook.php?record_id=1605&page=433>.

40. For more information about iron fertilization of the oceans see, for example, Phillip W. Boyd et al., "Mesoscale Iron Enrichment Experiments 1993–2005: Synthesis and Future Directions", *Science*, vol. 315, no. 5812 (2007), pp. 612–617.

41. For more information, see David W. Schnare, *A Framework to Prevent the Catastrophic Effects of Global Warming Using Solar Radiation Management (Geo-engineering)*. Supplement to the Testimony before the United States Senate, Committee on Environment and Public Works, Washington DC, Submitted to the Record – October 3, 2007 (2007); available at <http://thehardlook.typepad.com/thehardlook/files/schnare_supplemental_testimony_a_framework_for_geoengineering.pdf>.

42. For more information about geoengineering in general see, for example, Andy Jones, Jim Haywood and Olivier Boucher, "Climate Impacts of Geoengineering Marine Stratocumulus Clouds", *Journal of Geophysical Research* (2008), p. 114; Phillip J. Rasch, Simone Tilmes, Richard P. Turco, et al., "An Overview of Geoengineering of Climate Using Stratospheric Sulphate Aerosols", *Philosophical Transactions of the Royal Society A,* vol. 366 (2008), pp. 4007–4037; Alan Robock, "20 Reasons Why Geoengineering May Be a Bad Idea", *Bulletin of Atomic Scientists*, vol. 64, no. 2 (2008), pp. 14–18, 59; Kevin E. Trenberth and Aiguo Dai, "Effects of Mount Pinatubo Volcanic Eruption on the Hydrological Cycle as an Analog of Geoengineering", *Geophysical Research Letters, vol.* 34 (2007), p. L15702. See also a specialized site on geoengineering, available at <http://www.realclimate.org>.

43. See study by Tim M. Lenton and Naomi E. Vaughan, "The Radiative Forcing Potential of Different Climate Geoengineering Options", *Atmospheric Chemistry and Physics Discussions*, vol. 9 (2009), pp. 2559–2608, available at <http://www.atmos-chem-phys-discuss.net/9/2559/2009>.

44. Convention on the Prohibition of Military or Any Other Hostile Use of Environmental Modification Techniques, Geneva, 19 May 1977, entered into force 5 October 1978, 1108 UNTS 151; available at <http://www.fas.org/nuke/control/enmod/text/environ2.htm>. See also Jean Dean, "Iron Fertilization: A Scientific Review and International Policy Recommendations", *SPG Environs Environmental Law & Policy Journal*, vol. 32, no. 2 (2009), pp. 321–345.

45. See Lakshman D. Guruswamy, "A New Framework: Post-Kyoto Energy and Environmental Security", *Colorado Journal of International Environmental Law & Policy*, vol. 16, no. 2 (2005), pp. 333–353, p. 348.

46. *International Energy Outlook*, Chapter 7: Energy Related Carbon Dioxide Emissions (2007); available at <http://www.eia.doe.gov/oiaf/ieo/emissions.html>.

47. See *World Bank Statement, Ministerial Segment – COP11 – Montreal 4* (2005); available at <http://siteresources.worldbank.org/essdnetwork/resources/ministerialsegmentcop11Montreal.pdf>.

48. The United States signed an agreement with India to supply nuclear technology to India for civilian use, regardless of its non-participation in and exclusion from NPT, as a nuclear state. To facilitate the execution of the Agreement, the US Congress passed the United States–India Peaceful Atomic Energy Cooperation Act in December 2006, also known as the Hyde Act.

49. *IPCC Fourth Assessment Report (AR4), Climate Change 2007*: Working Group III Report, p. 325.

50. Michael B. Gerrard, "Global Climate Change: Legal Summary", American Law Institute–American Bar Associations Continuing Legal Education, ALI-ABA Course of Study, 4–6 February 2009, p. 256.

51. Alexander E. Farell et al., "A Low-carbon Fuel Standard for California, Part 2: Policy Analysis" (University of California Berkley Transportation Sustainability Research Center, 2007); available at <http://www.energy.ca.gov/low_carbon_fuel_standard/uc_lcfs_study_part_2-final.pdf>.

52. See "Revised Negotiating Text", p. 132.
53. Global surface temperature increased 0.74 ± 0.18 °C $(1.33 \pm 0.32$ °F) during the last century. IPCC, *Climate Change 2007: The Physical Science Basis.* Contribution of Working Group I to the Fourth Assessment Report of the Intergovernmental Panel on Climate Change – Summary for Policy Makers (2007); available at <http://ipcc-wg1.ucar.edu/wg1/report/ar4wg1_print_spm.pdf>.
54. UNFCCC, arts. 2 and 4(e).
55. UNFCCC, *The Nairobi Work Programme on Impacts, Vulnerability, and Adaptation to Climate Change* (2007); available at <http://unfccc.int/files/adaptation/sbsta_agenda_item_adaptation/application/pdf/nwp_brochure.pdf>.
56. UNFCCC, *Nairobi Work Programme on Impacts, Vulnerability and Adaptation to Climate Change, Subsidiary Body for Scientific and Technological Advice,* Thirtieth session, Bonn, 1–10 June 2009, FCCC/SBSTA/2009/L.2, 5 June 2009; available at <http://unfccc.int/documentation/documents/advanced_search/items/3594.php?rec=j&pripref=6000052 86#beg>.
57. See, for example, *Climate Change and Natural Disasters: Scientific Evidence of a Possible Relation between Recent Natural Disasters and Climate Change,* DG Internal Policies of the Union – Policy Department Economic and Scientific Policy, European Parliament, Briefing Note, IP/A/ENVI/FWC/2005-35, IPOL/A/ENVI/2002-19 (2005); available at <http://www.europarl.europa.eu/comparl/envi/pdf/externalexpertise/ieep_6leg/naturaldisasters.pdf>.
58. See, for example, *Wildfire 2007: Regional Session C: Europe, Southeast Europe, Mediterranean, North Africa and Caucasus,* a Report by the FIRE GLOBAL – Global Fire Monitoring Center (GFMC) (2007), p. 2; available at <http://www.fire.uni-freiburg.de/sevilla-2007/session-c-europe-report-en.pdf>. See also *Workshop on Forest Fires in the Mediterranean Region: Prevention and Regional Cooperation,* Sabaudia, Italy, 13–15 May 2008; available at <http://www.fao.org/docrep/010/k2891e/k2891e06.htm>: "After the fires of the 2007 summer, with more than 500,000 hectares burned only in Italy and Greece and the loss of around 90 persons, a resolution of the European Parliament came out in September 2007 on fires and floods which underlines some areas for further activity (extraordinary Community Funds, going beyond the EU Monitor Information Center (MIC), better use of the Solidarity Fund, enhanced strategies, more prevention)."
59. See *Human Impact Report – Climate Change – The Anatomy of a Silent Crisis,* a Report by the Global Humanitarian Forum (Geneva, 2009), p. 11, p. 13; available at <http://www.eird.org/publicaciones/humanimpactreport.pdf>.
60. See John Vidal, "Climate Change Will Overload Humanitarian System, Warns Oxfam" (2009); available at <http://www.guardian.co.uk/environment/2009/apr/21/climate-change-natural-disasters/print>.
61. Compare the figure of 200 million refugees estimated by Norman Myers in the Stern Report: Nicholas Stern, *Stern Review on the Economics of Climate Change: Executive Summary* (London: HM Treasury, 2007); available at <http://www.hm-treasury.gov.uk/sternreview_index.htm>. Christian Aid predicts that a further 1 billion people will be forced from their homes between now and 2050. See *Human Tide: The Real Migration Crisis,* a Report by Christian Aid (May 2007); available at <http://www.christianaid.org.uk/Images/human-tide.pdf>. See also *Environmentally Displaced People – Understanding the Linkage between Environmental Change, Livelihoods and Forced Migration,* a Report by the Refugee Studies Centre, Oxford Department of International Development, University of Oxford (2008); available at <http://www.reliefweb.int/rw/lib.nsf/db900sid/OCHA-7GMHJF/$file/rsc_Nov2008.pdf?openelement>.
62. See Alexandra Berzon, "Tuvalu is Drowning" (Salon, 2006); available at <http://www.salon.com/news/feature/2006/03/31/tuvalu>; Alex Kirby, "Pacific Islanders Fleeing Ris-

ing Seas", BBC News, 9 October 2001; available at <http://news.bbc.co.uk/2/hi/science/nature/1581457.stm>; Andrew Simms, "Farewell Tuvalu" *The Guardian*, 29 October 2001; available at <http://www.guardian.co.uk/comment/story/0,3604,582445,00.html>.

63. See, for example, United States Army Corps of Engineers, "Environmental Assessment and Finding of No Significant Impact", Section 117: Expected Erosion Control Project – Kivalina, Alaska, 2007.

64. Visit the official website of the Alliance of Small Island States (AOSIS); available at <http://www.sidsnet.org/aosis>.

65. See *Migration, Climate Change and the Environment*, a Report by IOM (2009); available at <http://www.iom.int/jahia/webdav/shared/shared/mainsite/policy_and_research/policy_documents/policy_brief.pdf>.

66. For more details of catastrophic scenarios, see Kurt M Campbell et al., *The Age of Consequences: The Foreign Policy and National Security Implications of Global Climate Change* (Center for Strategic & International Studies and Center for a New American Security, 2007).

67. "National Intelligence Assessment on the National Security Implications of Global Climate Change to 2030", statement for the Record of Dr Thomas Fingar, 24 June 2008, House Permanent Select Committee on Intelligence/House Select Committee on Energy Independence and Global Warming, Office of the Director of National Intelligence, United States of America.

68. *Sudan Post-Conflict Environmental Assessment*, a Report by UNEP (Geneva, 2007); available at <http://www.unep.org/sudan>.

69. *Sahel: Region is "Ground Zero" for Climate Change*, Integrated Regional Information Networks, UN Office for the Coordination of Humanitarian Affairs (Geneva, 2008); available at <http://www.irinnews.org>.

70. *From Conflict to Peacebuilding – The Role of Natural Resources and the Environment* (United Nations Environment Programme, 2009), p. 9; available at <http://www.unep.org/publications/search/pub_details_s.asp?ID=3998>.

71. See, for example, Speech by NATO Secretary-General, Jaap de Hoop Scheffer, on security prospects in the High North (2009); available at <http://www.nato.int/docu/speech/2009/s090129a.html>.

72. See "Security Council Holds First-ever Debate on Impact of Climate Change on Peace, Security, Hearing over 50 Speakers", Security Council 5663rd Meeting, Security Council SC 9,000 (2007); available at <http://www.un.org/news/press/docs/2007/sc9000.doc.htm>.

73. Regarding the rights of the indigenous peoples and gender under conditions of climate change, which are outside the scope of this chapter, see, respectively, IUCN, *Indigenous and Traditional Peoples and Climate Change*. Issue Paper (2007); available at <http://www.ohchr.org/english/issues/climatechange/docs/iucn.pdf>; IUCN, *Gender Aspects of Climate Change* (2008); available at <http://www.iucn.org/en/news/archive/2007/03/7_gender_climate_change.pdf>.

74. International Covenant on Civil and Political Rights, 16 December 1966, entered into force 23 March 1976, 999 UNTS 171.

75. International Covenant on Economic, Social and Cultural Rights, 16 December 1996, entered into force 3 January 1976, 993 UNTS 3.

76. Universal Declaration of Human Rights, GA. Resolution 271 A, at 71 UN GAOR, 3rd Session, 1st plenary meeting. UN Doc. A/810 on 12 December 1948.

77. See, for example, European Convention for the Protection of Human Rights and Fundamental Freedoms, Rome, 4 November 1950, entered into force 3 September 1953, 213 UNTS. 222.

78. *Report of the Office of the High Commissioner for Human Rights on the Relationship Between Climate Change and Human Rights*, Human Rights Committee (2009), A/HRC/10/61.

79. "Human Rights and Climate Change", Human Rights Council, Resolution A/HRC/10/L (30 March 2009).
80. IPCC, *Climate Change 2007: The Physical Science Basis*, p. 5.
81. N.L. Poff et al., *Aquatic Ecosystems & Global Climate Change, Potential Impacts on Inland Freshwater and Coastal Wetland Ecosystems in the United States*, Pew Center on Global Climate Change (2002); available at <http://www.pewclimate.org/docuploads/aquatic.pdf>; Robert W. Adler, "Freshwater: Sustaining Use by Protecting Ecosystems", *Environmental Law Reporter News & Analysis* (2009), pp. 10309–10315, p. 11311.
82. Bryson Bates, Zbigniew W. Kundzewicz, Shaohong Wu and Jean P. Palutikof (eds), *Climate Change and Water*, Technical Paper of the Intergovernmental Panel on Climate Change (Geneva, 2008); available at <http://www.ipcc.ch/pdf/technical-papers/climate-change-water-en.pdf>.
83. A right to development was first officially proclaimed by the United Nations in the 1986 Declaration on the Right to Development, UNGA Resolution 41/128, 1986. It was further recognized in the African Charter on Human and Peoples' Rights and reaffirmed in the 1993 Vienna Declaration and Programme of Action. Those instruments are, however, soft law instruments, and the concept of this right remains controversial, with commentators disputing whether it is a right at all. Up to the present, discussions by international institutions involving the right to development have provided a forum for reflection on human rights and development in general that is certainly comprehensive and useful for future legislative and policy development regarding climate change law.
84. See, for example, Paul Baer et al., *The Greenhouse Development Rights Framework – The Right to Development in a Climate Constrained World*, revised second edition (Berlin: Heinrich Böll Foundation, Christian Aid, EcoEquity and the Stockholm Environment Institute, 2008).
85. On the development of a GDR framework, see Baer et al., *The Right to Development in a Climate Constrained World*. According to this research the threshold is schematically set at US$9000 per capita at purchasing power parity. The GDR framework also offers pointers for determining the level at which different countries should cap their GHG emissions and emphasizes the importance of technology transfer, swift and substantial adaptation funding, and other forms of assistance. The authors of the study perceive that, for the system to work, levies would be imposed on wealthy countries, calculated on the basis of excess GHG usage.
86. "Petition to the Inter-American Commission on Human Rights Seeking Relief from Violations Resulting from Global Warming Caused by Acts and Omissions of the United States", submitted by Sheila Watt-Cloutier, with the support of the Inuit Circumpolar Conference on behalf of the Arctic Region of the United States and Canada, 7 December 2005, p. 70.
87. See International Council on Human Rights Policy, *Climate Change and Human Rights: A Rough Guide* (2008), p. vii; available at <http://www.ichrp.org>; Svitlana Kravchenko and John E. Bonine, *Human Rights and the Environment: Cases, Law, and Policies* (Durham, NC: Carolina Academic Press, 2009).

8

A new ocean to govern: Drawing on lessons from marine management to govern the emerging Arctic Ocean

Timo Koivurova and Sébastien Duyck

Nearly half of the Arctic Ocean is currently covered by a permanent ice cap that grows and shrinks seasonally, with maximum cover in March and minimum cover in September. The extent of summer sea ice has been declining over the past fifty years by an average of 8 per cent a decade,[1] and on 15 September 2007 the ice cap was 22 per cent smaller than it was in 2005, the previous record year.[2] The 2007 record went beyond the computer model predictions used to prepare the *Fourth Assessment Report* of the Intergovernmental Panel on Climate Change in 2007.[3]

Partly as a result of reduced sea ice, the Arctic seems to be on the verge of a new era of development. The improved access to the region will likely result in an expansion of oil and gas, minerals and fisheries resource extraction, as well as an expansion of shipping and tourism. All of these commercial activities entail significant environmental, social and cultural issues. According to some researchers, a scramble for resources is under way,[4] with the Arctic Ocean coastal states competing to see who gets to claim most of the seabed. Even though this line of thinking seems to exaggerate the realities in the region and, in particular, to forget that the Arctic states have complied rather well with the United Nations Convention on the Law of the Sea,[5] it is true that the perceived competition for hydrocarbon reserves has triggered a new type of policy discussion on how the Arctic, in particular the Arctic Ocean, should be governed.

This chapter tries to tease out principles that could be used to address, more sustainably, the challenges in governing the Arctic Ocean. A crucial resource to this end is the recently published report of the Arctic Council's

The future of international environmental law, Leary and Pisupati (eds),
United Nations University Press, 2010, ISBN 978-92-808-1192-6

Best Practices in Ecosystems-based Oceans Management in the Arctic (BePOMAr) project;[6] the project's findings allow us to examine whether an approach to Arctic marine management that draws on past and current experience is enough to counter the considerable challenges that managing the Arctic Ocean entails. Our argument is that, while BePOMAr has much to offer, we cannot content ourselves to rely solely on the type of experience it cites if we are to deal with rapid change such as that affecting the Arctic Ocean.

Before studying ideal principles for Arctic Ocean management, it is important to introduce the Arctic Council, the prevailing intergovernmental forum in the Arctic, and to examine the recent dynamics in Arctic governance, where various states and the European Union are recasting their Arctic policies in the face of a rapidly changing ocean.

Introduction to the present arctic intergovernmental cooperation and its marine work

Before one can study the emergence of the Arctic Council, which has also done marine-related work, it is necessary to define the Arctic. This is a complex question since several different criteria can be presented for drawing the southernmost boundary of the region. Possible natural boundaries are, for instance, the tree line (the northernmost boundary where trees grow) or the 10 °C isotherm (the southernmost location where the mean temperature of the warmest month of the year is below 10 °C). In Arctic-wide cooperation, the Arctic Circle has been used as a criterion for membership, with only those states invited to participate in cooperation that possess areas of territorial sovereignty above the Circle.

The same complexity applies to the Arctic marine areas, since no such definition is available. A widely used one is that adopted by the Arctic Monitoring and Assessment Programme (AMAP) of the Arctic Council, which uses the working definition of marine areas north of the Arctic Circle (66°32'N), and north of 62°N in Asia and 60°N in North America (as modified to include the marine areas north of the Aleutian chain, Hudson Bay, and parts of the North Atlantic Ocean, including the Labrador Sea).[7] There is no universally accepted definition of Arctic Ocean. It does seem generally accepted, however, that there are only five coastal states, namely, Canada, Denmark (through Greenland), Norway, the Russian Federation and the United States.

Emergence of the Arctic Council

The initial idea of Arctic-wide cooperation was launched in 1987 in Murmansk by Soviet Secretary-General Michail Gorbachev. He proposed that the Arctic states could initiate cooperation in various fields, one being protection of the Arctic environment.[8] The idea was developed further when Finland convened a conference of the eight Arctic states in Rovaniemi in 1989 to discuss the issue. After two additional preparatory meetings – in Yellowknife, Canada, and Kiruna, Sweden – the eight Arctic states, as well as other actors, met again in Rovaniemi in 1991 to sign the Rovaniemi Declaration, by which they adopted the Arctic Environmental Protection Strategy (AEPS).[9]

The AEPS identified six priority environmental problems facing the Arctic: persistent organic contaminants, radioactivity, heavy metals, noise, acidification and oil pollution. It also outlined the international environmental protection treaties that apply in the region and, finally, specified actions to counter the environmental threats. The eight Arctic states established four environmental protection working groups: Conservation of Arctic Flora and Fauna (CAFF), Protection of the Arctic Marine Environment (PAME), Emergency Prevention, Preparedness and Response (EPPR) and the Arctic Monitoring and Assessment Programme (AMAP). After the signing of the Rovaniemi Declaration and the AEPS, three ministerial meetings were held in this first phase of Arctic cooperation, generally referred to as the AEPS process. The meetings were held in 1993 (Nuuk, Greenland), 1996 (Inuvik, Canada) and 1997 (Alta, Norway). Between the ministerial meetings, cooperation was guided by senior Arctic officials (SAO), typically officials from the foreign ministries of the Arctic states. The final AEPS ministerial was held after the establishment of the Arctic Council and focused on integrating the AEPS into the structure of the Council.

The Arctic Council was established in September 1996 in Ottawa, Canada, where the Arctic states signed the Declaration on the Establishment of the Arctic Council and issued a joint communiqué to explain the newly created body.[10] With the founding of the Council came changes in the forms of Arctic cooperation that had been based on the AEPS document, changes that extended the terms of reference beyond the previous focus on environmental protection. The Council was empowered to deal with "common Arctic issues, in particular issues of sustainable development and environmental protection in the Arctic".[11] This yielded a very broad mandate, since "common issues" can include almost any international policy issue; however, the Declaration provides in a footnote that "the Arctic Council should not deal with matters related to military security".[12] Environmental cooperation is now included as a principal focus within the mandate of the Council,[13] with the four environmental protection working groups that started as part of AEPS cooperation continuing under the umbrella of the Council.[14] The second "pillar" of the Council's mandate is cooperation on sustainable development,[15] whose terms of reference were adopted in the second ministerial meeting of the Council, held in 2000 in Barrow, Alaska, and which is managed by the Arctic Council Sustainable Development Working Group (SDWG).[16]

The Declaration amends and elaborates the rules on participation set out in the AEPS. It provides for three categories of participants: members, permanent participants and observers. The eight Arctic states are members; the three organizations representing the indigenous peoples of the Arctic are permanent participants.[17] The Declaration also lays down the criteria for acquiring the status of observer[18] and permanent participant, as well as the decision-making procedure for determining those statuses.[19]

The decision-making procedure of the Arctic Council, which developed in AEPS cooperation, is made more explicit in the Declaration. Article 7 provides: "Decisions of the Arctic Council are to be by consensus of the Members." In art. 2, "member" is defined as including only the eight Arctic states. Decision-making by consensus is to be undertaken only after "full consultation"[20] with the permanent participants, i.e. the organizations of the Arctic indigenous peoples. Although the permanent participants do not have formal decision-making power, they are clearly in a position to exert much influence in practice on the decision-making of the Council.[21]

The work of the Arctic Council is much dictated by its chair states. The first was Canada (1996–1998), followed by the United States (1998–2000), Finland (2000–2002), Iceland (2002–2004), Russia (2004–2006) and Norway (2006–2009);[22] the current chair is Denmark. Since the Council has no permanent secretariat, the chair state has a great deal of freedom to choose its priorities during its tenure, which hampers the formation of long-term policies. (The three Scandinavian states have created a semi-permanent secretariat, to function in Tromsø, Norway, until 2012).[23] The Arctic Council has also created certain programmes of its own, such as the Arctic Council Action Plan to Eliminate Pollution in the Arctic (ACAP), which recently became the sixth working group, and the Arctic Climate Impact Assessment (ACIA). The Council has carried out many ambitious scientific assessments in addition to the ACIA, the most recent being the oil and gas assessment released in 2008 and the Arctic Marine Shipping Assessment in 2009.[24] Both the AEPS and the Arctic Council have been established by declarations and thus Arctic-wide cooperation has been based on soft law from its very inception.[25]

The Arctic Council's marine work

The Arctic Council is engaged in various kinds of activities related to the Arctic marine environment, in particular through the AMAP and PAME working groups, but to some extent through CAFF's projects as well. The main driver in the Council's marine policy is PAME's Arctic Marine Strategic Plan (AMSP), which urges actions on many fronts. The AMSP[26] identifies the largest drivers of change in the Arctic as climate change and increasing economic activity.

The AMSP encourages the Arctic states to develop guidelines and procedures for port reception facilities for ship-generated wastes and residues; to examine the adequacy of the Arctic Council's Oil & Gas Guidelines, which led to the third revision of the guidelines, endorsed by the April 2009 ministerial;[27] to identify potential areas where new guidelines and codes of practice for the marine environment are needed; to promote application of the ecosystem approach; to support the establishment of marine protected areas, including a representative network (work which is still to be commenced);[28] to call for periodic reviews of both international and regional agreements and standards; and to encourage implementation of contaminant-related conventions or programmes and possible additional global and regional actions. PAME has also regularly reviewed the IMO's Polar Code (*Guidelines for Ships Operating in Ice-covered Waters*), which are soon to be adopted as guidelines applicable to both polar regions. A process has also been set in motion to make these guidelines legally binding.[29]

One of the important outcomes of the April 2009 ministerial meeting was the BePOMAr project, which highlighted some of the best practices in Arctic marine area management and encouraged the use of certain principles in future marine governance work in the region. Later in the chapter we will examine the BePOMAr principles to ascertain whether they could form the best basis for managing the vulnerable and unique marine ecosystems of the Arctic Ocean.

Evaluation

The Arctic Council has done marine-related work, but clearly there are limits to what the Council can do as a soft-law body, that is, one not empowered to take legally binding decisions, and as an organization with an ad hoc funding base. Nevertheless, it is important to keep in mind that there are various international treaties that apply to the Arctic Ocean because one or more of the Arctic states are parties to them.[30] Since ice still covers much of the Arctic Ocean, these treaties are at present more theoretical than practically applicable. The most important instrument is the United Nations Convention on the Law of the Sea (UNCLOS), together with its implementing agreements.[31] Of the five coastal states of the Arctic Ocean, the United States is the only one that is not a party to the UNCLOS; nevertheless, the US considers itself bound by most of the provisions of the Convention as a matter of customary international law.[32]

Hence, in the Arctic Ocean, it is still very much the coastal states that are responsible for managing the ocean, which they do on the basis of the law of the sea and the UNCLOS and all related agreements. Unlike the Southern Ocean in Antarctica, the Arctic Ocean is to a large extent subject to the sovereign rights and jurisdiction of its coastal states and art. 234 of the LOS Convention even accords those states expanded powers to control shipping in the ice-covered areas.[33] However, the central Arctic Ocean is high seas, and this area may well contain two fairly small pockets of deep seabed area after the coastal states have fixed the outer limits of their continental shelves on the basis of recommendations from the Commission on the Limits of Continental Shelf.[34] There are also some unresolved disputes over the legal status of certain areas, some of which have a significant bearing on Arctic Ocean governance.[35]

Current dynamics of Arctic Ocean policy and law

It was the 2008 Ilulissat meeting in Greenland of the five coastal states of the Arctic Ocean that sparked genuine discussion on future Arctic governance. The meeting was mainly designed to explain to the rest of the world that there is no scramble for resources going on in the Arctic, as had been widely portrayed in the media after the Russians planted their flag underneath the North Pole. In fact, quite the opposite is the case: the position is one of orderly development. Even though the original intention of the meeting was to highlight that the coastal states are acting in accordance with their duties under the law of the sea, as they in fact are, the meeting still provoked reaction among various Arctic stakeholders.[36]

The states perceived that the Arctic Ocean was on the threshold of significant changes as a result of climate change and melting sea ice, and thus: "By virtue of their sovereignty, sovereign rights and jurisdiction in large areas of the Arctic Ocean the five coastal states are in a unique position to address these possibilities and challenges."[37] The states also projected themselves as protectors of the environment and of indigenous and other local inhabitants in the Arctic Ocean area:

> Climate change and the melting of ice have a potential impact on vulnerable ecosystems, the livelihoods of local inhabitants and indigenous communities ... By virtue of their sovereignty, sovereign rights and jurisdiction in large areas of the Arctic Ocean the five coastal states are in a unique position to address these possibilities and challenges ... The Arctic Ocean is a unique ecosystem, which the five coastal states have a stewardship role in protecting. Experience

has shown how shipping disasters and subsequent pollution of the marine environment may cause irreversible disturbance of the ecological balance and major harm to the livelihoods of local inhabitants and indigenous communities.[38]

The Arctic Ocean coastal states saw "no need to develop a new comprehensive international legal regime to govern the Arctic Ocean":[39]

Notably, the law of the sea provides for important rights and obligations concerning the delineation of the outer limits of the continental shelf, the protection of the marine environment, including ice-covered areas, freedom of navigation, marine scientific research, and other uses of the sea. We remain committed to this legal framework and to the orderly settlement of any possible overlapping claims. This framework provides a solid foundation for responsible management by the five coastal States and other users of this Ocean through national implementation and application of relevant provisions.[40]

Even though Denmark insisted at the 2007 Narvik SAO meeting, prior to the Ilulissat meeting, that coastal state cooperation would not compete with the Arctic Council, the meeting caused friction among the Council members.[41] Iceland has been the most concerned of the three states (the others being Finland and Sweden) left out of this meeting. It expressed its concern in the Narvik SAO meeting[42] and also in the August 2008 Conference of the Arctic parliamentarians.[43] This is, of course, no surprise. The Ilulissat Declaration seems to outline an agenda for cooperation between the coastal states of the Arctic Ocean regarding high-level ocean policy issues, potentially challenging the Arctic Council, with its eight members, broad circumpolar focus and soft-law efforts in the areas of environmental protection and sustainable development.

The Greenland meeting also provoked a reaction from one of the strongest of Arctic Council permanent participants, the Inuit Circumpolar Council (ICC), as well as national Inuit leaders, who in their "Statement issued by Inuit Leaders at the Inuit Leaders' Summit on Arctic Sovereignty"[44] outlined their concerns over the meeting of the five coastal states:

Concern was expressed among us leaders gathered in Kuujjuaq that governments were entering into Arctic sovereignty discussions without the meaningful involvement of Inuit, such as the May, 2008 meeting of five Arctic ministers in Ilulissat, Greenland. The Kuujjuaq summit noted that while the Ilulissat Declaration asserts that it is the coastal nation states that have sovereignty and jurisdiction over the Arctic Ocean, it completely ignores the rights Inuit have gained through international law, land claims and self-government processes. Further, while the ministers strongly supported the use of international mechanisms and international law to resolve sovereignty disputes, it makes no reference to those international instruments that promote and protect the rights of indigenous peoples.

But the ICC and the Inuit leaders were also critical of the present Arctic governance:

We recognized the value of the work of the Arctic Council and asked ICC, through its permanent participant status on the Council ... We further noted the meaningful and direct role that indigenous peoples have at the Arctic Council, while at the same time expressing concern that the Council leaves many issues considered sensitive by member states off the table, including security, sovereignty, national legislation relating to marine mammal protection, and commercial fishing.

They also cited their own justification for being strongly involved in Arctic governance:

We took note of various declarations and statements made by governments and industry regarding overlapping claims and assertions of Arctic sovereignty without full regard to Inuit concerns and rights. We further asserted that any claim of sovereignty that nation states may make is derived through the use and occupancy by Inuit of lands and seas in the Arctic ... Various aspects of what sovereignty means for Inuit were discussed. There was agreement among us that the foundation of Inuit sovereignty begins at home, and that only through Inuit well-being and the development of healthy and sustainable communities can meaningful sovereignty be achieved. To achieve these goals, we called upon Arctic governments to be active partners in creating such a foundation.

Thereafter, they clarified their position should a new governance arrangement be negotiated:

We called upon Arctic governments to include Inuit as equal partners in any future talks regarding Arctic sovereignty. We insisted that in these talks, Inuit be included in a manner that equals or surpasses the participatory role Inuit play at the Arctic Council through ICC's permanent participant status.

The Inuit can be viewed as favouring a stronger governance arrangement than the present Arctic Council, since they direct serious criticism towards the Council's inability to tackle sensitive issues. Even though they naturally make their own case – that Inuit should be included in any future talks on Arctic governance – they also refer to indigenous peoples' rights in general and the Arctic Council's permanent participant status in particular. One possible view that emerges from their statement is that any future governance arrangement should make the present permanent participants of the Council partners in equal standing to the eight Arctic Council member states.

On 9 October 2008, the EU Parliament[45] adopted a resolution in which it first took note of the Greenland meeting (para. I) and then established its Arctic agency in the following terms:

> Whereas three of the EU's Member States, and a further two of the EU's closely-related neighbours participating in the internal market through the EEA Agreement, are Arctic nations, meaning that the EU and its associated states comprise more than half the numeric membership of the Arctic Council.

For the EU Parliament, the ultimate governance solution should be one that involves a broader group of countries and the region's indigenous peoples:

> Suggests that the Commission should be prepared to pursue the opening of international negotiations designed to lead to the adoption of an international treaty for the protection of the Arctic, having as its inspiration the Antarctic Treaty, as supplemented by the Madrid Protocol signed in 1991, but respecting the fundamental difference represented by the populated nature of the Arctic and the consequent rights and needs of the peoples and nations of the Arctic region; believes, however, that as a minimum starting-point such a treaty could at least cover the unpopulated and unclaimed area at the centre of the Arctic Ocean (paragraph 15).[46]

Given that the EU has no Arctic coastline, but does have potentially significant navigational and fishery interests in the region, establishing a more inclusive governance arrangement for the Arctic would suit the Union's interests better than the "of-the-sea" approach embraced by the five coastal states, or even the approach of the Arctic Council, which rests on the difference between Arctic and non-Arctic states. This strategic choice by the Parliament of having an inclusive governance arrangement for the Arctic is amply reflected in the resolution: it suggests the governance model for the Arctic draw on the Antarctic Treaty System (ATS), a very inclusive arrangement in that it is, in principle, open to all states who conduct scientific research in Antarctica.[47] As a minimum requirement, the Parliament proposes the conclusion of a treaty covering the unpopulated and unclaimed area at the centre of the Arctic Ocean. Although worded incorrectly in legal terms,[48] this suggestion entails an inclusive approach to Arctic governance since all states possess rights and interests in the high seas and deep seabed of the Arctic Ocean, under the law of the sea.

Even though the European Parliament made the above-mentioned suggestion to the European Commission, the latter did not respond to the proposal in its November 2008 Communication. The Commission did, however, provide an interesting starting point for its Arctic policy by first diagnosing the problem: "The main problems relating to Arctic govern-ance include the fragmentation of the legal framework, the lack of effec-tive instruments, the absence of an overall policy-setting process and gaps in participation, implementation and geographic scope."[49] The Commis-sion then proposed that one remedy for tackling such problems would be to:

> explore the possibility of establishing new, multi-sector frameworks for inte-grated ecosystem management. This could include the establishment of a net-work of marine protected areas, navigational measures and rules for ensuring the sustainable exploitation of minerals.[50]

Non-Arctic coastal states (China, South Korea and Japan) and the European Commission have expressed their interest in becoming part of the established Arctic intergovernmental forum, currently by applying for observership status from the Arctic Council. The Council did not approve permanent observerships for China or the European Commission in its last ministerial meeting.

Even though there clearly is a new dynamic in Arctic governance, the reaction of the Arctic Ocean coastal states has been less than enthusiastic – as shown by the rejection of observership status for China and the European Commission. The recent Arctic policy documents of the United States and Russia have been very much in line with the Ilulissat Declara-tion in that they view the current Arctic Council and the law of the sea as an adequate solution for the Arctic. The US policy considers that the Arctic Council "should remain a high-level forum devoted to issues within its current mandate"[51] but a certain desire for proactive regulation that would enhance governance in the changing Arctic can be found in the document:

> Consider, as appropriate, new or enhanced international arrangements for the Arctic to address issues likely to arise from expected increases in human activity in that region, including shipping, local development and subsistence, exploitation of living marine resources, development of energy and other resources, and tourism.[52]

Evaluation

In a very short time, the discussions of Arctic governance have moved from being a topic of scholarly attention and NGO advocacy to featuring on the agendas of states and the European Union. It would, however, be a mistake to think that there are rapid changes ahead in Arctic governance. The established Arctic actors – especially the Arctic Council's eight member states – are defending the status quo, arguing that the Arctic, and the Arctic Ocean in particular, can be governed best by the Council, the law of the sea – the UNCLOS in particular – and related multilateral environmental agreements.[53]

However, it is important to note that the Council is defending this approach as an ideal approach for governance, not one dictated by political realities. The Arctic Ocean coastal states have taken the same tack, representing themselves in the Ilulissat Declaration as stewards of the unique Arctic Ocean ecosystem in the face of unprecedented change in the region. With all of the major players subscribing to the same approach, one would do well to ask whether that approach is in fact the best one for governing the fragile Arctic Ocean ecosystem.

Experience in marine management in the Arctic

Even though the Arctic Council does not possess a strong mandate in the area of marine policy, it has recently taken a step forward in providing guidance on Arctic marine governance by endorsing the conclusions of the BePOMAr. Although BePOMAr has not received much publicity, its conclusions will likely constitute a milestone in the activities of the Arctic Council in ocean management. The BePOMAr project was initiated during the Norwegian chairmanship of the Arctic Council in 2006.[54] The project report builds on the expertise of both the Sustainable Development Working Group and the Protection of the Arctic Marine Environment Working Group. Rather than drawing on abstract principles and concepts from existing international regulatory instruments, the report relies on the experiences in ocean management of seven of the Arctic states and identifies best practices.[55] The report presents the national approaches of each of the participating states to ocean management, as well as an indigenous perspective on the issue. Initially, the objective of the project was to deliver a set of lessons from past experience and to foster mutual learning and understanding.

The authors of the report decided midway through their work to provide a more recommendatory perspective on the issue of ocean management in the Arctic through a short conclusion specifying core elements and common themes in ecosystems-based oceans management.[56] After the review of its conclusions by the two working groups involved, at the SAO meeting in Kautokeino in October 2008, the report was submitted to the sixth ministerial meeting in Tromsø, in April 2009. The ministerial formally welcomed the report and endorsed its conclusions.[57] Given that the Arctic Council is a political forum rather than an international organization with legal capacity – the competence to make legally binding decisions – such an endorsement gave strong status to the conclusions of the report.

The geographic scope of the report covers "Arctic waters". However, most of the policies examined in the document relate specifically to the Arctic Ocean.[58] The rationale underpinning the BePOMAr project is recognition of the fact that the cumulative impact of multiple uses of the Ocean can only be addressed through an ecosystems-based approach to ocean management.[59] As early as 2004, the Arctic Marine Strategic Plan identified an ecosystems-based approach as the best approach for managing the Arctic Ocean.[60]

Based on the study of the national marine policies of the seven participating states and of the contributions by indigenous peoples, the authors of the report identified six key principles whose implementation in practice have proven particularly useful. These principles are:

1. The flexible application of effective ecosystem-based ocean management, which entails consideration given to local circumstances, and the conception of ocean management as a process rather than a designed state;
2. The requirement of integrated and science-based decision-making, thus constituting a comprehensive approach to ocean management, including through transboundary sharing of information and the involvement of all levels of government;
3. National commitment to ecosystem-based oceans management, through the redaction of a management plan and the establishment of a structure in order to guarantee the holistic approach;
4. The necessity for area-based approaches and transboundary perspectives, the definition of the geographic scope of policies should be based on the natural range of ecosystems;
5. Stakeholder and Arctic residents' participation is an additional key element, thus including the human dimension of the ecosystems, and providing for public participation;
6. Adaptive management, in order to respond to changes of natural circumstances, in particular in the context of climate change.[61]

These six principles constitute further practical guidance for the member states of the Arctic Council. The practices identified reinforce the findings of the AMSP on the implementation of ecosystem-based ocean management in the Arctic Ocean in the context of climate change.

Critical evaluation

The approach adopted by the BePOMAr study – identifying best practices from currently implemented policies – offers the advantage of being a pragmatic course of action rather than an abstract exercise. The pragmatic focus can be seen in the study being confined to the Arctic region, whereby it identifies only practices that have already proven their value in the very particular conditions prevailing there. Finally, and given the Arctic Ocean coastal states' express reluctance to accept additional international regulations applicable to the region's natural resources,[62] a principled approach to further international cooperation might constitute a more viable step forward than the immediate development of a formal legal instrument.

However, the approach adopted by the BePOMAr project has two major shortcomings. First, by focusing solely on the past and present experiences of the Arctic States in ocean management, the report fails to propose forward-looking solutions. Given that the regional impacts of climate change render the Arctic Ocean one of the fastest evolving marine environments in recent history, exclusive reliance on traditional and tested principles and solutions will fail to provide an adequate solution to the challenges facing the regional environment. Indeed, most of the economic activities anticipated for the Arctic in the future have either not materialized as yet or occur on a much smaller scale today. The conclusions of the report thus endorse the application of principles applied at present to what will be a different economic and environmental situation. This lack of ambition in providing innovative solutions contrasts with the apparent readiness of the Arctic states to adopt a proactive approach to cooperation and governance in the face of a changing climate.[63]

Second, the report does not provide an incisive analysis of the global context in relation to marine management. While the introduction makes brief mention of some international legal agreements and the conclusion evokes references in major multilateral environmental instruments to the importance of ecosystem-based management, such references do not serve as a basis for the identification of principles of an ecosystems-based approach to ocean management.[64] Accordingly, when assessing the core elements of ecosystem-based ocean management in general, the report identifies only those elements that have actually been recognized as principles of an ecosystems-based approach to ocean management and implemented by some of the Arctic states. By relying exclusively on regional experiences, the report fails to learn from principles of international environmental law that have been identified in international instruments but not necessarily emphasized in the context of Arctic environmental governance.

The rapid development of new economic activities in the Arctic region – including hydrocarbon and mineral resources exploitation, shipping, fisheries and tourism – will constitute the main challenge to the effective implementation of the principles identified in the report. Indeed, regulatory frameworks are more effective when implemented prior to the establishment of strong economic interests. In this regard, the ATS constitutes a specific regional experience from which the Arctic coastal states could learn, in order to further develop the regulatory framework in their region. However, the Antarctic regime should not been seen as a facie solution for the Arctic context, for the two polar regions differ in certain key respects: the Arctic has local populations, in particular indigenous peoples, and practically all land area in the Arctic is under the sovereignty of eight states, whereas the Antarctic has no sovereigns; and the Arctic has an extensive set of norms applicable to the region.[65]

Nevertheless, these differences should not mean ignoring the similarities between the two regions. The Antarctic regime has been developed proactively. The Convention on the Conservation of Antarctic Seals,[66] the Convention on the Conservation of Antarctic Marine Living Resources[67] (CCAMLR), and the Convention on the Regulation of Antarctic Mineral Resources Activities[68] (CRAMRA) each rely heavily on a proactive approach in the regulation of the conservation and exploitation of the resources which they cover. Where the exploitation of mineral resources is concerned, the Protocol on Environment Protection to the Antarctic Treaty relies on a more "extreme approach," since all economic activity is prohibited until the absence of unacceptable harm for the local environment has been demonstrated.[69]

The Arctic currently represents a similar context in that an increase in and diversification of economic activities – and thus the scale of their impact on the local environment – is expected in the midterm. Indeed, until climate change further modifies the natural circumstances prevailing in the region, new economic activities will remain marginal as the ice still renders navigation and the exploitation of local resources hazardous.

The precautionary approach, the core of the development of the Antarctic regime,[70] constitutes a premier example of a proactive regulatory approach in international environmental law. This approach is one of the central components of international environmental law. It has been described as "the most prominent – and perhaps the most controversial – development in international environmental law in the last two decades".[71] As it has been both adopted in many multilateral environmental agreements and referred to in the judgments of international tribunals, scholars have made the case that it possesses the status of customary law.[72] Principle 15 of the Rio Declaration provides a definition of the precautionary approach:

> In order to protect the environment, the precautionary approach shall be widely applied by States according to their capabilities. Where there are threats of serious or irreversible damage, lack of full scientific certainty shall not be used as a reason for postponing cost-effective measures to prevent environmental degradation.[73]

In the context of marine ecosystems, international agreements have also urged implementation of the approach. Although the UNCLOS does not refer to the approach, it is mentioned in the international instruments related to fisheries management.[74]

In relation to the Arctic Ocean more specifically, the precautionary approach has also been recognized as a key component in the management of natural resources and the conservation of the marine environment. The precautionary approach has indeed been an element of many multilateral agreements specifically addressing the Arctic environment, such as the Fur Seal Convention[75] and the Polar Bear Agreement.[76] The approach has also been implemented through the North Atlantic Salmon Conservation Organization (NASCO), which in 1998 adopted the Agreement on Adoption of a Precautionary Approach[77] and the subsequent 1999 Action Plan for Application of the Precautionary Approach.[78] Finally, the Convention for the Protection of the Marine Environment of the North-East Atlantic[79] (the OSPAR Convention), which covers a small section of the Arctic Ocean, also espouses the precautionary approach, recognizing it as a legal principle. According to art. 2.2(a), the parties to the Convention shall apply:

> the precautionary *principle*, by virtue of which preventive measures are to be taken when there are reasonable grounds for concern that substances or energy introduced, directly or indirectly, into the marine environment may bring about hazards to human health, harm living resources and marine ecosystems, damage amenities or interfere with other legitimate uses of the sea, even when there is no conclusive evidence of a causal relationship between the inputs and the effects. (emphasis added)

The repeated references to the precautionary approach in the international agreements related to both polar regions not only confirm the relevance of the implementation of this approach, but also can be seen as contributing to the recognition of the precautionary approach as a general principle of international environmental law.[80]

The BePOMAr report notes that the precautionary approach has been recently affirmed as a legal principle in Norway in relation to environmental protection.[81] Furthermore, and while not explicitly elevating the approach to the status of a principle as such, all but one of the seven national regimes of marine management studied in the BePOMAr project refer to the implementation of the precautionary approach in the description of various aspects of their domestic maritime policies.[82] Although the principle provides for a very effective approach in the management of marine ecosystems, it entails ambiguous elements and, until now, has not been widely implemented in the case of oceans other than in fisheries management.[83] The approach has also been invoked by the US Congress, which in October 2007 considered the need for international cooperation regarding the migratory, transboundary and straddling fish stocks in the Arctic Ocean.[84] In a Joint Resolution with the House of Representatives, the Senate invited the United States government to co-operate with the other Arctic nations in order to negotiate an agreement managing the regional fisheries, establish the appropriate international organization or organizations, and reinforce the implementation of the existing provisions under the UN Fish Stock Agreement.[85] An interesting component of the joint resolution was the recommendation that the fisheries in the Arctic Ocean be frozen at their present extent until such an agreement can be reached at the regional level. The need for the effective implementation of the precautionary approach – and to possibly recognize it explicitly as a legal principle – in the Arctic region is further highlighted by the considerable degree of scientific uncertainty regarding the pace and consequences of climate change for local ecosystems.[86] Indeed, while recent scientific assessments pointed to the possibility of ice-free summers in the Arctic before the end of the century,[87] the latest scientific assessments currently highlight the alarming fact that such a situation could occur as early as 2030.[88] In addition, there is also a significant range of uncertainty concerning the quantities of natural resources located in the region and the scale of economic opportunities generated by environmental changes. The recognition of this high level of uncertainty should urge a science-driven approach such as that highlighted in the conclusions of the BePOMAr report, but more specifically oriented towards anticipatory decisions and the implementation of the precautionary principle.

Conclusions

There is no doubt that the Arctic Council's BePOMAr project has done important work by identifying the six principles for stronger Arctic marine and, particularly, ocean management. This principled approach to marine management should guide the way in which the Arctic Ocean coastal states exercise their self-proclaimed environmental stewardship over the Arctic Ocean ecosystem. In the Ilulissat meeting, the coastal states announced their readiness to regulate proactively, that is, before economic activities spread into the ice-covered regions, but not through a comprehensive international treaty. This approach gives those states ample room to commence and continue regulatory efforts in their coastal regions on the basis of the principles identified in this chapter.

The BePOMAr principles – together with proactive and precautionary approaches in use in the Antarctic Treaty System and OSPAR – could indeed frame future actions by the Arctic Ocean coastal states. Such an approach is suitable for the time being, given that the Arctic Ocean sea ice will be opening in the near future, primarily in areas under the marine jurisdictions of the five coastal states. However, when the projected melting of the Arctic Ocean extends to high seas, more difficult questions may have to be addressed: in principle, all countries of the world and their fishing and commercial fleets can make use of many parts of the Arctic Ocean, in particular the large high seas area at the centre of the Ocean. The coastal states could thus also consider what types of solutions might be available to engage other countries in Arctic Ocean governance in the future.

Notes

1. Julienne Stroeve, Marika Holland, Walt Meier, Ted Scambos and Mark Serreze, "Arctic Sea Ice Decline: Faster than Forecast", *Geophysical Research Letters*, vol. 34 (2007), pp. 1–5.
2. See press release from the National Snow and Ice Data Center (NSIDC), "Arctic Sea Ice Shatters All Previous Record Lows" (2007); available at: <http://nsidc.org/news/press/2007_seaiceminimum/20071001_pressrelease.html>.
3. See news release from the National Center for Atmospheric Research (2007); available at <http://www.ucar.edu/news/releases/2007/seaice.shtml>.
4. Scott G. Borgerson, "Arctic Meltdown, the Economic and Security Implications of Global Warming", *Foreign Affairs* (March/April 2008), p. 65.
5. See Timo Koivurova, "Do the Continental Shelf Developments Challenge the Polar Regimes?", in Gudmundur Alfredsson and Timo Koivurova (ed.), *The Yearbook of Polar Law, Volume 1* (Leiden: Brill Publishers, 2009), pp. 477–497.
6. Håkon Hoel (ed.), *Best Practices in Ecosystems Based Oceans Management in the Arctic* (BePOMAr), Report Series no. 129 (Norwegian Polar Institute, 2009).
7. Arctic Monitoring and Assessment Programme, geographical coverage; available at <http://www.amap.no/aboutamap/geocov.htm>.
8. Gorbachev proposed that a nuclear-weapon-free zone be declared in northern Europe, naval activity be limited in the seas adjacent to northern Europe, peaceful cooperation be the basis for utilizing the resources of the Arctic, scientific study of the Arctic has great significance for all humankind, the countries of the North cooperate in matters of environmental protection, and the Northern Sea Route be opened by the Soviet Union to ice-breaker-escorted passage.
9. The history of the negotiation process is studied in Monica Tennberg, *The Arctic Council: A Study in Governmentality* (Rovaniemi: University of Lapland, 1998), pp. 53–61. The AEPS is reproduced in 30 *ILM* 1624 (1991).
10. The 1996 Declaration on the Establishment of the Arctic Council. The Declaration is reproduced in 35 *ILM* 1385–1390 (1996).
11. Ibid., art. 1(a).
12. Ibid., p. 3, fn.
13. Ibid., art. 1(b).
14. Ibid. Article 1(b) reads: "The Arctic Council is established as a high level forum to ... b. oversee and coordinate the programs established under the AEPS on the Arctic Monitoring and Assessment Programme (AMAP); Conservation of Arctic Flora and

Fauna (CAFF); Protection of the Arctic Marine Environment (PAME); and Emergency Prevention, Preparedness and Response (EPPR)."

15. Ibid. Article 1(c) reads: "The Arctic Council is established as a high level forum to ... c. adopt terms of reference for, and oversee and coordinate a sustainable development program."

16. The home page of the SDWG is at <http://portal.sdwg.org>.

17. Article 2 of the Declaration on the Establishment of the Arctic Council enumerates the following as permanent participants: "The Inuit Circumpolar Conference, the Saami Council and the Association of Indigenous Minorities of the North, Siberia and the Far East of the Russian Federation." Three organizations have since been accepted as permanent participants: the Aleut International Association, the Gwich'in Council International and the Arctic Athabascan Council.

18. Article 3 of the Declaration reads: "Observer status in the Arctic Council is open to: a) non-Arctic states; b) inter-governmental and inter-parliamentary organisations, global and regional; and c) non-governmental organisations that the Council determines can contribute to its work."

19. Article 2(2) reads: "Permanent participation is equally open to other Arctic organisations of indigenous peoples with majority Arctic indigenous constituency, representing: a. a single indigenous people resident in more than one Arctic State; or b. more than one Arctic indigenous people resident in a single Arctic state." Decisions by the Arctic states on whether this criterion is fulfilled must be unanimous. Article 2 also states: "the number of Permanent Participants should at any time be less than the number of members".

20. Ibid., art. 2.

21. Timo Koivurova and Leena Heinämäki, "The Participation of Indigenous Peoples in International Norm-making in the Arctic", *Polar Record*, vol. 42, no. 221 (2006), pp. 101–109.

22. In the Scandinavian chair-period, Norway, Denmark and Sweden organize the ministerial meetings during the spring rather than fall, as previously.

23. See the Norwegian, Danish, Swedish common objectives for their Arctic Council chairmanships 2006–2012 (2007); available at <http://arctic-council.org/article/2007/11/common_priorities>.

24. See the *Arctic Council Arctic Marine Shipping Assessment 2009 Report* (2009); available at <http://arctic-council.org/filearchive/amsa2009report.pdf>.

25. For a comprehensive account of the evolution of the Arctic Council, see Timo Koivurova and David VanderZwaag, "The Arctic Council at 10 Years: Retrospect and Prospects", *University of British Columbia Law Review*, vol. 40, no. 1 (2007), pp. 121–194.

26. *Arctic Marine Strategic Plan* (2004), p. 8; available at <http://web.arcticportal.org/uploads/bi/d8/bid8eronocy8atetm8kzoq/pame-bklingur-a4.pdf>.

27. See <http://arctic-council.org/filearchive/Arctic%20Offhsore%20Oil%20and%20Gas%20Guidelines%202009.pdf>.

28. See Timo Koivurova, "Governance of Protected Areas in the Arctic", *Utrecht Law Review*, vol. 5, no. 1 (2009), pp. 44–60.

29. Maritime Safety Committee, 86th session, agenda item 26, MSC 86/26, 12 June 2009, at 23.32. (On file with the authors.)

30. Convention for the Prevention of Pollution from Ships (MARPOL 73/78), Oslo, 15 February 1973, 1340 UNTS 184 as amended by the Protocol 1978 which entered into force 2 October 1983; Convention on the Prevention of Marine Pollution by Dumping of Wastes and Other Matter, London, 13 November 1972, entered into force 30 August 1975, 1046 UNTS 120, (London Convention); Convention on Persistent Organic Pollutants, Stockholm, 23 May 2001, entered into force 17 May 2004, 40 ILM 532; Global Pro-

gramme of Action for the Protection of the Marine Environment from Land-based Activities, Washington DC, 3 November 1995, UNEP(OCA)/LBA/IG.2/7; International Convention on the Regulation of Whaling (ICRW), Washington DC, 2 December 1946, entered into force 10 November 1948, 161 UNTS 72; the Agreement on the Conservation of Polar Bears, Oslo 15 November 1973, entered into force 26 May 1976, 13 ILM 13 (1974); Convention on the Conservation of Migratory Species of Wild Animals, Bonn, June 1979, entered into force 1 November 1983, 19 ILM 15 (1980); Convention on Biological Diversity, Rio de Janeiro, 5 June 1992, entered into force 29 December 1993, 1760 UNTS 79; 31 ILM 818 (1992); and International Convention on Oil Pollution Preparedness, Response and Co-Operation, London, 30 November 1990, entered into force 13 May 1995, 1891 UNTS 51; 30 ILM 773 (1991).

31. United Nations Convention on the Law of the Sea, Montego Bay, 10 December 1982, entered into force 16 November 1994, 1833 UNTS 397; Agreement relating to the Implementation of Part XI of the UNCLOS, New York, 28 July 1994, entered into force 28 July 1996, 33 ILM 1309; and Agreement for the Implementation of the Provisions of the UNCLOS Relating to the Conservation and Management of Straddling Fish Stocks and Highly Migratory Fish Stocks, New York, 4 December 1995, entered into force 11 December 2001.

32. As new Secretary of State, Hillary Clinton has committed to make the ratification of the UNCLOS one of her priorities. See transcript of Hillary Clinton's confirmation hearing; available at <http://www.cfr.org/publication/18225/transcript_of_hillary_clintons_confirmation_hearing.html>.

33. Article 234 reads: "Coastal States have the right to adopt and enforce non-discriminatory laws and regulations for the prevention, reduction and control of marine pollution from vessels in ice-covered areas within the limits of the exclusive economic zone, where particularly severe climatic conditions and the presence of ice covering such areas for most of the year create obstructions or exceptional hazards to navigation, and pollution of the marine environment could cause major harm to or irreversible disturbance of the ecological balance. Such laws and regulations shall have due regard to navigation and the protection and preservation of the marine environment based on the best available scientific evidence."

34. Since the US is not yet a party to the UNCLOS, it cannot make a submission to the Commission on the Limits of the Continental Shelf.

35. There are few still pending disputes over the delimitation of maritime borders, namely those between the United States and the Russian Federation, between the US and Canada in the Beaufort Sea and between Russia and Norway in the Barents Sea. Because of the process of drawing the outermost limits of the continental shelves of Arctic Ocean coastal states, there may also be areas of the seabed that two or even three states perceive as belonging to their continental shelf. The status of the waters and seabed surrounding the Svalbard islands is also controversial, Norway perceiving the status of these areas differently from other contracting states to the Svalbard Treaty. Finally, the legal status of Northwest passage(s) is disputed and to some extent also portions of the Northern Sea Route.

36. For a study over how the Arctic Ocean coastal states have followed their Law of the Sea Convention duties in establishing the outer limits of their continental shelves, and how this process may impact on the Arctic Council, see Koivurova, "Do the Continental Shelf Developments Challenge the Polar Regimes?"

37. The Ilulissat Declaration (2008), p. 1; available at <http://arctic-council.org/filearchive/Ilulissat-declaration.pdf>.

38. Ibid., pp. 1–2.

39. Ibid., p. 2.

40. Ibid., p. 1.
41. *Final Report of the Narvik SAO Meeting 2007* (2007); available at <http://arctic-council. org/filearchive/Narvik%20-final%20report-%2023Apr08.doc>.
42. During discussion at the Narvik SAO meeting, ibid. (18.1), "Iceland expressed concerns that separate meetings of the five Arctic states, Denmark, Norway, US, Russia and Canada, on Arctic issues without the participation of the members of the Arctic Council, Sweden, Finland and Iceland, could create a new process that competes with the objectives of the Arctic Council. If issues of broad concern to all of the Arctic Council Member States, including the effect of climate change, shipping in the Arctic, etc. are to be discussed, Iceland requested that Denmark invite the other Arctic Council states to participate in the ministerial meeting. Permanent participants also requested to participate in the meeting. Denmark responded that the capacity of the venue may be an issue."
43. The Conference statement, in para. 39, "Notes the information from the Danish delegation concerning the Ilulissat Declaration, and the concerns of the Icelandic delegation regarding full participation of all states of the Arctic Council." Conference Report (2008), p. 36; available at: <http://www.arcticparl.org/_res/site/file/files%20from%20 8th%20conference/Conference_Report_Fairbanks_final.pdf>.
44. Statement issued by Inuit Leaders at the Inuit Leaders' Summit on Arctic Sovereignty, Kuujjuaq, Canada (6–7 November 2008): "Arctic Sovereignty Begins with Inuit"; available at <http://www.sikunews.com/art.html?artid=5711&catid=2>.
45. *European Parliament resolution of 9 October 2008 on Arctic governance* (2008); available at: <http://www.europarl.europa.eu/sides/getdoc.do?pubref=-//ep//text+ta+p6-ta-2008-0474+0+doc+xml+v0//en>.
46. The Commission did not follow this suggestion by the EU Parliament, but provided that "The full implementation of already existing obligations, rather than proposing new legal instruments should be advocated. This however should not preclude work on further developing some of the frameworks, adapting them to new conditions or Arctic specificities." *Communication from the Commission to the European Parliament and the Council – The European Union and the Arctic Region*, Brussels, COM(2008) 763; available at: <http://ec.europa.eu/maritimeaffairs/pdf/com08_763_en.pdf>.
47. See the provision on membership in article IX.2 of the Antarctic Treaty, Washington DC, 1 December 1959, entered into force 23 June 1961, 402 UNTS 71 (1961).
48. The EU Parliament speaks of the "unclaimed area at the centre of the Arctic Ocean", meaning types of areas beyond national jurisdiction, the deep seabed (the Area) and the high seas. First, if the Parliament refers to the deep seabed, this cannot said to be an unclaimed area since the coastal states do not claim their continental shelf for it is a natural prolongation of the land mass into the sea. Hence, the deep seabed is a result of what remains after the coastal states have drawn the outer limits of their continental shelves. Second, high seas cannot be subjected to sovereignty claims under the law of the sea. It would thus have been legally correct to speak, for instance, of "areas beyond national jurisdiction at the centre of the Arctic Ocean". It is also a bit odd that the Parliament speaks of this area as "unpopulated", given that it is referring to the core of an ice-covered Ocean.
49. *Communication from the Commission to the European Parliament and the Council – The European Union and the Arctic Region.*
50. Ibid., p. 12.
51. US Arctic Region Policy 2009, "National Security Presidential Directive/NSPD-66", Homeland Security Presidential Directive/HSPD-25, January 9, 2009, Arctic Region Policy. (On file with the authors.)
52. Ibid., C 5b.

53. For a forthcoming account, see Timo Koivurova, "Limits and Possibilities of the Arctic Council in a Rapidly Changing Scene of Arctic Governance", *Polar Record* (2009), published online by Cambridge University Press, doi:10.1017/S0032247409008365, 08 Sep 2009.

54. See the report of the SAO, *Report of Senior Arctic Official to Ministers at the Fifth Arctic Council Ministerial Meeting* (2006); available at <http://archive.arcticportal. org/287/01/sao-reportto_ministers.pdf>.

55. All the member states of the Arctic Council except Sweden participated, Sweden considering its marine management activities as not being of "oceanic" character.

56. This decision was taken at the February 2008 meeting of the authors in Washington, DC.

57. See Arctic Council, *Tromsø Declaration* (2009), p. 7; available at <http://arctic-council. org/filearchive/Tromsoe%20Declaration-1.pdf>.

58. The report also includes analysis of the ocean management policies of the Arctic Council states, thus also including marine areas located outside the Arctic Ocean such as the Baltic Sea in the case of the Finnish policy.

59. *PAME Working Group Meeting Report No: II-2007*, Agenda Item 8: Project Document on Best Practices in Ecosystems-based Oceans Management in the Arctic (2007); available at <http://web.arcticportal.org/uploads/ot/nb/otnbzpwwbxkpxruusaowkg/pame-report-ii-2007.pdf>.

60. *Arctic Marine Strategic Plan*, p. 8.

61. Hoel, *Best Practices in Ecosystems Based Oceans Management in the Arctic*, pp. 111–112.

62. See extract from the Ilulissat Declaration reproduced above.

63. The Ilulissat Declaration.

64. Hoel, *Best Practices in Ecosystems Based Oceans Management in the Arctic*, pp. 8–9, p. 10.

65. As is well known, seven states have made sovereignty claims over the Antarctic continent, but they have agreed not to consolidate these into full sovereignty on the basis of the 1959 Antarctic Treaty.

66. Convention on the Conservation of Antarctic Seals, London, 1 June 1972, entered into force 11 March 1978, 11 ILM 251 (1972).

67. Convention on the Conservation of Antarctic Marine Living Resource, Canberra, 20 May 1980, entered into force 7 April 1982, 1329 UNTS 48; 19 ILM 841 (1980).

68. Convention on the Regulation of Antarctic Mineral Resource Activities, Wellington, 2 June 1988, not yet in force, 27 ILM 868.

69. Protocol on Environment Protection to the Antarctic Treaty, art. 7, Madrid, 40 October 1991, entered into force 14 January 1998, 30 ILM 1.

70. Rosie Cooney, *The Precautionary Principle in Biodiversity Conservation and Natural Resource Management: An issues paper for policy-makers, researchers and practitioners* (Gland: IUCN, 2004), p. 21.

71. Jonathan B. Wiener, "Precaution", in Daniel Bodansky, Jatta Brunnée, Hellen Hey (eds), *The Oxford Handbook of International Environmental Law* (Oxford: Oxford University Press, 2007), pp. 597–612, p. 599.

72. See Philippe Sands, *Principles of International Environmental Law*, 2nd edn (Cambridge: Cambridge University Press, 2003), p. 273.

73. Rio Declaration on Environment and Development, Principle 15, 1992, 31 ILM 874.

74. See 1995 UN Agreement for the Implementation of the Provisions of the United Nations Convention on the Law of the Sea of 10 December 1992 relating to the Conservation and Management of Straddling Fish Stocks and Migratory Fish Stocks, 34 ILM 1542, in force 11 December 2001, article 6 and the FAO Code of Conduct, art. 6(5).

75. Convention between Great Britain, Japan, Russia and the United States respecting Measures for the Preservation and Protection of Fur Seals in the North Atlantic Ocean, in force 7 July 1911, treaty no longer in force, 214 ConTS 80.

76. Agreement on the Conservation of Polar Bears.

77. CNL(98)46, Agreement on Adoption of a Precautionary Approach (1998); available at <http://www.nasco.int/pdf/agreements/pa_agreement.pdf>.

78. CNL(99)48, *Action Plan for Application of the Precautionary Approach* (1999); available at <http://www.nasco.int/pdf/nasco_res_actionplan.pdf>.

79. Convention for the Protection of the Marine Environment of the North-East Atlantic, Ostend, June 2007, not yet into force.

80. Donald R. Rothwell, *The Polar Regions and the Development of International Law* (Cambridge: Cambridge University Press, 1996), p. 401.

81. Hoel, *Best Practices in Ecosystems Based Oceans Management in the Arctic*, p. 46.

82. Besides Sweden, which is not included in the report, Finland is the only state which does not refer to the precautionary approach.

83. David VanderZwaag, "The Precautionary Principle and Marine Environmental Protection: Slippery Shores, Rough Seas, and Rising Normative Tides", *Ocean Development & International Law*, vol. 33, no. 2 (2002), pp. 165–188.

84. US Senate Joint Resolution 17, Directing the United States to initiate international discussions and take necessary steps with other Nations to negotiate an agreement for managing migratory and transboundary fish stocks in the Arctic Ocean 110th Congress, 5 October 2007.

85. Ibid., paras. 1 and 2.

86. For a discussion of the relation between the degree of uncertainty and the proportionality of precautionary measures, see Nicolas de Sadeleer, *Environmental Principles: From Political Slogans to Legal Rules* (Oxford: Oxford University Press, 2002), pp. 167–172.

87. Intergovernmental Panel on Climate Change, *Assessment Report 4* (Cambridge: Cambridge University Press, 2007).

88. Muyin Wang and James E. Overland, "A Sea Ice Free Summer Arctic within 30 Years?", *Geophysical Research Letters*, vol. 36 (2009).

9

Moving beyond the tragedy of the global commons: The Grotian legacy and the future of sustainable management of the biodiversity of the high seas

Rosemary Rayfuse

The Grotian ideal and the freedom of the seas

Freedom of the seas. Considered one of the fundamental principles of international law, it embodies the notion that the oceans cannot be occupied or appropriated by anyone and that freedom of navigation and exploitation of the high seas and its resources cannot be interfered with or restricted in any way. Originally expounded by Hugo Grotius in his now famous treatise, *Mare Liberum*,[1] the principle is arguably of considerably longer lineage,[2] having had its origins in the principle of freedom of navigation accepted in Roman and Greek law.[3] During the Middle Ages, as piracy spread and sea power grew, security concerns resulted in attempts by maritime powers to appropriate areas of the sea.[4] However, the principle was revived by Grotius to lend support to the claims of the Dutch East India Company to its right to trade in the East Indies and to take Portuguese ships in prize, and in support of Dutch arguments against the restrictions being placed on their fishery by the British.[5] To Grotius the seas were vast, limitless, inexhaustible of use and, because they could not be occupied by anyone, neither were they subject to appropriation by anyone.[6] The sea, he said, was "a public thing", "the common property of all".[7]

Not everyone agreed with Grotius. Almost immediately, English and European lawyers set out to refute the argument that the seas were open to all. Thus began what has been called "the battle of the books"[8] in which some argued for a *mare clausum*[9] against the Grotian assertions of

The future of international environmental law, Leary and Pisupati (eds),
United Nations University Press, 2010, ISBN 978-92-808-1192-6

a *mare liberum*.[10] Throughout the remainder of the seventeenth century and a good part of the eighteenth the pretence of a *mare liberum* was dropped in favour of new scrambles for wealth and power, predominantly manifested in trading monopolies and in claims to exclude foreigners from coastal fishing areas.[11] However, as trade became more lucrative, the industrial revolution led to technological advances, and British sea power – followed by that of the United States – came to the fore, the doctrine was revived.[12] For much of the nineteenth and twentieth centuries the clarion call of seafaring nations was "freedom of the seas".

Retreat from the Grotian ideal: Restricting the freedom of the seas

While it may be true that the Grotian ideal of a *mare liberum* reached its zenith in the nineteenth and twentieth centuries, during the latter half of the twentieth century, ecological, economic, political and ideological developments gave rise to fundamental challenges to this freedom. Resolution of many of these challenges was articulated, first in the 1958 Geneva Conventions on the Law of the Sea,[13] and then in the 1982 United Nations Convention on the Law of the Sea[14] (the "Law of the Sea Convention", LOSC or UNCLOS) and its implementing agreements of 1994[15] and 1995.[16] Today, the freedom is not unfettered; an ever-increasing range of restrictions, embodied in numerous treaties and rules of customary international law, exist on the freedom. These restrictions can broadly be grouped into three categories: geographical restrictions; participant restrictions; and activity restrictions.

Geographical restrictions relate to the area in which the freedom of the seas can be exercised, in other words *where* the freedom exists. In Grotius's conception, the seas in which the freedom was to be exercised lapped at the very shores of the land masses of states. Today, the physical area of ocean space in which the freedom may be exercised has been radically reduced. Indeed, the freedom is no longer even referred to as one "of the seas". The "freedom of the seas" is now generally referred to as the "freedom of the *high* seas", a freedom to be exercised only in that geographic area of waters which lie outside the radically expanded areas under the national jurisdiction of states; in other words, in "all parts of the sea that are not included in the exclusive economic zone, in the territorial sea or in the internal waters of a State, or in the archipelagic waters of an archipelagic State".[17] These geographical restrictions were not easily won. They are, however, now firmly entrenched in the LOSC and in customary international law, and give coastal states jurisdiction over the living and non-living resources out to 200 nautical miles as well as the continental shelf resources out to the geomorphological limit of the continental shelf.[18] Exploitation of the non-living resources of the deep seabed, beyond the limits of the continental shelf, is administered by the International Sea-Bed Authority (ISBA).[19]

The second set of restrictions relate to participants in activities on the seas, in other words *who* may exercise the right of the freedom of the seas. While in theory anyone can exercise the freedom,[20] in practice, not everyone is entitled to its full and unfettered enjoyment. Only ships flying the flag of a state, whose nationality they thereby acquire, are entitled to full participation,[21] and even they are limited by rules of conduct such as the prohibitions on piracy,[22] transportation of slaves[23] and unauthorized broadcasting.[24] Stateless vessels and vessels engaged in conduct which violates rules of international law may not be afforded the same privileges and protections.[25]

The third category encompasses restrictions which have been placed on the behaviour of those seeking to exercise the freedom of the seas. In other words, these are restrictions relating to conduct, or to *what* can be done in the exercise of the freedom, and in what manner. In some respects it is arguable that the freedom of the seas is today much wider than the Grotian conception which was limited to the freedom of navigation and, arguably, fishing.[26] While including these two freedoms, art. 87 of the LOSC lists a number of other activities which are considered as part of the overall freedom: overflight, laying submarine cables and pipelines, construction of artificial islands and other installations, and scientific research. However, freedom requires regulation if it is to be maintained. Regulation bespeaks restriction. Developing appropriate and acceptable restrictions on freedom requires the difficult accommodation of multiple and complex competing interests. The bare listing of these high seas freedoms (including activities unthought-of in Grotius's day) masks the numerous restrictions which have, in fact, developed on the freedom of activity on the high seas.

The primary determinants for the restrictions that have developed on the exercise of high seas freedoms have included political and economic security matters, broadly defined, and – importantly – the spectre of exhaustibility of natural resources.[27] The LOSC, itself, imposes a number of restrictions on the exercise of high seas freedoms, including the general conditions that they be exercised for peaceful purposes and with due regard for the interests of other states. However, it also imposes a number of specific restrictions including the duties to protect and preserve the marine environment, to conserve marine living resources, and to cooperate for these purposes. Numerous other sectoral treaty regimes regulate various other aspects of high seas uses such as dumping,[28] discharge of marine pollution by shipping,[29] safety of navigation[30] and fishing.[31]

The failure of the Grotian ideal: The exhaustibility of marine biodiversity and the problem of the tragedy of the commons

Despite the adoption of the LOSC and related treaties, the high seas and its living resources have not been protected from the adverse consequences of human activities. In the case of fisheries, more than 75 per cent of the world's fish stocks are reported as already fully exploited or overexploited (or depleted and recovering from depletion)[32] and increasing numbers of marine species are considered threatened or endangered.[33] Moreover, inadequate management, destructive fishing practices such as bottom trawling, and illegal, unregulated and unreported fishing (IUU fishing) are to blame for a whole range of adverse effects on fish stocks and dependent and associated species and ecosystems, including excessive by-catch of non-targeted species and damage to vulnerable marine ecosystems such as deep-sea cold water corals and seamount ecosystems.[34]

Other existing and emerging ocean uses also pose threats to the marine environment and its biodiversity from, for example, increasing ship source pollution, marine debris and noise pollution, acoustic thermometry, seabed mining, bioprospecting and marine scientific research which perturbs the marine environment. Climate change, too, threatens the oceans. Ocean acidification as a result of increased absorption of carbon dioxide by the oceans threatens a range of marine species, while ocean temperature changes are already wreaking havoc on the geographical distribution and continued existence of others.[35] In addition, human attempts to geo-engineer solutions to climate change through, for example, proposed large-scale ocean fertilization projects may have disastrous consequences for the marine environment as a whole.[36]

In short, the Grotian ideal of freedom based on the notion of inexhaustibility has proven a chimera. In recent years concern has been growing that the current international management arrangements are inadequate to ensure conservation and management of the high seas marine environment and its biodiversity. The international community has thus begun to explore possible reforms to the high seas legal regime, aimed at curbing the excesses of the Grotian ideal in favour of improving the conservation and management of marine biodiversity within areas beyond national jurisdiction.

The developing legal regime for the protection of high seas marine biodiversity

"Mind the gap"

The focus on conservation and sustainable use of marine biodiversity has predominantly emerged from the annual meetings of the United Nations Informal Consultative Process on Oceans and the Law of the Sea (UNIC-POLOS) which, since 1999, has discussed a range of ocean issues and suggested a number of initiatives aimed at improving oceans governance. In 2004, on the recommendation of UNICPOLOS, the UN General Assembly established an Ad Hoc Open-ended Informal Working Group specifically to study issues relating to the conservation and sustainable use of marine biological diversity beyond areas of national jurisdiction (BBNJ Working Group).[37] Other multilateral bodies, such as the Conference of the Parties to the Convention on Biological Diversity (CBD COP), regional fisheries management organizations (RFMOs), the Food and Agriculture Organization (FAO) and its Committee on Fisheries (COFI), and the International Maritime Organization (IMO), have also been engaged in discussions on improving protection of high seas biodiversity and the marine environment.

Within the BBNJ Working Group, attention has focused on how best to carry forward the implementation of the legal framework provided by the LOSC in a manner that is consistent with the mandates of existing international bodies and forums. It will be recalled that the LOSC obliges states to protect and preserve the marine environment,[38] including rare and fragile ecosystems, and imposes particular requirements on states to cooperate on a global and regional basis in the formulation and elaboration of the international rules necessary to achieve these ends.[39] Since its first meeting in 2006, numerous proposals have been discussed in the BBNJ Working Group aimed at finding the *modus operandi* to give content to these obligations in order to improve the conservation of high seas biodiversity. This has included consideration of the means of dealing with related issues such as IUU fishing and marine genetic resources and the inter-linkages between the marine genetic resources of the deep seabed, the biodiversity of the water column and the non-living resources beyond national jurisdiction.[40] However, while there may be consensus among states on the need to promote international cooperation and coordination to achieve long-term conservation of high seas biodiversity, there is, as yet, no agreement on the legal and institutional mechanisms required to meet this objective.

The developing legal regime for the protection of high seas marine biodiversity

"Find the gap"

At a very basic level, dispute exists over the fundamental question of whether any governance or regulatory gaps do, in fact, exist in the legal framework.[41] Some argue that the LOSC, even by its own terms, is not comprehensive. They point to the deliberate exclusion of comprehensive regulation of high seas fisheries during the LOSC negotiations and the subsequent negotiation of the 1995 UN Fish Stocks Agreement (FSA) as evidence of this. Others argue that the LOSC already provides a comprehensive legal regime for oceans governance and that all that is lacking is adequate implementation of its norms.[42]

This polarization of positions is particularly evident in the dispute over the question of the legal status of marine genetic resources and whether existing legal arrangements and management tools sufficiently cover their conservation and sustainable use. Many states anticipate potentially lucrative returns from the exploitation of marine genetic resources for industrial, cosmetic, pharmaceutical and other biotechnical applications and are therefore pressing for international agreement on an access and benefit-sharing regime in respect of marine generic resources beyond national jurisdiction. China and the G77 group of developing countries argue that marine genetic resources of the high seas and the Area[43] should be regarded as part of the common heritage of mankind and subject to a similar access and benefit-sharing regime to that which applies to the mineral resources of the Area under the LOSC and the Part XI Implementing Agreement.[44] They note that UNGA Resolution 27/49 of 1970[45] declares all resources of the Area to be the "common heritage of mankind" and assert that this should include living resources as well as mineral resources. Developed countries, on the other hand, strongly resist the extension of the common heritage of mankind principle beyond its specific application to mineral resources, as currently articulated in Part XI of the LOSC. Rather, they take the position that the high seas regime for marine living resources under Part VII of the LOSC applies to the living resources of the Area, including marine genetic resources. Still others argue that, while the Part VII regime applies to the living marine genetic resources of the high seas water column, there is no regime applicable to the living marine genetic resources of the deep seabed.[46]

Various studies have identified a plethora of governance, regulatory and implementation gaps in the high seas regime, which is best described as fragmented, both sectorally and geographically.[47] Governance gaps are gaps in the international institutional framework and include the absence of institutions at the global, regional or sub-regional level as well as in-consistent mandates of existing organizations and mechanisms. Regula-tory gaps are those that arise as a result of non-existent or inadequate regulation of activities at a global, regional or sub-regional level, while implementation gaps refer to failures by states to implement their inter-national obligations.

Governance gaps arise as a result of the combined operation of the principle of high seas freedoms and the fundamental principle of the sov-ereign equality of states. The central challenge for effective high seas gov-ernance stems from the Grotian notion of the high seas as a common property, open-access regime with equal right of user. The high seas are, by definition, open for legitimate and reasonable use by all states and may not be appropriated to the exclusive sovereignty of any one state. No single user can have exclusive rights over any of the common prop-erty resources and no state can prevent any other state from joining in the exploitation of these resources. Once "captured", a common property resource becomes the exclusive property of the exploiter, who then de-rives any commercial or other benefit therefrom. High seas fisheries are the quintessential example of a common property resource – and provide a vivid demonstration of the shortcomings of a common property regime. However, all high seas users have the potential, whether realized or not, to interfere with the rights and interests of other users and potentially to harm, whether purposely or not, the marine environment.

The high seas regime of freedom and its corollary of exclusive flag state jurisdiction[48] leads, as we now know, to two related governance problems. First, unbridled exercise of the freedom leads inexorably to overexploitation and the tragedy of the commons. Second, flag state juris-diction is ineffective in halting or addressing this tragedy. In the absence of any international rule-making structure, individual sovereign states take decisions to exploit or enforce in their own interest rather than that of the international community. States may refrain from becoming party to particular treaties, or they may object to and therefore "opt out" of any particularly onerous measures adopted by treaty bodies of which they are a party. Despite growing recognition of the benefits of peer re-view and performance audit, no effective international machinery exists to hold states accountable for their failure to engage with or comply with generally accepted measures. Those international organizations that do exist are only as effective as their weakest or most reluctant member state, and may be wholly undermined by non-member states.

Regulatory gaps are both substantive and geographical in nature. They include geographical gaps in high seas coverage by RFMOs and arrange-ments which may not apply to any or all fisheries within the relevant geo-graphical area. Indeed, many high seas areas are not covered by RFMOs

at all. In addition, there is little coordination and cooperation between
the fisheries regimes and between the fisheries and environmental sectors. Substantive regulatory gaps include the absence of reference to dis-
crete high seas fish stocks in the FSA and lack of clarity on the interaction
between the regime of the high seas and the regime of the outer continental shelf. Existing and emerging high seas activities such as marine scientific research, bioprospecting for marine genetic resources, laying of
cables and pipelines, carbon dioxide sequestration, floating installations
and deep-sea tourism are not regulated at all. Finally, no global rules
exist to elaborate on the requirements in the LOSC and the 1992 Convention on Biological Diversity[49] (CBD) for environmental impact assessment for any of the existing or emerging high seas activities or uses.

With respect to implementation gaps, in the high seas context many
states have failed to adequately implement and enforce the duties in the
LOSC to cooperate in the protection and preservation of the marine environment and the conservation and sustainable use of marine biodiversity. States have also failed to adequately assess, monitor and control the
activities of both their nationals and of processes and activities relating
to the high seas which are otherwise under their jurisdiction and control.
The failure of members of RFMOs and other sectoral or global agreements and arrangements to adequately implement and enforce their obligations under these agreements and arrangements is notorious.

"Fill the gap"

Even if agreement can be reached on the existence of gaps in the high
seas regime, however, the question remains as to how best to fill these
gaps. Proposals within the BBNJ Working Group have ranged from doing
nothing, to improving implementation of existing relevant obligations, to
increasing adherence to existing international instruments and strengthening existing bodies, to a European Union proposal for a new Implementation Agreement to develop a more specific framework to address
conservation and sustainable use of marine biodiversity in areas beyond
national jurisdiction.[50]

The key objectives of the proposed Implementation Agreement would
be to ensure the effective conservation and sustainable use of marine
biodiversity through the application of modern principles and approaches, including the principle of equity and integration, precaution
and ecosystem-based approaches, and the requirements of prior and ongoing impact assessment, in order to assist states to deliver on their
WSSD[51] and CBD commitments on biodiversity loss, vulnerable ecosystems and establishing marine protected areas (MPAs) networks. It is
envisaged that the Implementation Agreement would incorporate the re-

quirements of an integrated precautionary approach, taking into account the impact of all human activities. It would facilitate and enhance, rather than detract from or replace, cooperation and coordination between existing regulatory frameworks and bodies, and would be consistent with the LOSC and without prejudice to the sovereign rights of coastal states over their maritime zones. The Implementation Agreement would provide for the establishment of MPAs based on identification and designation of vulnerable marine ecosystems and species, using the best available scientific information and the precautionary principle, and measures adopted in respect of these MPAs would similarly be based on the best scientific information available and the precautionary principle. Measures would also need to be coherent and compatible with measures taken within national maritime zones.

Other commentators have suggested an even more far-reaching restructuring of the high seas regime through the adoption of a new global, comprehensive, legally binding agreement to provide for one integrated system for addressing all identified regulatory and governance gaps and not just the establishment of MPAs.[52] It is envisaged that such a new agreement would ensure that modern conservation principles, such as the ecosystem approach and precautionary principle, are incorporated and applied in all existing global and regional agreements relevant to areas beyond national jurisdiction. It would provide rules for current and future unregulated activities and improve regulation of increasing impacts from traditional uses such as shipping and military activities (for example, from underwater noise). The proposed agreement would require the application of modern conservation tools such as environmental impact assessments and marine spatial planning, and would provide for effective compliance and enforcement mechanisms at both the global and the regional level in respect of all human activities in areas beyond national jurisdiction. It would also provide rules or a process to coordinate regulation of interactions between activities in the high seas water column and those on the extended continental shelf of coastal states.

In terms of institutional design for a comprehensive integrated high seas regime, at least two approaches have been suggested: a decentralized and a centralized model. A decentralized regime could be established through adoption of an international instrument setting out the relevant principles and criteria to be applied globally, but leaving specific authority for implementation of those requirements to the mandate of existing or new regional or global sectoral agreements. These would include existing RFMOs and the ISBA, as well as global sectoral agreements such as the London (Dumping) Convention,[53] London Protocol[54] and MARPOL,[55] and regional agreements such as the OSPAR Convention[56] and the Antarctic Treaty[57] and its Environmental Protocol.[58] The instrument could also call for the establishment of other integrated regional oceans management organizations (ROMOs) where none exist. The instrument would set out the principles and criteria to be adopted and applied by these various agreements and the terms of the coordination and cooperation between them. The advantage of such a regime would be the enhancement of global-scale cooperation by making it a breach of international law not to comply with the rules of the other existing (or new) agreements. In other words, since the corollary of a right to do something is the right not to do something, states would still retain the right not to utilize the high seas. However, if they chose to do so, the exercise of their right to utilize the high seas would have to be in accordance with the rules adopted by the relevant regional or sectoral organization. Enforcement would be the responsibility of the various regional and sectoral regimes, and all parties to those regimes would exercise an enforcement power on behalf of the international community as a whole.

A centralized model would see the establishment by global agreement of a new International Oceans Authority (IOA) or similar body to govern and manage all high seas uses and activities. Adoption of a global mechanism with both legal and institutional elements could be used to coordinate and integrate the parallel strands of sectoral and regional marine environmental protection activity, and would not necessarily supplant it. In this respect the IOA would act as the institutional focal point to provide best practice guidance and global endorsement of decisions and measures adopted by regional or sectoral agreements. It would be responsible for progressing coordination and cooperation between these regional and sectoral agreements and would have the ultimate power of oversight to ensure their efficacy and compliance with best management practices. Where regional or sectoral organizations and their members failed to enforce compliance, the IOA could step in to do so. It would also be responsible for overseeing and reviewing assessments and monitoring of the environmental impact of existing, new and emerging uses and activities to ensure they do not cause damage to the marine environment or unduly interfere with the rights of other users. The IOA could be empowered either to take measures directly or to recommend the taking of measures by relevant regional or sectoral bodies.

However, even assuming one fully integrated and enforceable regime is desirable, the likelihood of achieving such a result, even in the mid to long term, is slim. The EU proposal for an Implementation Agreement has yet to achieve sufficient support for the convening of a diplomatic negotiating process, having been bogged down by the dispute over the legal status of marine genetic resources and the demands of the G77 and

China for the development of an access and benefit-sharing regime as a component part of any such comprehensive agreement.[59] Nevertheless, many states have signalled their support for the objective of increased integration. In addition, they have signalled their support for the application, within existing sectoral policy frameworks, of modern policy instruments and tools, such as area-based management tools and environmental impact assessments, for the conservation and sustainable use of marine biodiversity in areas beyond national jurisdiction.[60] Thus the focus of discussions appears to have shifted to an identification of the range of short- and medium-term solutions that are available to states at both the sectoral and global level.

Short-term actions include those targeted to urgently address specific issues and might include the adoption of UNGA resolutions, codes of conduct, pilot initiatives, scientific studies and upgrading existing bodies. Medium-term actions include the reform or expansion of the existing legal and institutional framework at the regional level, through, for example, the expansion or establishment of new regional seas agreements and RFMOs, or region-specific agreements, protocols or annexes for unregulated activities, or requiring environmental impact assessment. Other possibilities include the development of new global or sectoral issue-based instruments and other processes to address specific governance, regulatory or implementation gaps.

Since 2004 some progress on improving high seas governance arrangements for the conservation of marine biodiversity has been made. Indeed, establishment of the BBNJ Working Group, itself, has been a significant step in bringing the issue of the need for improved high seas governance arrangements to the fore. Issues discussed in the Working Group have had a direct bearing on discussions in both the General Assembly and UNICPOLOS. Progress has been particularly evident with regard to the impacts of unsustainable and destructive fishing practices.[61]

In 2004 the UN General Assembly called on states to take action, including the possible interim prohibition of destructive fishing practices, to protect vulnerable marine ecosystems, including seamounts, hydrothermal vents and cold water corals in areas beyond national jurisdiction.[62] In 2006 the UN General Assembly adopted Resolution 61/105, which specifically addressed the impacts of bottom fishing on vulnerable marine ecosystems and called on states to take immediate action, both individually and through RFMOs, to sustainably manage fish stocks and protect vulnerable marine ecosystems, and established a timeframe in which those actions were to be taken.[63]

The FAO has also been active, adopting guidelines for the management of deep-sea fisheries in the high seas[64] and a global agreement on port state measures aimed at combating illegal, unreported and unregulated fishing.[65] Work is currently under way on the development of a global record of fishing vessels,[66] the articulation of criteria for assessing flag state performance and the actions that may be taken against vessels flagged in states not meeting those criteria.[67] Each of these initiatives is aimed at improving the regulatory framework for compliance and enforcement in high seas fisheries and thereby contributing to the conservation and sustainable management of high seas biodiversity.

RFMOs have also responded to the need to improve the conservation of high seas biodiversity. As a result of calls made during the 2006 Review Conference of the FSA,[68] a number of RFMOs have undergone performance reviews aimed at identifying lacunae in both their mandate and in the implementation of their mandate. In some cases, RFMOs have renegotiated their constitutive treaties to bring their mandates into line with modern conservation and management principles.[69] RFMOs have also begun to adopt measures to protect vulnerable high seas ecosystems, particularly seamounts, from the adverse effects of fishing operations[70] and have continued in their efforts to combat IUU fishing and its detrimental effects on high seas fish stocks and dependent and associated ecosystems.

In the broader biodiversity context, progress has been made in the CBD towards the development of scientific criteria for the identification of ecologically and biologically significant marine areas in need of protection (including areas beyond national jurisdiction), and on biogeographical classification systems for selecting areas to establish representative networks of MPAs.[71] The ISBA has adopted regulations on Prospecting and Exploration for Polymetallic Nodules in the Area[72] and is working on similar regulations on prospecting and exploration for polymetallic sulfides and cobalt-rich ferromanganese crusts in the Area. The parties to the London Convention and London Protocol have confirmed that proposed ocean fertilization activities fall within their mandate, and they are working on guidelines for the conduct of such activities.[73] The CBD has also called on states to ensure that ocean fertilization activities are not carried out until an adequate scientific basis on which to justify such activities has been demonstrated by the conduct of appropriately approved and managed small-scale studies.[74]

Despite this progress, as recognized by the BBNJ Working Group in 2008, efforts are "still needed in order to conserve and sustainably use marine biodiversity beyond areas under national jurisdiction and achieve the goals set by the international community, including at the World Summit on Sustainable Development and the 2005 World Summit".[75] The UNGA continues to call upon states to urgently consider ways to integrate and improve, based on the best available scientific information and the precautionary approach, the management of risks to marine biodiversity and to develop and facilitate the use of diverse approaches and tools for doing so.[76]

A number of options have already been suggested by commentators, such as: adoption of global or region-specific agreements on environmental impact assessment and marine spatial planning; development of regional seas agreements providing comprehensive oceans management for specific regions where none currently exists and/or a series of annexes or protocols to existing agreements that provide detailed rules for currently unregulated activities and measures for the conservation and sustainable use of marine biodiversity; or adoption of actor-specific agreements for unregulated activity. In addition, recognizing the fundamental importance of scientific knowledge to sound oceans management, commentators have also pointed to the need to expand the scope of existing regional scientific advisory bodies, such as the International Council for the Exploration of the Sea (ICES), the North Pacific Marine Science Organization (PICES) and the Scientific Committee on Antarctic Research (SCAR), and to establish new advisory bodies to provide advice to regional oceans management institutions on cumulative impacts in specific oceanic areas, including areas beyond national jurisdiction. Some have even called for the establishment of an Inter-governmental Panel on the Oceans.[77]

There is also growing momentum for the adoption by the UNGA of a Declaration of the Principles of High Seas Governance, to set out more clearly and explicitly the basic principles that the international community has already established and agreed to in existing legal and policy instruments in relation to the use and exploitation of the high seas.[78] The principles that have been identified include, importantly, a "conditional", as opposed to unrestricted, freedom of the seas, and the responsibility of states to act as stewards of the global marine environment. Other principles identified include the duties of cooperation, protection and preservation of the marine environment, and the requirement of sustainable and equitable use, as well as the requirements of a science-based approach to management, the application of the precautionary and ecosystem approaches, and the requirements of public availability of information and transparent and open decision-making processes. As is immediately clear, it is already recognized that the freedom of the seas is no longer unfettered. Whatever steps are taken to integrate and improve high seas governance and the conservation and sustainable use of marine biodiversity, the result will be the placement of further restrictions on the so-called freedom of the high seas.

A post-Grotian paradigm for high seas governance and the sustainable management of marine biodiversity in areas beyond national jurisdiction

Given the plethora of restrictions that now exist on the freedom of the seas, it can be asked whether, 400 years after the *Mare Liberum*, the law of the sea has progressed to the point that the principle of "freedom of the seas" should be retired entirely from the pantheon of fundamental principles of international law. This then begs the question as to what the juridical basis of modern high seas governance for the sustainable management of marine biodiversity might be.

One view posits the replacement of the principle of freedom with the principle of the common heritage of mankind.[79] The major characteristics of the common heritage principle are generally identified as the elements of non-appropriation, international management, shared benefits and reservation for peaceful purposes.[80] A common heritage regime therefore differs fundamentally from a common property regime in that it allows all states to participate in the benefits gained from exploitation of a resource, even if they do not or cannot participate in that exploitation.

However, expanding the application of the common heritage of mankind regime to the high seas in general is a difficult proposition. Both the definition and the scope of the common heritage principle are matters of deep contention and its legal status is doubtful.[81] While state practice and *opinio juris* clearly demonstrate acceptance of the elements of non-appropriation, international management and peaceful purposes,[82] the concept of benefit-sharing is in direct opposition to the exclusive ownership notion inherent in the capture-based common property regime. Extension of the concept of benefit-sharing makes application of the common heritage principle objectionable to many, as evidenced by the intractable debates over the legal status of marine genetic resources in areas beyond national jurisdiction.

While, to a casual observer, the divide between the common property and common heritage camps may seem irreconcilable, it is possible that it may be bridged without direct application of, but with reference to, the underlying concept of public trusteeship or stewardship inherent in the common heritage principle and other principles of international law relating to cooperation and sustainable development.[83] The idea of a public trusteeship in international law is nothing new[84] and, indeed, we may have long been practicing international public trusteeship in some aspects of high seas governance without realizing or admitting it.[85] Importantly, the trusteeship model does not presuppose that all revenues and benefits *must* be shared on a common heritage basis. In other words, it does not require the redistribution of revenues back to individual states to do with as they please. Rather, revenues received by the trust are reinvested back into the trust property, either for the purpose of managing the trust more effectively or for conducting remediation of damaged trust property. Revenues may be provided to individual states to assist with capacity-building to ensure their ability to respect the terms of the trust, but not for other purposes. The trusteeship model therefore seems to straddle the divide between the common heritage and common property principles. There is thus no inherent reason why the concept cannot be applied as the juridical basis for establishment of a twenty-first-century coherent, integrated, global system of fiduciary oceans governance which regulates *access* and *use* (as opposed to access and benefit-sharing) in the common interest and concern of all.

Conclusion

The history of the law of the sea has been one of oscillation between freedom and restriction. Even as Grotius was expounding his famous postulate, restrictions on the freedom existed or were being claimed. Indeed, no sooner had Grotius enunciated the principle of absolute freedom than he found himself defending restrictions on it. Pushing for success in their pretensions in the East Indies, the Dutch sought to establish and maintain, by force of arms if necessary, their own monopoly over navigation and trade in the area.[86] Likewise, while the Dutch contested the whaling monopoly which James I had given to an English company over the waters around Spitzbergen, they did so primarily in order that they might establish their own whaling monopoly there.[87] Grotius was called in to argue in support of both these propositions which on their face, at least, were directly contrary to the position he had taken in his *Mare Liberum* of 1609. While there is some debate over the extent of his self-contradiction,[88] it is now generally accepted that the *Mare Liberum* was written as a legal opinion and not as a doctrinal work intended to ossify the legal agenda for centuries to come.[89]

While the influence of the *Mare Liberum* on the doctrine of the law of the sea has been both considerable and lasting, in the twenty-first century, the gradual, but now urgent, admission of the reality of the exhaustibility of marine biodiversity in areas beyond national jurisdiction militates in favour of a reappraisal of the Grotian ideal and leads inexorably towards its significant diminution. Indeed, the case for a new global, comprehensive, legally binding agreement seems strong. In a perfect world, such an agreement would provide the most direct route towards addressing all, or at least most of, the governance and regulatory gaps that have been identified; it would overcome the current lack of cooperation and coordination, coherency and consistency across global, sectoral and regional regimes; and it would help to confront some of the root causes of inadequate implementation of the current regime by providing the framework for comprehensive, cross-sectoral, integrated protection, modern management approaches and tools, as well as effective compliance and enforcement powers.

Admittedly this is not a perfect world. Some progress has been made, although much remains to be done before the precise parameters of the new regime are fully determined. Nevertheless, the international community has accepted the need for an integrated and improved legal regime for the conservation and sustainable management of marine biodiversity in areas beyond national jurisdiction, to better protect the interests of the international community as a whole. Such a regime will need to significantly modify many aspects of the freedom of the high seas if we are to finally free ourselves from the detrimental consequences of the Grotian legacy and achieve real long-term conservation and sustainable management and use of high seas biodiversity in areas beyond national jurisdiction.

Notes

1. Hugo Grotius, *Mare Liberum* or *The Freedom of the Seas or the Right Which Belongs to the Dutch to take Part in the East Indian Trade* (1608), translated by Ralph Van Deman Magoffin (Oxford: Oxford University Press, 1916).
2. On the pre-Grotian history of the principle see, for example, Ram P. Anand, *Origin and Development of the Law of the Sea* (The Hague: Martinus Nijhoff, 1982), especially chs. 1–3; C. John Colombos, *The International Law of the Sea* (London: Longman, 1954), pp. 39–44; Thomas W. Fulton, *The Sovereignty of the Sea* (Edinburgh: Blackwood and Sons, 1911), especially chs. 1–4; Pitmann B. Potter, *The Freedom of the Sea in History, Law and Politics* (London: Longman, 1924). A useful summary is given in W. Frank Newton, "Inexhaustibility as a Law of the Sea Determinant", *Texas International Law Journal*, vol. 16, no. 3 (1981), pp. 369–432.
3. Anand, *Origin and Development of the Law of the Sea*, p. 34. Numerous authors, however, make the point that the Greeks and Romans did not attempt to claim ownership of the sea despite using and exploiting it extensively. See, for example, Potter, *The Freedom of the Sea in History, Law and Politics*; Coleman Phillipson, *The International Law and Custom of Ancient Greece and Rome* (London: Macmillan & Co., 1911), pp. 376–378; and Percy T. Fenn Jr., "Justinian and the Freedom of the Sea", *American Journal of International Law*, vol. 19, no. 4 (1925), pp. 716–727.
4. Fulton, *The Sovereignty of the Sea*, pp. 3–6.
5. Anand, *Origin and Development of the Law of the Sea*, pp. 76–82; Frans De Pauw, *Grotius and the Law of the Sea*, translated by P.J. Arthern (Brussels: Editions de l'Institute de Sociologie, Université de bruxelles, 1965), pp. 20–21; see also Johanna K. Oudendijk, "Status and Extent of Adjacent Waters", *Nova et Vetera Juris Gentium* (Leyden: A. W. Sijthoff, 1970), reproduced in L.E. Van Holk and C.G. Roelofsen (eds), *Grotius Reader* (The Hague: TMC Asser Institute, 1983), ch. 1.

6. Grotius, *Mare Liberum*, p. 27. "[T]hat which cannot be occupied, or which never has been occupied, cannot be the property of anyone, because all property has arisen from occupation." In addition, "all that which has been so constituted by nature that although serving some one person it still suffices for the common use of all other persons, is today and ought in perpetuity to remain in the same condition as when it was first created by nature".

7. Ibid., p. 28.

8. This term is used by Anand, *Origin and Development of the Law of the Sea*, p 101. A full description of the "juridical controversies" and the books published in response to the *Mare Liberum* is found in Fulton, *The Sovereignty of the Sea*, ch. IX.

9. The most famous English proponent of the *mare clausum* at the time was John Selden, *Mare Clausum* sev *De Dominio Maris Ivribvsque ad Dominium praecipve spectantibus Assertio brevis et methodica* (Of the Dominion or Ownership of the Sea) (Cosmopoli, 1615, translated by Marchamont Nedham, London, 1652, republished at The Hague, 1653). Selden appears to have made use of the work of Sir John Boroughs and his book *The Sovereignty of the British Seas*. Boroughs' book was not, however, published until 1651. See the Preface to the 1920 edition (Edinburgh: W. Green & Son), edited by Thomas C Wade. Other proponents of the *mare clausum* included William Welwood, *An Abridgment of all Sea-Lawes*, ch xxvii (London, 1613, republished by Teatrvm Orbis Terrarvm Ltd, Amsterdam, 1972). Another distinguished opponent of Grotius was the Portuguese monk and scholar, Seraphin de Freitas, whose *De Justo Imperio Lusitanorum Asiatico adversus Grotii Mare Liberum* appeared in 1625.

10. Anand sums this battle up using a pithy quote: "Writers from practically all the European countries – Portuguese, Spanish, German, Italian, Danish and French – 'played national politics and took part in this literary campaign on the side of a closed sea. Everywhere purely political products were involved, merely dressed in the arguments of international law'." Anand, *Origin and Development of the Law of the Sea*, p. 107, quoting Christian Muerer, *The Program of the Freedom of the Sea: A Political Study in the International Law,* translated from German by Leo J. Frachtenberg (Washington, DC, 1919), p. 9.

11. See Anand, *Origin and Development of the Law of the Sea*, pp. 124–135; and Herbert A. Smith, *The Law and Custom of the Sea* (London: Stevens and Sons, 1959), p. 58.

12. Authors cite Lord Stowell in the *Le Louis* [1817] 2 Dods 210, 243: "all nations have an equal right to the unappropriated parts of the ocean for their navigation" and Judge Story in *The Marianna Flora* [1826] 1 Wheaton 1, 43: "upon the ocean, in time of peace, all possess an entire equality. It is the common highway of all, appropriated to the use of all, and no one can vindicate to himself a superior or exclusive prerogative there" as evidence of the acceptance of the principle. See Colombos, *The International Law of the Sea*, p. 54; and D.P. O'Connell, *The International Law of the Sea* vol. 1 (Oxford: Clarendon Press, 1982), pp. 19–20.

13. Prior to 1958 and the convening of the first United Nations Conference on the Law of the Sea (UNCLOS I), the bulk of the rules relating to the law of the sea existed only as rules of customary international law, supplemented by a number of treaties relating to issues such as pollution, safety of life at sea and collisions. The great achievement of UNCLOS I was the adoption of four conventions relating to: (1) the Territoral Sea and the Contiguous Zone, 516 UNTS 205; (2) the High Seas, 450 UNTS 82; (3) Fishing and Conservation of the Living Resources of the High Seas, 559 UNTS 285; and the Continental Shelf, 499 UNTS 311. Collectively these treaties are known as the 1958 Geneva Conventions on the Law of the Sea.

14. Adopted on 10 December 1982 at the conclusion of the 12 years of negotiations which comprised the Third United Nations Conference on the Law of the Sea (UNCLOS III),

Montego Bay, 10 December 1982, in force 16 November 1994, 1833 UNTS 397. The Second UN Conference on the Law of the Seas (UNCLOS II), which convened in 1960 to discuss the issue of the breadth of the territorial sea and the associated issue of fishery limits, resolution of which had eluded negotiators at UNCLOS I, had resulted in failure.

15. 1994 Agreement on the Implementation of Part XI of the 1982 Law of the Sea Convention, 33 ILM 1309 (commonly referred to as the "Part XI Implementing Agreement").

16. 1995 Agreement for the Implementation of the Provisions of the United Nations Convention on the Law of the Sea of 10 December 1982, Relating to the Conservation and Management of Straddling Fish Stocks and Highly Migratory Fish Stocks, 4 August 1995, entered into force 11 December 2001, 24 ILM 1542 (1995) (commonly referred to as "the UN Fish Stocks Agreement" or "the FSA").

17. LOSC, art. 86.

18. Ibid., arts. 56, 57, 76 and 77.

19. Ibid., arts. 156 and 157.

20. Ibid., art. 87 provides that "the high seas are open to all States".

21. Ibid., art. 91.

22. Ibid., arts. 100–105.

23. Ibid., art. 99.

24. Ibid., art. 109.

25. Ibid., arts. 92 and 110.

26. See William E. Butler, "Grotius and the Law of the Sea", in Hedley Bull, Benedict Kingsbury and Adam Roberts (eds), *Hugo Grotius and International Relations* (Oxford: Oxford University Press, 1992), pp. 209–220, pp. 217–218.

27. For an extensive discussion of the development of inexhaustibility as a determining factor in the development of restrictions on the high seas, see W. Frank Newton, "Inexhaustibility as a Law of the Sea Determinant".

28. 1972 Convention for the Prevention of Marine Pollution by Dumping of Wastes and Other Matter, London, 13 November 1972, entered into force 30 August 1975, 1046 UNTS 120 (commonly referred to as "the London (Dumping) Convention"); and the 1996 Protocol to the Convention on the Prevention of Marine Pollution by Dumping of Wastes and Other Matter of 29 December 1972, London, 7 November 1996, entered into force 13 May 2004, 36 ILM 1 (1997), (commonly referred to as the "London Protocol").

29. For example, the 1973 International Convention for the Prevention of Pollution from Ships, as amended by the 1978 Protocol (MARPOL 73/78), Oslo, 15 February 1973, 1340 UNTS 184.

30. For example, the 1972 Convention on the International Regulations for Preventing Collisions at Sea, London, 20 October 1972, entered into force 15 July 1977, 1977 *UKTS* 77; and the 1974 International Convention for the Safety of Life at Sea, London, 17 June 1960, entered into force 26 May 1965, 1184 UNTS 2.

31. There are ten multilateral treaties establishing regional fisheries management organizations (RFMOs) which regulate (some but not all) fisheries on the high seas. Five RFMOs deal with straddling fish stocks: the Commission on the Conservation of Antarctic Marine Living Resources (CCAMLR), the Northwest Atlantic Fisheries Organization (NAFO), the North-east Atlantic Fisheries Commission (NEAFC), the North Pacific Anadromous Fish Commission (NPAFC) and the South East Atlantic Fisheries Organisation (SEAFO). Five deal with tuna stocks: the Commission for the Conservation of Southern Bluefin Tuna (CCSBT), the Inter-American Tropical Tuna Commission (IATTC), the International Commission for the Conservation of Atlantic Tuna (ICCAT), the Indian Ocean Tuna Commission (IOTC) and the Western and Central Pacific Fisheries Commission (WCPFC).

32. FAO, *2006 State of World Fisheries and Aquaculture* (SOFIA) (2007); available at <http://www.fao.org/docrep/009/A099e/A099e00.htm>.
33. IUCN, *Red List of Threatened Species*; available at <http://www.iucnredlist.org>.
34. For a summary of the adverse effects of unsustainable fisheries see, for example, the *Report of the Secretary General on Sustainable fisheries, including through the 1995 Agreement for the Implementation of the Provisions of the United Nations Convention on the Law of the Sea of 10 December 1982 relating to the Conservation and Management of Straddling Fish Stocks and Highly Migratory Fish Stocks, and related instruments*, UN Doc. A/63/128, July 2008, para. 82.
35. See *Joint statement of the Co-Chairpersons of the Ad Hoc Open-ended Informal Working Group to study issues relating to the conservation and sustainable use of marine biological diversity beyond areas of national jurisdiction*, UN Doc. A/63/79, 16 May 2008, paras. 12–15 (hereafter BBNJ Report 2008).
36. See, for example, Rosemary Rayfuse, Mark Lawrence and Kristina Gjerde, "Ocean Fertilisation and Climate Change: the Need to Regulate Emerging High Seas Uses", *International Journal of Marine and Coastal Law*, vol. 23, no. 2 (2008), pp. 297–326.
37. UNGA Resolution 59/24, 17 November 2004, para. 73. The mandate of the BBNJ Working Group is: (a) to survey the past and present activities of the United Nations and other relevent international organizations with regard to the conservation and sustainable use of marine biological diversity beyond areas of national jurisdiction; (b) to examine the scientific, technical, economic, legal, environmental, socioeconomic and other aspects of these issues; (c) to identify key issues and questions where more detailed background studies would facilitate consideration by states of these issues; and (d) to indicate, where appropriate, possible options and approaches to promote international cooperation and coordination for the conservation and sustainable use of marine biological diversity beyond areas of national jurisdiction.
38. LOSC, art. 192.
39. Ibid., art. 194 and 197.
40. See *Report of the Ad Hoc Open-ended Informal Working Group to study issues relating to the conservation and sustainable use of marine biological diversity beyond areas of national jurisdiction*, (hereafter BBNJ Report 2006) UN Doc. A/61/65, 20 March 2006; and BBNJ Report 2008.
41. BBNJ Report 2008, para. 9.
42. *Earth Negotiations Bulletin*, Summary Report of UNICPOLOS Eighth Meeting, 25–27 June 2007; available at <http://www.iisd.ca/oceans/icp8/compilatione.pdf>.
43. The Area is defined in the LOSC as "the sea-bed and ocean floor and subsoil thereof, beyond the limits of national jurisdiction".
44. See *Report on the Work of the United Nations Open-ended Informal Consultative Process on Oceans and the Law of the Sea at its eighth meeting* (hereafter UNICPOLOS Report 2007), UN Doc. A/62/169, 30 July 2007, para. 73.
45. Declaration of Principles Governing the Sea-Bed and the Ocean Floor, and the Subsoil Thereof, Beyond the Limits of National Jurisdiction, GA Resolution 2749(XXV), UN Doc. A/8028, 17 December 1970.
46. UNICPOLOS Report 2007, para. 74. For a comprehensive discussion of the debate see Alexander Proelss, "Marine Genetic Resources under UNCLOS and the CBD", *German Yearbook of International Law*, vol. 51 (2009), pp. 417–446.
47. See, for example, Erik Jaap Molenaar, "Addressing Regulatory Gaps in High Seas Fisheries", *International Journal of Marine and Coastal Law*, vol. 20, no. 3–4 (2005), pp. 533–567; Rosemary Rayfuse, David Freestone, Kristina Gjerde and David VanderZwaag, "Co-Chairs Report of the Workshop on High Seas Govenance for the 21st Century" (2007); available at <http://www.iucn.org/themse/marine/pubs/pubs.htm>; see also Kristina

Gjerde, Harm Dottinga, Sharelle Hart, et al., "Regulatory and Govenance Gaps in the International Regime for Conservation and Sustainable Use of Marine Biodiversity in Areas beyond National Jurisdiction" (2008); available at <http://www.iunc.org/downloads/iucn_marine_paper_1_2.pdf>.

48. In a world of sovereign equal states, the necessary corollary of the equal right of user is the obligation not to interfere with vessels of other flag states. This duty to refrain from interference leads inexhorbly to the principle of exclusivity of flag state jurisidiction, which is embodied in art. 92 of the LOSC: "Ships shall sail under the flag of one State only and, save in exceptional cases expressly provided for in international treaties, or in this Convention, shall be subject to its exclusive jurisdiction on the high seas." For a discussion of the limits of this principle see Rosemary Rayfuse, *Non-Flag State Enforcement in High Seas Fisheries* (The Hague: Martinus Nijhoff, 2004); and R. Rayfuse, "Regulation and Enforcement in the Law of the Sea: Emerging Assertions of a Right to Non-flag State Enforcement in the High Seas Fisheries and Disarmament Contexts", *Australian Yearbook of International Law*, vol. 24 (2005), pp. 181–200.

49. Rio de Janeiro, 5 June 1992, entered into force 29 December 1993, 1760 UNTS 79; 31 ILM 818 (1992).

50. First articulated at the BBNJ Working Group in 2006, the proposal was subsequently elaborated on in an EU statement to the seventh meeting of UNICOPLOS in 2007 and the BBNJ Working Group meeting in 2008. See BBNJ Report 2006, BBNJ Report 2008 and UNICPOLOS Report 2007.

51. The Johannesburg Plan of Implementation that was adopted by the World Summit on Sustainable Development calls for the implementation of the ecosystem approach in all fisheries by 2010 and the establishment, by 2012, of a network of representative MPAs, including in areas beyond national jurisdiction. See Johannesburg Plan of Implementation, Chapter IV, *Protecting and Managing the Natural Resource Base of Economic and Social Development*, paras. 30(d) and 32(c); available at <http://www.un.org/esa/sustdev/documents/WSSD_POI_PD/English/POIChapter4.htm>.

52. See Rosemary Rayfuse and Robin Warner, "Securing a Sustainable Future for the Oceans beyond National Jurisdiction: The Legal Basis for an Integrated Cross-sectoral Regime for High Seas Governance for the 21st Century", *International Journal of Marine and Coastal Law*, vol. 23, no. 3 (2008), pp. 399–421.

53. 1972 Convention for the Prevention of Marine Pollution by Dumping of Wastes and Other Matter.

54. 1996 Protocol to the Convention on the Prevention of Marine Pollution by Dumping of Wastes and Other Matter.

55. 1973 International Convention for the Prevention of Pollution from Ships .

56. Convention for the Protection of the Marine Environment of the Northeast Atlantic, Paris, 22 September 1992, entered into force on 25 March 1998, 32 ILM 1069 (1993).

57. Antarctic Treaty, Washington DC, 1 December 1959, entered into force 23 June 1961, 402 UNTS 71 (1961).

58. 1991 Protocol on Environmental Protection to the Antarctic Treaty, Madrid, 4 October 1991, entered into force 14 January 1998, 30 ILM 1461 (1991).

59. The intractability of the debate is particularly evident in the division of opinion expressed during the eighth meeting of UNICPOLOS, where states were unable to adopt a consensus text on the outcome of the meeting because of their differences on this issue. See UNICPOLOS Report 2007.

60. See BBNJ Report 2006 and BBNJ Report 2008.

61. For a review see David Freestone, "Problems of High Seas Governance", in Davor Vidas and Peter J. Schei (eds), *The World in Globalisation: Challenges and Responses* (The Hague: Martinus Nijhoff), 2010.

62. UNGA Resolution 59/25, 17 November 2004, para. 66.

63. UNGA Resolution 61/105, 8 December 2006 paras. 80–91. For reports on implementation of these resolutions see, for example, *IUCN study regarding implementation of UNGA Resolution 61/105*, paras. 83–90 with respect to deep sea bottom fishing on the high seas (IUCN, 2009); and Matthew Gianni, *Review of the implementation of the UNGA agreement to protect deep-sea ecosystenms on the high seas* (Deep Sea Conservation Coalition, 2009); available at <http:www.savethehighseas.org>. See also the *Report of the Secretary General on Actions taken by states and regional fisheries management organisations and arrangements to give effect to paras. 83–90 of General Assembly Resolution 61/105 of 8 December 2006 on Sustainable Fisheries*, (hereafter Secretary General's Report on Implementation of Resolution 61/105) 64th Session, Advanced and unedited text; available at <http://www.un.org/Depts/los/general_assembly/documents/fisheriesreport64sessionadvanceunedited.pdf>.
64. FAO, "International Guidelines for the Management of Deep-sea Fisheries in the High Seas", in *Report of the Technical Consultation on International Guidelines for the Management of Deep-Sea Fisheries in the High Seas* (Rome: FAO, 2009), p. 39.
65. The final text of the Draft Agreement on Port State Measures to Prevent, Deter and Eliminate Illegal, Unreported and Unregulated Fishing was approved by the Technical Consultation to Develop a Legally-binding Agreement on Port States Measures in August 2009. The text is available at <ftp://ftp.fao.org/docrep/fao/meeting/017/k5919e1.pdf>. The text was endorsed by the FAO Committee on Constitutional and Legal Matters at its meeting in September 2009 and has been forwarded to the FAO Council for subsequent transmission to the Conference for approval under Article XIV, para. 1 of the FAO Constitution. Adoption of the text is therefore expected to take place at the 36th Session of the FAO Conference, to be held in November 2009. See *Report of the 88th Session of the FAO Committee on Constitutional and Legal Matters*, 23–25 September 2009, FAO Doc CL 137/5; available at <http://www.fao.org/UNFAO/Bodies/CCLM/cclm88/index_en.htm>.
66. *Report of the Expert Consultation on the Development of a Comprehensive Global Record of Fishing Vessels*, Rome, 25–28 February 2008; available at <ftp://ftp.fao.org/docrep/fao/010/i0149e/i0149e00.pdf>.
67. *Report of the Expert Consultation on Flag State Performance*, Rome 23–26 June 2009. See also Rosemary Rayfuse, "Non-flag State Enforcement and Protection of the Marine Environment: Responding to IUU Fishing", in Myron H. Nordquist, Tommy T.B. Koh and John N. Moore (eds), *Freedom of the Seas, Passage Rights and the 1982 Law of the Sea Convention* (The Hague: Martinus Nijhoff, 2009), pp. 573–600; and Rosemary Rayfuse, "The Anthropocene, Autopoeisis and the Disingenuousness of the Genuine Link: Addressing Enforcement Gaps in the Legal Regime for Areas beyond National Jurisdiction", in Alex G. Oude Elferink and Erik Jaap Molenaar (eds), *The Legal Regime for Areas beyond National Jurisdiction: Current and Future Development* (The Hague: Martinus Nijhoff, 2010).
68. *Report of the Review Conference on the Agreement for the Implementation of the Provisions of the United Nations Convention on the Law of the Sea of 10 December 1982 relating to the Conservation and Management of Straddling Fish Stocks and Highly Migratory Fish Stocks*, UN Doc. A/CONF.210/2006/15, 5 July 2006.
69. NEAFC, NAFO and the IATTC have all adopted "renewed" treaties.
70. NEAFC was the first RFMO to close areas to bottom fishing. NAFO and CCAMLR have also adopted measures incorporating some form of regulation of fishing in areas identified as vulnerable marine ecosystems. For a review of actions taken by RFMOs, see the Secretary-General's Report on Implementation of Resolution 61/105.
71. Decision IX/20 Marine and coastal biodiversity, para. 10 and Annex I and II, 2008; available at <http://www.cbd.int/decision.cop.?id=11663>.
72. ISBA/6/A/18; available at <http://www.isa.org.jm/en/documents/mcode>.

73. See resolution LC-LP.1 (2008) of the thirtieth Consultative Meeting of Contracting Parties to the London Convention and the third Meeting of the Contracting Parties to the London Protocol on the regulation of ocean fertilization in which the Contracting Parties agreed, *inter alia*, that the scope of the London Convention and Protocol includes ocean fertilization activities and that, given the present state of knowledge, ocean fertilization activities, other than for legitimate scientific research, should not be allowed, and that scientific research proposals should be assessed on a case-by-case basis using an assessment framework to be developed by the scientific groups under the LC and LP, and also agreed that, to this end, such other activities should be considered as contrary to the aims of the LC and LP and should not currently qualify for any exemptions from the definition of dumping in art. III(1)(b) of the LC and art. 1(4.2) of the LP. *International Maritime Organization* Doc LC 30/16, annex 6.

74. Decision IX/16 C, Biodiversity and Climate Change, 2008, available at <http://www.cbd.int/doc/decisions/cop-09/cop-09-dec-16-en.pdf>, in which the parties, *inter alia*, bearing in mind the ongoing scientific and legal analysis occurring under the auspices of the LC and LP, requested parties and urged other governments, in accordance with the precautionary approach, to ensure that ocean fertilization activities were not carried out until there was an adequate scientific basis on which to justify such activities, including an assessment of associated risks, and that a global, transparent and effective control and regulatory mechanism was in place for those activities, with the exception of small-scale scientific research studies within coastal waters, and stated that such studies should be authorized only if justified by the need to gather specific scientific data, should be subject to a thorough prior assessment of the potential impacts of the research studies on the marine environment, should be strictly controlled and should not be used for gathering and selling carbon offsets or for any other commercial purposes.

75. BBNJ Report 2008, para. 8.

76. UNGA Resolution on Oceans and the law of the sea, A/Res/ 63/111, 12 Feb 2009, paras. 132–134.

77. See Kristina Gjerde, Harm Dottinga, Sharelle Hart, et al., *Options for Addressing Regulatory and Governance Gaps in the International Regime for the Conservation and Sustainable Use of Marine Biodiversity in Areas beyond National Jurisdiction*, IUCN Marine Law and Policy Paper (2008); available at <http://cmsdata.iucn.org/downloads/iucn_marine_paper_2.pdf>

78. See the Ten Principles for High Seas Governance adopted by the IUCN at its 4th World Congress in Barcelona in October 2008, available at <http://cmsdata.iucn.org/downloads/10_principles_for_high_seas_governance___final.pdf>. See also David Freestone, "Modern Principles of High Seas Governance: The Legal Underpinnings", *Environmental Policy and Law*, vol. 39, no. 1 (2009), pp. 44–49.

79. This is the view held by China and the G77 states. Usually referred to in the context of regulatory regimes for resources in global commons, the common heritage of mankind principle has most famously been applied in respect of the deep seabed in Part XI of the LOSC, which gives jurisdiction over all rights in the resources, defined as "solid, liquid or gaseous resources, *in situ* in the Area at or beneath the seabed", to mankind as a whole. Activities in the Area are to be organized and controlled by the ISBA which is responsible for administering the resources of the Area.

80. Patricia Birnie and Alan Boyle, *International Law and the Environment*, 2nd edn (Oxford: Oxford University Press, 2002), p. 143.

81. Particularly given the revision of Part XI by the 1994 Implementing Agreement, which largely removed the benefit-sharing provisions for deep seabed mining. See Kemal Baslar, *The Concept of the Common Heritage of Mankind in International Law* (The Hague: Martinus Nijhoff, 1998), pp. 1–7; David Leary, *International Law and the Genetic*

Resources of the Deep Seabed (The Hague: Martinus Nijhoff, 2007), pp. 98–101; and Nico Schrijver, *Sovereignty over Natural Resources: Balancing Rights and Duties* (Cambridge: Cambridge University Press, 1997), p. 468.

82. As evidenced in the role and powers of the ISBA in managing exploration for deep seabed minerals beyond national jurisdiction which are generally accepted by states.

83. Rayfuse and Warner, "Securing a Sustainable Future for the Oceans beyond National Jurisdiction".

84. Phillipe Sands, "Public Trusteeship for the Oceans", in Tafsir M. Ndiaye and Rudiger Wolfrum (eds), *Law of the Sea, Environmental Law and Settlement of Disputes: Liber Amicorum Judge Thomas A. Mensah* (The Hague: Martinus Nijhoff, 2007), pp. 521–544. The use of the trust analogy is reflected in the proposals for, *inter alia*, a Global Commons Trust Fund, a high-seas fisheries trust, and a World Ocean Public Trust, and the recommendation, in 1998, by the Independent World Commission on the Oceans that "the 'high seas' be treated as a public trust to be used and managed in the interests of present and future generations". See, for example, Christopher D. Stone, "Mending the Seas through a Global Commons Trust Fund", in John M. Van Dyke, Durwood Zealke and Grant Hewison (eds), *Freedom for the 21st Century: Ocean Governance and Environmental Harmony* (Washington, DC: Island Press, 1993); Ross Shotton, *Managing the World's High Seas Fisheries: A Proposal for the High Seas Fisheries Trust*, Paper submitted to the Workshop on High Seas Governance for the 21st Century, New York, 17–19 October 2007; available at <http://www.iucn.org/themes/marine/high-seas-workshop-oct07.html>; M. Gorina-Ysern, Kristina Gjerde and Michael Orbach, "Ocean Governance: A New Ethos through a World Ocean Public Trust", in Linda K. Glover, Sylvia A. Earle and Graeme Kelleher (eds), *Defying Oceans End; An Agenda for Action* (Washington, DC: Island Press, 2004), pp. 197–212; Independent World Commission on the Oceans, *The Ocean: Our Future* (Cambridge: Cambridge University Press, 1998), p. 17.

85. The FSA, for example, purports to make RFMOs the stewards, custodians or trustees of high seas fisheries resources, not only for their members but for the entire international community. Open access continues, but those who exercise that access must do so subject to rules for sustainable management adopted by the regional stewards: FSA, arts. 8–17.

86. See *Origin and Development of the Law of the Sea*, pp. 95–98.

87. See Fulton, *The Sovereignty of the Sea*, pp. 181–187, 193–4.

88. Hersch Lauterpacht considered it to be "not far-reaching" while Telders considered it a "*volte-face*". See Hersch Lauterpacht, "The Grotian Tradition in International Law", *British Yearbook of International Law*, vol. 50 (1946) and Benjamin M. Telders, *Verzamelde Geschriften*, II, p. 121, cited in De Pauw, *Grotius and the Law of the Sea*, p. 68. Kwiatkowska considers it to have been "a gradual rather than a fundamental" change, while Oudendijk finds that while Grotius "certainly didn't reverse his principles, still the modification of his opinion regarding maritime sovereignty can be seen as at least the *beginning* of a *volte face*, which eventually could be completed by others". See Barbara Kwiatkowska, "Hugo Grotius and the Freedom of the Sea", in *Hugo Grotius: 1583–1983, Maastricht Hugo Grotius Colloquium, 31 March 1983* (1984), pp. 23–31, p. 28; and Oudendijk, "Status and Extent of Adjacent Waters", p. 49. Oudendijk and others attribute his changes to his political experience during the intervening years and to the pragmatism of accounting for existing state practice (Oudendijk, p. 49). That Grotius did not consider this a *volte face* may be evidenced by a comment written in a letter by Sir Kenelm Digby in January 1636 regarding the possibility of a reply by Grotius to Selden's book, *Mare Clausum*. According to Sir Kenelm, no reply should be expected. Grotius had written *Mare Liberum* "as a Hollander, and is exceedingly glad to see the contrary proved": Fulton, *The Sovereignty of the Sea*, p. 375.

89. Grotius's own biographer was most harsh in passing this judgement on him: "It is a plea of an advocate – from first to last – of an advocate, too, whose client is his own fatherland fighting desperately to avoid sentence of political death. Its conclusions are based on facts and arguments generally most partially selected and marshalled, and these are frequently presented with a much too unrestricted rhetoric. It is, moreover, often so abstract and academic as to have but little relation to the actual facts and conditions of real life. Only its own age and conditions made it possible." See W.S.M. Knight, "Seraphin de Freitas: Critic of Mare Liberum", *Transactions of the Grotius Society*, vol. 11 (1926), p. 4, quoted in Anand, *Origin and Development of the Law of the Sea*, p. 104. For an argument that Grotius was only doing his job and that he did so as any good advocate would, see G. Ladreit de Lacharrière, "The Controversy Surrounding the Consistency of the Position Adopted by Grotius", in *International Law and the Grotian Heritage* (The Hague: TMC Asser Institute, 1985), pp. 207–213. See also George A. Finch, *Preface to De Jure Praedae Commentarius* (Oxford: Oxford University Press, 1950), pp. xii–xv. Indeed, Grotius is not the only one who has been subjected to this criticism. According to Fulton, "It may be noted that those who took part in it on the one side or the other, including some of the most learned men of their age, were in large measure inspired by patriotic motives. National interests as much as lofty ethics or legal principles were at its root": Fulton, *The Sovereignty of the Sea*, p. 340. Blum puts it thus: "There is good reason to believe that the respective attitudes taken up by these two scholars [Grotius and Selden], and later by their disciples and followers, were largely influenced by the national pretensions and other vested interests of their countries": Yehuda Z. Blum, *Historic Titles in International Law* (The Hague: Martinus Nijhoff, 1965), p. 242. Bynkershoek states more critically, "... some were led astray by their patriotic feelings, some by the tempting vision of commercial freedom, some by a desire to curry favour, some, finally, by the offer of rewards by their state". Cornelius van Bynkershoek, *De Dominio Maris Dissertatis* (Margoffin translation, 1923), p. 29.

Part III

New emerging issues for international environmental law

10

Emerging technologies: Nanotechnology

David Leary and Balakrishna Pisupati

Introduction

Nanotechnology is science and engineering resulting from the manipulation of matter's most basic building blocks: atoms and molecules.[1] Nanotechnology is the understanding and control of matter at dimensions of roughly 1 to 100 nanometres, where unique phenomena enable novel applications. One nanometre is one billionth of a metre and is the width of approximately ten atoms.[2] To put that into perspective, a sheet of paper is about 100,000 nanometres thick.[3]

Scientific research across a range of disciplines, including physics, chemistry and biology, has advanced to such a stage that it is now possible to engineer matter at this scale, either by making particles or matter uniformly smaller, or by scaling up matter using nano-sized building blocks.[4] By working at the molecular or atomic level it is possible to create materials with properties with a wide range of new applications. This convergence of scientific disciplines is leading to a multiplication of applications in fields as diverse as materials manufacturing, computer chips, medical diagnosis, biotechnology, energy and national security.[5]

Nanotechnology is best described as a "platform technology".[6] One area where this platform technology is showing promising signs is in responding to climate change. Nanotechnology will not, by itself, have a dramatic impact on climate change, but its incorporation into larger systems,[7] such as the hydrogen-based economy, solar power technology or next-generation batteries, potentially could have a profound impact on

The future of international environmental law, Leary and Pisupati (eds),
United Nations University Press, 2010, ISBN 978-92-808-1192-6

energy consumption and hence greenhouse gas emissions. A recent report commissioned for the United Kingdom government recognizes that nanotechnology has the potential to contribute to efforts to reduce harmful greenhouse gas emissions and therefore assist in responding to climate change in a range of areas, including: the development of efficient hydrogen-powered vehicles; enhanced and cheaper photovoltaics or solar power technology; the development of a new generation of batteries and supercapacitors (i.e. devices that can store and subsequently release electricity) which could make the more widespread use of electric cars a reality; improved insulation of buildings; and fuel additives that could enhance the energy efficiency of motor vehicles.[8]

Nanotechnology has been identified by industry and governments globally as a priority area of research.[9] For example, since 2000 the US Federal Government has invested more than $1 billion a year in nanotechnology research, with similar amounts having been invested by industry in that country.[10] Other developed countries have also invested heavily in nanotechnology research and development. For example, in 2004 the Japanese government invested ¥97.1 billion while the German government invested €290 million in nanotechnology research and development in the same year.[11] By 2004, venture capitalists had invested in excess of US$1 billion in nanotechnology companies worldwide, and the Organisation for Economic Co-operation and Development (OECD) estimates that, by 2014, nanotechnology will represent 15 per cent of all global manufacturing output.[12]

These projections are strongly supported by data on nanotechnology-based products already available on the market. The most comprehensive data published so far are the various inventories on nanotechnology published by the Woodrow Wilson International Centre for Scholars as part of their Project on Emerging Nanotechnologies.[13] As of 25 August 2009, the Woodrow Wilson nanotechnology consumer products inventory contains some 1015 products or product lines,[14] including cosmetics, food and beverages, clothing, personal care, sporting goods, agriculture, automotives and sunscreens.[15]

While there are potentially many benefits offered by nanotechnology, there are also emerging concerns about the potential risks that nanotechnologies present to humans and the environment, and about the ability of current legal and regulatory regimes to sustainably manage those risks. The complexity of the technology and the properties related to nanoparticles have raised a series of questions on the safety of the technology, which have led to calls for a range of responses including better testing, monitoring and evaluation of the technology as well as appeals to more clearly define legal and regulatory regimes for this technology. In this chapter we explore some aspects of these emerging debates and offer some thoughts on the challenges nanotechnology poses in the context of the overall aim of this book to contribute to debate on the future of international environmental law.[16]

In that context we briefly outline some of the main concerns that have been raised in relation to nanotechnology. Discussion in this first section will be brief as these issues have already been canvassed at length in the published literature.[17] We then go on to consider some of the recent broad policy and regulatory developments with respect to nanotechnology at both the domestic and international level. This analysis will highlight that the response of policymakers, regulators and legal systems is very much a work in process. We then go on to offer some concluding thoughts on possible future directions for international policymakers in responding to the emergence of this new issue for international environmental law and policy.

A sketch of the key concerns

As noted above, there are emerging concerns about the potential risks that nanotechnologies present to humans and the environment, and the ability of current regulatory regimes to sustainably manage those risks. As nanotechnologies are an emergent field of science and technology, it is not yet clear precisely what risks they pose to humans, animal health and the broader environment.[18] As Kuzma and VerHage have observed:

> the risks could be practically zero or they could be significant, depending on the properties of a particular product and exposure levels. For the most part, no one knows. Few risk assessments have been done that allow one to predict what happens when these very small materials, some designed to be biologically active, enter the human body or are dispersed in the environment.[19]

The most significant issues raised so far relate to the toxicity of manufactured nanoparticles. The concerns about the potential toxicity of nanomaterials relate to their small size and their novel properties and their ability to enter the human body and reach vital organs via the blood.[20] There are major gaps in scientific understanding of how nanoparticles act, their toxicity and basic risk management techniques such as how to measure and monitor exposure to nano-particles.[21] However, as the UK Royal Commission on Environmental Pollution in its 2008 report on nanotechnology has observed, so far there is no "evidence of actual ecological damage or harm to humans resulting from exposure to manufactured nanomaterials".[22] But the actual level of risk remains an area of great uncertainty and, as the same inquiry observed:

With our extremely limited understanding regarding exposure levels and patterns, as well as our ignorance of the toxicology of nanomaterials, we cannot be confident of knowing whether effects are occurring or will in future occur in the wider environment.[23]

Clearly, many more rigorous scientific studies and risk assessments still need to be undertaken to confirm or refute initial concerns and, perhaps more significantly, to clearly delineate the nature and scale of the risks potentially associated with the use of nanotechnology.

Given the sophisticated and expensive nature of nanotechnology research and development, ethical issues exist concerning the ability of less developed countries to benefit from and sustainably manage such advances in technology. Less developed countries such as China, India, South Korea, Iran and Thailand are also active in many aspects of nanotechnology research and development.[24] But it is so far unclear whether developing countries will be able to readily fully exploit the opportunities of this technology. What role, for example, will patents have in either facilitating or hindering access to and transfer of nanotechnology? Perhaps more importantly, given the hightech nature and sophisticated science behind nanotechnology, the question arises whether developing countries have the capacity to properly assess and manage those risks.

A related issue that complicates consideration of appropriate regulatory responses is that, so far, there is no generally agreed definition of what nanotechnology is and what it is not; debate in relation to nanotechnology has become confused because no one can agree on a clear definition.[25] It may seem an oxymoron but, in some respects, it might even be reasonable to argue that there is no single technology that we can rightly call nanotechnology. As one witness before a recent parliamentary enquiry into nanotechnology in Australia observed:

Nanotechnologies are not a simple technique. There are a whole range of sciences from material science, biotechnology, medicine, physics and chemistry, to health care and so on. They certainly all aim to manufacture nanomaterials at the nano scale ... That is what they have in common. We could just as well have labelled this new field as "new developments in chemistry, physics, material science and biotechnologies at the atomic scale." We did not because it is too cumbersome. We have shorthanded [sic] this to "nanotechnology," so we tend to see nanotechnology as a label these days for the phenomenon rather than the science. It is a phenomenon that describes an immense range of technologies.[26]

The wide range of techniques and technologies encompassed in the term nanotechnology makes shaping a regulatory response to nanotechnology even more complicated. If scientists, academic commentators and policymakers alike cannot agree on a definition, or indeed if nanotechnology means different things to different "experts", what then is the general public to make of both the opportunities and the potential risks of nanotechnology? The extent to which the public and, perhaps more importantly, civil society (which has a major role to play in shaping public responses and attitudes to nanotechnology) fully understands both the technology that lies behind nanotechnology and the potential risks and benefits offered by nanotechnology is unclear. Indeed, in some sections of civil society and in the community more broadly, there appears to be an emerging visceral response to nanotechnology which is both sceptical and, in some cases, outright hostile. In part this is motivated by genuine and reasonable concerns about the scientific uncertainty surrounding the potential risks to human health and the environment posed by nanotechnology; in part there is also a lack of understanding of the new technology.

For example, in much of the debate concerning nanotechnology to date, sections of civil society have often relied on quite emotional comparisons between asbestos and nanotechnology. But is it fair to regard all nanotechnology (i.e. the "whole range of sciences", as the witness before the parliamentary enquiry cited above describes it) as presenting the same risk, akin to that of asbestos? The simple answer is: probably not. In fact, on the available evidence it is arguable that the comparisons with asbestos are probably only valid when talking about carbon nanotubes. In its 2004 report on nanoscience and nanotechnologies, the United Kingdom's Royal Society highlighted the similarities between carbon nanotubes and asbestos and recommended further detailed scientific studies to assess the potential of harm resulting from possible human exposures in the laboratory and the workplace.[27] But in much of the recent public debate, all nanotechnology is lumped together. It is increasingly being categorized as similar to asbestos, in support of calls for a moratorium on nanotechnology.[28]

Whether those concerns are well founded remains to be seen. So far, on the scientific evidence it appears simply wrong to liken all nanotechnology to asbestos. There are concerns with some forms such as carbon nanotubes, and appropriate science-based policy and regulatory responses need to be developed to respond to those risks. But developing an entire regulatory framework for nanotechnology on the assumption that all nanotechnology poses the same level of risk is an entirely inappropriate way to proceed and is at odds with science-based risk management.

In approaching regulation of nanotechnology we really need to consider two key questions that lie at the heart of the regulation of nanotechnology applications and products:

Does the nanotechnology create something new and currently unknown to the applicable regulatory regime? Does the unprecedented small scale of the nanotechnology application or product make a currently known material, process or product significantly different, from the perspective of regulatory goals? If the answer to one or both of these questions is yes for a given nanotechnology application, then regulatory changes are likely to be required. If neither of those two conditions exist for a given nanotechnology application, then the existing regulatory framework can effectively handle the application.[29]

This suggests that regulators need to consider the need for regulation on a case-by-case basis rather than perhaps developing one blanket regulatory regime for all nanotechnology.

Clearly for public trust and enthusiasm for nanotechnology to be maintained, it is vital that developments in nanotechnology occur against the backdrop of a robust, transparent and efficient regulatory regime. To some extent, lessons learned from the experience of dealing with other technologies, such as biotechnology and genetically modified organisms, is relevant here. For example, greater education of the public about nanotechnology appears needed; ensuring that the science of nanotechnology is understood by the public will help them to assess its benefits, in turn aiding consideration of suitable regulatory frameworks for the development and deployment of this technology.

Against that background we now turn to consider recent policy and regulatory responses to nanotechnology.

Emerging regulatory and policy responses

It is indisputable that we still do not fully understand either the potential risks of nanotechnology or how policymakers and regulators should appropriately respond to the emergence of nanotechnology. Clearly, more detailed research is required on the nature of the potential risks associated with nanotechnology before we can truly say that proper safeguards are in place. However, now that concerns about potential risks have emerged, it has been increasingly recognized that there needs to be closer examination of the regulatory implications of nanotechnology.

To date, no national government has formulated regulations that apply specifically to nanotechnology or nanomaterials. The only nanotechnology-specific legislative instrument that the authors are aware of globally is that adopted by the City of Berkeley, California, USA. Effective 15 December 2006, an ordinance amended the provisions of the City's Municipal Code dealing with hazardous materials to require manufacturers, researchers and other businesses to file written disclosure plans that identify their production or use of nanoparticles.[30]

While no nanotechnology specific legislation has been enacted by national governments, in several jurisdictions there is clearly an emerging scrutiny of the legal and policy implications of nanotechnology. This includes major reviews in the United Kingdom, within the European Community, Australia and the United States. These major reviews include the work of the UK Royal Commission on Environmental Pollution in its Report on *Novel Material in the Environment: the case of nanotechnology*;[31] the Commission of the European Communities regulatory review of European Union legislation relevant to nanotechnology,[32] an independent review of the effect of nanotechnologies on Australia's regulatory frameworks, commissioned by the Australian government;[33] and a Parliamentary inquiry conducted in the Australian state (province) of New South Wales.[34] In the United States in early 2007, the Environmental Protection Agency (EPA) issued a White Paper on Nanotechnology which considers the future role of the EPA in environmental issues that may emerge from current and future developments in nanotechnology.[35] Apart from these detailed reviews, policymakers in Austria, Canada, the Czech Republic, Denmark, Finland, Germany, Ireland, Japan, South Korea, the Netherlands, New Zealand, Norway, the Slovak Republic, Spain, Switzerland, Russia, Singapore and Thailand all appear aware of the need to consider the regulatory implications of nanotechnology and, to varying degrees, seem to be considering what, if any, regulatory response may be necessary in their areas of national jurisdiction.[36]

A detailed examination of developments in each of these countries is beyond the scope of this chapter. But it is worth noting two key themes that seem to run through each of the major reviews undertaken so far. First, all these reviews, to varying degrees, acknowledge that there is an urgent need for a rapid improvement in scientific understanding of the risks of nanotechnology, especially in areas underpinning risk assessment and risk management under existing regulatory frameworks, such as legislation dealing with handling of hazardous chemicals, and occupational health and safety and allied worker protection.[37] For example, the European Commission in its review highlighted four priority areas for research:

- Data on toxic and eco-toxic effects as well as test methods to generate such data;
- Data on uses and exposures throughout the life cycle of nanomaterials or products containing nanomaterials, as well as exposure assessment approaches;
- Characterization of nanomaterials, development of uniform standards and nomenclature, as well as analytical measurement techniques; and
- For occupational health aspects, the effectiveness of a range of risk management measures including process enclosure, ventilation, and

personal protective equipment such as respiratory protective equipment and gloves.[38]

Second, to varying degrees these reviews have all concluded that existing legislation in these countries appears to provide adequate regulatory frameworks for managing known risks. But they all acknowledge that further amendments to existing legislation may be required in the future, as greater scientific understanding of the risks of nanotechnology emerges. In Australia, for example, the review of that country's regulatory framework observed that, while existing legislation appears to regulate issues of concern associated with nanotechnology, specific amendments may be required in future, but the precise nature of these changes to the law will not be known until new knowledge on hazards, exposure and monitoring tools becomes available.[39]

Clearly, therefore, the need for further or amended regulation will only become clear once our scientific understanding is increased. For the mid to long term, the priority should be on addressing gaps in scientific knowledge in relation to the risks of nanotechnology, rather than gaps in the law and regulatory frameworks, per se. With greater scientific understanding, appropriate legal and regulatory responses can evolve over time; this means regulators should be striving to create "adaptive management systems that can respond quickly and effectively as new information becomes available".[40]

Emerging international debates on nanotechnology

The main focus of discussion so far in this chapter has been the response of domestic legal and regulatory systems. What, if any, action has been taken at the international level to respond to emerging concerns in relation to nanotechnology? How do international developments relate to the emerging response of regulators under domestic legal and regulatory systems?

A significant body of international environmental law already seeks to regulate hazardous and dangerous substances. A detailed examination of how international environmental law regulates hazardous and dangerous substances is beyond the scope of this chapter, but several treaties with potential application to nanotechnology are worth noting. The three most important treaties are the 1989 Basel Convention on the Control of Transboundary Movement of Hazardous Wastes (Basel Convention),[41] the 1998 Rotterdam Convention on the Prior Informed Consent Procedure for Certain Hazardous Chemicals and Pesticides in International Trade (Rotterdam Convention),[42] and the 2001 Stockholm Convention on Persistent Organic Pollutants (Stockholm Convention).[43] The Basel

Convention regulates the transboundary movement of hazardous waste and establishes a prior informed consent procedure where, for certain types of hazardous waste, consent for import must be given by the receiving country. Under art. 4(1)(b) of the Basel Convention, parties must not allow exports to countries where the import of such waste has been prohibited by the receiving country. A similar prior informed consent procedure is also applied to certain chemicals and pesticides under the Rotterdam Convention. The Stockholm Convention, on the other hand, seeks to restrict or eliminate altogether the production and use of certain persistent organic pollutants (POPs). Where this is not possible, the Stockholm Convention seeks to ensure that wastes containing POPs are managed safely and in an environmentally sound manner.

However, these treaties only apply to substances that are listed in annexes to the original treaty or which have subsequently been listed in accordance with procedures set out in the relevant treaty. As far as the authors are aware, to date there has not been any attempt to list substances based on nanotechnology under any of the treaties mentioned above. Even if such attempts were to be made, the application of these treaties to nanotechnology is problematic. The lack of clear scientific data on the risks of nanotechnology presents an obstacle, albeit one arguably in part addressed by a precautionary approach. The fact that transboundary movement of such substances would be restricted or prohibited outright, or that their production might be controlled under these treaties if they were listed, suggests that listing appears unlikely in the near future.

More importantly, all three treaties rely on listing of certain substances (waste, chemicals and pesticides) because of the inherent chemical properties of these substances and the harm they present for humans and the natural environment. But in the case of nanotechnology it is not so much the chemical composition of the substances in issue, rather their small size (i.e. on the "nano" scale they pose a risk). Some substances or materials may pose no risk or a manageable risk to human health and the environment when ordinarily used, but might pose a significant risk only at the "nano" scale.

In any event the Rotterdam Convention, in particular, will in all likelihood have only limited application to nanotechnology. Article 2 of the Rotterdam Convention specifically provides that it does not cover, *inter alia*, "pharmaceuticals, including human and veterinary drugs", "chemicals used as food additives" and "food". The Rotterdam Convention would therefore not apply to some of the most controversial uses of nanotechnology.

Existing international treaties therefore do not appear, to date, to provide adequate mechanisms to address the issues surrounding nanotechnology.

Unlike previous environmental issues considered by the international community, the examination of the regulatory implications of nanotechnology at the international level has largely taken place outside the formal United Nations system. Consideration of nanotechnology within the UN has been, at best, rudimentary and fragmented; that is to say there has been no integrated or coordinated consideration of nanotechnology within the UN system. To the extent that there has been consideration, it has largely been ad hoc and confined to particular aspects of the debate within the remit or mandate of individual international organizations.

For example, despite having a wide mandate on a range of environmental issues, the main UN organization dealing with environmental issues, the United Nations Environment Programme (UNEP), so far has had only a passing role to play in debate surrounding nanotechnology. This work has mainly centred on raising awareness of the issue rather than contributing substantively to new initiatives. In 2007 UNEP's fourth annual report on the changing global environment (*GEO Year Book 2007*) highlighted the urgent need to adopt appropriate assessment and legislative processes to address the unique challenges presented by nanomaterials and their life cycles.[44] As well as stressing both the potential risks and benefits offered by nanotechnology, that report also highlighted a number of policy recommendations for future actions by nations and international organizations including, *inter alia*, the need to: standardize nomenclature and test protocols for assessing risks associated with nanotechnology; evaluate the potential environmental and human health impacts of nanotechnology, giving priority to nanotechnology already being mass produced and potentially released into the environment; identify, evaluate and share private sector risk management methods and best practices relating to worker safety and materials handling procedures; and study what lessons can be learned from the existing knowledge and experience related to environmental health issues.[45]

Significantly this cursory UNEP study also recognized that a high priority must be attached to sensitizing national regulatory and environmental agencies to the potential opportunities and risks of nanotechnology. It similarly endorses the need for action to educate the public about the benefits and risks of nanotechnology, raise awareness, and provide access to information about the health and environmental impacts.[46]

More recently the *UNEP Year Book 2009*[47] devotes slightly more than one page to nanotechnology, and that document merely summarizes much of the existing literature.

The United Nations Educational, Scientific and Cultural Organization (UNESCO) has considered some of the ethical issues surrounding nanotechnology. One of UNESCO's main roles is to function as a laboratory of ideas and a standard-setter to forge universal agreements on emerging ethical issues.[48] "UNESCO also serves as a clearing-house for the dissemination and sharing of information and knowledge, while helping Member States to build their human and institutional capacities in diverse fields."[49] Consistent with that mandate in considering the implications of nanotechnology, UNESCO, through the work of the World Commission on the Ethics of Scientific Knowledge and Technology (COMEST) and the International Bioethics Committee (IBC), has largely focused on the ethical implications of nanotechnology. The issues of nanotechnology and ethics were first explored during the Third Session of COMEST in Rio de Janeiro in December 2003. In 2005 a group of experts was established in order to assist COMEST to draft a potential policy document in regard to ethics and nanotechnology. This group of experts was composed of members from South Korea, Canada, New Zealand, Japan, the Netherlands, China, Germany and Brazil. Key outputs from this work has included a number of short papers on the ethical implications of nanotechnology.[50]

The Food and Agriculture Organization of the United Nations (FAO) has a mandate to raise levels of nutrition, improve agricultural productivity, better the lives of rural populations and contribute to the growth of the world economy.[51] Although the FAO has a wide mandate with respect to food and agriculture issues, it has so far had little role to play in the debate concerning the regulatory implications of nanotechnology in food and agriculture. However, in response to concerns raised by member countries on the possible food safety implications of the application of nanotechnology to food and agriculture, the FAO and the World Health Organization (WHO) convened a series of experts meetings on the issue in 2008 and 2009. Essentially marking the beginning of detailed consideration by the FAO and the WHO, the experts meetings aim to develop a common view of actual and anticipated nanotechnology applications in the food and agriculture sectors, and of the regulatory implications. One of the main outcomes of this process is expected to be agreement on priority actions that are needed to control potential food safety hazards associated with nanotechnology applications in food and agriculture. This process will also possibly develop guidance on the possible roles of the FAO and WHO in promoting sound governance of food safety issues linked to nanotechnology applications.[52] At the time of writing, further information on the outcomes of these meetings was not yet available from the FAO.

The WHO is the main directing and coordinating authority for health within the United Nations system. Its mandate is to provide leadership on global health matters, shaping the health research agenda, setting norms and standards, articulating evidence-based policy options, providing technical support to countries and monitoring and assessing health trends.[53] Yet, like the FAO, the WHO has so far had little role to play in the emerging debate on nanotechnology, and currently has no dedicated programme or project on nanotechnology. Its work to date on this issue has essentially involved providing updates to member states on the work of the OECD and the International Organization for Standardization (ISO) (see discussion below), principally through its involvement with the Intergovernmental Forum on Chemical Safety.

The Intergovernmental Forum on Chemical Safety was created by the International Conference on Chemical Safety held in Stockholm in April 1994, and provides "an overarching mechanism for cooperation among governments, intergovernmental and non-governmental organizations for the promotion of chemical risk assessment and the environmentally sound management of chemicals".[54] Its secretariat is based at the WHO. The most recent meeting of the Intergovernmental Forum on Chemical Safety, held in Senegal in September 2008, adopted the *Dakar Statement on Manufactured Nanomaterials*,[55] which contained some twenty-two recommendations that are largely aspirational or hortatory in nature, adding little if anything to the emerging debate.

In a separate development, nanotechnology was also considered at the second session of the International Conference on Chemicals Management (ICCM), held under the framework of the programme of work under the Strategic Approach to International Chemicals Management (SAICM) which was created under the Johannesburg Plan of Implementation, adopted at the World Summit on Sustainable Development in 2002.[56] SAICM "is a policy framework to promote chemical safety around the world" whose objective is "the achievement of the sound management of chemicals throughout their life cycle so that, by 2020, chemicals are produced and used in ways that minimize significant adverse impacts on human health and the environment".[57]

Resolution II/4 on Emerging Policy Issues[58] adopted at the second session of the ICCM devoted some eleven paragraphs to nanotechnology. But this resolution contained no substantive new initiative, focusing instead on the need for information sharing, participation by all stakeholders (e.g. policy-makers, industry, civil society and trade unions) and dialogue with other existing processes. Resolution II/4 invited governments and other stakeholders to develop a report that focuses on nanotechnologies and manufactured nanomaterials including, in particular, issues of relevance to developing countries and economies in transition, and to make the report available to the Open-ended Working Group at its first meeting and to the International Conference on Chemicals Management at its third session.[59]

Apart from these very rudimentary programmes, there has been little substantive examination of the regulatory implications of nanotechnology within the UN system. In fact, by far the most advanced developments with respect to the consideration of the regulatory implications of nanotechnology are occurring outside of formal UN processes.

Within the OECD for example, in 2005 a process was established to facilitate exchange of information on the development of regulation of nanotechnology and to assist OECD member countries in developing regulatory frameworks, and this process is ongoing. Similarly, in March 2007 the OECD's Committee on Scientific and Technological Policy established a Working Party on Nanotechnology. The objective of this Working Party is to promote international cooperation that facilitates research, development and responsible commercialization of nanotechnology in member countries and in non-member economies.[60] A work programme is under development to address some of the main policy challenges and will include: work on statistics and indicators of nanotechnology; examination of the business environment for nanotechnology; work to foster international collaboration in nanotechnology research; work on public perceptions towards nanotechnology and the engagement of stakeholder communities in the debate on nanotechnology; as well as a dialogue on policy strategies to spread good policy practices towards the responsible development of nanotechnology.[61] In 2006 the OECD also established a Working Party on Manufactured Nanoparticles which is currently looking at international cooperation in health and environmental safety-related aspects of manufactured nanomaterials.

The most significant developments so far, however, have occurred under the auspices of the International Organization for Standardization or ISO, the world's largest developer and publisher of international standards. The ISO is a non-governmental organization which is essentially a network of national standards institutes of 157 countries with a central Secretariat in Geneva, Switzerland.[62]

In 2005 the ISO established a new technical committee, ISO/TC 229 Nanotechnologies, hosted by the United Kingdom, to develop international standards for nanotechnologies.[63] The mandate of this committee is to examine standardization in the field of nanotechnologies that includes either or both of the following:

(1) Understanding and control of matter and processes at the nanoscale, typically, but not exclusively, below 100 nanometres in one or more dimensions where the onset of size-dependent phenomena usually enables novel applications [and] (2) Utilizing the properties of nanoscale materials that differ from the properties of individual atoms, molecules, and bulk matter, to create improved materials, devices, and systems that exploit these new properties.[64]

The initial work of this committee will be in three broad areas: (1) terminology and nomenclature standards to provide a common language for scientific, technical, commercial and regulatory processes; (2) measurement and characterization standards to provide an internationally accepted basis for quantitative scientific, commercial and regulatory activities; and (3) health, safety and environmental standards to improve occupational safety, and consumer and environmental protection, promoting good practice in the production, use and disposal of nanomaterials, nanotechnology products and nanotechnology-enabled systems and products.[65] As at 19 October 2009, two international standards relating to nanotechnology have now been published by the ISO.[66] Another forty or so standards were under development.[67]

As noted earlier in this chapter, one of the key threshold issues that needs to be considered is the development of a clear definition of what is and what is not nanotechnology. The work of the ISO in developing international standards dealing with terminology and nomenclature will help in providing a common language for scientific, technical, commercial and regulatory debates surrounding nanotechnology. Likewise the development of measurement and characterization standards to provide an internationally accepted basis for quantitative scientific, commercial and regulatory activities provide a vital first step in assisting in enhanced understanding of the risks of nanotechnology. Scientists and in turn regulators cannot hope to fully understand the risks of nanotechnology and shape appropriate policies in response unless these appropriate agreed standards are in place to measure that risk.

Both developed and developing country experts are involved in the development of the ISO standards. Currently thirty-two countries[68] are participating in the work of ISO TC 229, while another ten countries[69] are formally involved as observers. Because the ISO is composed of member standards organizations, participation is through those various national standards organizations, which may or may not include some representation or formal involvement of national and provincial governments, as well as industry representatives. The ISO does not function as an intergovernmental organization as its members are not governments per se, although governments are involved in the work of national standards organizations to various degrees.

For the foreseeable future the ISO and, in particular ISO TC 229, appears to be the main international forum for debate on technical issues relating to nanotechnology. While the standards developed by the ISO have no binding legal effect, per se, they will act as guides to international best practice into the future and may ultimately be incorporated into national regulatory regimes. It is too early to say whether these standards will be adequate, but the involvement of the ISO in developing such standards is a promising first step in assisting existing regimes to adapt to the new challenges of nanotechnology.

A related development which is taking place at the same time as the work of the ISO is the emergence of voluntary standards that have been developed by industry, often in partnership with the NGO community. There are, for example, a number of initiatives under way to develop interim voluntary standards for the safe production, use and disposal of nanotechnology.[70] These include the Voluntary Reporting Scheme for engineered nanoscale materials sponsored by the government of the United Kingdom[71] and joint industry and civil society initiatives such as the Environmental Defense-DuPont Nano Partnership Nano Risk Framework.[72] How these voluntary schemes will ultimately be incorporated in more formal legislative regimes remains unclear. But engagement by industry together with civil society should also be seen as a positive development which should be encouraged.

Conclusion – Responding to nanotechnology: Is new international environmental law required or might we opt for a cluster of governance mechanisms?

The response of regulators under domestic legal systems and at the international level is very much a work in progress. Given the state of scientific understanding of the potential risks of nanotechnology (not forgetting also its huge potential for benefits) it is still too soon to judge whether existing legal and regulatory mechanisms will be adequate to manage those risks (while also facilitating the benefits). It is true that management of health, safety and environmental issues surrounding nanotechnology will need to be part of an ongoing process of adaptive management, at both the domestic and international level. As scientific understanding of both the risks and the benefits of nanotechnology develops, so legal and policy responses will also need to adapt.

Developments, both internationally and within individual legal and regulatory systems, will be closely linked. Importantly for the purposes of the aims of this book (i.e. to consider new challenges for international environmental law) it appears increasingly obvious that international responses to nanotechnology relate not so much to law, per se, but perhaps fall under the broader idea of international governance for nanotechnology.

In Chapter 1 of this book, we noted that Edith Brown Weiss has suggested we are witnessing the emergence of a "kaleidoscopic" international legal and political system.[73] It may be that, in the long term, initiatives outside the UN system such as the development of standards by the ISO and voluntary industry initiatives will provide a cluster of governance mechanisms for the safe and sustainable management of nanotechnology.

The idea of a governance response to nanotechnology (in a "kaleidoscopic" international legal and political system or otherwise), as opposed to a strictly legal response, is consistent with similar debates that have been emerging in relation to the appropriate form of response under domestic regulatory frameworks. Thus, for example, the likes of Bowman and Hodge,[74] drawing on the earlier work of Ayres and Braithwaite[75] and Grabosky,[76] have posited a framework for understanding regulatory options for nanotechnology, suggesting "a continuum of regulatory mechanisms was possible from hard law at one extreme through licensing and codes of practice to 'soft' self-regulation and negotiation in order to influence behaviour at the other".[77] This is the so-called enforcement pyramid.[78]

Others, such as Grabosky,[79] have proposed a three-dimensional pyramid that goes "beyond the depiction of instruments available to state regulatory authorities, to incorporate the other institutions which comprise regulatory system-regulated entities themselves and their industry associations, and third parties, both public interest institutions and commercial actors".[80] In this context, Bowman and Hodge have proposed a conceptual model for the regulatory frontiers of nanotechnology that recognizes that, while hard law (such as legislation and treaties) may be at the centre of regulatory concerns, it is not the only possible response.[81] Significantly, as Bowman and Hodge recognize, "a regulatory response will be made within the broader context of public policy concerns and international norms in which stakeholder dialogue occurs" and that this stakeholder dialogue should incorporate a "wide range of social and ethical issues as well as the scientific and commercial matters usually dominating the nanotechnology discourse".[82]

This model suggests that, rather than considering nanotechnology as requiring one single regulatory response to deal with all issues, it may be that there will be several regulatory regimes specific to particular issues or forms of nanotechnology. This thus suggests that regulation of nanotechnology may involve more than just a new piece of nanotechnology-specific legislation or treaty, and may in fact include a range of possible regulatory responses extending across the whole enforcement pyramid and its multiple legal domains. A view of future regulation of nanotechnology as requiring a governance response does not, of course, exclude a role for law, and international environmental law in particular. New or existing international environmental treaties (such as those discussed above) may form part of future regulatory frameworks for nanotechnology. But they need not be the only regulatory mechanisms that may be appropriate into the future. Law, and international environmental law in particular, will only be part of an overall international governance response to the emergence of nanotechnology, as it will be for other new technologies and new environmental challenges.

Notes

1. Kristen Kulinowski, "Nanotechnology: From 'Wow' to 'Yuck'?", in Geoffrey Hunt and Michael Mehta (eds), *Nanotechnology: Risk, Ethics and Law* (London: Earthscan, 2006), pp. 13–24.

2. Oakdene Hollins, *Environmentally Beneficial Nanotechnologies: Barriers and Opportunities* (2007), p. 9; available at <http://www.defra.gov.uk/environment/quality/nanotech/documents/envbeneficial-report.pdf>.

3. Australian Research Council, *Nanotechnology Network*; available at <http://www.ausnano.net/content/about>.

4. Commonwealth Department of Industry, Tourism and Resources, *Smaller, Cleaner, Cheaper, Faster, Smarter. Nanotechnology Applications and Opportunities for Australian Industry* (2002), p 3; available at <http://www.innovation.gov.au/Industry/nanotechnology/documents/occasionalpapersmallercleanercheaperfastersmarter20051111120225.pdf>.

5. OECD and Allianz, *Small sizes that matter: Opportunities and risks of nanotechnologies*; available at <https://www.oecd.org/dataoecd/37/19/37770473.pdf>.

6. Oakdene Hollins, *Environmentally Beneficial Nanotechnologies*, p. 9.

7. Ibid.

8. Ibid.

9. Australian Research Council, *Nanotechnology Network*.

10. UK Council for Science and Technology, *Nanosciences and Nanotechnologies: A Review of Government's Progress on its Policy Commitments* (2007); available at <http://www.cst.gov.uk/cst/news/Files/nano_review.pdf>.

11. Ibid.

12. Australian Research Council, *Nanotechnology Network*.

13. See <http://www.nanotechproject.org/inventories>.

14. See <http://www.nanotechproject.org/inventories/consumer/analysis_draft>.

15. Ibid.

16. Our focus here is on the environmental issues. Other implications of nanotechnology including military applications and human rights implications, such as privacy, etc., are outside the scope of this chapter.

17. See, for example, Hunt and Mehta, *Nanotechnology: Risk, Ethics and Law*; and Fritz Allhoff (ed.), *Nanoethics: The Ethical and Social Implications of Nanotechnology* (Hoboken, NJ: Wiley-InterScience, 2007).

18. Roland Clift, "Risk Management and Regulation in an Emerging Technology", in Hunt and Mehta, *Nanotechnology: Risk, Ethics and Law*, pp. 140–153.

19. Jennifer Kuzma and Peter VerHage, *Nanotechnology in Agriculture and Food Production: Anticipated Applications* (2006); available at <http://www.nanotechproject.org/publications/archive/nanotechnology_in_agriculture_food>.

20. OECD and Allianz, *Small sizes that matter: Opportunities and risks of nanotechnologies*.

21. Australian Senate, Community Affairs References Committee, *Report on Workplace Exposure to Toxic Dust* (2006); available at <http://www.aph.gov.au/senate/committee/clac_ctte/completed_inquiries/2004-07/toxic_dust/report/report.pdf>.

22. United Kingdom, Royal Commission on Environmental Pollution, *Twenty-seventh Report: Novel Materials in the Environment: The case of nanotechnology* (2008), p. 27; available at <http://www.rcep.org.uk/reports/27-novel%20materials/27-novelmaterials.htm>.

23. Ibid., p. 34.

24. UK Council for Science and Technology, *Nanosciences and Nanotechnologies: A Review of Government's Progress on its Policy Commitments*.

25. See K. Eric Drexler, "Nanotechnology: From Feynman to Funding", in Hunt and Mehta, *Nanotechnology: Risk, Ethics and Law*, pp. 25–41, p. 25.

26. Professor Graeme Hodge, Evidence, *Report of Proceedings before Standing Committee on State Development Inquiry into Nanotechnology in New South Wales, New South Wales Parliament* (2008), p. 21; available at <http://www.parliament.nsw.gov.au/Prod/parlment/committee.nsf/0/1cea57e011cad31bca25743a00080972/$FILE/080428%20Uncorrected%20Transcript.pdf>.

27. See The Royal Society & The Royal Academy of Engineering, *Nanoscience and Nanotechnologies: Opportunities and Uncertainties* (Plymouth: Royal Society, 2004), p. 43; available at <http://www.nanotec.org.uk/report/Nano%20report%202004%20fin.pdf>.

28. See, for example, media reports such as "Nanotechnology is the Next Asbestos, Union Says", *ABC News*, 14 April 2009; available at <http://www.abc.net.au/news/stories/2009/04/14/2541876.htm>; "Nanotechnology the New Asbestos?", *Food Navigator USA*, 17 June 2009; available at <http://www.foodnavigator-usa.com/Financial-Industry/Nanotechnology-The-new-asbestos>.

29. Jeffery H. Matsuura, *Nanotechnology regulation and policy worldwide* (Boston, Artech House, 2006).

30. City of Berkeley, Municipal Code, §§ 15.12.040 and 15.12.050. A copy of this code can be accessed at <http://codepublishing.com/ca/berkeley>. For a brief examination of these provisions see Arnold & Potter LLP, *Client Advisory-City of Berkeley's Ordinance Regulating Nanotechnology raises key issue* (2007); available at <http://www.arnoldporter.com/resources/documents/Arnold&PorterCA-CityofBerkeleysOrdinanceRegulatingNanotechnology_030207.pdf>.

31. The Royal Commission on Environmental Pollution is an independent standing body established in 1970 to advise the Queen, Government, Parliament, the devolved administrations and the public on environmental issues. The Commission delivers its advice in the form of reports, which are submitted to the Queen and to Parliament. See United Kingdom, Royal Commission on Environmental Pollution, *Twenty-seventh Report: Novel Materials in the Environment: The case of nanotechnology* (2008); available at <http://www.rcep.org.uk/reports/27-novel%20materials/27-novelmaterials.htm>.

32. See Commission of the European Communities, *Communication from the Commission to the European Parliament, the Council and the European Economic and Social Committee: Regulatory Aspects of Nanomaterials* [SEC (2008) 2036], 2008; available at <http://ec.europa.eu/nanotechnology/pdf/comm_2008_0366_en.pdf>.

33. See Karinne Ludlow, Diana Bowman and Graeme Hodge, *A Review of Possible Impacts of Nanotechnology on Australia's Regulatory Framework* (2007); available from <http://www.innovation.gov.au/Industry/Nanotechnology/Documents/MonashReport2008.pdf>.

34. See Parliament of New South Wales, Standing Committee on State Development, *Nanotechnology in New South Wales*, Report no. 33 (2008). A copy of this report and transcripts of evidence before the inquiry is available at <http://www.parliament.nsw.gov.au/Prod/parlment/committee.nsf/0/60ce9a9b34382dc5ca2573aa00045168>.

35. US Science Policy Council, *Final Nanotechnology White Paper* (2007); available at <http://www.epa.gov/OSA/nanotech.htm>.

36. For a review of the latest developments in each of these jurisdictions see OECD Environment Directorate, Joint Meeting of the Chemicals Committee and the Working Party on Chemicals, Pesticides and Biotechnology, *Current Developments/Activities on the Safety of Manufactured Nanomaterials/Nanotechnologies* (ENV/JM/MONO (2008) p. 29, 2008; available at <http://www.olis.oecd.org/olis/2008doc.nsf/linkto/nt0000799e/$file/jt03257288.pdf>.

37. Commission of the European Communities, *Communication from the Commission to the European Parliament, the Council and the European Economic and Social Committee: Regulatory Aspects of Nanomaterials*, p. 9.

38. Ibid.

39. Ludlow et al., *A Review of Possible Impacts of Nanotechnology on Australia's Regulatory Framework*, p. 5.
40. United Kingdom, Royal Commission on Environmental Pollution, *Twenty-seventh Report: Novel Materials in the Environment: The case of nanotechnology*, p. 72.
41. Convention on the Control of Transboundary Movement of Hazardous Wastes and their Disposal, Basel, 22 March 1989, entered into force 5 May 1992, 28 ILM 657 (1989).
42. Convention on the Prior Informed Consent Procedure for Certain Hazardous Chemicals and Pesticides, Rotterdam, 11 September 1998, entered into force 24 February 2004, 38 ILM 1 (1999).
43. Convention on Persistent Organic Pollutants, Stockholm, 22 May 2001, entered into force 17 May 2004, 40 ILM 532 (2001). The 1990 Convention Concerning Safety in the Use of Chemicals at Work (ILO No 170), Geneva, 25 June 1990, entered into force 11 April 1993, might also be relevant but is not examined here.
44. United Nations Environment Programme, *GEO Year Book 2007: An Overview of Our Changing Environment* (2007); available at <http://www.unep.org/geo/yearbook/yb2007/pdf/gyb2007_english_full.pdf>.
45. Ibid.
46. Ibid.
47. United Nations Environment Programme, *UNEP Year Book 2009: New Science and Developments in our Changing Environment* (Nairobi: UNEP, 2009).
48. UNESCO, *Research: nanotechnology* (2008); available at <http://portal.unesco.org/shs/en/ev.php-url_id=6314&url_do=do_topic&url_section=201.html>.
49. Ibid.
50. For an overview of this work and for links to copies of these various reports see ibid.
51. FAO, available at <http://www.fao.org>.
52. FAO–Codex Alimentarius Commission, *Report-Joint FAO/WHO Food Standards Programme, Codex Alimentarius Commission, Thirty First Session*, Agenda Item 15, 2008, available at <ftp://ftp.fao.org/codex/CAC/CAC31/al3109Ge.pdf>.
53. World Health Organization, "About WHO"; available at <http://www.who.int/about/en>.
54. For a detailed overview of the work and operations of the Intergovernmental Forum on Chemical Safety, see International Institute for Sustainable Development, *A Brief Introduction to the Intergovernmental Forum on Chemical Safety* (2003); available at <http://www.iisd.ca/process/chemical_management-ifcsintro.htm>.
55. The *Dakar Statement on Manufactured Nanomaterials* is contained in World Health Organization, Intergovernmental Forum on Chemical Safety, *Final Report of the Sixth Session of the Intergovernmental Forum on Chemical Safety*, /FORUM-VI/07w, 2008, available at <http://www.who.int/ifcs/en>.
56. Strategic Approach to International Chemicals Management, "Introducing SAICM"; available at <http://www.saicm.org/index.php?menuid=2&pageid=256>.
57. Ibid.
58. *Report of the International Conference on Chemicals Management on the Work of its Second Session, Resolution II/4*; advanced draft copy available at <http://www.saicm.org/index.php?menuid=9&pageid=392&submenuheader=.
59. Ibid., para. 9.
60. OECD, "Science and Technology Policy: Nanotechnology"; available at <http://www.oecd.org/site/0,3407,en_21571361_41212117_1_1_1_1_1,00.html>.
61. OECD, *The OECD's Work on Nanotechnology*; available at <http://www.oecd.org/document/36/0,3343,en_2649_34269_38829732_1_1_1_1,00.html>.
62. International Organization for Standardization, *About ISO* (2009); available at <http://www.iso.org>.
63. Ibid.

64. International Organization for Standardization, *Standards Development-TC 229*; available at <http://www.iso.org/iso/iso_technical_committee.html?commid=381983>.
65. International Organization for Standardization, *Business Plan ISO/TC 229 Nanotechnologies*; available at <http://isotc.iso.org/livelink/livelink/fetch/2000/2122/4191900/4192161/TC_229_BP_2007-2008.pdf?nodeid=6356960&vernum=0>.
66. These are ISO/TR 12885: 2008 – Health and safety practices in occupational settings relevant to nanotechnologies and ISO/TS 27687: 2008 Nanotechnologies – Terminology and definitions for nano-objects – Nanoparticle, nanofibre and nanoplate. See <http://www.iso.org/iso/iso_catalogue/catalogue_tc/catalogue_tc_browse.htm?commid=381983&published=on> for further details.
67. For details see <http://www.iso.org/iso/iso_catalogue/catalogue_tc/catalogue_tc_browse.htm?commid=381983&development=on>.
68. This includes national standards organizations from Argentina, Australia, Austria, Belgium, Brazil, Canada, China, Czech Republic, Denmark, Finland, France, Germany, India, Iran, Israel, Italy, Japan, Kenya, South Korea, Malaysia, Mexico, the Netherlands, Norway, Poland, Russia, Singapore, South Africa, Spain, Sweden, Switzerland, United Kingdom and the United States.
69. This includes national standards organizations from Egypt, Estonia, Hong Kong, Ireland, Kazakhstan, Morocco, Romania, Slovakia, Thailand and Venezuela.
70. Scott Walsh, John Balbus, Richard Denison and Karne Florini, "Nanotechnology: Getting it Right the First Time", *Journal of Cleaner Production*, vol. 16, no. 8–9 (2008), pp. 1018–1020.
71. United Kingdom Department for Environment Food and Rural Affairs, *Nanotechnologies*; available at <http://www.defra.gov.uk/environment/nanotech/index.htm>.
72. DuPont-Environment Defense Fund, *Nano Risk Framework*; available at <http://nanoriskframework.com/page.cfm?tagID=1095>.
73. Edith Brown Weiss, "International Law in a Kaleidoscopic World", paper presented at the Second Biennial General Conference of the Asian Society of International Law, Tokyo, 1–2 August 2009, copy on file with author.
74. Ibid.
75. Ian Ayres and John Braithwaite, *Responsive Regulation: Transcending the Deregulation Debate* (New York: Oxford University Press, 1992).
76. Peter N. Grabosky, "Discussion Paper: Inside the Pyramid: Towards a Conceptual Framework for the Analysis of Regulatory Systems", *International Journal of the Sociology of Law*, vol. 25 (1997), pp. 195–201.
77. Dianne Bowman and Graham Hodge, "Nanotechnology: Mapping the Wild Regulatory Frontier", *Futures*, vol. 38, no. 9 (2006), pp. 1060–1073, p. 1068.
78. Ibid.
79. Grabosky, "Inside the Pyramid".
80. Ibid, p. 98.
81. Bowman and Hodge, "Nanotechnology: Mapping the Wild Regulatory Frontier", p. 1064.
82. Ibid.

11

Legal frameworks for emerging technologies: Bioenergy

Richard L. Ottinger and Victor M. Tafur

Bioenergy is energy produced from vegetation. It may be in the form of ethanol (e.g. distilled from corn, sugar cane, etc.), biodiesel (e.g. from palm oil, soy beans, jatropha, etc.), for use as biofuels to power vehicles or for power to produce electricity or industrial processes; non-vehicular bioenegy may also be derived from wood chips. In this chapter we explore the risks and benefits of biofuels before going on to look at standards that have been developed to address some of the risks of biofuels. We also explore options for implementation of bioenergy standards through both international and national environmental law.

Potential benefits

Bioenergy has the potential of being a uniquely advantageous resource for the economic development of developing countries and rural areas of all countries not served by electricity grids, areas constituting a population of approximately 1.6 billion people.[1] Most such areas in developing countries are in the tropics, where bioenergy feedstocks can be readily and affordably grown. Local labour can be used and local jobs can be created. Some of the feedstocks can be grown on marginal land[2] and some require few fertilizers or pesticides.[3] Some bioenergy feedstocks can enrich the soil and prevent erosion. Usually no sophisticated processing equipment or experts need to be imported, but the most vulnerable developing countries will need financial assistance and expertise for education and training.

The future of international environmental law, Leary and Pisupati (eds),
United Nations University Press, 2010, ISBN 978-92-808-1192-6

For all countries, use of bioenergy can reduce greenhouse gas (GHG) emissions by replacing high-emitting fossil fuels, and they can relieve dependence on imported oil from less stable regions, thus providing increased energy security. The cost of importing oil places a heavy burden on developing countries, and when oil costs are high, biofuels can often be economically advantageous for all countries.

Risks

There are, however, significant risks associated with the growing and processing of bioenergy feedstocks, including the following:[4]
1. *Energy balance* – Production of bioenergy can consume more energy than the use of fossil fuels if significant fossil fuel is required for fertilizers, pesticides, production fuelling and transportation to processing centres and then to markets.[5]
2. *GHG emissions* – Related to energy balance, some bioenergy production can emit as much or more GHG emissions than direct utilization of fossil fuels.[6] Critically, if forests or peat bogs, substantial GHG sinks, are destroyed for bioenergy feedstock planting, reductions in GHG emissions will not be offset – indeed, considerable increases in GHG emissions can result, as happened in Indonesia and Malaysia.[7]
3. *Food impacts* – Planting bioenergy feedstocks so as to displace food crops or occupy lands needed for food production can contribute to food price increases and shortages. There has been a great deal of controversy over the extent of these effects from the heavy use of corn, soy beans and other food crops as bioenergy feedstocks.
4. *Water impacts* – Many bioenergy feedstocks require substantial amounts of water for irrigation, and this can cause water shortage problems where water supplies already are scarce, particularly where wasteful spray irrigation is utilized. Pollution of water supplies can also occur.
5. *Soil impacts* – Planting of monocultures for production of bioenergy feedstocks can deplete the nutrients in the soil, thus making feedstock growth unsustainable and limiting the soil's use for other production.[8]
6. *Indirect land use impacts* – The conversion of valuable forests, peat bogs and productive agricultural lands that act as carbon sinks to large bioenergy plantations can cause more environmental costs than benefits. However, in assessing the environmental impacts of indirect land use from bioenergy production, comparison should be made against the environmental impacts of fossil, nuclear and other fuel production.

7. *Biodiversity impacts* – The loss of biodiversity arising from indirect land use impacts can have significant environmental impacts.
8. *Air impacts* – In many countries, feedstock residues are burned to facilitate the growth of the crops, causing substantial air pollution.[9]
9. *Invasive species* – Some bioenergy feedstocks have invasive characteristics that could crowd out other agricultural uses.[10]
10. *Labour impacts* – In some countries, child labour is employed to harvest feedstocks, and workers are exploited by payment of substandard wages, intolerable working conditions, unreasonable quotas and lack of resources to provide healthcare for workers suffering job-related injuries and diseases.[11]
11. *Equity impacts* – Large bioenergy plantation owners sometimes expropriate lands long used by local farmers, and foreign developers sometimes pay inadequate compensation to the countries or communities for the land they develop for bioenergy, creating the potential for a new kind of colonialism.[12] These large developers also frequently ignore rural area bioenergy development in areas that are highly in need of the economic opportunity and energy supplies that bioenergy can provide.

In addition to the risks described above, other essential requirements for successful bioenergy project development may be lacking:

1. *Education and training* – Many developing countries lack officials with sufficient knowledge of bioenergy production and marketing to permit successful project implementation. They often lack agricultural extension services to educate and train local farmers in sustainable bioenergy production. There may be scant infrastructure to process biofuels and get them efficiently utilized locally or transported to markets.
2. *Maintenance* – Developers may not take responsibility for long-term maintenance of equipment they supply or the provision of spare parts where there are equipment failures, and local farmers and their representatives may lack the contractual expertise to acquire them.
3. *Research and development (R&D)* – There is a great need for R&D on the most sustainable feedstocks, biofuel production methodologies and on multi-cropping; indeed, there is a serious lack of R&D into the most efficient and environmentally sound methods for all agricultural production.[13] Agricultural experts have recommended significant expansion of support for the research centres of the Consultative Group of International Agricultural Research (CGIAR) to form the scientific basis for expansion of sustainable bioenergy.[14]
4. *Public involvement and transparency* – The affected public often is not involved in proposed bioenergy projects from the start of planning through execution of the project, creating serious risks of lack of acceptance and unsustainable practices. To enable meaningful public

involvement, all information on a project, costs and risks as well as benefits, must be provided to the affected public in a form that is readily understandable. An environmental impact assessment process can be critically helpful.

5. *Legal framework* – The necessary legal system is often lacking to govern contractual agreements and to regulate the sustainability, environmental and social aspects described above, with an independent judiciary to interpret and apply the legislation. An official body needs to be charged with issuing regulations to carry out the legal provisions.

6. *Enforcement/Corruption* – The required enforcement structure is not always in place, with appropriate penalties for violations and sufficient numbers of adequately paid and trained personnel to ensure that laws are complied with. Provision is also needed for independent auditors to perform audit inspections at least annually, and to publish reports on the observance of relevant laws and regulations.

Standards

To address these risks, standards are being developed to assure the sustainability of bioenergy production. The most thorough and participatory work on formulating the principles and criteria for sustainable biofuels standards has been carried out by the Roundtable on Sustainable Biofuels (RSB) under the aegis of the École Polytechnique Fédérale de Lausanne.[15] The RSB proposals are organized round the twelve principles listed below, and detailed criteria have been developed for each principle.[16] The RSB process is uniquely open, so that any interested party can participate and make recommendations.

The RSB principles are:

1. Biofuel production shall follow all applicable laws of the country in which they occur, and shall endeavour to follow all international treaties relevant to biofuels production to which the relevant country is a party;

2. Biofuels projects shall be designed and operated under appropriate, comprehensive, transparent, consultative, and participatory processes that involve all relevant stakeholders;

3. Biofuels shall contribute to climate change mitigation by significantly reducing GHG emissions as compared to fossil fuels;

4. Biofuel production shall not violate human rights or labour rights and shall ensure decent work and the well-being of workers;

5. Biofuel production shall contribute to the social and economic development of local, rural and indigenous peoples and communities;

6. Biofuel production shall not impair food security;

7. Biofuel production shall avoid negative impacts on biodiversity, ecosystems, and areas of high conservation value;
8. Biofuel production shall promote practices that seek to improve soil health and minimize degradation;
9. Biofuel production shall optimize surface and groundwater resource use, including minimizing contamination or depletion of these resources, and shall not violate existing formal and customary water rights;
10. Air pollution from biofuel production and processing shall be minimized along the supply chain;
11. Biofuels shall be produced in the most cost-effective way. The use of technology must improve production efficiency and social and environmental performance in all stages of the biofuel value chain; and
12. Biofuel production shall not violate land rights.[17]

These principles and accompanying criteria as requisites for standards are well enunciated in the RSB analysis, currently embodied as a near-final draft called Version Zero.[18] In the following discussion we focus on the options for implementation of bioenergy standards through both international and national environmental law.

Implementation

Implementation measures must be adequate to address the risks mentioned above, but simple enough to be acceptable, affordable (or financeable) and capable of execution by developing countries. This is a major challenge. It may be necessary to have two implementation regimes, one for developed countries and one for less developed countries, with a longer phase-in period and provision for financial and technical assistance for the latter. Different implementation measures might also be indicated for large bioenergy plantations and small rural developments so that agro/petro giants do not further dominate developing country agricultural and resource development, and to protect the energy and development needs of poor rural farmers.

The subject may be too controversial now to enable implementation by a binding treaty. However, to guarantee the required GHG reductions recommended by the Intergovernmental Panel on Climate Change (IPCC) to avoid the projected catastrophic consequences of climate change, a binding treaty may eventually be required. Successful treaties have been adopted to address several environmental threats such as for reduction of chlorofluorocarbon (CFC) and hydrofluorocarbon (HFC) emissions in the Montreal Protocol,[19] and for elimination of trade in endangered species in the CITES treaty.[20] As desirable as a treaty might be

for addressing bioenergy production risks, treaties take a long time to negotiate and the negotiation outcome is uncertain. The bioenergy industry
is already large and growing rapidly, with many countries having set ambitious legislative quantitative goals.[21] So, to address the risks quickly
enough to significantly promote sustainable bioenergy production, voluntary standards and incentives will probably have to be adopted. Voluntary standard implementation options (premised on their inclusion of
significant sustainability standards and the adoption of a meaningful cap-
and-trade programme or carbon tax to set a realistic price on GHG emissions) include the following:

1. *Pricing* – Pricing is critical to the promotion of sustainable biofuels. If
   the standards are so stringent as to make sustainable bioenergy unaffordable, it will not be purchased, nor will the standards be implemented. This problem may be overcome by adopting standards less
   costly to implement, by providing tax relief, or by increasing the subsidy for sustainable bioenergy to the point where it will be competitive
   with other fuels.

   If the negotiations following the COP 15 Copenhagen climate conference establish a meaningful and enforceable cap-and-trade (or carbon tax) programme, setting a price on GHG emissions, some of the
   bioenergy implementation challenges may be resolved in the marketplace. For example, cutting forests or digging up peat bogs to produce
   bioenergy feedstocks may become prohibitively expensive. But note
   that the cap-and-trade provisions will apply for the foreseeable future
   only to developed countries, so the price strictures will make unsustainable bioenergy more expensive only for them to purchase, not for
   developing countries to produce. Tax relief for sustainable bioenergy
   could be an additional price incentive.

2. *Subsidies* – Reduction or removal of the large subsidies for petrol, coal
   and nuclear power would make bioenergy more competitive. Many
   countries provide subsidies for production of biofuels. These subsidies
   could be made conditional on compliance with sustainability standards.

3. *Certification* – Certification that bioenergy products are sustainable
   could be a useful tool. It would require a monitoring and evaluation
   programme that could be difficult and expensive, but detailed provisions for such a programme are provided by the Voluntary Carbon
   Standard (VCS) Program[22] that could be adapted for bioenergy.

4. *Labelling* – Labelling of bioenergy production as conforming to sustainability standards is an option, serving as a significant sales promotion incentive if widely accepted, such as the "Energy Star©" labelling
   system in the United States,[23] or the Forest Stewardship Council (FSC)
   certification on "responsible forestry management", and the related

Rainforest Alliance Certification (RAC) seal.[24] One could go further to assign label gradations, such as silver, gold and platinum labels for bioenegy meeting progressively higher standards such as has been adopted in the United States for "LEEDS" standards for energy efficiency in buildings.[25] The difficulty, when applied to bioenergy, is that the high-standard products are likely to be priced out of the market, there being few customers willing to pay for the superior environmental performance. So it is vital that the basic "sustainable" standard be stringent enough to address the most important environmental and social equity risks.

5. *Incentives* – Various kinds of incentives beyond labelling could be adopted, such as tax relief for sustainable products, as indicated above, or subsidies such as those being considered for forest preservation and reforestation under the Reducing Emissions from Deforestation and Forest Degradation (REDD) programme that were discussed at the Copenhagen negotiations. The REDD programme is elaborated in the case studies below.

6. *"Social Seal"* – In 2005, Brazil enacted a sophisticated law dealing with the sustainability of its sugar cane ethanol in regard to both its environmental and social impacts, discussed further in the case studies below.[26] For example, the law requires all sugar plantations to plant 20 per cent of their crop land each year with soil-enriching non-sugar crops, prohibits planting in protected forest areas such as the Amazon, and has stringent labour protection provisions. Most innovatively, Brazil has established a "Social Seal", providing strong tax incentives for biodiesel producers who obtain a specified percentage of their products from small rural farmers who are most in need of the health and gender protections and energy and economic development obtainable from bioenergy. But there remain serious problems in compliance and enforcement of these provisions.[27]

7. *Import standards and the WTO* – A more stringent implementation measure would be to negotiate an agreement among bioenergy importers that they will not import bioenergy products that are not certified as sustainable. RSB has been exploring these possibilities with importers. There are considerable enforcement problems in many developing countries deriving from inadequate numbers of trained environmental enforcement personnel and underpayment of such personnel that makes them vulnerable to corruption. These obstacles are difficult to overcome internally, but for the large producers and processors, the inability to export products not certified as sustainable would be an effective deterrent to these problems. An example is the CITES programme discussed below and the Generalized System of Preferences (GSP) under the WTO enabling clause.[28] The GSP

programme provides duty-free entry into developed markets for exports from designated beneficiary developing countries, and additional exports from least-developed beneficiary countries. "The GSP may allow developed nations to condition the receipt of benefits under the GSP on the fulfillment of certain conditions..."[29] Conditioning the GSP for sustainable biofuels would provide an incentive for international production of sustainable biofuels in developing countries.

The GSP programme is not without limitations. The justification for the programme as it would pertain to biofuels is subject to uniform application for "similarly-situated GSP beneficiaries", meaning countries with the same "development, financial and trade needs" intended to be addressed by the programme.[30] Also there must be a substantial correlation between the preferential treatment to the benefited party and the need alleviated by the GSP programme. The beneficiaries are also subject to annual trade ceilings known as competitive need limitations (CNLs).[31] Exceeding these CNLs automatically strips the benefited party of its GSP eligibility, unless it belongs to the list of least-developed GSP countries.[32]

8. *Financing* – The financing of bioenergy programmes for developing countries is of major concern, particularly in the less developed countries. The mechanisms by which biofuel projects are financed can have a critical impact on environmental outcomes. The reality is that most biofuel projects in developing countries are and will be funded by large local landholders and multinational agribusinesses seeking major profits from exploitation of developing country feedstocks. The need for sound standards and effective implementation of those standards is therefore fundamental and essential.

The programmes of the World Bank, GEF, regional banks, UNDP, UNEP, other international agencies and overseas development assistance from countries and companies can be important in funding research on more sustainable feedstocks and processing methodologies, for funding demonstration projects, and for assisting with education and training programmes. Such funds are grossly inadequate to finance significant bioenergy development in the less developed countries, however. Environmental considerations for the approval and implementation of biofuel projects funded under these schemes are also inadequate.

The Clean Development Mechanism (CDM), Emission Trading (ET) and Joint Implementation (JI) mechanisms of the Kyoto Protocol[33] should be of material funding assistance for these purposes. To date there are few bioenergy projects under consideration for the Kyoto Protocol mechanisms, however, of which CDM should be the most promising.[34] The primary reasons are the burdensome CDM requirements for determining a baseline and additionally, a monitoring methodology, and a method of validation.[35] Other barriers include difficulties in calculating the GHG reduction and high abatement costs.[36] The approval processes, besides being burdensome and expensive, require expertise not possessed in many less developed countries.

Financing by commercial banks is mainly viable for large-scale enterprises. However, for some banks it is unappealing because of the lack of knowledge by bank officers of GHG emission reduction technologies, their costs and benefits, and the risks involved. Commercial banks and investment firms have begun to finance some biofuel enterprises, however.

Microfinancing, that is, loans by institutions specializing in small community development loans, is an appealing scheme for small-scale biofuel projects, particularly in rural communities. The success of this method of financing has been demonstrated by the innovative Grameen Bank, developed in Bangladesh and now spreading rapidly to other developing countries. It has an energy lending subsidiary, Grameen Shakti, that has funded loans, primarily to village women, to finance solar, wind and bioenergy projects.[37]

The formulation of implementation regimes for bioenergy standards has already commenced or is being considered by a number of established international voluntary standards agencies. The International Organization for Standardization (ISO), the European Centre for Standardization (CEN)[38] and the Food and Agricultural Organization (FAO)[39] are exploring bioenergy certification standard implementation in addition to the RSB. The Inter-American Development Bank (IADB) has developed a Biofuels Environmental Sustainability Scorecard based on the RSB criteria.[40] The World Bank (WB) and World Wildlife Fund (WWF), with the International Union for the Conservation of Nature (IUCN), are developing a WB/WWF Biofuels Environmental Scorecard seeking to measure the impact of biofuels on the environment.[41] In addition, the United Nations Environment Programme has developed Environmental Due Diligence of Renewable Energy Projects Guidelines for Biomass Systems based on Energy Crops (UNEP SEFI) to provide investors and lenders with guidance on identifying and managing environmental risks.[42]

Case studies

Some case studies of successful voluntary and mandatory standards programmes will be discussed below, including voluntary forest protection and maintenance standards under several regimes; the Social Seal programme in Brazil; endangered species under CITES; depletion of the ozone layer in the Montreal Protocol on Substances that Deplete the Ozone Layer; and various voluntary labelling programmes such as the Energy Star© programme for environmental soundness[43] and the LEEDS® programme for the efficiency of buildings.[44] These studies demonstrate the feasibility of obtaining international agreement to address important environmental threats as precedents that can be applied to obtaining either binding or voluntary agreements on standards addressing the environmental and social concerns in relation to bioenergy projects.

The advantages of binding agreements over voluntary agreements, so highly touted for the climate change agreement, are in our opinion highly overblown. There is as much chance of a widely accepted voluntary standard being observed as of a less accepted binding standard.

Voluntary forest programmes

There are three quite successful voluntary agreements setting standards on forest conservation and sustainable management. Their success depended on the importance of sustainable forest management, the many benefits that well-managed forests offer for reducing GHG emissions and adaptation to climate change, preserving biodiversity, and reducing air and water pollution. They also attracted membership because, like biofuels, poor environmental management became the subject of considerable public criticism and good management could enhance the reputation of the forest owners and managers. They set a good example of what might be done to implement bioenergy standards.

The three major forest standards programmes are under the auspices of the Sustainable Forestry Initiative (SFI), the Forest Stewardship Council (FSC) and the American Tree Farm System.[45] "In the U.S. 107 million acres representing 14% of total U.S. forests are certified. 25% of private forestlands are certified."[46]

The Sustainable Forestry Initiative (SFI) is an organization established by the members of the American Forest and Paper Association to promote sustainable forestry. It created a non-profit Sustainable Forestry Board to oversee SFI standards development and certification in the United States and Canada. In addition, an umbrella organization, the Programme for the Endorsement of Certification (PEFC), was founded in 1999 to supervise the SFI programmes, contributing to their success and acceptance as reliable.[47] The latest standard contains thirteen objectives including forest management, procurement of wood and fibre, public reporting, continuous improvement and mitigating illegal logging.[48]

The American Tree Farm System® (AFTS), sponsored by the American Forest Foundation, promotes sustainable forests, watershed and healthy habitats among private forestry owners. Currently it involves 27.5 million acres of private forestland and 87,000 family forest owners in forty-six states. Under its standards and guidelines for certification, forest owners must develop a management plan based on strict environmental standards and pass an inspection by an AFTS forester every five years.

The FSC is an international non-profit organization whose members, from more than seventy countries, represent social, economic and environmental interests in forestry issues. FSC has set standards covering these issues, which have been applied in over fifty-seven countries worldwide.

Social Seal in Brazil

One of the most interesting implementation innovations is the Social Seal adopted for biodiesel production in Brazil.[49] Under this programme, substantial tax incentives are provided to biodiesel producers who meet specified social criteria and purchase specified percentages of their production from small family farmers, with greater incentives going to biodiesel from the poorer areas of the country.

This is an innovation model unique in the world, stimulating the partnership between government, family farmers, social movements and biodiesel-producing companies. The Social Seal defines different levels of financial incentives, stronger in the poorer North, Northeast and semi-arid regions in Brazil, including complete exemption from certain taxes for biodiesel producers that acquire oilseeds from family farmers. Brazil's National Petroleum, Natural Gas and Biofuels Agency (ANP) publishes technical specification norms for biodiesel and promotes public auctions to stimulate offers of biodiesel and to foster development of a domestic biodiesel market. Only companies that receive the Social Seal can participate in the auctions. Thirteen auctions have been held (from 2005 to February 2009), where Petrobras[50] has been the main purchaser.[51]

The key criteria with which the biodiesel producing companies must comply to receive the Social Seal are:

- Acquire feedstock from family farmers[52] in minimum percentages calculated on the feedstock acquisition cost, regionally differentiated;
- Provide a Technical Assistance Plan including the participation of a qualified technician and contracts or accords with institutions that will teach the family farmers; and
- Enter into contracts with the family farmers, negotiated by the representative of the family farmers, specifying duration, total value of feedstock purchases, price agreements and assurance of feedstock delivery, purchase guarantees, and the name of the organization that represents the family farmers in the agreement.[53]

The feedstock acquisition provisions include soil analysis of the family farmer's soils, selection of feedstocks, effects on other farm agricultural production, resources given to the family farmers, technical assistance and training of the family farmers.[54] Some guiding principles for coverage by the Technical Assistance Plan include the effect on food security; sustainability of the production systems, emphasizing respect for the local culture and knowledge of the feedstock, and necessary growing and processing regimens required; expected income generation; and the effect on women, youth and rural poverty reduction. The contracts undertaken can be entered into with the family farmers or their cooperatives, but with the participation of at least one representative of the family farmers, who could be one of several Brazilian labour unions or farmer federations in the negotiations.[55]

The Social Seal is an important and innovative step towards the sustainability of biodiesel production in Brazil, where the family farmers constitute a high component of the strategic stakeholders. Since the start of the programme, however, problems have emerged. The most impoverished family farmers have been facing structural problems such as lack of access to adequate credit, insurance, and technical and agricultural extension services.[56]

One of the objectives of the Social Seal programme is to reduce regional disparities, providing biodiesel producers in poorer areas better fiscal incentives and producing oilseeds suitable to each region.

Brazil has sixty-five biodiesel plants,[57] thirty of which have the Social Seal. However, the majority of biodiesel production plants are being installed in the Centre-West region, characterized by mechanized farming of grains, mostly soybean. Therefore, the participation of those family farmers with the lowest incomes has been well below expectations. In 2007, according to preliminary data from the Ministry of Agrarian Development, around 30,000 low-income farmers were effectively participating,[58] much fewer than the 200,000 initially expected.[59]

Finally, a research study presented indications that the control mechanisms of the Social Seal are not capable of preventing family farmers from being used by large producers to obtain financial incentives for themselves rather than for the local farmers.[60] Small farmers, even with their representatives, do not have the necessary knowledge and clout to be able to negotiate favourable contracts to sell the small farmers' feedstocks in a market that is dominated by large biodiesel operators.[61]

To address these problems, more, better trained and paid environmental staff need to be employed, the agricultural extension service needs to be augmented, periodic independent audits of the programme are required, and stiff penalties should be imposed for violations of the Social Seal legislation.

Despite the problems encountered, the implementation of the Social Seal is a unique opportunity to promote the social inclusion of family farmers in biodiesel production, and could be advantageously applied to other renewable fuels in developing countries, including Brazil's burgeoning bioethanol programme.

Convention on International Trade in Endangered Species

The CITES treaty prevents market trading in specified endangered species. Its trade restrictions have been referred to as "the most successful of all international treaties regarding wildlife conservation".[62] This success is based on the international acceptance of a list of endangered species, and the enactment of legislation by parties imposing criminal penalties for import of those species.[63]

The usefulness of the CITES example for biofuels is to demonstrate the feasibility of concluding a multilateral treaty to remedy widely recognized environmental problems, with criminal prosecution for violations.

In the United States, a one-time thriving market for endangered species and their products,[64] CITES is enforced through the Endangered Species Act[65] and the Lacey Act.[66]

Endangered species and their products that are marketable are generally distinguishable from legally taken species, and genetic testing exists to establish proof of violation of trading bans. Unlike endangered species, blending of biofuel products would make import restrictions more difficult because of the problems in determining the origins of particular biofuels. Import restrictions would have to be placed on all blended biofuels, any of which violate sustainability standards.

The CITES functions, in large part, because of broad participation of the international community and has had success in curbing lucrative markets for endangered species in the United States and Europe. Even with CITES enforcement, the existence of black markets in places such as Hong Kong confounds the authorities and threatens to undermine the effectiveness of the treaty.[67]

While the proposed voluntary biofuels regulatory systems will not criminalize violations, the choice will be left to the consumer. The systems will rely on consumers' willingness to pay more for good behaviour and on the commercial advantages of sustainability certification for producers, as in the case of any voluntary standard implementation.

Montreal Protocol

The Montreal Protocol, like the CITES agreement, is a treaty rather than an informal agreement, and it sets mandatory standards for its signatories rather than voluntary standards. Both these treaties contain important lessons on how to successfully obtain international consensus on adoption of standards to mitigate environmental risks and damages such as those involved in the production of bioenergy.

The Montreal Protocol emanated from a broad consensus of scientific studies demonstrating cancer threats from ozone depletion caused by emissions from widely used consumer sprays and refrigerants. Success in obtaining international acceptance of the treaty was attributed to careful planning in preparing for the treaty; obtaining wide agreement in the scientific community on the unremedied dangers of ozone depletion; the education of the public on the issues involved, thus getting vocal support from citizens and NGOs; and persuading industry to support the treaty and to create less harmful alternatives.[68] The openness and inclusiveness of the Protocol preparations is very much like the attributes of the RSB preparation on biofuels.

The treaty was adopted, signed by countries representing more than 85 per cent of the banned emissions, and as a result CFCs have been virtually eliminated. CFCs are also significant GHGs, so double benefits have been achieved at very little cost. The HFCs[69] that replaced them recently have been found also to be virulent GHGs and treaty revisions are being negotiated for their elimination as well.

Labelling examples

A number of national and international labelling programmes that could be utilized for biofuels have been used to inform the public of risks and to promote cleaner products from other sectors.

Energy Star©

The Energy Star© labelling programme[70] was started by the US Department of Energy to recognize companies and products with superior environmental and energy-saving attributes. Specified standards have to be met to earn the right to use the label, and a committee of experts was formed to make decisions as to compliance with these standards. The standards are valued by companies marketing in the United States as a means of advancing sales of their products.

According to the Department of Energy, "Last year alone, Americans, with the help of [Energy Star©], saved enough energy to power 10 million homes and avoid greenhouse gas emissions from 12 million cars – all while saving $6 billion."[71]

LEEDS®

The LEEDS® certification and labelling programme[72] is a voluntary programme established by the US Green Building Council, a private non-profit association formed by the US building industry, to reward builders for construction of buildings that meet specified environmental and energy efficiency standards. Certification is performed by an independent committee of experts, can be labelled as such, and is highly valued internationally as a promotional asset.

A major difference of LEEDS® from the Energy Star© programme, however, is that points are awarded under LEEDS® for various environmental and efficiency attributes; according to the points awarded, silver, gold and platinum labels are designated in accordance with criteria such as sustainability of the site, energy and water efficiency, GHG emissions, indoor air quality, etc. This system might be very attractive for biofuel labels because there are so many risk elements that must be addressed. However, if higher levels of certification are accompanied by increased prices, it would undermine the programme unless offsetting subsidies were adopted.

In all labelling programmes, there must be sufficient public interest in purchasing the "green" products certified by the labels to induce many manufacturers and marketers to seek label approvals, and thus improve product sales and improve the environmental attributes of their production and products.

As with the CITES discussed above, application of these labelling programmes to biofuels is complicated by the difficulty of distinguishing conforming and non-conforming biofuels in blends, so that biofuels would have to be rejected for the labels if any part of the product failed to meet the prescribed sustainability standards.

Indonesian palm oil programme

Indonesia initiated a programme for utilizing palm oil for biodiesel production through the planting of large-scale palm oil plantations by cutting down forests and digging up peat bogs. This programme is replacing forests in Indonesia at an alarming rate, wiping out 80–100 per cent of wildlife in the affected area, forcing local communities from their land and destroying their livelihoods. Indonesian forests are disappearing at a rate of more than 2 million hectares a year – an area half the size of Belgium.[73]

Indonesia holds the global record for increasing GHG emissions through deforestation, putting it third in GHG emissions behind the United States and China. During the last fifty years, over 74 million hectares of Indonesia's forests have been destroyed – logged, burned, degraded, pulped – and its products shipped round the planet. Also, every year, 1.8 billion tonnes (Gt) of GHG emissions are released by the degradation and burning of Indonesia's peat lands – 4 per cent of global GHG emissions from less than 0.1 per cent of the land on Earth.[74] Indonesia is now seeking to remediate these problems through its project Palm Oil, Timber & Carbon Offsets (POTICO) programme, initiated with the World Resources Institute. The project's goal is to curb new oil palm plantations from being created by clearing virgin or primary forests and digging up peat bogs.[75]

Reducing emissions through deforestation and forest degradation

Tropical deforestation worldwide causes about 20 per cent of the world's GHG emissions by eliminating important carbon sinks. Tropical rainforests are known to absorb almost 5 billion tonnes of carbon dioxide from the Earth's atmosphere.[76] To curb the disastrous destruction of tropical forests and to work towards utilizing forests in mitigation of climate change, as well as conserving them for future generations, the United Nations commenced discussions on the introduction of the REDD mechanism (Reducing Emissions through Deforestation and Forest Degradation) as a part of its Bali Action Plan, in 2006.

The REDD mechanism is envisaged as a joint partnership among the FAO, UNDP, UNEP and other stakeholders.[77] REDD policies offer incentives to local farmers in developing countries to reduce their deforestation rates.[78] Local people in heavily forested areas such as in Indonesia, Brazil and even recently recognized forested areas of Africa[79] are often referred to as "stewards of the forests".[80] They are the ones who daily work in the forests and who are best equipped to protect them. However, their livelihoods often involve the utilization and consequent destruction of these areas. But if these local people are given incentives which will protect the forests while also serving their economic needs, then forest conservation may be successful.

Great care must be given in designing a REDD programme to assure against reversion of the forest preservation being financed, and against fraudulent preservation claims. A system of auditing, verification and monitoring is needed. Both satellite monitoring and ground inspections can be used for these purposes. Stiff penalties will need to be provided for intentional deviations (as opposed to fires, earthquakes and other natural disasters that may result in deforestation).

Norway announced at the Bali Climate Conference that it would create a massive forest protection fund to promote the REDD programme, committing 3 billion Norwegian kroner per year to this initiative.[81]

The first REDD demonstration project is a contract between Norway and Tanzania, executed in 2009.[82] The Norwegian Ministry of Foreign Affairs (MFA) agreed to make a maximum of 13.5 million kroner available, to be used exclusively for financing forestry preservation in Tanzania. The

MFA agreed to make additional funds available for advisory services in financial management and training. The Institute of Resources Assessment (IRA), part of the University of Dar es Salaam, agreed to implement the project. The IRA took over responsibility for administering the available funds, based on the REDD strategy, in a way that the funds could be accounted for. To ensure this, the IRA agreed to submit timely reports to the MFA on the use of the funds and project progress. This reporting requirement is crucial to ensuring that the funds are being used appropriately. Additionally, the contract contains a clause allowing MFA to cancel and reclaim its funds if the IRA does not fulfil its contract obligations. This is an important mechanism for reducing corruption and ensuring the proper use of funds.

In advance of REDD funding, Norway initiated a fund for preservation of tropical forests, starting with an Amazon Fund to assist Brazil in protecting its Amazon forests. In Copenhagen, Norway committed to increase its Amazon Fund to $150 million for 2010, and US President Obama endorsed this initiative as a good way of going forward with tropical forest preservation.[83]

Adoption of a REDD programme would be very important, not only in mitigating GHG emissions, but in preserving biodiversity. The Convention on Biological Diversity has incorporated the issue of biofuel production and use into its programme of work, in particular by addressing the destruction of biodiversity through deforestation, thus supporting the REDD programme.[84]

The developed countries and companies participating in the REDD programme will have to assist with the costs of implementation, as was done in the Norway-Tanzania project, to make project implementation feasible for the less developed countries. Unfortunately, at the most recent United Nations Forestry Forum on REDD, the parties were unable to agree on financing of the programme.[85]

Conclusion

Well-considered standards are being formulated by RSB and other international organizations to define the requirements for sustainable bioenergy production. Many of the principal biofuel producing and purchasing countries have adopted a variety of implementation options for effectuating such standards, and a number of international environmental treaties deal with particular aspects of this production. A lot of work remains to be done to develop international consensus on which standards and implementation measures should be adopted.

Acknowledgements

The authors thank Robert Goldstein, who edited this paper. Robert Goldstein is an Adjunct Professor at Pace Law School and a law professor at the US Military Academy, West Point, New York. The authors gratefully acknowledge the contributions of Lily Henning, Nana O. Safo, Kavitha Mukund, Silvia Blajberg Schaffel, T. David Wand, Ethan B. Spaner, Alexander N. Gastman and Gabriella Machado de Sant'Anna Carvalho to this chapter. The authors express gratitude to John Costenbader, Yves de Soye and Nadine McCormick of IUCN and Alexander Koch of UNEP for their helpful comments and reviews.

Notes

1. UN Economic and Social Council (ECOSOC), Sub-Commission on Energy (UN-Energy), 2007, "Sustainable Bioenergy: A Framework for Decision Makers", UN Doc. TC/D/A1094E/1/4.07/2000.
2. UN Environment Programme (UNEP), Roundtable on Bioenergy Enterprise in Developing Regions, *Background Paper: Empowering Rural Communities by Planting Energy*, 2007; available at <http://www.uneptie.org/energy/activities/rbe/pdf/Background.pdf>.
3. International Risk Governance Council, *Policy Brief: Risk Governance Guidelines for Bioenergy Policies* (2008), p. 13; available at <http://www.irgc.org/IMG/pdf/IRGC_PB_Bioenergy_WEB-2.pdf>.
4. For a good critique of these risks, however, see R. Brooke Coleman, New Fuels Alliance, *Biofuel Critics Stray from the Facts* (2008); available at <http://www.worleyobetz.com/Portals/2/Repository/4%20Common%20Misperceptions.613436da-27d8-465d-919f-d03e3817c6fb.pdf>.
5. ECOSOC, "Framework for Decision Makers", p. 48.
6. But see Catherine V. Clute (ed.), *Epowerviews, IEA Task 39 Report T39-TR1, An Examination of the Potential for Improving Carbon/Energy Balance of Bioethanol* (2009); available at <http://www.globalrfa.org/pdf/improving_carbon_iea_task_39.pdf>.
7. Henry Lee, William C. Clark and Charan Devereaux, *Biofuels and Sustainable Development: Report of An Executive Session on the Grand Challenges of a Sustainability Transition* (2008), pp. 5–6; available at <http://belfercenter.ksg.harvard.edu/files/biofuels%20and%20sustainable%20development.pdf>.
8. International Risk Governance Council, *Risk Governance Guidelines*, p. 44.
9. Ibid., p. 30.
10. Ibid., p. 29.
11. Andrea Rossi and Yianna Lambrou, Food and Agriculture Organization of the United Nations (FAO), *Gender and Equality Issues in Liquid Biofuel Production: Minimizing the Risks to Maximize the Opportunities* (2000), p. 14; available at <ftp://ftp.fao.org/docrep/fao/010/ai503e/ai503e00.pdf>.
12. ECOSOC, "Framework for Decision Makers", p. 27.
13. National Research Council, Transitioning to Sustainability Through Research and Development on Ecosystem Services and Biofuels: Workshop Summary (2008); available at <http://www.nap.edu/catalog/12195.html>.

14. Lee et al., Biofuels and Sustainable Development, pp. 12–14.
15. See <http://cgse.epfl.ch/page65660.html>.
16. See École Polytechnique Fédérale de Lausanne Centre, *Roundtable on Sustainable Biofuels* (2008); available at <http://www.bioenergywiki.net/images/f/f2/Version_zero.pdf>.
17. See *Guidance for RSB P&C 12 (Land Rights)*; available at <http://www.bioenergywiki.net/guidance_for_rsb_P%26C_12_(land_rights)>.
18. *Global principles and criteria for sustainable biofuels production – Version Zero*; available at <http://cgse.epfl.ch/webdav/site/cgse/shared/Biofuels/VersionZero/Version%20Zero_RSB_Std_en.pdf>.
19. The Montreal Protocol on Substances that Deplete the Ozone Layer as either adjusted and/or amended in London 1990, Copenhagen 1992, Vienna 1995, Montreal 1997, Beijing 1999; available at <http://www.unep.org/ozone/pdfs/Montreal-Protocol2000.pdf>.
20. Convention on International Trade in Endangered Species of Wild Fauna and Flora, Washington DC, 3 March 1973, entered into force 1 July 1975, 993 UNTS 24 (CITES).
21. For example, the European Community in 2003 adopted a Directive to require biofuels for 2 per cent of EU transport fuels by 2005, 5.75 per cent by 2010 and 10 per cent by 2020. The United States has also adopted similar requirements. These requirements pose grave environmental and social risks since they were made without consideration of the environmental and social problems with biofuel feedstocks and processes enunciated above, or even the feasibility of the adopted requirements. They already have contributed to pressures on food prices, destruction of forests and resulting biodiversity impacts. See John Lewis, *Leaping Before They Looked: Lessons from Europe's Experience with the 2003 Biofuels Directive* (2007); available at <http://www.catf.us/publications/view/96>; and Lee et al., *Biofuels and Sustainable Development*, p. 12.
22. See <http://www.v-c-s.org>. The VCS Program provides a robust, new global standard and programme for approval of credible voluntary offsets. VCS offsets must be real (have happened), additional (beyond business-as-usual activities), measurable, permanent (not temporarily displace emissions), independently verified and unique (not used more than once to offset emissions). VCS has placed the burden of monitoring and reporting on the individual participants. All data from the project must be compiled and maintained by the individual participating organization and then a verifier selects samples of data and information to be validated. VCS registries and a central project database must be maintained that is open to the public. See <http://www.v-c-s.org/about.html>.
23. For the "Energy Star©" labelling system, see <http://www.energystar.gov>; and on the FSC certification and RAC seal, see <http://www.ra.org>.
24. See <http://www.rainforest-alliance.org/certification.cfm?id=main>.
25. See <http://www.usgbc.org>.
26. See <http://www.mre.gov.br/de/english/temas/biocombustiveis_09ing-programabrasileirobiodiesel.pdf>.
27. Ibid. See also *An In-Depth Look at Brazil's "Social Fuel Seal"* (2007); available at <http://news.mongabay.com/bioenergy/2007/03/in-depth-look-at-brazils-social-fuel.html>, describing social reasoning for obtaining biofuels from different geographic areas.
28. Enrique Rene de Vera, "The WTO and Biofuels: The Possibility of Unilateral Sustainability Requirements", *Chicago Journal of International Law*, vol. 8, no. 2 (2007–2008), pp. 661–680; available at <http://www.allbusiness.com/environment-natural-resources/pollution-environmental/8897080-1.html>.
29. Ibid., p. 676.
30. World Trade Organization, Report of the Appellate Body, European Communities-Conditions for the Granting of Tariff Preferences to Developing Countries, WTO Doc. no. WT/DS246/AB/R, 7 April 2004 (EC-Tariff Preferences).

31. The Office of the United States Trade Representative, *The US Generalized System of Preferences (GSP) Program: Increasing Exports from 131 Countries* (1974, updated 8 March 2010); available at <http://www.ustr.gov/trade-topics/trade-development/preference-programs/generalized-system-preference-gsp>.
32. Ibid.
33. See <http://www.unfccc.int/kyoto_protocol/mechanisms/items/1673.php>.
34. The CDM provides that developed country signatories to the Kyoto Protocol can obtain tradable Emissions Trading Rights for qualified investments made in developing countries to finance specified GHG emission reduction measures.
35. Masdjidin Siregar, *Is CDM a Necessary Condition for Biofuel Development?* (2008); available at <http://www.uncapsa.org/Flash_Detail.asp?VJournalKey=702>. Siregar notes that the limited number of biofuel projects included in the CDM project portfolio is "caused by the fact that no crop-based biofuel baseline methodology has been approved by the CDM Executive Board". See also Stefan J.A. Bakker, *Can the CDM assist biofuel production and deployment?* (2006); available at <http://www.globalbioenergy.org/bioenergyinfo/bioenergy-and-trade/detail/en/news/1482/icode/12/>.
36. Siregar, *Is CDM a Necessary Condition for Biofuel Development?*
37. See <http://www.gshakti.org>.
38. See <http://www.cen.eu/cenorm/sectors/sectors/utilitiesandenergy/index.asp>.
39. See <http://www.fao.org>.
40. See <http://iadb.org/scorecard>.
41. See Zarina Geloo, *World Bank releases draft standards for biofuels* (2008); available at <http://www.ipsterraviva.net/tv/IUCN2008/currentNew.aspx?new=1200>.
42. See <http://sefi.unep.org/English/home/publications.html>.
43. See <http://www.energystar.gov>.
44. See <http://www.usgbc.org/leed>.
45. BIOstock Blog, "Forest Certification Programs: FSC, SFI, and Tree Farm" (2008); available at <http://biostock.blogspot.com/2007/06/forest-certification-programs-fsc-sfi.html>.
46. Ibid.
47. Ibid.
48. Ibid.
49. N°5.297/04, later modified by Decree N°5.457/05.
50. Also known as The Brazilian National Oil Company.
51. N°5.297/04, later modified by Decree N°5.457/05.
52. Family farmers are defined in law as farmers that hold an area no more than four modules (modulos fiscais: unit of measure in hectares), using predominantly labour from the family (N°5.297/04, later modified by Decree N°5.457/05).
53. Published in February 2009, revoked the Normative Instruction No 01/2009 from the MDA.
54. Ibid. According to the Normative Instruction, some restrictions apply.
55. Ibid.
56. G. Potengy, K. Kato, D.S. Sousa, et al., *Plano de Ação Para o Fornecimento de Oleaginosas em Candeias, Montes Claros e Quixadá Para a Petrobras*, Relatório Final (Lima: GEI/IE/UFRJ e COPPE/UFRJ, 2007).
57. March 2009; see <http://www.anp.gov.br/biocombustiveis/capacIdade_plantas.asp>.
58. See <http://www.biodiesel.gov.br>.
59. See <http://www.anp.gov.br/biocombustiveis/capacIdade_plantas.asp>. See also <http://www.mda.gov.br/saf/index.php?sccid=362>.
60. See Ricardo Abramovay, *A Political Cultural Approach to the Biofuels Market in Brazil* (São Paulo: University of São Paulo, Faculty of Economics and Administration, 2008); available at <http://www.econ.fea.usp.br/abramovay>.

61. Catherine A.G. Garcez and João Nildo de Souza Vianna, "Brazilian Biodiesel Policy: Social and Environmental Considerations of Sustainability", *Energy*, vol. 34, no. 5 (2009), pp. 645–654.
62. Michelle A. Peters, "The Convention on International Trade in Endangered Species: An Answer to the Call of the Wild", *Connecticut Journal of International Law*, vol. 10 (1985), pp. 169–191, p. 177, citing Simon Lyster, *International Wildlife Law* (Cambridge: Cambridge University Press, 1985), pp. 239–242 p. 240.
63. Peters, "The Convention on International Trade in Endangered Species: An Answer to the Call of the Wild", p. 180.
64. There remains, arguably, a thriving market in particular products from endangered species, notably ivory. See *HSUS Investigation: Illegal Ivory Trade in Our Own Backyard* (2002); available at <http://www.hsus.org/wildlife/wildlife_news/hsus_investigation_illegal_ivory_trade_in_our_own_backyard.html>.
65. 16 USC § 3371, et seq.
66. 18 USC §42; 16 USC §§ 3371–3378.
67. See generally Mara E. Zimmerman, "The Black Market for Wildlife: Combating Transnational Organized Crime in the Illegal Wildlife Trade", *Vanderbilt Journal of Transnational Law*, vol. 36 (2003), pp. 1657–1689; available at <http://www.velaw.com/lawyers/MaraZimmerman.aspx>.
68. Conversation with Ambassador Richard Benedick of Battelle Northwest Laboratories and President of the National Council of Environmental Scientists, a principal negotiator of the Protocol.
69. CFCs are chlorofluorinated hydrocarbons and HFCs are hydrochlorofluorinated hydrocarbons. HFCs at first were approved as less dangerous substitutes for CFCs. HFCs were then found to pose unacceptable risks, so they are being included in the treaty ban, and other benign substitutes are being adopted.
70. See <http://www.energystar.gov>.
71. See <http://www.energystar.gov/index.cfm?c=about.ab_index>.
72. See <http://www.usgbc.org/leed>.
73. Palm Oil and Rainforest Deforestation; see <http://www.mongabay.com/external/foe_palm_oil.htm>.
74. Greenpeace, "How the Palm Oil Industry is Cooking the Climate" (2007); available at <http://www.greenpeace.org.uk/files/pdfs/forests/cooking-the-climate-1.pdf>.
75. World Resources Institute, Project POTICO, "Palm Oil, Timber & Carbon Offsets in Indonesia"; available at <http://www.wri.org/project/potico>.
76. "Tropical Rain Forests Absorb 5 bn Tonnes of CO_2" (2009); available at <http://www.igovernment.in/site/tropical-rain-forests-absorb-5-bn-tonnes-of-co2/?section=environment>.
77. See <http://www.undp.org/mdtf/un-redd/overview.shtml>.
78. "What's Needed for Strong REDD Policy?"; available at <http://www.ucsusa.org/global_warming/solutions/forest_solutions/recognizing-forests-role-in.html>.
79. A recent study found a carbon sink in Africa's forests that removes approximately 1.2 billion of the 4.8 billion tonnes of CO_2 removed from the atmosphere by forests every year: Planet Earth Online, *Scientists Show African Forests are Major Carbon Sinks* (2009); available at <http://planetearth.nerc.ac.uk>.
80. Hemant R. Ojha and Bhola Bhattarai, *Making REDD Work for the Forest-Dependent Poor: Civil Society Perspectives from the South* (2008); available at <http://research.yale.edu/gisf/tfd/pdf/stakeholders/Nepal%20civil%20society%20REDD.pdf>.
81. See <http://www.development-today.com/Forests_and_REDD>.
82. Available at <http://www.norway.go.tz/Development/Climate+Change/FirstREDDContract.htm>.

83. *Norway Increases Amazon Funding* (2009); available at
    <http://copenhagenforestupdates.blogspot.com/2009/12/norway-increases-amazon-
    funding.html>.
84. Decision IX/1, para. 31, of the 9th Meeting of the Conference of Parties of the Conven-
    tion on Biological Diversity (CBD COP9), May 2008. See also Decisions IX/2 and IX/5;
    available at <http://www.cbd.int>.
85. "UNFF8 Negotiations Last All Night. Forests in Changing Environment Resolution
    Adopted. Decision on Financing Forwarded to UNFF9"; available at <http://www.iisd.
    ca/forestry/unff/unff8>.

12

Synthetic biology and synthetic genomics

Michele S. Garfinkel and Robert M. Friedman

Introduction

In the nearly four decades since the introduction of recombinant DNA as the key technique for manipulating DNA in the laboratory, the technology has spread to virtually all sectors of biological research and development. Scientists have become adept at controlling the expression of genes to study cancer, human development, animal behaviour, evolution and many other biological phenomena.

In some cases, scientists have spent more time manipulating the DNA rather than doing an actual experiment. At the same time, the cost of directly synthesizing DNA from its component parts has dropped significantly. This combination makes synthesis very attractive to researchers. Further, over the last decade or so, more engineers have become interested in biology, for a variety of reasons. Although recombinant DNA techniques have collectively been referred to as "biological engineering", these new entrants to the field truly want to impose engineering principles on biology. Whether or not they will succeed remains to be seen. But the attempts to do so have resulted both in new ways of looking at the field, and in bringing to the forefront some problems that had not been fully confronted for recombinant DNA technologies.

Although the idea of a "synthetic biology" has been in various literature at least as long as "recombinant DNA", synthetic biology and synthetic genomics, a related technology, have been analysed in their current forms for about the last ten years. Synthetic biology is frequently described

The future of international environmental law, Leary and Pisupati (eds),
United Nations University Press, 2010, ISBN 978-92-808-1192-6

rather than defined, or it is defined differently by the various constituencies interested in it. Practitioners may describe it by its functions, including the ability to construct new biological components, design those components and redesign existing biological systems. At the very least, these descriptions generally take into account both biological and engineering features.

Synthetic genomics is a limited set of technologies that make it possible to construct a molecule of DNA of any specified sequence and nearly any length, up to the size of a whole genome. Older technologies exist for constructing relatively short pieces of DNA which could be put together in the laboratory to make long pieces. Newer technologies allow for the direct synthesis of very long pieces of DNA; these technologies are generally proprietary and are held by for-profit firms.

These are technologies that will be or already have been shown to be extremely powerful. But synthetic biology and synthetic genomics are quintessential dual-use technologies: they may be used in ways that advance science and improve society, but they may also be used maliciously. This is true of many of the tools of biotechnology, including classical recombinant DNA, but the speed and relatively low cost of synthesizing DNA directly has raised particular concern for the biosafety and biosecurity communities.

Further, these technologies may in some cases raise culture- or religion-specific questions about what life is, whether it is hubristic to try to "create" life, and who gets to make those decisions. Questions about unfair distribution of the results of research using these techniques, and concerns about potential environmental impacts of accidental or planned release of synthesized organisms, have been raised. Many of these questions have been raised about biotechnology in general and applications of recombinant DNA, particularly with respect to genetically modified plants and animals.

These questions and concerns have attracted the attention of a wide variety of stakeholders, policymakers, and other professional communities, including non-governmental organizations, academic researchers, elected officials and international bodies. These individuals and groups are still in the process of enumerating the full scope of their concerns. In a few select and well-defined cases, mechanisms for oversight and regulation have begun to be discussed. How to deal with more general ethical, philosophical and theological concerns remains to be discussed in a much more rigorous way.

Synthetic biology also gives rise to a more specific problem. All emerging technologies present potential legal implications. In some cases, the concerns may be about whether a new technology might cause old laws to be interpreted in different ways. In other cases, the technologies may be unique, so that they somehow fall outside current regulations, and thus new laws may be needed to deal with them. These concerns are of course amplified in the realm of international law. Synthetic biology appears to precipitate many of these concerns among bodies that deal with the legal consequences of the introduction of new technologies or applications using those technologies.

Here we first describe the science and engineering of synthetic biology and synthetic genomics. We next illustrate several potential applications or benefits that have been enumerated by the community developing the technologies, as well as potential risks accompanying the use of these technologies. We consider emerging societal concerns about those risks and benefits. Finally, we describe potential mechanisms of governance and oversight of these benefits and risks, both generically and in the context of international law.

The science and engineering of synthetic genomics and synthetic biology

The techniques that would be necessary for constructing a cell truly from scratch are disparate, and at very different stages of being understood or developed. For example, to make a eukaryotic cell (a cell with a nucleus, such as those found in animals, including human beings), one would need to synthesize a large number of individuals chromosomes, grow a variety of cell membranes, find a way to incorporate those membranes into various organelles, build any number of ribosomes and transcription factors, and then combine all of these parts together into a single cell.[1] While at some time in the distant future such an approach might be possible, for now, it is more realistic to look at the construction of viruses, which have very small genomes, and the construction of small or medium-sized bacteria.[2] The construction of viral genomes is relatively straightforward; the construction of a bacterium should be much simpler than constructing an animal cell. Even then, researchers are more focused on the critical step of constructing the chromosome of a given bacterium from component DNA parts. Thus, governance questions for the moment focus most productively on that step, which is sometimes called synthetic genomics, the construction of very long molecules of DNA of any sequence and in lengths up to the size of full genomes.

De novo synthesis of gene-length DNA is not a particularly new technology. The first chemical synthesis of a gene was described by Har Gobind Khorana and colleagues in papers published in the early 1970s.[3] To accomplish this, each nucleotide subunit of DNA was attached to a previous one in a chemical reaction set up by the researchers. It was a laborious task, taking two years for Khorana and at least 17 co-workers to assemble the 207 base-pair gene for a transfer RNA. However, its implications were quickly recognized by Khorana: "Since the sequence is generated by chemical synthesis, there is full choice in the subsequent manipulation of the sequence information. This ability is the essence of the chemical approach to the study of biological specificity in DNA and RNA."[4] As with recent synthetic biology, the two sides of the coin are building and understanding.

While this basic technique, the chemical joining of one subunit to the next, has been essentially maintained over the last thirty-five years, various improvements and automation steps have allowed researchers to build ever-longer molecules of DNA, both more rapidly and with more accuracy. By the mid-1990s Willem Stemmer and his co-workers were able to directly synthesize a gene plus a vector (a piece of DNA that allows the gene of interest to be transferred into a host microorganism, such as a bacterium, and to replicate in that host) of approximately 2700 base-pairs. They were able to accomplish this in days, and could repeat the process at will, allowing for applications from the study of evolution to the discovery and testing of new drugs.

A major change in how scientists, engineers and policymakers think about DNA synthesis was precipitated by the introduction of automated DNA synthesis machines. Rather than spending their time building new molecules using tedious biotechnology approaches, scientists can simply order the DNA they need for an experiment. Since the early 1980s, oligonucleotides (short pieces of DNA, up to about 75 base-pairs in length) could be ordered from companies at low prices. These oligonucleotides can be used in a variety of experimental approaches and developmental applications, and in fact could themselves be strung together to make full-length genes. The techniques to do that, however, have until recently remained somewhat idiosyncratic, almost at the craft level. Several laboratories have recently used much-improved techniques to assemble genes and genomes from oligonucleotides. Wimmer and colleagues constructed a poliovirus (about 7700 nucleotides long) from a series of oligonucleotides; this took about a year.[5] Just over a year later, Smith and colleagues constructed a bacterial virus called phiX174, about 5400 base-pairs, in just over two weeks.[6]

Producing genomes using oligonucleotides, however, remains laborious and still requires training and skills. The introduction of machines that can synthesize molecules thousands of nucleotides in length (around the size of a gene), or even tens of thousands of nucleotides in length, meant that, with no training in biology, an individual could obtain a genome at least the length of a virus such as poliovirus, or the pieces of influenza virus. For now, these technologies are proprietary and are used only in firms that sell these long pieces of DNA. Companies and the researchers using those services have reported error-free constructions of up to 52,000 base-pairs.[7]

The availability of protocols describing how to carry out the synthesis of genes and genomes from oligonucleotides, and the ability of researchers to order full-length genes or genomes from a firm and have them delivered within six weeks, has given the research community confidence that it can make significant advances in areas such as human health, the production of alternative fuels, improved crops and so on. This is partly because synthetic genomics allows for a much more direct construction of the desired DNA to test (eliminating the need to troubleshoot failed experiments) and to be able to modify experiments quickly when the results are genuinely negative.

For now, either of these techniques remain somewhat expensive (ordering genes or genomes from companies can cost several US dollars per base-pair; joining oligonucleotides in the laboratory still requires fairly skilled personnel). But costs are rapidly decreasing for either approach, particularly for ordering genes or genomes from firms, and taken together, the constellation of speed, ease of manipulation and affordability is a prime concern for those concerned about biosecurity and, to a degree, biosafety. Further, it brings society closer to needing to deal with less well-defined but no less important concerns, such as the philosophical, theological and legal issues surrounding the use of synthesis techniques.

Benefits

While it is impossible, a priori, to predict the exact outcomes, and thus benefits, of the application of new technologies to research problems or to specific societal concerns, it is possible at least to reasonably extrapolate the advances that could be brought about by such technologies.

The potential benefits of synthetic biology, as currently described, are not necessarily vastly different from those originally envisaged for the use of recombinant DNA technologies: new drugs, faster vaccine manufacturing and a cleaner environment. However, the decades of experience since the publications by Berg, Boyer, Cohen and their colleagues on techniques that led to relatively easy handling of DNA molecules have also shown that, as with many technologies, benefits can be over-promised, risk can be understated, and the timelines for either of these can be completely misunderstood.

While certainly synthetic biology has had its share of uncontextualized promises of benefits, in general the field seems to have focused on areas where technology has not quite succeeded in providing society with useful products. These are areas that, while some may disagree on the approach, virtually all can agree are serious societal issues, either already with us or soon to emerge.

Alternative fuels

The production of carbon-neutral energy sources, particularly for liquid transportation fuels, is a good example of an application that conceivably could be carried out using standard biotechnological or other approaches, but which the community of those practicing synthetic biology have been able to identify as one that could overwhelmingly benefit from these new approaches. Consolidated bioprocessing (CBP) of biomass from the cellulose of plants has always been a goal of those studying alternative energy sources. The goal of all CBP approaches is to combine to one microorganism a series of enzymatic steps that normally would occur in physically different locations (e.g. moving materials from tank to tank to introduce new enzymes) or from the sequential introduction of microorganisms to conduct each step. While it may be impossible to combine every step needed to convert cellulosic biomass to ethanol into one microorganism, any reduction in the number of individual steps would bring the cost of ethanol closer to that of gasoline without needing to use food crops for its production. Research from a variety of microbial discovery programmes should contribute to the discovery of various pathways that might eventually be consolidated.

New drugs

Biotechnology has long had the potential to produce new or improved drugs. That potential has gone largely unrealized as the diseases that biotechnology has tried to target are extremely complicated, and biologically based therapeutics frequently do not work as expected once they enter clinical trials. Synthetic biology, in itself, cannot solve those problems. Where it may be powerful, though, is in the production of drugs that are difficult or expensive to manufacture; or in cases where the ability to test large numbers of different candidates exists but the drugs themselves do not exist. The former case frequently includes, for example, drugs that must be harvested from plants; the latter includes the important class of therapeutics including antibiotics.

There is already one example of the use of synthetic biology for the improved manufacture of a drug normally harvested from a plant. Artemisinin, an antimalarial drug, is currently manufactured using techniques that have not changed in decades, and involves the extraction of the drug from sweet wormwood. The metabolic process in the plant that leads to the production of artemisinin cannot be replicated in any straightforward fashion using conventional laboratory techniques.

One laboratory in particular, that of Jay Keasling, has used at least some synthetic biology techniques (along with some that biotechnologists have been using for decades) to add several metabolic steps to a (naturally occurring) yeast pathway, resulting in the reliable production of artemisinic acid, which is easy to harvest from the yeast in fermenters. This precursor can then be chemically converted to the antimalarial drug, artemisinin. The laboratory is currently testing methods to scale up this manufacture; that may itself include using synthetic genomics to "stabilize" yeast in the scale-up.[8]

There is promise as well for producing novel antibiotics, which is becoming ever more critical as bacteria gain resistance to known antibiotics, while at the same time basic research on antibiotics has dropped over the last several decades. A paper by Kodumal and colleagues[9] described in detail the total synthesis of a 32,000 base-pair polyketide synthase gene cluster. The polyketide drugs include, not only antibiotics, but also transplant rejection suppressors and potential anti-cancer drugs). Synthesizing variants of polyketide synthase may allow for the downstream synthesis in vivo of slight variants of antibiotics. By pairing this technology with various supporting technologies to allow the rapid screening of drug activities, it is imaginable that variants of such genes could be constructed and tested with great rapidity.

New diagnostics and rapid vaccine development

One of the problems in older genetic technologies with respect to vaccine or diagnostic development is the difficulty in being able to set up large numbers of tests against pathogens, in a limited period of time. The ability to construct large numbers of, for example, viral genomes that differ just slightly (perhaps even by one nucleotide) from a pathogenic version, that could be used as a vaccine would significantly speed vaccine development. The related ability to produce specific sequences of DNA (or perhaps its protein product) to use as a diagnostic is also a target for synthetic biology.

An example of these potential applications is the severe acute respiratory syndrome virus (SARS), a coronavirus. SARS emerged and disappeared rapidly in 2003. Although the primary infection route in that epidemic was from civet cats to human beings, there may also have been bat-to-human transmission. Although the precise strain that killed so many people at that time is probably no longer a threat, a similar strain could certainly emerge and spread as well. Ralph Baric, a leader in the SARS-CoV field, used genome sequences from the publicly available

National Library of Medicine's sequence database to make a synthetic virus that can infect bats, and which he and his colleagues can now easily modify to test as a vaccine strain if and when a new SARS strain emerges.[10]

Bio-based manufacturing

As one approach to decreasing the use of precious resources such as petroleum and to assist in the adoption of less impactful manufacturing processes in general, industrial researchers are looking carefully at the possibility of "white" biotechnology, where plants or microbes could be engineered to produce raw materials that today are produced chemically. The manufacture of plastics, for example, could be made more environmentally friendly by engineering pathways in plants to produce types of plastics, or their precursors.[11]

Engineering specific metabolic pathways

While this last benefit is at some level the most obscure, in some ways it best captures the spirit of what synthetic biologists claim to want to accomplish. Currently throughout the world, scientists are participating in metagenomic surveys of microbes. Specifically, microorganisms are being collected by different teams from, for example, oceans[12] and acid mines.[13] This type of survey can identify thousands of new species and millions of new genes. However, most of the microorganisms collected for these surveys cannot grow under laboratory conditions. Thus, the "metagenome" of any given sample is defined by the entirety of the DNA sequence. Using extremely sophisticated computing approaches, these bulk sequences can be sorted out to define both individual genes and, to a large degree, which genes have come from the same microbe.

Because these microorganisms generally cannot be cultured and because there is so little DNA in the samples that it is frequently used in its entirety to be analysed at the sequence level, it is only by using synthetic genomics techniques (i.e. taking the digital sequence and synthesizing the actual DNA for use) that these sequences can then be tested for various biological properties.

Although no novel microbe has been constructed by combining many of these sequences, the engineering part of synthetic biology anticipates doing exactly this.[14] Various genes or multi-gene signal transduction pathways could be inserted into an already existing microbial platform (as is now done for simple expression of single gene in, for example, *E. coli*), or, in the future, into an empty bacterial shell.

Molecular biology research

Although more mundane than the other benefits discussed here, improvements in basic laboratory research are a critical application of these new technologies, especially synthetic genomics. As an enabling technology, DNA synthesis has already been shown to save time in the laboratory; in the next five to ten years, it should begin to save money as well. Synthetic genomics has already become a powerful tool for research in laboratories studying molecular evolution, defining regulators of gene expression and studying the minimal molecular requirements for life.[15]

Risks

The risks of synthetic biology or synthetic genomics have generally been described in two classes: one taking in concerns about biosecurity and biosafety; the other having to do with more philosophical or cultural concerns. These have sometimes been called respectively "hard" risks and "soft" risks (referred to by some as "physical" and "non-physical" risks).

Biosecurity and biosafety

Malicious intent

The synthetic biology community itself, in addition to other stakeholders, recognized early on that this technology could introduce risks to society along with the potential benefits. These risks derive from the dual-use nature of the research and applications. For example, research by scientists to understand how to make a better vaccine could contribute to a bioterrorist's understanding of how to make a virus that can elude such a vaccine. This generic type of risk has long been understood (nuclear power/nuclear weapons; knives for cutting food/knives for stabbing) but a risk involving biology has a further dimension: newly constructed organisms can replicate.

These types of concerns were recognized as long ago as 1975, at the Asilomar Conference on Recombinant DNA, where scientists considered safety issues arising from the then-emerging technology. Prior to the start of the meeting, however, the organizers decided specifically not to address concerns around misuse by malicious groups, as the laboratory biosafety concerns alone seemed difficult enough to work through.[16] But in a post-September 11 world, concerns about bioterrorism and biosecurity not only could no longer be placed to the side, but rather became the focus of much policy analysis.

In the United States especially, and in other countries as well, certain aspects of biosecurity have been discussed and presented publicly in great detail, and some of the aspects of particular concern are being dealt with, or may soon be dealt with, either through self-governance by both providers and users of the raw materials, or potentially in the near future through regulation. We focus specifically on issues where synthetic genomics can be distinguished from recombinant DNA technologies or biotechnologies generally.

A major concern is the possibility of an individual with malicious intent ordering DNA from a synthesis firm with the purpose of constructing pathogenic viruses, or perhaps bacteria. This could be done in a number of different ways. Because at least some firms now have the ability to synthesise stretches of DNA up to 50,000 base-pairs, many viral DNA sequences could simply be ordered directly. For very large viruses, such as smallpox, just a few separate orders could supply such an individual with all of the genetic material necessary to then carry out a few simple ligation steps to synthesize an entire virus.

Alternatively, if such an individual wanted to avoid easy detection, another possibility would be to order a large number of oligonucleotides (very short pieces of DNA, around 40–100 nucleotides in length). Although technically much more difficult, it is possible to string many of these together to synthesize a viral genome. As noted above, this exact technique was used by Wimmer and colleagues to synthesize an infectious poliovirus and by Smith and colleagues to synthesize the bacteriophage phiX174.

The industry as a whole is very aware of the type of concerns that these possibilities generate. The vast majority of DNA synthesis firms that focus on gene or genome-length synthesis already screen incoming DNA orders. The technical requirements for screening long stretches of DNA for malicious intent are in fact not overly arduous. In the United States, several government agencies have been considering for several years now whether or not to require such firms to screen, whether or not they would need to report any potential malicious sequence, to whom such information should be reported, and so on.

Oligonucleotide orders, on the other hand, would be technically very difficult to screen. Comparing very short sequences against databases of gene or genome-length sequences can lead to high rates of false-positive reporting. While gene firms can afford a few extra days to examine orders (as it already takes at least several weeks to synthesize a gene or genome), oligonucleotide suppliers can turn an order around as fast as overnight; any additional time for screening and determining if an order is truly malicious or not carries a real additional cost to the company.

Even if policies and mechanisms could be put into place to prevent individuals or non-state groups with malicious intent from ordering DNA, if those individuals were motivated enough, they could in fact synthesize pathogen DNA themselves. The same machines that power oligonucleotide supply companies are readily available. Oligonucleotide synthesizers are a mature technology, and can be purchased from laboratory supply houses, by resale from businesses such as LabX, and even on general auction sites such as eBay. In the United States, there are essentially no restrictions on individuals owning such machines or ordering the chemical supplies necessary to carry out oligonucleotide synthesis.

In addition to governments that have expressed concerns about such technologies, several organizations interested in the governance of these technologies have released reports describing various options and recommendations. The present authors, along with Endy and Epstein, authored the report *Synthetic Genomics: Options for Governance*[17] in which we outline a number of options for the governance of firms selling gene- and genome-length DNA, oligonucleotides and oligonucleotide synthesizers.

Legitimate researchers

An additional risk is related to biosafety; that is, the possibility of an accident in a research or manufacturing laboratory, where there is no nefarious intent, yet individuals, communities or the environment could suffer in the event of an unplanned release of synthesized microorganisms.

Scientists have been working with genetically modified organisms, specifically microorganisms, for decades, and the professional biosafety community has used these experiences in evaluating the risks of employing specific techniques while working with particular microorganisms. However, one issue that clearly will need more attention is how to evaluate the possibility of emergent risks from combining genes or signal transduction pathways (a series of events in the cell resulting in a specific change, such as the modification of a protein, dependent on the action of several genes in a coordinated fashion) that are being combined in novel ways.

The intentional or unintentional release of synthesized microbes into the environment has raised concerns from a wide variety of stakeholders. The accidental release of a truly novel organism would be highly problematic, as by definition there would be no prior knowledge of how it would function in an uncontrolled environment. However, most legitimate researchers work with organisms that are difficult to propagate, even in the highly controlled environment of the laboratory, and it is unlikely that any microorganism engineered for research would survive if released.

The larger concern is about micoorganisms that have been engineered specifically so that they can be released into the environment. In the United States, any planned release would be subject to the same regulations as other genetically modified organisms, and would be overseen as appropriate by the Environmental Protection Agency, the Food and Drug Administration, and/or the Department of Agriculture. Any approval would require a series of laboratory and field tests.

Students and amateurs

One of the hallmark projects of the synthetic biology community is the International Genetically Engineered Machine (iGEM) competition.[18] Although most well-known by its once-a-year jamboree where teams gather to compete for various prizes, this is a year-round project of the associated BioBricks™ non-profit organization. Starting as a competition of just a few teams several years ago, the last competition saw over eighty teams numbering around 1000 participants working over the course of the year on projects relevant to new energy sources, new vaccines, and basic research and discovery. The participants are generally college students, although at least one team of all high-school students, under the direction of college students, has participated.

iGEM is linked both practically and analytically with the BioBricks™ Foundation and Registry of Parts. Although currently the parts in the Registry are only used by iGEM participants, the idea of modular parts that are easily available to hobbyists (or researchers) is of course one of the underlying promises of the whole approach of synthetic biology. For the moment, these parts do not necessarily work exactly as described, and synthesizing a "new" microorganism or vaccine that does something truly useful is unlikely to happen any time in the near future. However, as those approaches are improved, either by amateurs or professionals, the prospect of anyone being able to do synthetic biology will be that much closer.

Although there is a long history of amateur scientists making significant contributions, both to the scientific knowledge base and to society, genetic biotechnologies have always been tools of the scientific elite. The laboratories necessary to conduct the research and the chemicals needed to carry out experiments were expensive, difficult to set up, and generally needed the type of infrastructure that could only be provided by a university or firm. Over the last several decades, many of these costs have dropped.

More important, though, is a change in attitude about who should have access to these construction technologies. Partly this is due to the entry of engineers into what was once a field populated almost solely by biologists. Partly there is the more transparent sharing of information that has been made possible by the internet. Part of the attitude is the adoption of a "hacker" mentality (although, in this case, the hackers are benign rather than malicious).

As noted above, oligonucleotide synthesizers and the chemicals needed to synthesize DNA can be delivered, literally, to a garage, and, while hard numbers are difficult to come by, it seems that there is a significant community of hobbyist biotechnologists.[19]

Other societal risks

Unlike biosecurity or biosafety risks, societal risks are the constellation of concerns that the use of these technologies may cause non-specific yet real harms. In other fields these have sometimes been referred to as the "ELSI" (ethical, legal, and social implications) of a technology. Initial reactions to or analyses of synthetic biology have identified a number of related issues as well, particularly in the philosophical and theological realms.

Creating life

For now, synthetic biologists have not "created" anything. The work that has been done until now is focused on replicating already existing genomes (such as building poliovirus from scratch,[20] or constructing the *Mycoplasma genitalium* genome[21]), or on modifying existing cells to produce useful products (such as building and inserting into yeast pathways to produce the artemisinin precursor, artemisinic acid).

Even when removed from the realm of reconstructing, though, what "creating life" means is problematic, as researchers (or those with malicious intent) can only start their experiments from what is known already about how to build cells. This has been dealt with in a cursory way[22] and is a critical baseline issue for allowing discussions about what "creating life" means to move forward in useful ways.

With those caveats, though, the idea of creating life is of course one of the most controversial, and trenchant, in discussion about potential non-physical harms of synthetic biology. The main concern that emerges is that of "playing god". That view has at least two components. Theologians, religious leaders and members of religious groups may express these concerns from the perspective of how a particular religion or group of religions view creation, per se. At the same time, even those who hold no particular religious view may share a concern that creating life is hubristic, even if it could be made safe.

Unfair access and distribution

Another worry, voiced especially by a wide range of non-governmental civil society organizations, is that the applications (benefits) of synthetic biology will accrue mostly or exclusively to those who can afford them, namely, rich individuals or countries. While this type of concern is very much a general one with respect to new technologies, it is of marked concern with synthetic biology as many of the applications would seem to be of a type that could be more useful precisely to those who could not afford them. For example, alternative energy sources could mitigate at least some burning of biomass; the production of inexpensive artemisinin could lessen the impacts of malaria; the rapid development of vaccines could stop emergent diseases that frequently impact developing areas disproportionately.

Certainly this type of maldistribution of benefits has been recognized, at least in the case of artemisinin. The funder (the Gates Foundation), the researcher (Jay Keasling and his colleagues) and the probable producer of the final product (Sanofi-Aventis) all agreed that the drug would be distributed at cost.[23] While that could potentially still be too expensive for individuals in poor countries, it certainly allows for the possibility of large-scale buyers being able to purchase and distribute the drug in bulk. How often this type of agreement could be struck remains to be seen.

Additionally, there are some arguments that, as well as unfair distribution of benefits, there can be unfair distribution of risks, and these arguments can be seen in the histories of some other emerging technologies. For example, a decade ago, when the possibility of robust research on human embryonic stem cells became a reality, one of the concerns was that poor women would be exploited for their eggs.

Ownership

Intellectual property rights are particularly complex in synthetic biology. As Rai and Boyle have noted,[24] there are at least two parts to this problem, neither of which will be easily resolved. First, intellectual property law has found it difficult, in the last thirty years in general, to deal with several emerging technologies. Biotechnology law, software law (where software is frequently considered to be an analogue of what synthetic biologists are trying to do), and the way that, for example, the United States Patent and Trademark Office has dealt with new technologies, collectively may simply not work for synthetic biology. At the same time, "openness" is a goal and a hallmark of the synthetic biology community. But what openness means exactly has not been fully explicated. It might mean putting information into public domains and thus make such information not property; or it may mean using intellectual property rights in order to create a commons. This would be similar to the situation in software development; however, software developers generally work under a copyright framework, whereas copyright might not work for synthetic biology.

Further, there are a number of synthetic biology firms operating for profit, and in at least some of those cases, patent applications have already been entered, and these are on both process and product.[25] Particularly in the field of alternative fuel discovery and development, many recognizable, for-profit names can be found collaborating with or funding academic or non-profit research.[26]

But as with other issues in synthetic biology, patenting and profiting have been discussed at great length with respect to other biotechnologies and it is unclear how synthetic biology would be different, if it should be and, if so, whether the power of the technology is enough to move policymakers to start to rethink current oversight and regulation. One example that has received significant attention is the patent filed at both USPTO and WIPO by researchers at the J. Craig Venter Institute, titled Minimal Bacterial Genome.[27] The filing of the patent has been criticized both by some non-governmental organizations[28] and by individuals in the scientific community.[29] Although some of these criticisms are reminiscent of discussions focused on ownership of genetically modified organisms, these newer discussions also are very focused on the relationship of the process to the product. In the United States, that very issue is about to come under Supreme Court review for a non-biological system.[30]

Governance of risks and benefits

A significant amount of analytical work has already been done on the governance of biosecurity and biosafety risks. In the United States, the National Research Council (NRC) has had studies from several committees on many biosecurity-related issues, including the openness of genetic sequence databases.[31] The best-known and perhaps most influential of all of these NRC reports, *Biotechnology Research in an Age of Bioterrorism*[32] (commonly called the Fink Report after the head of the committee), was the basis for establishing the National Science Advisory Board for Biosecurity (NSABB). The NSABB has, to date, released several reports on biosecurity concerns, both directly and indirectly related to synthetic biology, including on the synthesis of select agents.[33] Several research and security agencies are now looking at the recommendations from the Fink Report and from NSABB in considering new policies and oversight.

The US Department of Energy (DoE) has long been an important funder of synthetic biology and synthetic genomics. In 2004 DoE's

Biological and Environmental Research Advisory Committee published a report that noted the potential need for some kinds of oversight or regulation for synthesis, and also the importance of researchers to be aware of the wide variety of concerns that accompany these technologies.[34]

Many non-governmental and academic organizations have carried out analyses and evaluations. Our study, discussed above, and other studies have considered the safety and security issues, and there has been some preliminary work on the potential societal impacts. In 2004, following the first International Meeting on Synthetic Biology (SB 1.0) George Church, a researcher at Harvard and considered to be one of the founders of current approaches to synthesis, proposed that DNA synthesizers be subject to oversight and/or regulation, and that DNA firms should screen orders for select agent sequences. At the second such meeting, SB 2.0, participants issued a statement to ask the scientific and engineering communities to take steps to deal with the security concerns, especially focusing on screening DNA sequence orders for malicious intent (one idea was that researchers would only purchase DNA from companies that screened using some kind of approved software).

The need for screening orders is something that firms themselves have recognized. The International Consortium for Polynucleotide Synthesis (ICPS) and International Association: Synthetic Biology (IASB) are, respectively, US-founded and Europe-founded consortia of companies that supply gene- and genome-length DNA. The founders of ICPS and members of the synthetic biology and security communities described a potential framework for screening of orders,[35] and IASB has sponsored workshops on biosecurity and has published several reports on possible approaches to screening.[36]

For those companies that now screen for potentially malicious sequences, no approved or agreed-upon software yet exists. Approaches range from the use of commercial software (e.g. BlackWatch from Craic Computing[37]), to the use of public databases such as that in the National Library of Medicine. At least in the United States and in various European countries, discussions are ongoing as to how to structure oversight and potential regulation of this industry.

Even if screening were to be carried out industry-wide, a serious problem remains: some individuals (specifically, legitimate researchers) need to have access to such DNA. This implies a need for screening of individuals, as well as screening sequences. In our report, we discuss a number of ways to achieve this. Keeping in mind that gene synthesis firms can spare a few days to do some kind of user check, while oligonucleotide suppliers may be financially hurt by any delay, options include approval of users by institutional safety officers (much the same way that users of radionuclides must now be approved) or the use of identity-check software (similar to VeriSign, used in some online transactions). Certainly such identity checks could be done in the absence of screening software, but our analyses showed that using these together was a much more powerful mitigator of potential malicious uses, while imposing only moderate additional burdens on researchers and institutions.

Finally, if, despite these approaches to lowering the risk of malicious uses, an act of bioterrorism were to occur, it will be critical for public health and law enforcement officials to be able to at least try to trace the origin of a pathogen. Thus, one additional governance option discussed in our report is that firms should be required to store records of the orders they have received (and, before the fact, should only ship orders to legitimate addresses). There has been discussion about aggregating order information from various firms in real time for inspection by law enforcement (e.g. by the FBI in the United States) but this possibility raises questions for firms who are concerned about their proprietary transactions with customers.

The governance of additional societal impacts, including benefits, will likelier be messier and even more difficult than dealing with security and safety. As early as 1971 (before the Asilomar meeting), in describing the content of a talk in a conference session that he was organizing, Sidney Fox wrote: "As such processes [of synthetic biology] are brought under control in the laboratory, they have increasing implications for society and its philosophy."[38] Nearly forty years later, those implications still permeate discussions about synthetic biology, yet very few answers or options for how to approach them have been widely accepted.

Our analyses of current concerns about societal impacts of synthetic genomics specifically date to a 1999 paper in which Clyde Hutchison and his colleagues describe an experiment in which they defined a minimal set of genes needed for the functioning of a very small bacterium, *Mycoplasma genitalium*.[39] The list of such a set can be thought of in several ways, all of which may raise discomfort or controversy. Is it a definition of life? Or perhaps a shopping list for someone trying to create life? In the paper the researchers note especially this latter implication, and because it would be such an obvious, not to mention important experiment to do, an ethics study was immediately commissioned and the results published at the same time as the minimal genome study. At the time, the group found nothing inherently unethical in synthetic genomics, in this particular case the building of a bacterial chromosome: "The prospect of constructing minimal and new genomes does not violate any fundamental moral precepts or boundaries..." The authors then, however, go on immediately to add: "[constructing minimal and new genomes] does raise questions that are essential to consider before the technology advances further".[40]

Particularly since the event of 11 September 2001, in the United States, overlapping safety and ethical concerns have emerged; diverse groups and individuals have expressed concern over synthetic genomics research with respect to a broad array of issues, not just biosafety and biosecurity.

In Europe, the Rathenau Institute issued a report noting a wide range of issues specific to research communities, more general societal issues, and the overlaps of those.[41] Importantly, the European Group on Ethics in Science and New Technologies (EGE) has undertaken a major study on synthetic biology.[42] The EGE directly advises the European Commission and can influence legislation and policy-setting.

In the United Kingdom, the Royal Society has been conducting research and organizing panels on the science and ethics of synthetic biology,[43] and the Biotechnology and Biological Research Council commissioned a report to detail issues ranging from bioterrorism to global justice.[44]

One area that clearly will require more attention, as engineers and scientists become more adept with these new techniques, is the ethics of synthesizing truly new genomes or organisms. For the moment, this is not a particularly pressing concern (scientists are puzzled as to how to construct single signal transduction pathways, let alone the tens or hundreds of them that would be needed to make something truly new), but it is an issue that crops up in many discussions and is thus worthy of rigorous analysis. In our report we considered, in detail, general issues that will need to be taken up by institutional oversight boards as synthetic biology become more widespread.

While in our earlier report we only touch on the complexities of formal risk assessment with respect to emerging technologies generally and synthetic genomics in particular, we note here that there is a significant literature on the nature of risk assessment and scientific uncertainty. There are many papers both on the precautionary principle, and on what is called science-based regulation. For example, a paper on "science-based precaution" by Charles Weiss provides a particularly cogent explication of these views as well as a model for a combined or hybrid approach to risk assessment that could well facilitate adaptive management of new technologies.[45]

Finally, it is worth noting that several commentators have suggested that one way to avoid at least some of the risks is to have as many legitimate researchers, users and amateurs working on the positive applications as possible (sometimes called a "proactionary" approach, to distinguish it from "precautionary" approaches). Although this idea has been discussed to some degree in general literature on innovation theory, in this particular case a more rigorous analysis is needed.

Oversight and regulation: International law

Synthetic biology cannot be regulated as a single entity. It uses a collection of techniques and materials that are commonly used throughout biology. Further, the suppliers of the materials are found worldwide. More generally, the risks and the benefits of applications of these technologies could be global, but there is concern that these will be unequally distributed, with rich countries gaining benefit and poor countries absorbing most of the risk. Many international non-governmental organizations as well as governmental bodies have looked at governance options, particularly legal approaches, that could be used for regulating synthetic biology.

The critical issue likely to arise internationally, as it is beginning to in the United States, is whether synthetic biology and synthetic genomics are essentially the same as genetic modification technologies with respect to governance, or if they are genuinely new and need new oversight or regulation.

The international biosecurity community has longstanding concerns about synthetic biology. The Biological and Toxin Weapons Convention[46] is following developments closely, as it is of course concerned that synthetic biology could contribute further to the expansion of biological weapons of mass destruction (WMD). To a large extent, the Convention is focused on state-sponsored terrorism. While there are governance options that can take this into account, if a nation were intent on carrying out a WMD programme using synthetic genomics, there is likely little that could stop it.

Other societal impacts are also taken up through a variety of international treaties or conventions. Although research on intellectual property and access issues in synthetic biology and synthetic genomics specifically is just beginning, there is a significant literature on intellectual property issues on the products of biotechnology generally, and as those issues are dealt with in international settings. Longstanding problems, including that of patent thickets (a developer needing to get permission from many owners in order to construct something new) may become bottlenecks for synthetic biology. These types of issues have already been taken up to some degree by the World Intellectual Property Organization and the European Patent Office, in addition to the US Patent Office.[47]

With respect specifically to access and benefit sharing of genetic resources within the Convention on Biological Diversity, synthetic biology (and, more pointedly, synthetic genomics) has been discussed at some length. A number of side events on the topic have been held both at Ad Hoc Working Group on Access and Benefit Sharing[48] meetings and at the Subsidiary Body on Scientific, Technical, and Technological Advice.[49]

Synthetic biology carries with it many of the same problems for international bodies as genetically modified organisms do in general. Particularly with respect to biosafety and international commerce, synthesized microorganisms do not necessarily pose new problems, although there may be concerns within countries or regions with regard to which agencies should handle such organisms.[50]

But there is a major difference (at the moment, only a potential difference) that, as scientists' skills in manipulating synthesized organisms develop, any direct analogy between genetic modification and synthesis could break down almost completely. One of the goals of some synthetic biologists is to be able to construct organisms that, while not fully from scratch, would include a variety of signal transduction and other metabolic pathways from different organisms, collected into one organism, to confer upon it a variety of traits not found together in nature. Beside the more philosophical or theological question of whether constructing such an organism is equivalent to "creating life", and what the policy-relevant questions of that observation would be, is the more practical question: who would have ownership of a microorganism constructed that way? A key aspect of guidance on access and benefit-sharing of genetic resources is that geographical origins of genetic material must be disclosed in patent applications.[51] What will this mean if a newly constructed chromosome has fifty geographical origins? Although no one has yet built such a chromosome, it is not beyond the realm of possibility. Many open-access databases that describe gene sequences and the possible functions of those genes already exist; a goal of the providers of those databases is that they be used for understanding how cells work, precisely by building them from component parts.

At the same time, an apparent goal of the synthetic biology community as a whole is to act fairly and to work to mitigate disparities. Access and benefit-sharing principles operate to resolve some of those parallel goals; other principles may need to be introduced to ensure that scientists and engineers can carry out their work while the goals and values of other communities and nations are included in the development of any governance mechanisms.

Conclusion

While not wholly new technologies, synthetic biology and synthetic genomics introduce novel problems for those concerned about the governance of biotechnologies generally. In the realm of environmental law especially, particularly with respect to planned releases of synthesized organisms, it will be critical to determine where synthetic biology specifically differs from genetic modification. At the same time, societal concerns about the technologies that cannot necessarily be resolved through legal and regulatory means will nonetheless have to be taken into account by policymakers.

Notes

1. Peter Aldhous, "Countdown to a Synthetic Lifeform", *New Scientist*, iss. 2611 (2007), pp. 6–7.
2. Chemistry and scale: the basic subunit of nucleic acids is the nucleotide. When joined chemically to each other these may be ribonucleic acid (RNA) or deoxyribonucleic acid (DNA). Depending on the situation they may be single-stranded or double-stranded. The classic double helix is base-paired DNA. Oligonucleotides are sequences of about 25–100 nucleotides. Genes range greatly in size but for purposes of this discussion are in the range of hundreds to thousands of nucleotides in length. Genomes can range from very small viral genomes (5,000 base-pairs for some viruses that infect bacteria; 7,700 RNA nucleotides for poliovirus) to large viruses or small bacteria (186,000 base-pairs in the smallpox virus; 500,000 base-pairs for the chromosome of a small bacterium such as *Mycoplasma genitalium*) to large bacteria (5,000,000 base-pairs for a "typical" bacterium such as anthrax or *E. coli*). The human reference genome is about 3 billion base-pairs, and plants can have genomes in the tens of billions base-pairs.
3. See K.L. Agarwal, H. Buchi, M.H. Caruthers, et al., "Total Synthesis of the Gene for an Alanine Transfer Ribonucleic Acid from Yeast", *Nature*, vol. 227 (1970), pp. 27–34. See also H. Gobind Khorana, K.L. Agarwal, H. Buchi, et al., "Total Synthesis of the Structural Gene for an Alanine Transfer Ribonucleic Acid from Yeast", *Journal of Molecular Biology*, vol. 72, no. 2 (1972), pp. 209–217.
4. H.G. Khorana, "Total Synthesis of a Gene", *Science*, vol. 203, no. 4381 (1979), pp. 614–625.
5. Jeronimo Cello, Aniko V. Paul and Eckard Wimmer, "Chemical Synthesis of Poliovirus cDNA: Generation of Infectious Virus in the Absence of Natural Template", *Science*, vol. 297, no. 5583 (2002), pp. 1016–1018.
6. Hamilton O. Smith, Clyde A. Hutchison III, Cynthia Pfannkoch and J. Craig Venter, "phiX174 Bacteriophage from Synthetic Oligonucleotides", *Proceedings of the National Academy of Sciences USA*, vol. 100, no. 26 (2003), pp. 15,440–15,445.
7. *Blue Heron Biotechnology Announces Delivery of 52kb Gene*, Press Release (2007); available at <http://www.blueheronbio.com/company/press/mar26-07.html>.
8. Dae-Kyun Ro, Eric M. Paradise, Mario Ouellet, et al., "Production of the Antimalarial Drug Precursor Artemisinic Acid in Engineered Yeast", *Nature*, vol. 440, no. 7086 (2006), pp. 940–943.
9. Sarah J. Kodumal, Kedar G. Patel, Ralph Reid, et al., "Total Synthesis of Long DNA Sequences: Synthesis of a Contiguous 32-kb Polyketide Synthase Gene Cluster", *Proceedings of the National Academy of Sciences USA*, vol. 101, no. 44 (2004), pp. 15,573–15,578.
10. Susan Hardy, *SARS, before Its Big Leap*, Endeavors Magazine (2009); available at <http://research.unc.edu/endeavors/spr2009/sars_big_leap.php>.
11. Biotechnology Industry Organization, *New Biotech Tools for a Cleaner Environment* (2004/2005); available at <http://bio.org/ind/pubs/cleaner2004>.
12. Douglas B. Rusch, Aaron L. Halpern, Granger Sutton, et al., "The Sorcerer II Global Ocean Sampling Expedition: Northwest Atlantic through Eastern Tropical Pacific", *Public Library of Science Biology*, vol. 5, no. 3 (2007), pp. 398–431, (e77).

13. Brent J. Baker, Gene W. Tyson, Lindsey Goosherst and Jillian F. Banfield, "Insights into the Diversity of Eukaryotes in Acid Mine Drainage Biofilm Communities", *Applied and Environmental Microbiology*, vol. 75, no. 7 (2009), pp. 2192–2199.
14. Thomas F. Knight, "Engineering Novel Life", *Molecular Systems Biology*, vol. 1 (2005), doi:10.1038/msb4100028.
15. See Jack W. Szostak, David P. Bartel and P. Luigi Luisi, "Synthesizing Life", *Nature*, vol. 409, no. 6818 (2001), pp. 387–390; and Leon Y. Chan, Siriam Kosuri and Drew Endy, "Refactoring Bacteriophage T7", *Molecular Systems Biology*, vol. 1 (2005), doi:10.1038/msb4100025.
16. Michael Rogers, "The Pandora's Box Congress", *Rolling Stone*, vol. 189, 19 June 1975, pp. 37–77.
17. Michele S. Garfinkel, Drew Endy, Gerald L. Epstein and Robert M. Friedman, *Synthetic Genomics: Options for Governance* (2007); available at <http://www.jcvi.org/cms/fileadmin/site/research/projects/synthetic-genomics-report/synthetic-genomics-report.pdf>.
18. *iGEM: International Genetically Engineered Machine: Yearly Competition Site*; available at <http://2009.igem.org/main_page>.
19. Jeanne Whalen, "In Attics and Closets, 'Biohackers' Discover their Inner Frankenstein", *The Wall Street Journal*, 12 May 2009; available at <http://online.wsj.com/article/SB124207326903607931.html>.
20. Cello et al., "Chemical Synthesis of Poliovirus cDNA".
21. Hutchinson et al., "Global Transposon Mutagenesis and a Minimal Mycoplasma Genome".
22. Joachim Boldt and Oliver Müller, "Newtons of the Leaves of Grass", *Nature Biotechnology*, vol. 26, no. 4 (2008), pp. 387–389.
23. Steve Hamm, "Cheaper Artemisinin to Fight Malaria", *Business Week*, 26 January 2009.
24. Arti K. Rai and James Boyle, "Synthetic Biology: Caught between Property Rights, the Public Domain, and the Commons", *Public Library of Science Biology*, vol. 5, no. 3 (2007), pp. 389–393, e58.
25. M. Bhatia, M.C.M. Cockrem, S.B. Del Cardayre and F.A. Sanchez-riera, "Reduction of the Toxic Effect of Impurities from Raw Materials by Extractive Fermentation", United States Patent and Trademark Office File Number 20090084025 (2009).
26. *BP Selects Strategic Partners for Energy Biosciences Institute* (2007); available at <http://www.bp.com/genericarticle.do?categoryId=2012968&contentId=7028142>.
27. John I. Glass, H.O. Smith, C.A. Hutchinson, et al., "Minimal Bacterial Genome", United States Patent and Trademark Office File Number 20070122826 (2007).
28. ETC Group, *Patenting Pandora's Bug* (2007); available at <http://www.etcgroup.org/en/materials/publications.html?pub_id=631>.
29. Jocelyn Kaiser, "Attempt to Patent Artificial Organism Draws a Protest", *Science*, vol. 316, no. 5831 (2007), p. 1557.
30. United States Patent and Trademark Office, *Bilski v. Doll* (2009); available at <http://www.uspto.gov/main/homepagenews/2009jun26.htm>.
31. Committee on Genomics Databases for Bioterrorism Threat Agents, *Seeking Security: Pathogens, Open Access, and Genome Databases* (Washington, DC: National Academies Press, 2004).
32. Committee on Research Standards and Practices to Prevent the Destructive Application of Biotechnology, *Biotechnology Research in an Age of Bioterrorism* (Washington, DC: National Academies Press, 2004).
33. National Science Advisory Board for Biosecurity, *Addressing Biosecurity Concerns Related to the Synthesis of Select Agents* (2006); available at <http://oba.od.nih.gov/biosecurity/pdf/Final_nsabb_Report_on_Synthetic_Genomics.pdf>. A select agent is a biological agent or toxin listed in 42 CFR Part 73, 7 CFR Part 331 and 9 CFR Part 121,

or the HHS and USDA Select Agents and Toxins List, according to the NIH/USDA list of definitions; available at <http://grants.nih.gov/grants/glossary.htm#S>, resulting from legislation enacted post-9/11, post-anthrax.

34. United States Department of Energy, *Synthetic Genomes: Technologies and Impact* (Biological and Environmental Research Advisory Committee, 2004); available at <http://www.sc.doe.gov/ober/berac/SynBio.pdf>.

35. Hans Bügl, John P. Danner, Robert J. Molinari, et al., "DNA Synthesis and Biological Security", *Nature Biotechnology*, vol. 25, no. 6 (2007), pp. 627–629.

36. *IASB Develops Security Measures for Use of Synthetic Biology* (2008); available at <http://www.ia-sb.eu/tasks/sites/synthetic-biology/assets/File/press-kit/press_release_workshop_biosecurity_en.pdf>.

37. *BlackWatch: Hazardous Biological Agent Sequence Detection*; available at <https://biotech.craic.com/blackwatch/>.

38. Sidney W. Fox, "Living Systems: Synthesis, Assembly, Origins", *Science*, vol. 174, no. 4011 (1971), pp. 858–859.

39. Clyde A. Hutchison III, Scott N. Peterson, Steven R. Gill, et al., "Global Transposon Mutagenesis and a Minimal Mycoplasma Genome", *Science*, vol. 286, no. 5447 (1999), pp. 2165–2169.

40. Mildred K. Cho, David Magnus, Arthur L. Caplan, Daniel McGee, Ethics of Genomics Group, "Ethical Considerations in Synthesizing a Minimal Genome", *Science*, vol. 286, no. 5447 (1999), pp. 2087–2090.

41. Huin de Vriend, *Constructing Life: Early Social Reflections on the Emerging Field of Synthetic Biology*, Working Document 97 (The Hague: Rathenau Institute, 2006); available at <http://www.lisconsult.nl/images/stories/Downloads/wed97_constructing_life_2006.pdf>.

42. *Activities—European Group on Ethics in Science and New Technologies* (2009); available at <http://ec.europa.eu/european_group_ethics/activities/index_en.htm>.

43. *Science Issues: Synthetic Biology*; available at <http://royalsociety.org/landing.asp?id=1230>.

44. Andrew Balmer and Paul Martin, *Synthetic Biology: Social and Ethical Challenges* (May 2008); available at <http://www.bbsrc.ac.uk/organisation/policies/reviews/scientific_areas/0806_synthetic_biology.pdf>.

45. Charles Weiss, "Scientific Uncertainty and Science-based Precaution", *International Environmental Agreements: Politics, Law, and Economics*, vol. 3, no. 2 (2003), pp. 137–166.

46. The State Parties to the Convention, *Convention on the Prohibition of the Development, Production and Stockpiling of Bacteriological (Biological) and Toxin Weapons and on Their Destruction* (1975); available at <http://www.opbw.org/convention/documents/btwctext.pdf>.

47. Berthold Rutz, "Synthetic Biology through the Prism of Scenarios", *Biotechnology Journal*, vol. 2, no. 9 (2007), pp. 1072–1075.

48. Convention on Biological Diversity, *Working Group on Access and Benefit Sharing*; available at <http://www.cbd.int/convention/wgabs.shtml>.

49. Convention on Biological Diversity, *Subsidiary Body on Scientific, Technical and Technological Advice*; available at http://www.cbd.int/sbstta/>.

50. Franco Furger, *From Genetically Modified Organisms to Synthetic Biology: Legislation in the European Union, in Six Member Countries, and in Switzerland – Paper Commissioned for Synthetic Genomics: Risks and Benefits for Science and Society* (2007); available at <http://dspace.mit.edu/handle/1721.1/39655>.

51. Commission on Intellectual Property Rights, *Integrating International Property Rights and Development Policy* (London: CIPR, 2003), pp. 85 ff.

13

Conclusion

David Leary and Balakrishna Pisupati

The future of international environmental law is very much linked to the future of global environmental governance. As we noted at the beginning of this book, the emphasis on environmental governance should be focused on how environmental governance can be improved as we move towards achieving "good" environmental governance, however we measure that.

There are many aspects to the question of how we may improve global environmental governance. One aspect we highlighted in our introduction is so-called "treaty congestion". We noted that there are very real concerns about the impact of "treaty congestion" on the ability of states to respond to the ever-increasing number of environmental challenges, and this is most visible in the case of developing countries and small island states (SIDS) in particular. Ann Powers demonstrated this quite clearly in her analysis of the challenges faced by SIDS in the context of both climate change and pollution.

This suggests that, in the future, rather than viewing new laws emerging from environmental diplomacy conducted by nation-states as the end game, our focus should instead be on considering what will bring about the most effective resolution of existing and new and emerging environmental challenges. This necessarily entails looking beyond law as a solution to international environmental problems.

Of course, to say that future debates should be about global environmental governance rather than having a strict focus only on international environmental law is not to deny a significant role for international envi-

The future of international environmental law, Leary and Pisupati (eds),
United Nations University Press, 2010, ISBN 978-92-808-1192-6

ronmental law into the future, when that law is effectively implemented. International environmental law can and has been effective in dealing with many of the global environmental challenges we face. In Chapter 3, Susan Shearing has highlighted that, despite the many and varied challenges faced by developed and developing countries alike, it is possible to achieve good environmental governance through many existing treaty regimes. In the case of biodiversity, she highlighted that, notwithstanding the many and varied challenges to biodiversity conservation and sustainable use, a number of the key mechanisms identified in the CBD are to an extent facilitating the objectives of the Convention. In a similar vein, Tulio Scovazzi highlighted the success of the series of legal instruments applying to the protection of the Mediterranean environment, the so-called Barcelona system, and how it has served as a model for the development of law in other regions.

The fact that we can point to success stories in some areas of international environmental law, but not in all, highlights further the importance to good environmental governance of the "diverse efforts of communities at every level", as Rosenau has suggested.[1] Maximizing the impact of these "diverse efforts" of course assumes the maximum involvement and engagement of all the relevant stakeholder communities. As Donna Craig and Michael Jeffery highlighted in their analysis, the right to public participation in the decision-making process, access to justice and a range of other factors have a significant role to play in fostering "good environmental governance". As they indicated, environmental governance is very much about "relationships and interactions among government and non-government structures, procedures and conventions, where power and responsibility are exercised in making environmental decisions".[2] It is, as their analysis emphasized, very much about "*how* the decisions are made" and how "communities" and other stakeholders participate. Conceived at the local level, this is straightforward, but of course when one talks of global environmental governance it is far more problematic, especially if, as Edith Brown Weiss has suggested, we are witnessing the emergence of a "kaleidoscopic" international legal and political system.[3] How to accommodate and balance the needs and aspirations of all stakeholders and communities is, and will continue to be, a major challenge for the future of international environmental law, and beyond, for international environmental governance more broadly.

This necessarily suggests that, at its core, environmental governance is also a question of human rights. Gudmundur Alfredsson, in his contribution, has shown how environmental issues and human rights are closely interrelated. This, of course, has been known for some time; it is at the heart of the "efficient synthesis" of development and environmental concerns that have been at the core of international debates on the environment since at least Stockholm, if not much earlier. But human rights will also be at the core of international environmental law and good global environmental governance into the future.

This suggests that the future of international environmental law will be dominated very much by the debates surrounding this "efficient synthesis"; about bridging the north-south divide. As in the past, so in the future, bridging the north-south divide will be a significant factor in determining the success or failure of both international environmental law and global environmental governance more broadly. This is most vividly illustrated by the failure of Copenhagen to produce any meaningful progress in shaping a truly global and effective response to climate change. Michael Gerrard and Dionysia-Theodora Avgerinopoulou distilled the essence of this in two neat sentences towards the end of their chapter when they observed: "The developing world will not accept measures that seriously impede its development. The developed world will not accept measures that seriously diminish current lifestyles." Reconciling these two seemingly contradictory broad positions will be the key to tackling the global environmental challenges presented by climate change and many other pressing global environmental problems. It will be no easy task.

While much of the debate on environmental governance and the development of new international environmental law has traditionally taken place within the UN system, as discussion in Part III of this book has highlighted, the monopoly of the UN system itself is increasingly coming under challenge. Responses emerging to many new environmental challenges such as those associated with nanotechnology, bioenergy and synthetic genomics and biology, for example, are occurring outside the existing state-centric UN system. It may well be that, in the long term, initiatives outside the UN system, such as the development of standards by the ISO for nanotechnology or voluntary industry initiatives in the areas of biofuels, nanotechnology and synthetic genomics, will provide a cluster of governance mechanisms for these emerging technologies.

As we highlighted in Chapter 10, the idea of a governance response to nanotechnology, for example, (in a "kaleidoscopic" international legal and political system or otherwise) as opposed to a strictly legal response is consistent with similar debates that have been emerging in relation to the appropriate form of response under a number of domestic regulatory frameworks for environmental issues. Regulatory options for emerging technologies such as nanotechnology and synthetic genomics, for example, may involve "a continuum of regulatory mechanisms ... from hard law at one extreme through licensing and codes of practice to 'soft' self-regulation and negotiation in order to influence behaviour at the other".[4] International environmental law is therefore no different to domestic law in that respect. What appears to be different for both international environmental law and global environmental governance into the future, though, is an increasing role for non-state actors. Meaningful stakeholder engagement in these processes will be just as important in this context as it is in any other.

In some areas, such as governance of the oceans, for example, shaping responses to global environmental challenges may also involve challenging long-held assumptions about what international law is or should be. As Rosemary Rayfuse's analysis in Chapter 9 has shown, the realization of the exhaustibility of marine biodiversity in areas beyond national jurisdiction challenges traditional dogma in international law that the seas should be free for all to exploit. Nothing less than a paradigm shift appears to be needed in shaping our response to environmental issues in the oceans. But, as Timo Koivurova and Sébastien Duyck highlighted in their chapter, nation-states are not necessarily going to accept such a paradigm shift overnight. There will need to be a long-term evolution rather than an overnight revolution.

The future response of international environmental law (and international environmental governance more broadly) to existing and emerging environmental challenges is therefore of necessity going to be a multifaceted and multidimensional evolutionary process, drawing on existing mechanisms in many cases, and enhancing them or developing totally new ways of responding with new actors and new tools in others.

The future of international environmental law (as part of overall global environmental governance), like the global environment it seeks to protect for future generations, will be a dynamic and ever-changing phenomenon. The key challenge for states and all other stakeholders and actors will be to keep up with the rapid pace of change.

Notes

1. James Rosenau, "Governance in a New Global Order", in David Held and Anthony McGrew (eds), *The Global Transformations Reader: An Introduction to the Globalization Debate* (Cambridge: Polity Press, 2003), pp. 223–235, p. 224.
2. Richard E. Saunier and Richard A. Meganck, *Dictionary and Introduction to Global Environmental Governance* (London: Earthscan, 2009), p. 3.
3. Edith Brown Weiss, "International Law in a Kaleidoscopic World", paper presented at the Second Biennial General Conference of the Asian Society of International Law, Tokyo, 1–2 August 2009, copy on file with author.
4. Dianne Bowman and Graham Hodge, "Nanotechnology: Mapping the Wild Regulatory Frontier", *Futures*, vol. 38, no. 9 (2006), pp. 1060–1073, p. 1068.

Index